ZAGAT®

Paris
Restaurants
2010/11

LOCAL EDITOR
Alexander Lobrano
LOCAL COORDINATOR
Mary Deschamps
STAFF EDITOR
Carol Diuguid

Published and distributed by
Zagat Survey, LLC
4 Columbus Circle
New York, NY 10019
T: 212.977.6000
E: paris@zagat.com
www.zagat.com

ACKNOWLEDGMENTS

We thank Axel Baum, Patrick and Sabine Brassart, Gilbert Brownstone, Erin Emmett, Juliet Faber, Claire Fitzpatrick-Quimbrot, Bertin Leblanc, Anne and Gérard Mazet, Bruno Midavaine, Denis Quimbrot, Troy Segal, Amy Serafin, Steven Shukow, Boi Skoi and François de la Tour d'Auvergne, as well as the following members of our staff: Josh Rogers (senior associate editor), Brian Albert, Sean Beachell, Maryanne Bertollo, Jane Chang, Sandy Cheng, Reni Chin, Larry Cohn, Alison Flick, Jeff Freier, Roy Jacob, Natalie Lebert, Mike Liao, Andre Pilette, Becky Ruthenburg, Sharon Yates, Anna Zappia and Kyle Zolner.

The reviews in this guide are based on public opinion surveys. The ratings reflect the average scores given by the survey participants who voted on each establishment. The text is based on quotes from, or paraphrasings of, the surveyors' comments. Phone numbers, addresses and other factual data were correct to the best of our knowledge when published in this guide.

Contents

Ratings & Symbols

Zagat Top Spot	Name	Symbols	Cuisine	Zagat Ratings			
				FOOD	DECOR	SERVICE	COST

Area, Address, Métro Stop & Contact*

Ⓩ Tim & Nina's ◐ *French/Thai* ▽ 23 | 9 | 13 | €15
6ᵉ | 604, rue de Buci (Odéon) | 01-23-45-54-32 | www.zagat.com

Review, surveyor comments in quotes

Jamais fermé, this "crowded" 6th-arrondissement cafe started the "French-Thai craze" (e.g. foie gras in pad Thai or lychee bouillabaisse); though it looks like a "historic garage" and T & N "never heard of credit cards or reservations" – yours in particular – the "*merveilleuse Bangkok-Brest cuisine*" draws delighted diners due to downmarket tabs.

Ratings   **Food, Decor** and **Service** are rated on the Zagat 0 to 30 scale.

0 – 9		poor to fair
10 – 15		fair to good
16 – 19		good to very good
20 – 25		very good to excellent
26 – 30		extraordinary to perfection
▽		low response | less reliable

Cost   Our surveyors' estimated price of a dinner with one drink and tip. Lunch is usually 25 to 30% less. For unrated **newcomers** or **write-ins,** the price range is shown as follows:

I	30€ and below	E	51€ to 80€
M	31€ to 50€	VE	81€ or above

Symbols

Ⓩ	highest ratings, popularity and importance
◐	serves after 11 PM
Ⓢ	closed on Sunday
Ⓜ	closed on Monday
⊄	no credit cards accepted

* When calling from outside France, dial the country code +33, then omit the first zero of the number listed.

Menus, photos, voting and more – free at ZAGAT.com

About This Survey

This **2010/11 Paris Restaurants Survey** is an update reflecting significant developments since our last Survey was published. It covers 1,022 restaurants in the Paris area, including 40 important additions. To bring this guide up to the minute, we've also indicated new addresses, phone numbers, chef changes and other major alterations. Like all our guides, this one is based on input from avid local consumers – 5,487 all told. Our editors have synopsized this feedback and highlighted (in quotation marks within reviews) representative comments. You can read full surveyor comments – and share your own opinions – on **ZAGAT.com,** where you'll also find the latest restaurant news plus menus, photos and more, all for free.

OUR PHILOSOPHY: Three simple premises underlie our ratings and reviews. First, we've long believed that the collective opinions of knowledgeable consumers are more accurate than the opinions of a single critic. (Consider, for example, that as a group our surveyors bring some 930,000 annual meals' worth of experience to this Survey. They also visit restaurants year-round, anonymously – and on their own dime.) Second, food quality is only part of the equation when choosing a restaurant, thus we ask surveyors to separately rate food, decor and service and report on cost. Third, since people need reliable information in a fast, easy-to-digest format, we strive to be concise and to offer our content on every platform. Our Top Ratings lists (pages 9–18) and indexes (starting on page 198) are also designed to help you quickly choose the *meilleur endroit chaque fois.*

ABOUT ZAGAT: In 1979, we started asking friends to rate and review restaurants purely for fun. The term "user-generated content" had not yet been coined. That hobby grew into Zagat Survey; 31 years later, we have over 375,000 surveyors and cover airlines, bars, dining, fast food, entertaining, golf, hotels, movies, music, resorts, shopping, spas, theater and tourist attractions in over 100 countries. Along the way, we evolved from being a print publisher to a digital content provider, e.g. **ZAGAT.com, ZAGAT.mobi** (for web-enabled mobile devices), **ZAGAT TO GO** (for smartphones) and **nru** (for Android phones). We also produce customized gift and marketing tools for a wide range of corporate clients. And you can find us on Twitter (twitter.com/zagatbuzz), Facebook and other social media networks.

JOIN IN: To improve our guides, we solicit your comments; it's vital that we hear your opinions. Just contact us at **nina-tim@zagat.com.** We also invite you to join our surveys at **ZAGAT.com.** Do so and you'll receive a choice of rewards in exchange.

MERCI: We're grateful to our local editor, Alexander Lobrano, a food and travel writer based in Paris, and our local coordinator, Mary Deschamps. Both Alec and Mary have worked with us for years. We also sincerely thank the thousands of surveyors who participated – all of our content is really "theirs."

New York, NY
May 19, 2010

Nina and Tim Zagat

What's New

There's good news from Paris. Even during a tough year, an exceptionally talented new generation of young chefs continues to arrive and demonstrate the culinary prowess of the French kitchen in a new century.

CREAM OF THE CROP: This year's biggest new sensations include Gregory Marchand's market-oriented bistro, **Frenchie,** and Shinichi Sato's tiny, loungey **Passage 53.** French chefs' fascination with Asia continued to gain momentum with the arrival of eateries like the bistro **KGB** from **Ze Kitchen Galerie**'s William Ledeuil and Adeline Grattard's fusion standout **Yam'Tcha** (the name means 'to drink tea' in Mandarin; Grattard cooked in Hong Kong before setting up shop near Les Halles). And the popularity and quality of Japanese food in Paris continues to grow with such openings as **Oto-Oto** and **Kiku,** while **Shan Gout** represents a fresh generation of more authentic Chinese restaurants.

WALLET-WATCHING: Cued by an ambient frugality, places all over town continue to offer good-value prix fixe menus, though only a few seem to be passing on to customers much of the savings from a recent cut in the TVA (national sales tax) designed to boost the restaurant business and make dining out in Paris more affordable.

GREEN WITH ENVY: The impact of the locavore movement in Paris and a shift toward environmentally sustainable eating can be seen all over the city. Chef Yannick Alléno introduced his 'terroir Parisien' prix fixe at **Le Dali** in the Hôtel Meurice, composed almost exclusively from seasonal produce sourced in the Ile de France, Alain Ducasse rebooted the menu at **Spoon** to favor non-threatened fish, whole grains and low-fat cooking, and the veggies of local produce star Joël Thiébault (whose farm is in the Yvelines, just outside of Paris) bagged bragging rights on menus too numerous to mention. On the horizon is a new organic eatery by architects Gilles & Boissier at La Grande Halle de La Villette that's expected to open in June with plans to source as much of its menu as possible from an adjacent garden.

 WINING AND DINING: This past year was another corker for oenophiles, with the red-hot popularity of wine bars and bistrots à vins showing no sign of cooling. Among the more notable arrivals were **Le Cru Rollin** in the 11th and **Vin Chai Moi** in the 1st.

SEE AND BE SEEN: The Costes brothers have struck again – this time in the heart of St-Germain-des-Prés – with **La Société,** their latest pricey, high-attitude posing perch (with fabulous decor by Christian Liaigre), and, together with chef Jean-François Piège (ex **Les Ambassadeurs**), a cool-operator redo of the old-timer **Thoumieux** in the 7th. **Les Enfants Terribles** opened just off the Champs-Elysées for the Golden Triangle's kissy-kissy set, and the team from **Le 404** has cooked up a real scene with **Derrière,** an instant only-in-Paris favorite of visitors from Bolly- and Hollywood.

Paris
May 19, 2010

Alexander Lobrano

Key Newcomers

Our editors' take on the year's top arrivals. See page 223 for a full list.

Arc | *New French* | hot spot with a killer view of guess what

Caffé dei Cioppi | *Italian* | cozy taste of Trastevere

Chez Grenouille | *Bistro* | traditional bistro for the 9th

Claude Colliot | *Bistro* | comeback of a creative chef

Derrière | *New French* | funky see-and-be-seen scene

Fourchette du Printemps | *Bistro* | out-of-the-way gem

Frenchie | *Bistro* | new star from a globe-trotting young talent

KGB | *Bistro* | Ze Kitchen Galerie annex

Kiku | *Japanese* | top-drawer Japanese

MBC | *New French* | creative, herb-loving cosmopolitan

Mon Oncle | *Bistro* | retro-hip bistro

Shan Gout | *Chinese* | authentic Sino standout

Tico | *Bistro/New French* | sleek modern bistro

Yam'Tcha | *Asian/New French* | East-meets-West sophisticate

As we go to press, the most eagerly awaited debut in Paris is Chicago-born Daniel Rose's **Spring,** which is set to reopen after a series of construction delays in a sleek duplex space near Les Halles. After leaving **Les Ambassadeurs** at the Hôtel de Crillon to completely re-vamp **Thoumieux,** Jean-François Piège will open an intimate gastro-nomic restaurant that's being created upstairs in the Hôtel Thoumieux early this summer, and **Le Chateaubriand**'s Inaki Aizpitarte will follow suit with a second table there, called **Le Dauphin,** in late spring. And speaking of Les Ambassadeurs, all eyes are on the chef who replaces Jean-François Piège there, Christopher Hache. He trained with Eric Briffard (**Le Cinq**) and Eric Frechon (**Le Bristol**) and was most recently at **La Grande Cascade.**

Though no chef has yet been announced for the restaurant at the Philippe Starck–redesigned Royal Monceau Hotel, set to reopen in June, *pâtissier extraordinaire* Pierre Hermé has been selected to supply the pastries. Young chef Bertrand Grébaut, who recently left **l'Agapé,** plans a place of his own at the end of the year, and a Yankee surge looks set for Paris with the arrival of a restaurant in the new Ralph Lauren boutique in Saint-Germain-des-Prés, expected in early sum-mer, and the news that **Chipotle,** the Denver-based Mexican chain, is scouting a Paris location. Later arrivals are expected to include Lyonnais chef Nicolas Le Bec's new brasserie at the Opéra Garnier and a possible new venue from avant-garde Bordelais chef Thierry Marx.

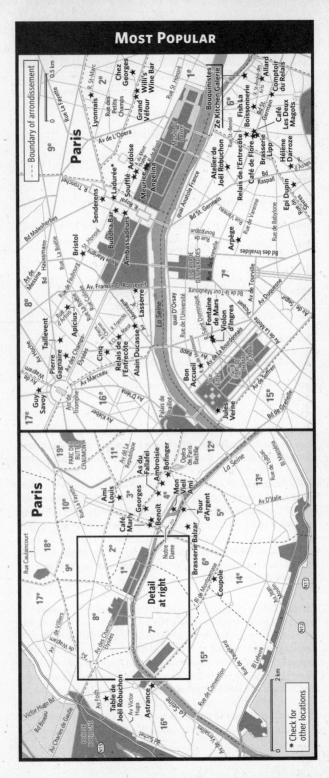

MOST POPULAR

Paris

2e — Chez Georges, Willi's Wine Bar, Grand Véfour, Lyonnais

9e — Rue St-Marc

Av de l'Opéra

Bouquinistes, Ze Kitchen Galerie, Fish La Boissonnerie, Café de Flore, Les Deux Magots, Comptoir du Relais, Allard, Brasserie Lipp, Hélène Darroze

Atelier de Joël Robuchon, Relais de l'Entrecôte, Epi Dupin

Ladurée*, Soufflé, Meurice, Angelina, Ardoise

Senderens, Buddha Bar, Ambassadeurs, Bristol

Arpège

7e

Taillevent, Apicius, Pierre Gagnaire, Cinq, Lasserre, Relais de l'Entrecôte, Alain Ducasse

Fontaine de Mars, Violon d'Ingres

8e

Guy Savoy

Bon Accueil, Tour Eiffel, Jules Verne

16e *17e*

15e

Paris

19e — PARC DES BUTTES CHAUMONT

11e — As du Fallafel, Ambroise, Bofinger, Opéra de Paris Bastille

12e

13e

Ami Louis, Georges, Café Marly, Benoît, Mon Vieil Ami, Tour d'Argent

10e *3e* *4e* *5e*

Brasserie Balzar, Coupole

6e *14e*

Notre Dame

Detail at right

18e *9e* *17e* *2e* *1er* *8e* *7e*

Table de Joël Robuchon, Astrance

16e *15e*

* Check for other locations

— — — Boundary of arrondissement

Menus, photos, voting and more - free at ZAGAT.com

Most Popular

1. Taillevent | *Haute*
2. Atelier Joël Robuchon | *Haute*
3. Grand Véfour | *Haute*
4. Alain Ducasse | *Haute*
5. Tour d'Argent | *Haute*
6. Cinq | *Haute*
7. Guy Savoy | *Haute*
8. Ladurée | *Classic French/Tea*
9. Jules Verne | *Haute*
10. Bofinger | *Brasserie*
11. Pierre Gagnaire | *Haute*
12. Ami Louis | *Bistro*
13. Relais/l'Entrecôte | *Steak*
14. Epi Dupin | *Bistro*
15. Brass. Lipp | *Brasserie*
16. Benoît | *Lyon*
17. Lasserre* | *Haute*
18. Meurice | *Haute*
19. Comptoir/Relais | *Bistro/Brass.*
20. Ambassadeurs | *Haute/New Fr.*
21. Table de Joël Robuchon | *Haute*
22. Angelina | *Tearoom*
23. Ambroisie | *Haute*
24. Café/Deux Magots | *Classic Fr.*
25. Bouquinistes | *New French*
26. Coupole | *Brasserie*
27. Ze Kitchen Galerie* | *Eclectic*
28. Bristol | *Haute*
29. Hélène Darroze* | *New Fr./SW*
30. Senderens* | *Brass./New French*
31. Soufflé | *Classic French*
32. Allard | *Bistro*
33. Astrance | *New French*
34. Bon Accueil | *Bistro*
35. Arpège | *Haute*
36. Chez Georges* | *Bistro*
37. Café de Flore | *Classic French*
38. Lyonnais* | *Lyon*
39. Brass. Balzar | *Brasserie*
40. Georges | *Eclectic*
41. Fish La Boissonnerie | *Provence*
42. Ardoise | *Bistro*
43. Buddha Bar* | *Asian*
44. As du Fallafel | *Israeli*
45. Apicius | *Haute*
46. Café Marly* | *Classic/New Fr.*
47. Fontaine de Mars* | *Southwest*
48. Willi's | *Wine Bar/Bistro*
49. Violon d'Ingres | *Bistro*
50. Mon Vieil Ami | *Bistro*

It's obvious that many of the above restaurants are among Paris' most expensive, but if popularity were calibrated to price, we suspect that a number of other restaurants would join their ranks. Thus, we have added two lists comprising 86 Best Buys on page 17 as well as Good-Value Prix Fixes on page 18.

---

* Indicates a tie with restaurant above

Top Food

²⁸ Taillevent | *Haute*
Cinq | *Haute*
Guy Savoy | *Haute*
Astrance | *New French*
Pierre Gagnaire | *Haute*
Ambroisie | *Haute*
Alain Ducasse | *Haute*
Atelier Joël Robuchon | *Haute*
Grand Véfour | *Haute*
Ambassadeurs | *Haute/New Fr.*

²⁷ Lasserre | *Haute*
Michel Rostang | *Classic French*
Braisière | *Gascony*
Bristol | *Haute*
Dominique Bouchet | *Haute*
Meurice* | *Haute*
Pré Catelan | *Haute*
Relais d'Auteuil | *Haute*

²⁶ Apicius | *Haute*
Trou Gascon | *Southwest*
Hiramatsu | *Haute/New Fr.*
Carré des Feuillants | *Haute*
Table de Joël Robuchon | *Haute*
Arpège | *Haute*
Espadon | *Classic French*

Pavillon Ledoyen | *Haute*
Villaret | *Bistro*
Jacques Cagna | *Haute*
Comptoir/Relais | *Bistro/Brass.*
Senderens | *Brass./New French*
Bistrot de l'Oulette | *Southwest*
Vin sur Vin | *New French*
Passiflore | *Asian/Classic French*
Stella Maris | *Classic French*

²⁵ Os à Moëlle | *Classic French*
Gérard Besson | *Classic French*
Régalade* | *Bistro*
144 Petrossian | *Seafood*
Grande Cascade* | *Haute*
Ami Louis | *Bistro*
Tour d'Argent | *Haute*
Relais Louis XIII | *Haute*
Hélène Darroze | *New Fr./SW*
Cagouille | *Seafood*
Isami* | *Japanese*
Temps au Temps | *Bistro*
Caviar Kaspia | *Russian*
Marius et Janette | *Seafood*
Violon d'Ingres* | *Bistro*
Ze Kitchen Galerie | *Eclectic*

BY CUISINE (FRENCH)

BISTRO (CONTEMP.)

²⁶ Villaret
Comptoir du Relais
²⁵ Temps au Temps
Violon d'Ingres
²⁴ Timbre

BISTRO (TRAD.)

²⁵ Régalade
Ami Louis
D'Chez Eux
²⁴ Bon Accueil
Voltaire

BRASSERIE

²³ Relais Plaza
Chez Les Anges
²² Garnier
²⁰ Stella
¹⁹ Coupole

CLASSIC

²⁷ Michel Rostang
²⁶ Espadon
Passiflore
Stella Maris
²⁵ Os à Moëlle

CONTEMPORARY

²⁸ Astrance
Ambassadeurs
²⁶ Hiramatsu
Senderens
Vin sur Vin

HAUTE CUISINE

²⁸ Taillevent
Cinq
Guy Savoy
Pierre Gagnaire
Ambroisie

Excludes places with low votes, unless otherwise indicated.

LYON

24	Benoît
21	Chez René
	Lyonnais
20	Aub. Pyrénées Cévennes
19	Moissonnier

OTHER REGIONS

27	Braisière	*Gascony*
24	Chez Michel	*Brittany*
	Chez L'Ami Jean	*Basque*
	Troquet	*Basque*
23	Pamphlet	*Basque*

PROVENCE

24	Casa Olympe
23	Chez Janou
22	Bastide Odéon
	Fish La Boissonnerie
18	Bistro de l'Olivier

SEAFOOD

25	144 Petrossian
	Cagouille
	Marius et Janette
24	Fables de La Fontaine
	Divellec

SHELLFISH

25	Marius et Janette
22	Dôme
	Garnier
20	Huîtrier Régis
	Stella

SOUTHWEST

26	Trou Gascon
	Bistrot de l'Oulette
25	Hélène Darroze
	D'Chez Eux
23	Pamphlet

STEAK

24	Relais de Venise
22	Relais/l'Entrecôte
20	Severo
18	Ribouldingue
17	Gavroche

WINE BARS/BISTROS

23	Bourguignon du Marais
22	Cave de l'Os à Moëlle
20	Enoteca
	Willi's Wine Bar
19	Louis Vin

BY CUISINE (OTHER)

CHINESE/ASIAN

21	Diep
	Chez Vong
20	Mirama
	Passy Mandarin
18	Davé

ECLECTIC

25	Ze Kitchen Galerie
23	Relais Plaza
22	Spoon Paris
	Market
	Comptoir

ITALIAN

23	Sormani
	L'Assaggio
22	Ostéria
	Stresa
21	Casa Bini

JAPANESE

25	Isami
23	Kinugawa/Hanawa
20	Yen
18	Inagiku
	Orient-Extrême

MIDDLE EASTERN

24	As du Fallafel
	Liza
21	Al Dar
	Al Diwan
19	Noura

MOROCCAN

22	404
	Mansouria
21	Comptoir
	Chez Omar
20	Atlas

SPANISH/LATIN AMER.

21	Anahuacalli
	Fogón
19	Bellota-Bellota∇
	Anahï
	El Palenque

TEA & DESSERTS

24	Jean-Paul Hévin
23	Ladurée
	Dalloyau
22	Soufflé
21	Mariage Frères

THAI

21	Thiou/Petit Thiou
20	Baan-Boran
	Blue Elephant
19	Banyan
17	Erawan

VIETNAMESE

23	Tan Dinh
22	Coin/Gourmets
20	Lac-Hong∇
18	Davé
	Palanquin

BY SPECIAL FEATURE

BRUNCH

24	Liza
22	404
	Market
	Jardin des Cygnes
21	Mariage Frères

HOTEL DINING

28	Cinq
	(Four Seasons George V)
	Pierre Gagnaire
	(Hôtel Balzac)
	Alain Ducasse
	(Plaza Athénée)
	Atelier Joël Robuchon
	(Hôtel Pont Royal)
	Ambassadeurs
	(Hôtel de Crillon)

LATE DINING

28	Atelier Joël Robuchon
26	Villaret
	Bistrot de l'Oulette
25	Os à Moëlle
	Caviar Kaspia

LIVE ENTERTAINMENT

27	Lasserre
23	Relais Plaza
	Bar Vendôme

22	Café Faubourg
20	Djakarta

SLEEPERS∇

26	Restaurant (Le)
25	Grand Venise
	Cave Gourmande/Mark Singer
	Magnolias*
	Cuisine

SUNDAY DINING

28	Cinq
	Atelier Joël Robuchon
	Ambassadeurs
27	Bristol
26	Table de Joël Robuchon

TRENDY

26	Comptoir du Relais
25	Ze Kitchen Galerie
24	Sensing
23	Aida∇
22	Chateaubriand

WINNING WINE LISTS

28	Taillevent
	Ambroisie
26	Vin sur Vin
25	Tour d'Argent
23	Macéo

BY ARRONDISSEMENT

1ST

28	Grand Véfour
27	Meurice
26	Carré des Feuillants
	Espadon
25	Gérard Besson

2ND

24	Liza
	Chez Georges
22	Fontaine Gaillon
	Drouant
21	Lyonnais

3RD

25	Ami Louis
23	Pamphlet
	Chez Janou
22	404
	Petit Marché

4TH

28	Ambroisie
26	Bistrot de l'Oulette
25	Isami
24	As du Fallafel
	Benoît

5TH

- 25 | Tour d'Argent
- 23 | Truffière
- Papilles
- Coupe-Chou
- Rôtiss. du Beaujolais

6TH

- 26 | Jacques Cagna
- Comptoir du Relais
- 25 | Relais Louis XIII
- Hélène Darroze
- Ze Kitchen Galerie

7TH

- 28 | Atelier Joël Robuchon
- 26 | Arpège
- Vin sur Vin
- 25 | 144 Petrossian
- Violon d'Ingres

8TH

- 28 | Taillevent
- Cinq
- Pierre Gagnaire
- Alain Ducasse
- Ambassadeurs

9TH

- 24 | Casa Olympe
- 23 | Ladurée
- 19 | Jean
- BE Boulangépicier
- Café de la Paix

10TH

- 24 | Chez Michel
- 19 | Brass. Julien
- 18 | Deux Canards
- Brass. Flo
- 17 | Chez Papa

11TH

- 26 | Villaret
- 25 | Temps au Temps
- 23 | Bistrot Paul Bert
- 22 | Chateaubriand
- Mansouria*

12TH

- 26 | Trou Gascon
- 20 | Biche au Bois

- 19 | Oulette
- Train Bleu
- 16 | Lina's

13TH

- 24 | Ourcine
- 23 | Avant Goût
- 21 | Petit Marguery
- 18 | Noveau Vill. Tao▽
- 16 | Chez Paul

14TH

- 25 | Régalade
- Cagouille
- 23 | Duc
- 22 | Dôme
- Crêperie de Josselin

15TH

- 25 | Os à Moëlle
- 24 | Troquet
- 22 | Cave de l'Os à Moëlle
- 21 | Fellini
- 20 | Villa Corse

16TH

- 28 | Astrance
- 27 | Pré Catelan
- Relais d'Auteuil
- 26 | Hiramatsu
- Table de Joël Robuchon

17TH

- 28 | Guy Savoy
- 27 | Michel Rostang
- Braisière
- 24 | Relais de Venise
- 23 | Sormani

18TH, 19TH & 20TH

- 19 | Famille
- 16 | Boeuf Couronné
- Baratin
- 15 | Lao Siam
- Moulin de la Galette

OUTSIDE PARIS

- 23 | Dalloyau
- 22 | Cazaudehore
- 21 | Bistrot d'à Côté
- 20 | Camélia
- 19 | Potager du Roy

Top Decor

29 Cinq	Georges
Grande Cascade	Costes
Grand Véfour	Guy Savoy
Ambassadeurs	Bouillon Racine
28 Pré Catelan	Kong
Lasserre	Maxim's
Meurice	Coupe-Chou
Tour d'Argent	404
Bristol	Pierre Gagnaire
Taillevent	Hiramatsu
Cristal Room	**24** Chalet des Iles
27 Alain Ducasse	Fermette Marbeuf
Train Bleu	Relais Louis XIII
Ombres	Liza
1728	Elysées
Espadon	Maison Blanche
Ambroisie	Michel Rostang
Lapérouse	Grand Colbert
26 Jules Verne	Bofinger
Laurent	Café Marly
Apicius	Ladurée
Pavillon Ledoyen	Atelier Joël Robuchon
Bar Vendôme	Arpège
Brass. Julien	**23** Jacques Cagna
25 Buddha Bar	Rest. du Musée d'Orsay

HISTORIC SPACES

Ambassadeurs	Jules Verne
Angelina	Lapérouse
Aub. Nicolas Flamel	Lasserre
Bofinger	Laurent
Café Les Deux Magots	Maxim's
Charpentiers	Pavillon Ledoyen
1728	Pré Catelan
Espadon	Relais Louis XIII
Grande Cascade	Tour d'Argent
Grand Véfour	Train Bleu

OUTDOORS

Absinthe	Maison de l'Amér. Latine
Bar Vendôme	Méditerranée
Bristol	Nabulione
Café Lenôtre	Pavillon Montsouris
Chalet/l'Oasis	Petite Cour
Chez Gégène	Pré Catelan
Closerie des Lilas	Rest. du Palais Royal
Grande Cascade	Romantica
Jardin des Cygnes	Saut du Loup
Jardins de Bagatelle	Terrasse Mirabeau

ROMANCE

Alain Ducasse
Ambassadeurs
Ambroisie
Astrance
Boudoir
Bristol
Caviar Kaspia
Coupe-Chou
Espadon
Gordon Ramsay
Grande Cascade
Grand Véfour
Guy Savoy
Joséphine/Dumonet
Jules Verne
Lapérouse
Lasserre
Meurice
Pavillon Ledoyen
Pré Catelan
Restaurant
Tour d'Argent

ROOMS

Ambassade/Auvergne
Ambassadeurs
Ambroisie
Blue Elephant
Boeuf Couronné
Brass. Mollard
Brass. Printemps
Chez Jenny
Cristal Room
1728
Guy Savoy
Ladurée (16, rue Royale)
Lapérouse
Liza
Maison Blanche
Maison Prunier
Market
Mori Venice Bar
Oth Sombath
Pré Catelan
Senderens
Train Bleu

VIEWS

Arc
Bar Vendôme
Bon Accueil
Bouquinistes
Caviar Kaspia
Cinq
Espadon
Fontaine de Mars
Fontaine Gaillon
Georges
Grande Cascade
Grand Véfour
Isami
Jules Verne
Lapérouse
Lasserre
Maison Blanche
Méditerranée
Pavillon Ledoyen
Petite Cour
Quai
Tour d'Argent

Top Service

28 Cinq
Ambassadeurs
Taillevent
Lasserre
Grand Véfour
Espadon

27 Pierre Gagnaire
Guy Savoy
Meurice
Alain Ducasse
Bristol
Astrance
Michel Rostang

26 Ambroisie
Grande Cascade
Pré Catelan
Apicius
Tour d'Argent
Hiramatsu
Florimond
Pavillon Ledoyen
Relais d'Auteuil

25 Jacques Cagna
Carré des Feuillants
Bar Vendôme

D'Chez Eux
Temps au Temps
Table de Joël Robuchon
Arpège
Elysées
Relais Louis XIII
Maupertu

24 Gérard Besson
Lapérouse
Angle du Faubourg
Atelier Joël Robuchon
Dominique Bouchet
Timbre*
Jules Verne
Trou Gascon

23 Laurent
Braisière
Ferme St-Simon
Villaret
Goumard
Table du Lancaster
Truffière
Maison du Jardin
Poule au Pot
Violon d'Ingres*

Best Buys

1. As du Fallafel
2. Cosi
3. Crêperie de Josselin
4. Breakfast in America
5. Lina's
6. A Priori Thé
7. Jean-Paul Hévin
8. Mariage Frères
9. Angelina
10. Chartier
11. BE Boulangépicier
12. Chez Marianne
13. Boulangerie Eric Kayser
14. Chez Papa
15. Ladurée
16. Loir dans la Théière
17. Dalloyau
18. Flore en l'Ile
19. Temps au Temps
20. Cave de l'Os à Moëlle
21. Chez Janou
22. Rest. du Musée d'Orsay
23. Chez Omar
24. Higuma
25. Bistrot d'Henri
26. Verre Volé
27. Paradis du Fruit
28. Polidor
29. Relais de Venise
30. Coin/Gourmets
31. Café Charbon
32. 404
33. Dame Tartine
34. Trumilou
35. Bistrot de l'Oulette
36. P'tit Troquet
37. Timbre
38. Bouillon Racine
39. Maison du Jardin
40. Restaurant Paul

OTHER GOOD VALUES

Accolade
Afaria
Agassin
Allobroges
Al Taglio
AOC
Astier
BAM
Bascou
Bon Saint Pourçain
Breizh Café
Briciola
Café Constant
Carte Blanche
Chantairelle
Chateaubriand
Chéri Bibi
Chez L'Ami Jean
Chez Marcel
Chez Ramulaud
Christophe
Comptoir du Relais
Cul de Poule

Duc de Richelieu
Ecailler du Bistrot
Entredgeu
Epi Dupin
Epigramme
Fines Gueules
Hier & Aujourd'hui
Huîtrerie Régis
Jadis
Mesturet
Pates Viventes
Poisson Rouge
Pré Verre
Pure Café
Racines
Reuan Thai
Sot l'y Laisse
Table d'Eugène
Temps des Cerises
Tricotin
Uitr
Vieux Chêne
Winch

GOOD-VALUE PRIX FIXES

Since prices can change, please call ahead to confirm.

DINNER (40€ & UNDER)

Affriolé 34	Ferme St-Simon 36
Agapes 33	Fish La Boissonnerie 35
Allobroges 34	Florimond 36
Ardoise 32	Garnier 35
Avant Goût 31	Graindorge 34
Beurre Noisette 32	Macéo 37
Bistro d'Hubert 34	Maison Courtine 38
Bistrot de l'Oulette 33	Maison du Jardin 30
Bistrot Paul Bert 32	Mansouria 30
Bon Accueil 31	Ourcine 32
Boudoir 27	Pamphlet 35
Boulangerie 30	Papilles 31
Casa Olympe 38	Parisiennes 30
Cave de l'Os à Moëlle 20	Pasco 24
Cave Gourmande/Mark Singer . .36	Poule au Pot 30
Chateaubriand 40	Pré Verre 27
Chez L'Ami Jean 32	P'tit Troquet 33
Chez Les Anges 34	Régalade 32
Chez Michel 30	Relais de Venise 23
Christine 40	Rest. de la Tour 26
Clos des Gourmets 35	Saveurs de Flora 38
Coin/Gourmets (1er) 28	Soufflé 30
Coupe-Chou 26	Table d'Eugène 32
Epi Dupin 34	Terrines de Gérard Vié 34
Fakhr el Dine 30	Tierny & Co. 34

LUNCH (30€ & UNDER)

A et M 30	Dôme du Marais 23
Agassin 23	Eugène 24
Allobroges 20	Fakhr el Dine 23
Astier 26	Fellini (1er) 25
Aub. Bressane 25	Ferrandaise 24
Aub. Pyrénées Cévennes 30	Fish La Boissonnerie 22
Baan-Boran 15	Glou 17
Bath's 25	Gorille Blanc 20
Bellini 28	Gourmand 28
Beurre Noisette 24	Issé 25
Biche au Bois 25	Lac-Hong 22
Bistrot d'à Côté 29	Maison du Jardin 30
Bistrot Paul Bert 16	Os à Moëlle 30
Blue Elephant 16	Parc aux Cerfs 30
Bon Accueil 27	Petit Marguery 26
Bouquinistes 28	Rest. de la Tour 26
Casa Bini 29	Rôtiss. d'en Face 29
Cave de l'Os à Moëlle 20	Soufflé 24
Chateaubriand 19	Temps au Temps 30
Chez Géraud 30	Timbre 22
Chez Maître Paul 29	Troquet 24
Chez Michel 30	Truffière 24
Clos des Gourmets 29	Villaret 27

RESTAURANT
DIRECTORY

	FOOD	DECOR	SERVICE	COST

Absinthe (L') 🏷 *Bistro* | 20 | 18 | 18 | €50

1er | 24, pl du Marché St-Honoré (Pyramides/Tuileries) | 01-49-26-90-04 |
www.michelrostang.com

Now "under the direction of Caroline Rostang", Michel's daughter,
this "stylish" place "decorated like a NYC loft" with exposed-brick
walls and a big clock face overlooks "one of the trendiest addresses
in Paris today" – the Marché Saint-Honoré, which makes it "a must,
even if the food is mediocre", as some snap; others, however, applaud the bistro cooking for its "inventive touch", as well as its
"friendly" (if "spotty") service and prices that are "relatively reasonable"; N.B. get there early to nab the "great terrace" seats.

Accolade (L') 🏷Ⓜ *Bistro* | – | – | – | M

17e | 23, rue Guillaume Tell (Péreire) | 01-42-67-12-67 |
www.laccolade.com

A former butcher shop has been transformed into an "intimate
neighborhood bistro" by a young couple – he's in the kitchen, turning out "good" contemporary French cuisine (after training under
chef Michel Rostang), and she's in the dining area, two "appealing"
rooms simply decorated with wood tables and brightly painted
walls; while still a sleeper, this *bonne adresse* is gradually garnering
plaudits from Porte de Champerret locals.

A et M, Restaurant 🏷 *Classic French* | ∇ 21 | 14 | 19 | €45

16e | 136, bd Murat (Porte de St-Cloud) | 01-45-27-39-60

This venue is one of several Parisian places where a Japanese chef
nails Classic French cuisine – though its "out-of-the-way" location
near the Porte de Saint-Cloud may feel halfway to Tokyo; fortunately, the dishes are "consistently" "well executed", the service is
"pleasant" and even if the modern decor is just "average", this
"great-value" restaurant co-owned by chefs Jean-Pierre Vigato
(Apicius) and François Grandjean (Marius) is "a place to go back to."

Afaria 🏷Ⓜ *New French/Southwest* | – | – | – | M

15e | 15, rue Desnouettes (Convention) | 01-48-56-15-36

On a quiet street in the 15th, young chef-owner Julien Duboué has
created a stir with this funky bistro that serves up some innovative
spins on Southwestern French fare (apple-infused blood sausage,
grilled duck in balsamic vinegar), along with tapas for grazing types;
the casual brown-and-white dining room is decked out in country
Basque fashion, with bare wood floors and red-glass lighting fixtures
to lure a lively local crowd.

Affriolé (L') 🏷Ⓜ *Bistro* | 22 | 15 | 19 | €48

7e | 17, rue Malar (Invalides/La Tour-Maubourg) | 01-44-18-31-33

Tucked away in a "quiet street in the 7th" is this "gastronomic pearl
with low prices" – that is, relative to the "excellent", frequently
changing bistro menu that's "modern without being too trendy";
"young professionals who look as good as the chef's offerings" dine
in its "hip, small" surrounds (with a facade that opens in summer)
and don't seem to mind that "service is frenetic, if affable"; N.B. a

post-Survey revamp ushered in a more contemporary look and may outdate the above Decor score.

Agapé (L') 🗗 *New French*   - | - | - | VE

17ᵉ | 51, rue Jouffroy d'Abbans (Wagram) | 01-42-27-20-18 | www.agape-paris.fr

Maitre d'hotel Laurent Lapaire has assiduously applied many of the lessons he learned from his former master, Alain Passard of L'Arpège, at this pricey place in a well-heeled residential corner of the 17th; newly hired chef Guillaume Barcaval, ex L'Ambroisie, brings an Haute-Cuisine touch to the short, appealing market menu, while the sleek setting of taupe walls and designer tableware (e.g. napkin rings by Andrée Putman) pleases a power crowd of execs at noon and a mix of expense-accounters and stylish locals of a certain age come dinnertime.

Agapes 🅼 *Classic/New French*   - | - | - | M

5ᵉ | 47 bis, rue Poliveau (St-Marcel) | 01-43-31-69-20 | www.restaurant-agapes.com

Beyond an appealing menu – a mix of contemporary French dishes like scallop tart glossed with curried olive oil and classics such as red wine–braised beef cheeks – what's memorable about this easygoing bistro is that it could be a country *auberge* deep in the woods, instead of deep in the Latin Quarter; friendly service and gentle prices augment the rustic air of its wood-beamed ceiling and exposed-stone walls.

Agassin (L') 🗗 *Classic/New French*   - | - | - | M

7ᵉ | 8, rue Malar (Invalides/La Tour-Maubourg) | 01-47-05-18-18

After a distinguished career that's included La Tour d'Argent and the old Anacréon, chef-owner André Le Letty beckons to the business types of the 7th with this intimate establishment, whose tasteful beige-and-burgundy decor is enlivened with photos of his native Brittany; though grounded in the classics – veal kidneys in mustard, sautéed scallops in rosemary *jus* – the French menu also has its innovative moments, especially with desserts.

Aida 🗗🅼 *Japanese*   ▽ 23 | 15 | 19 | €105

7ᵉ | 1, rue Pierre Leroux (Duroc/Vaneau) | 01-43-06-14-18 | www.aidaparis.com

As "trendy" as a sake cocktail, this "memorable" Asian near the Bon Marché serves "interesting, delectable" Japanese dishes to a select crowd of 20 well-heeled diners; the "minimally decorated", Kyoto-inspired interior allows clients "to focus on the Japanese food" (prix fixe or tasting menus) and the Burgundy list; men are requested to wear jackets, the pockets preferably stuffed with yen.

Aiguière (L') 🗗 *Classic French*   - | - | - | E

11ᵉ | 37 bis, rue de Montreuil (Faidherbe-Chaligny) | 01-43-72-42-32 | www.l-aiguiere.com

In a former roadhouse for Louis XIII's musketeers, this Classic French "on the eastern reaches" of the 11th might feel like "a trek" if you're not on horseback, but it's "worth it" for "seamless service" and cooking that's a "wonderful treat for the taste buds", washed down by a bottle from the "very fine cellar"; the Gustavian-style "rustic country" decor – pale yellow with blue checked curtains – is "cheerful."

Aimant du Sud (L') ●⊠ *Classic French* — | — | — | M

13ᵉ | 40, bd Arago (Les Gobelins) | 01-47-07-33-57

With a name that means 'magnet of the south', it's no surprise there's much Midi on the menu of this Classic French, "one of the better little bistros in the 13th"; service is "friendly but irregular", and if the kitchen "occasionally misses", the "good Basque wine list" restores a sunny disposition; N.B. the decor was recently redone.

⊠ Alain Ducasse au 28 | 27 | 27 | €187
Plaza Athénée ⊠ *Haute Cuisine*

8ᵉ | Plaza Athénée | 25, av Montaigne (Alma Marceau/ Franklin D. Roosevelt) | 01-53-67-65-00 | www.alain-ducasse.com

The legendary Alain Ducasse serves up "a meal of a lifetime" at his Paris flagship, an *ancien régime* meets high-tech" destination in the Plaza Athénée; "from the amuse-bouches to the delightful candy cart" and tea made from "live herbs snipped by white-gloved waiters", the Haute Cuisine is "probably similar to what the angels are eating", while "exceptional" service "without the starch" makes each diner feel like "the most important client in the world"; it's all "divine" – and though the bill can seem "hellish", consider it "tuition toward [learning] the art of eating."

Alcazar ● *New French* 19 | 22 | 19 | €56

6ᵉ | 62, rue Mazarine (Odéon) | 01-53-10-19-99 | www.alcazar.fr

Perhaps it's "not quite as trendy as it used to be" ("what once seemed fresh and modern now seems just big and brash"), but still it's "always interesting" to "take in the scene" at Terence Conran's Saint-Germain brasserie – and what a scene it is, with seats for 200 under a skylight roof; the New French food "isn't up to the panache of the place", but it's "pleasant" and "light" – and there's always the "buzzy bar", which compensates for the oft-"inattentive" service.

Al Dar ● *Lebanese* 21 | 13 | 18 | €40

5ᵉ | 8, rue Frédéric Sauton (Maubert-Mutualité) | 01-43-25-17-15 ⊠
16ᵉ | 93, av Raymond Poincaré (Victor Hugo) | 01-45-00-96-64

"Excellent, authentic" – if comparatively "expensive" – Lebanese food (including "the best baklava" in Paris) is the draw at these popular twins in the 5th and 16th, even if the "less-than-convincing atmosphere" has some saying it's "better to get the same dishes at the take-out counter"; still, the servers who "are always smiling" encourage frequent visits from expats and others ("we eat there so often the maitre d' asked if we owned a kitchen").

Al Diwan ● *Lebanese* 21 | 14 | 20 | €49

8ᵉ | 30, av George V (Alma Marceau/George V) | 01-47-23-45-45

Homesick Lebanese and other mezeholics find "a bit of old Beirut" at this "comfortable", "high-end" Middle Easterner in "a central lo-

	FOOD	DECOR	SERVICE	COST

cation" on the posh Avenue George V; most find the "feel and the food authentic and addictive", but those who deem the wood-paneled decor and prices a little too "fancy" head next door for "great", "reasonably priced" takeaway.

Alfred ☒ *Bistro*

| | - | - | - | M |

1er | 8, rue de Montpensier (Palais Royal-Musée du Louvre/Pyramides) | 01-42-97-54-40

Overlooking the Palais-Royal, this tiny dining room has quickly become a clubby insider's address for employees of the Ministry of Culture and performers from the Comédie Française; what attracts them is the cozy atmosphere, professional service and sincere, classic bistro cooking by a politician-turned-chef.

Alivi (L') *Corsica*

| | 16 | 15 | 15 | €44 |

4^e | 27, rue du Roi de Sicile (Hôtel-de-Ville/St-Paul) | 01-48-87-90-20 | www.restaurant-alivi.com

"Corsican cuisine, Corsican ambiance, Corsican waiters" characterizes the scene at this small spot "on a little lane" in the Marais; there's debate whether the fare is "original" or "uninspiring" – it may depend on whether you "skip the formula menu, strictly for tourists, and order à la carte"; all agree that the "staff's friendly" and the prices fair.

☑ Allard ☒ *Bistro*

| | 21 | 16 | 19 | €58 |

6^e | 41, rue St-André-des-Arts (Odéon) | 01-43-26-48-23 | www.restaurant-allard.com

"As traditional as tradition gets", this seventysomething Saint-Germain "institution" serves "rich, copious" bistro fare – including a signature duck with olives that "has no challenger" – amid a setting from "bygone times" that's so "cozy" you have to "climb over each other to get to your table"; the "old-time waiters" somehow manage to be both "amiable" and "grumpy", and overall the place oozes a "Gallic charm" only slightly diluted by the clientele ("if I wanted to eat with so many Americans, I could've stayed home").

Allobroges (Les) ☒ *Classic French*

| | ▽ 22 | 18 | 21 | €37 |

20^e | 71, rue des Grands-Champs (Buzenval/Maraîchers) | 01-43-73-40-00

Those who have journeyed to this "out-of-the-way gem" tucked away in the 20th "highly recommend" its "delicious", "carefully prepared" seasonal Classic French dishes at "great-value" prices, "soft lighting in a contemporary atmosphere" and "exceptional" service (even to the extent of "providing a chef's jacket to a rain-soaked customer"); best of all, the "trek from central Paris" renders it "non-touristy."

Al Mounia ☒ *Moroccan*

| | 17 | 16 | 14 | €46 |

16^e | 16, rue de Magdebourg (Trocadéro) | 01-47-27-57-28 | www.al-mounia.com

At this 16th-arrondissement Moroccan, the "absolutely stunning" atmosphere "instantly transports you to North Africa" – as, alas, do the "slow service" and "low seats"; though many find it "a little expensive", it's "reliable" for a "quality meal" à la Marrakech.

	FOOD	DECOR	SERVICE	COST

Alsace (L') ◐ *Alsace*

| 18 | 19 | 15 | €46 |

8ᵉ | 39, av des Champs-Elysées (Franklin D. Roosevelt) | 01-53-93-97-00 | www.restaurantalsace.com

Though it's a "tourist factory" on the Champs-Elysées, this "traditional brasserie" manages to turn out "edible, if not memorable" Alsatian food, including shellfish platters and "choucroute by the ton"; while the service "can go both ways", warm-weather visitors enjoy "people-watching from the outdoor seating (so very Parisian)", and nocturnal noshers find the 24/7 opening hours "ideal."

Al Taglio *Pizza*
| - | - | - | I |

11ᵉ | 2 bis, rue Neuve Popincourt (Parmentier/Oberkampf) | 01-43-38-12-00

In the up-and-coming Oberkampf quarter is this place where young hipsters come for a pizza the action – since it serves some 30 different varieties *al taglio* (by the slice); the atmosphere in the Milanese-modern setting of gray walls and red floors is always busy and friendly, but if you want to get a whole pie to go, you gotta call a day in advance.

Ambassade d'Auvergne *Auvergne*
| 20 | 18 | 20 | €47 |

3ᵉ | 22, rue du Grenier St-Lazare (Rambuteau) | 01-42-72-31-22 | www.ambassade-auvergne.com

"Come hungry" to this "cozy", country-style table in the 3rd, a "satisfying, belt-loosening experience" whose "rustic food" "at reasonable prices" is not only "good" but offers a snapshot of the "hearty", "salty" kitchens of the Auvergne; the "friendly service borders on the paternal", urging you to finish all the signature *aligot* (potatoes whipped with cheese curds and garlic), before diving into dessert.

☑ Ambassadeurs (Les) Ⓜ *Haute Cuisine/New French*
| 28 | 29 | 28 | €174 |

8ᵉ | Hôtel de Crillon | 10, pl de la Concorde (Concorde) | 01-44-71-16-16 | www.crillon.com

The "sumptuous" "gold and marble" surroundings of the Crillon hotel are "like being inside a jewel box", a "perfect showplace" for "inventive" New French Haute Cuisine and an 1,100-label wine list "*extraordinaire*"; the service is "choreographed to perfection" while remaining "refreshingly friendly", and though the experience may "relieve you of many euros", "you get a lot for the price" (and the "delight" of a lunch menu at 88€ is a relative deal); P.S. the post-Survey arrival of chef Christopher Hache, most recently of La Grande Cascade, may outdate the above Food score.

☑ Ambroisie (L') ⓈⓂ *Haute Cuisine*
| 28 | 27 | 26 | €158 |

4ᵉ | 9, pl des Vosges (Bastille/St-Paul) | 01-42-78-51-45 | www.ambroisie-placedesvosges.com

It's like "dining in a nobleman's home" at this "smoothly run", "aptly named" Haute Cuisine haven "serving food of the gods" along with a "top flight wine list" that helps to "rationalize" the "damage the bill inflicts"; "the most intimate of Paris' grand restaurants" (only 40 seats), it's also possibly the "toughest table in town" – and beware of "being exiled to the back room" – but "who wouldn't want to be king of the Place des Vosges, even just for a few hours?"

Amici Miei 🗷 🅼 *Pizza* | 19 | 13 | 13 | €33 |

11ᵉ | 44, rue Saint-Sabin (Bréguet-Sabin/Chemin-Vert) | 01-42-71-82-62 | www.amici-miei.net

Many fans of the "really good pizzas" thrown at this tiny place regret its move to larger digs in the 11th, saying the "charm got lost" – but the "high-strung service" stayed ("where's the warmth of Italy?"); still, those pining for pie concede it's a decent enough "neighborhood address."

☑ Ami Louis (L') 🅼 *Bistro* | 25 | 16 | 18 | €109 |

3ᵉ | 32, rue du Vertbois (Arts et Métiers/Temple) | 01-48-87-77-48

"Don't eat beforehand", as the "Pantagruelian portions" at this classic bistro make it "a scene from a classic food orgy", starring "superb foie gras", "orgasmic fries" and the world's "priciest", most "renowned" roast chicken; over the decades regulars, tourists and "many a VIP" have made this 3rd-arrondissement vet a "favorite", and if foes find it "a bit *fatigué*", scores see it as "blessedly unchanged", from the "shabby" interior to the "cranky French" service ("the waiters still toss your coat onto the overhead racks").

Ami Pierre (A l') ◐🗷🅼 *Mediterranean* | 17 | 15 | 16 | €37 |

11ᵉ | 5, rue de la Main-d'Or (Ledru-Rollin) | 01-47-00-17-35

Not much bigger than a cork, this "small, noisy" *bistrot à vins* near the Bastille claims a devoted following of vinophiles who, in between sips, soak up the "good, simple" Mediterranean cooking under the watchful eye of a "charming" owner.

Ampère (L') 🗷 *Bistro/Eclectic* | - | - | - | M |

17ᵉ | 1, rue Ampère (Wagram) | 01-47-63-72-05

Followers of chef-owner Philippe Detourbe, who disappeared for a few years after running an acclaimed restaurant in the 15th, have "welcomed" him back to this place north of the Parc Monceau, where he whips up an Eclectic array of "great bistro food" on "varied, highly creative menus"; clients commend "friendly service", pleasant surroundings and "reasonable prices" – in short, "what's not to like?"

Amuse Bouche (L') 🗷🅼 *New French* | 17 | 13 | 15 | €44 |

14ᵉ | 186, rue du Château (Gaîté/Mouton-Duvernet) | 01-43-35-31-61

This "charming, small" amuse-bouche "off the Avenue du Maine" in the 14th may be "a little out of the way" but its "original" New French menu has many murmuring "yum, yum" within the "*très fun*" environs; prices are judged "correct" and service "considerate", while the owner's family photos and copper pots help create a "cozy" feel.

Anahï ◐ *Argentinean* | 19 | 15 | 15 | €49 |

3ᵉ | 49, rue Volta (Arts et Métiers/Temple) | 01-48-87-88-24

"Chichi" carnivores from the fashion crowd congregate nightly at this Latin American, a former *boucherie* in the 3rd, where "meat

	FOOD	DECOR	SERVICE	COST

meat meat" is the name of the game, notably "choice Argentine steak"; though some find the "butcher-chic" decor a bit "creepy", this "high-volume" "hangout" is so much "fun" that nobody beefs about the "expensive" bill.

Anahuacalli *Mexican*

21	14	19	€41

5e | 30, rue des Bernardins (Maubert-Mutualité) | 01-43-26-10-20
Adoring amigos claim that this Latin Quarter cantina – "Margaritaville in the City of Light" – is "the only good Mexican" in Paris, with "genuine", "expertly prepared" south-of-the-border eats ("come early for the chiles rellenos, before they run out") and a "warm welcome" from the staff; if "the prices are high" given the "cramped" digs, a "pitcher or two of margaritas will help you forget" all that.

Andy Wahloo ●🗷Ⓜ *Moroccan*

▽ 14	22	12	€36

3e | 69, rue des Gravilliers (Arts et Métiers) | 01-42-71-20-38
The name of this "lively bar" in the Marais, adjacent to Le 404, means 'I have nothing' in Arabic (perhaps the mantra for the "really bad" service), but it also channels the spirit of that other Andy and his Factory with its North African Pop Art decor, "good music", "exotic" cocktails and "simple" Moroccan mezes that clients nibble while sitting on paint-can stools; it's the "perfect place to start an evening quietly with friends or to finish it, madly dancing."

🗷 Angelina 🗷 *Tearoom*

20	20	15	€28

1er | 226, rue de Rivoli (Concorde/Tuileries) | 01-42-60-82-00 | www.groupe-bertrand.com
"You can go for brunch if you want", but most "skip the food" at this "legendary" tea salon and go straight to the "otherworldly" African hot chocolate so thick "your spoon almost stands up in the cup", plus "decadently dense whipped chantilly" and the "famous Mont Blanc" for an added sugar rush; despite "surly service" and "long lines", this belle epoque address across from the Tuileries is eternally "crowded", mainly with tourists, who swear that once you've consumed their *chocolat chaud*, "everything else is just a beverage."

Angelo Procopio ●🗷 *Italian*

-	-	-	M

1er | 89, rue St-Honoré (Châtelet/Louvre-Rivoli) | 01-40-41-06-25
Chef Angelo Procopio, ex Il Viccolo, has a hit on his hands with this hip, casual dining room in a fashion-driven neighborhood just shy of Les Halles; the Italian menu changes daily but stars starters like Burrata cheese from Puglia with cherry tomatoes and fresh homemade pasta; reasonable prices and a cute little terrace out front when the sun shines means it's always packed.

Angle du Faubourg (L') 🗷 *Classic/New French*

24	21	24	€75

8e | 195, rue du Faubourg St-Honoré (Charles de Gaulle-Etoile/Ternes) | 01-40-74-20-20 | www.taillevent.com
The Vrinat family's "stylish" New French in the 8th is a "budget alternative" to their "celebrated" Taillevent, and yet there's "nothing second-rate" about the "edgy", "inspired" dishes in a "refreshingly different" contemporary setting, with "excellent wines" by the bot-

tle or glass and "well-paced" service; lunch hour sees a corporate crowd while evenings are more "serene", but day or night, the "nicely spaced tables" make this "great for business and/or romance."

Annapurna ◑▣ Indian ▽ 18 | 17 | 19 | €37

8e | 32, rue de Berri (George V/St-Philippe-du-Roule) | 01-45-63-91-62
While it "caters to French taste buds by extinguishing the heat and more complicated flavors", the refined curries and tandooris "certainly satisfy" at this upscale Indian – Paris' oldest – off the Champs; those in-the-know spend a bit more and "book the little 'Punjab' salon" where low tables are surrounded by tapestries and diners eat to the melodious accompaniment of a sitar player.

Antoine ◑ Bistro/Seafood – | – | – | E

16e | 10, av de New York (Alma Marceau) | 01-40-70-19-28 | www.antoine-paris.fr
A terrific view of the Eiffel Tower across the Seine and an appealing catch-of-the-day menu have made this cozy little riverside bistro a hit with well-heeled locals in the 16th; ladies who lunch and execs tuck into grilled sole, bouillabaisse and sea bass in the light and airy dining room, while power couples dominate at dinner.

AOC (L') ▣ Bistro 18 | 14 | 16 | €40

5e | 14, rue des Fossés St-Bernard (Cardinal Lemoine/Jussieu) | 01-43-54-22-52 | www.restoaoc.com
This Latin Quarter bistro run by a "lovely couple" is a "fantastic place to irritate your vegetarian friends" with "copious amounts of" "traditional" "country French cuisine" made with "top-notch meat" and other "fresh ingredients" (a mark of quality, 'AOC' indicates adherence to government standards), served by "pros who never lose their smile"; N.B. the Decor score doesn't reflect a recent freshening up.

✕ Apicius ▣ Haute Cuisine 26 | 26 | 26 | €135

8e | 20, rue d'Artois (George V/St-Philippe-du-Roule) | 01-43-80-19-66 | www.restaurant-apicius.com
It's easy to "fall in love" with "movie-star-handsome" chef-owner Jean-Pierre Vigato and his Haute Cuisine venue, a "stunning" mansion in the centrally located 8th with "spectacular decor" and a "hidden garden", plus "welcoming service" that's "close to perfection"; "but the food trumps all", "combining the very best of the French classics with creative modern influences"; in short, supporters swear this place "outshines" the rest, though "alas, it's impossible to get a reservation."

Apollo Eclectic – | – | – | M

14e | 3, pl Denfert Rochereau (Denfert-Rochereau) | 01-45-38-76-77 | www.restaurant-apollo.com
The "fantastic terrace" on the street-level concourse of a métro station in the 14th may be "super-nice in summer", but otherwise this Eclectic with "kitschy" "retro"-'70s decor fails to inspire: "Apollo was the god of prophesy – I wish that someone had prophesized that this place serves totally forgettable food."

	FOOD	DECOR	SERVICE	COST

A Priori Thé *Tearoom* — 16 | 19 | 15 | €24

2e | 35, Galerie Vivienne (Bourse/Palais Royal-Musée du Louvre) |
01-42-97-48-75

"Deliciously fresh and creatively prepared" cakes, scones and savories (including many meat-free, "great-for-vegetarians" varieties)
make this "adorable" little tearoom with a "gorgeous" skylight in the
"sparkling" Galerie Vivienne a perennial favorite – even, dare we
say, a priority – "between two shopping sessions" in the 2nd; "owned
by a cheery American expat", Peggy Hancock, for 30 years, it also
does "a nice Sunday brunch."

NEW Arc (L') ⑤ *New French* — - | - | - | M

8e | 12, rue de Presbourg (Charles de Gaulle-Etoile) | 01-45-00-78-70 |
www.larc-paris.com

Ensconced in a handsome 1854 Napoleon III private mansion, with
one of Paris' best views right onto the Arc de Triomphe at Etoile, this
upscale-casual restaurant/bar/club attracts lots of business types
at lunch with its well-spaced tables, impressive contemporary
French cuisine from chef Antony Germani (ex Joël Robuchon) and
reasonable 35€ menu; the '70s-style cocktail lounge and bar is a
meeting point for young trendies, while the garden-level nightclub is
popular with clubbing types on weekends.

Z Ardoise (L') Ⓜ *Bistro* — 24 | 13 | 19 | €41

1er | 28, rue du Mont-Thabor (Concorde/Tuileries) | 01-42-96-28-18 |
www.lardoise-paris.com

In a high-rent district of the 1st, "an abundance of Americans"
crowds into the "hole-in-the-wall" digs of this "perfect neighborhood bistro" for "marvelous, inventive" French food that "does not
require a chemistry degree and six hours to appreciate", delivered
by "friendly, bilingual" servers at an "unbelievable price"; the "minimal" decor is easy to ignore, but avoid the "basement hinterland."

Arome (L') ⑤ *Classic/New French* — - | - | - | M

8e | 3, rue St-Philippe-du-Roule (St-Philippe-du-Roule) | 01-42-25-55-98 |
www.larome.fr

Following up on the success of L'Ami Marcel, owner Eric Martins
moved on to this chic location in the 8th, which has eye-pleasing decor
of arched doorways, Murano lamps, chestnut tablecloths and an open
kitchen, from which waft the *aromes* of chef Thomas Boullault's
(ex Le Cinq) cuisine, which surfs from Classic to contemporary
French; the prix fixe lunch has made regulars of local business types,
while a valet service is the icing on the cake in the evenings.

Z Arpège (L') ⑤ *Haute Cuisine* — 26 | 24 | 25 | €187

7e | 84, rue de Varenne (Varenne) | 01-47-05-09-06 |
www.alain-passard.com

It's like "tasting such fundamental products as tomatoes, lobster,
potatoes for the first time" aver acolytes of the "astonishingly intense experience" provided by this Haute Cuisine temple in the 7th
arrondissement, where chef-owner Alain Passard has a "genius" for
turning even "simple vegetables" and seafood (no red meat) into a

| | FOOD | DECOR | SERVICE | COST |

"religious experience"; the "elegant" Lalique-paneled setting may seem "spare" ("beware the downstairs dining room"), "the service stiffly correct" and the bill the "most expensive" you've ever seen (after all, "an onion is just an onion") – unless, as many do, you think of the "food as art."

ⓏⒶ As du Fallafel (L') ◐ *Israeli*

| 24 | 7 | 14 | €13 |

4ᵉ | 34, rue des Rosiers (St-Paul) | 01-48-87-63-60

"Long lines" help you locate this "go-to location" for "fantastic falafels" "brimming with all the fixings" (including "transcendent" fried eggplant) and other Israeli eats, to be consumed "while traipsing in the Marais" or else sitting "shoehorned" inside; "service would have to improve to be indifferent and the place looks like a dump, but who cares" when you're noshing on "one of the most delicious inexpensive meals in Paris" – the town's Best Buy, in fact.

Asian ◐ *Asian*

| 16 | 18 | 15 | €49 |

8ᵉ | 30, av George V (Alma Marceau/George V) | 01-56-89-11-00 | www.asian.fr

"Grandiose", "dark"-lit Asiatic decor remains the main, if not "the only reason to visit" this once "trendy", now "touristy" bar/restaurant that's "quite expensive, as it's in the Champs-Elysées" area; though "they try hard", the Pan-Asian cuisine – "20% Thai, 20% sushi, 20% Chinese and the rest, indeterminate" – "just doesn't measure up", except possibly "for Sunday brunch", and the service could "drive even the Dalai Lama to drink."

Assiette (L') Ⓜ *Bistro*

| – | – | – | E |

14ᵉ | 181, rue du Château (Gaîté/Mouton-Duvernet) | 01-43-22-64-86 | www.restaurant-lassiette.com

"Mitterrand made it famous, but he is gone and so is the buzz", which may account for the low vote count of this veteran Montparnasse bistro; nevertheless, the simple Southwestern cooking – augmented with healthy touches by an Alain Ducasse–trained chef from Benoît – still thrills, and the "informal" 1930s butcher shop setting feels "fresh and stylish."

Astier *Bistro*

| 21 | 15 | 18 | €41 |

11ᵉ | 44, rue J.P. Timbaud (Oberkampf/Parmentier) | 01-43-57-16-35 | www.restaurant-astier.com

The "familial feel" of this "delightful" neighborhood bistro near the funky Rue Oberkampf owes as much to the "tightly packed" tables as to the "gargantuan cheese tray" "shared by all" – the culmination of a "consistently good" three-course meal of Classic French fare, from "fresh seafood" to "forgotten dishes" featuring offal, on a fixed-price menu that surveyors call "a steal."

Astor (L') Ⓩ *Haute Cuisine*

| 16 | 16 | 16 | €64 |

8ᵉ | Hôtel Astor | 11, rue d'Astorg (St-Augustin) | 01-53-05-05-20 | www.hotel-astor.net

Hotel guests and businesspeople frequent this "classy" '30s-style room in the corporate 8th for "attentive" service and Haute Cuisine that's "satisfying" if "not terribly original"; on the plus side: the "well-spaced tables allow for conversation", the prices, while still "dear", have actually dropped and it always helps that "they can make a good martini."

☒ Astrance (L') 🔒Ⓜ *New French* | 28 | 22 | 27 | €154 |

16ᵉ | 4, rue Beethoven (Passy) | 01-40-50-84-40

"Young, passionate" chef/co-owner Pascal Barbot "manages to wow the most blasé palates" with "inventive" New French cuisine that's "otherworldly", "intellectual" and always "surprising" (especially at dinner, when the "no-choice" tasting menu is the only option) at this "hard-to-get-into" table in the 16th, where a near-"flawless" staff with a "personal touch" services the small, "sophisticated" room; aesthetes argue "they could rethink the decor, but with bookings two months in advance, why – and when?"; N.B. open Tuesday–Friday only.

Atelier Berger (L') 🔒 *New French* | 21 | 17 | 17 | €48 |

1ᵉʳ | 49, rue Berger (Louvre-Rivoli) | 01-40-28-00-00 | www.restaurant-atelierberger.com

A Scandinavian chef-owner comes up with some "really fascinating combinations, like tuna tartare with black squid-ink sorbet" on the New French–with-Norwegian-notes menu at this duplex on the edge of Les Halles; sometimes the service and "surrealist" cuisine are "uneven", but overall, this "original" offers "good value for the money."

☒ Atelier de Joël Robuchon | 28 | 24 | 24 | €100 |
(L') ◑ *Haute Cuisine*

7ᵉ | Hôtel Pont Royal | 5, rue de Montalembert (Rue du Bac) | 01-42-22-56-56 | www.joel-robuchon.com

In the tony 7th, the idolized chef's "Asian-sleek" "canteen for the rich" has them queuing at the door, then sitting "on a stool at a counter" ("singles welcomed") and watching the kitchen turn out "sublime", "cutting-edge" Haute Cuisine; tapas-size portions offer "a great way to sample the offerings" from the Robuchon repertoire, though the "hearty of appetite" must be "prepared to pay a fortune"; cynics snap that the staff, while "attentive", displays "typical French insouciance", but the only really "irksome" item is the no-reservations policy (except for very early and very late).

Atelier Maître Albert (L') ◑ *Bistro* | 21 | 22 | 21 | €62 |

5ᵉ | 1, rue Maître-Albert (Maubert-Mutualité) | 01-56-81-30-01 | www.ateliermaitrealbert.com

"Redone nicely" since it became a Guy Savoy-run rotisserie a while back, this Latin Quarter site juxtaposes "traditional French" bistro cooking – it's "amazing how tasty roast chicken and mashed potatoes can be" – with an "edgy contemporary look and beautiful fireplace" to create a "dark", "smart atmosphere"; a few antagonists gripe about "the limited menu" and the "painful" bill, but most appreciate the "thoughtful food and glitzy crowd" ("even the servers look hip").

Atlas (L') Ⓜ *Moroccan*

	FOOD	DECOR	SERVICE	COST
	20	16	19	€42

5ᵉ | 12, bd St-Germain (Maubert-Mutualité) | 01-46-33-86-98

"On a cold winter night", this "brief stop in Morocco" with its "border-line kitsch" decor warms travelers with "homey choices" from the land of "sweet and tangy"; in fine weather "eat outside and watch the crowd" of the *Quartier Latin.*

Auberge Aveyronnaise ● *Aveyron*

	FOOD	DECOR	SERVICE	COST
	-	-	-	M

12ᵉ | 40, rue Gabriel Lamé (Cour St-Emilion) | 01-43-40-12-24

"If you're really hungry, this is the place to go for hearty fare" attest aficionados of the Auvergne area – e.g. *aligot* (cheesy whipped potatoes), blood sausage and Aubrac beef that's "better" than most; it may be in the modern Bercy district, but in between the decor (checkered tablecloths, huge fireplace) and "reasonable prices", it feels like it's smack-dab in the provinces.

Auberge Bressane (L') *Classic French*

	FOOD	DECOR	SERVICE	COST
	20	16	19	€47

7ᵉ | 16, av de la Motte-Picquet (Ecole Militaire/La Tour-Maubourg) | 01-47-05-98-37 | www.auberge-bressane.fr

A "loyal" clientele of "trendy people during the week and families on weekends" makes pilgrimage to this "authentic" provincial bistro for "heartwarmingly" Classic French dishes that are almost extinct in this "well-heeled" area near Ecole Militaire; with its "friendly", "relaxed vibe" and 1950s/Gothic château decor, it's "a great place to beat those Sunday-night blues"; P.S. "don't forget to preorder your soufflé."

Auberge Dab (L') ●Ⓩ *Brasserie*

	FOOD	DECOR	SERVICE	COST
	16	14	15	€56

16ᵉ | 161, av de Malakoff (Porte Maillot) | 01-45-00-32-22 | www.rest-gj.com

Come to this "honest", "practical" "neighborhood brasserie" for a "fresh" shellfish fix or some "consistent" classic dishes, served nonstop till 2 AM; fans find the well-heeled crowd from the surrounding 16th adds to the "old-fashioned charm" of the "typical decor"; but foes fume the place is "pretentious" and "overpriced for what it is."

Auberge de la Reine Blanche *Classic/New French*

	FOOD	DECOR	SERVICE	COST
	19	18	19	€39

4ᵉ | 30, rue St-Louis-en-l'Ile (Pont-Marie/St-Paul) | 01-46-33-07-87

"Cozy and charming", just like the Ile Saint-Louis where it's located, this "warm" little bistro is perfect for a low-key lunch or "casual dinner" of carefully cooked Classic and New French fare, served by an "inviting" staff; views vary as to whether the tight tables are "romantic" or "so small you risk eating your neighbors' dish", but prices are "very reasonable", given the "generous portions."

Auberge du Champ de Mars Ⓩ *Classic French*

	FOOD	DECOR	SERVICE	COST
	17	16	19	€40

7ᵉ | 18, rue de l'Exposition (Ecole Militaire) | 01-45-51-78-08

"Gracious hosts", a husband-and-wife team, attract American "visitors and loyal regulars" to this "homey" and enviably situated "little restaurant" near the Eiffel Tower; *hélas,* sliding scores support oppo-

	FOOD	DECOR	SERVICE	COST

nents who opine the "simple" Classic French fare is "ordinary" and the "wine list almost nonexistent."

Auberge du Clou (L') *Classic French*

| 16 | 12 | 14 | €53 |

9ᵉ | 30, av Trudaine (Anvers/Pigalle) | 01-48-78-22-48 | www.aubergeduclou.fr

Relatively new owners, and an even newer chef, have been working hard to dust off this 120-year-old auberge in the 9th arrondissement, named for the nails on which artists left paintings to pay for their meals; "good quality, traditional French [cuisine] with some interesting 'world' dishes" is served amid "old-fashioned" decor with fireplace and wood beams – but the trump card is the terrace that's heated in winter.

Auberge Etchégorry ⑤Ⓜ *Southwest*

| - | - | - | M |

13ᵉ | 41, rue Croulebarbe (Corvisart/Les Gobelins) | 01-44-08-83-51 | www.etchegorry.com

Cured hams and garlic braids hang from the ceiling of this bastion of Basque cooking, "worth a try" for "quality" Southwestern specialties such as *piperade* (a sweet pepper, onion and tomato sauté) or stuffed squid, all dished out with an equally sunny dose of hospitality; it occupies a "quiet" street in the 13th.

Auberge Nicolas Flamel ⑤ *Classic French*

| ▽ 23 | 23 | 25 | €54 |

3ᵉ | 51, rue de Montmorency (Arts et Métiers/Rambuteau) | 01-42-71-77-78 | www.auberge-nicolas-flamel.fr

The "distant past" seems like yesterday at this "historic" home – the city's oldest – built by an alchemist in the upper Marais in 1407; but medieval meanderings aren't the only reason for a pilgrimage to this "romantic treasure": young chef-owner Alain Al Geaam has refreshed the decor, brought in an "intelligent" staff and prepares "excellent" Med-accented French classics; best of all, clients won't have to turn lead into gold to pay for it all.

Auberge Pyrénées Cévennes

(L') ⑤ *Lyon/Southwest*

| 20 | 13 | 21 | €46 |

11ᵉ | 106, rue de la Folie-Méricourt (République) | 01-43-57-33-78

"Its cassoulet could be the best in the world – but all else is pretty good too" at this "honest neighborhood table" near the Place de la République; a "hoot of an owner" reigns amid an "atmospheric" aubergelike decor as "friendly servers" set down "generous portions" of Lyonnais and Southwest dishes; prices are rising, but most still find them "reasonable", and the overall vibe "simply marvelous."

Auguste ⑤ *Classic French*

| ▽ 25 | 24 | 23 | €80 |

7ᵉ | 54, rue de Bourgogne (Varenne) | 01-45-51-61-09 | www.restaurantauguste.fr

It's been an august period for this "young", "chic" table in the 7th run by chef Gaël Orieux, ex-second at the Hôtel Meurice; politicians and the beau monde quickly fill the 30 coveted seats in a "modern", "elegant" room with a poppy-red wall and gray wood floor, and consult the "delightful", "varying" menu of "creative" Classic French cuisine and mostly (if "not always consistently") "good service"; insiders insist "enjoy it before it becomes more of a celebrity", and while prices are still "reasonable" for this caliber of cooking.

Autobus Imperial (L') 🗷 *Classic French* | - | - | - | M |

1ᵉʳ | 14, rue Mondétour (Etienne Marcel/Les Halles) | 01-42-36-00-18 | www.autobus-imperial.fr

You don't need a ticket to ride what some contented commuters call "the best bang for your euro in Paris", a vast restaurant/lounge with an "original art nouveau interior" under a soaring ceiling with skylight; "one of the rare good addresses near Les Halles", it offers "traditional French fare, jazzed up by the youthful culinary staff"; sweet tooths should be sure to stop off at the tea salon, with its "desserts to die for"; N.B. it changed owners post-Survey.

Autour du Mont 🗷 Ⓜ *Seafood* | - | - | - | M |

15ᵉ | 58, rue Vasco de Gama (Lourmel) | 01-42-50-55-63

Near the Porte de Versailles, this cozy, "good seafooder" pulls a media crowd at noon – there are several TV studios nearby – and young working couples at night with an imaginatively prepared catch-of-the-day menu and a relaxed atmosphere; the marine-themed decor may be "a bit tacky", but the moderate prices have made it popular.

Autour du Saumon *Seafood* | 17 | 11 | 14 | €39 |

4ᵉ | 60, rue François Miron (St-Paul) | 01-42-77-23-08 🗷
9ᵉ | 56, rue des Martyrs (Pigalle/St-Georges) | 01-48-78-47-58
15ᵉ | 116, rue de la Convention (Boucicaut) | 01-45-54-31-16 🗷
17ᵉ | 3, av de Villiers (Villiers) | 01-40-53-89-00 🗷
www.autourdusaumon.eu

This salmon-seller has spawned a slew of venues that present a "pricey" but "good selection of smoked fish", plus other seafood specialties, in a "bright, uncluttered" nautical setting, almost "like being in a fishbowl"; while service is "efficient", those in a hurry can migrate to the adjoining boutique for products to go.

Avant Goût (L') 🗷 Ⓜ *New French* | 23 | 16 | 21 | €43 |

13ᵉ | 26, rue Bobillot (Place d'Italie) | 01-53-80-24-00 | www.lavantgout.com

"If you're willing to make the trip to the 13th, this bustling bistro will never disappoint – and sometimes it'll stun" say supporters; the New French cuisine is "original", even "surprising" ("where else would we have been inspired to try a pig pot-au-feu?"), and "for a heck of a price" too; while the "minimally decorated" dining room has been redone, still "the tables are mighty close together" and service swings from "smiling" to "surly."

Avenue (L') ◑ *New French* | 18 | 19 | 16 | €64 |

8ᵉ | 41, av Montaigne (Franklin D. Roosevelt) | 01-40-70-14-91 | www.restaurant-avenue.fr

"Extreme style" sums up this "place to see-and-be-seen in the heart of fashionland", aka the Avenue Montaigne; Jacques Garcia's "cool" baroque decor is backdrop to the "up-to-the-minute" New French menu, and while "always good" – if "sooo nouveau riche" in price – "it's secondary to the people-watching"; "if you're not famous, getting the attention of the model-waitresses can be tedious"; P.S. try to sit in the "lovely" "sidewalk-window area."

Azabu **M** *Japanese*   ▽ 24 | 17 | 17 | €52

6ᵉ | 3, rue André Mazet (Odéon) | 01-46-33-72-05

"For those who want to discover Japanese cuisine that goes beyond the clichés", this "rare find" in Saint-Germain offers "one of Paris' best teppanyaki" grills, manned by a chef who "cooks in front of you with great calm"; the "original" dishes include "melt-in-your-mouth fish" and a "surprising" foie gras, in a room decorated with Zen sobriety.

Baan-Boran **◐ ☒** *Thai*   20 | 14 | 17 | €39

1ᵉʳ | 43, rue de Montpensier (Palais Royal-Musée du Louvre) | 01-40-15-90-45 | www.baan-boran.com

"Thai food with a delicate touch" – including "typical dishes from different regions" – distinguishes this "authentic" Siamese standby in the 1st; amid a "nice, bright" – some say "sterile" – setting, patrons also praise the "non-pompous" servers; pity that the "portions seem kind of small."

Bacchantes (Les) **◐ ☒** *Wine Bar/Bistro*   - | - | - | M

9ᵉ | 21, rue de Caumartin (Havre-Caumartin/Opéra) | 01-42-65-25-35 | www.lesbacchantes.fr

Habitués "go back over and over again" to this "down-to-earth" wine bar/bistro conveniently located by the Opéra Garnier that serves late for a post-ballet bacchanalia; the "traditional French food" – "especially meat" – is washed down with a good selection of wines by the glass or bottle, amid rustic, low-key decor.

Ballon des Ternes (Le) **◐** *Brasserie*   15 | 13 | 14 | €54

17ᵉ | 103, av des Ternes (Porte Maillot) | 01-45-74-17-98

Located near the Porte Maillot, this "traditional brasserie" is a "convivial", if "slightly noisy" destination for "excellent shellfish" and other "respectable" French classics; however, most foes find the fare "costly for what it is", the service "middling" and even the "retro" belle epoque decor, consisting of wood paneling, glass partitions, moleskin banquettes and bric-a-brac, "uninteresting."

Ballon et Coquillages **◐** *Seafood*   - | - | - | M

17ᵉ | 71, bd Gouvion-St-Cyr (Porte Maillot) | 01-45-74-17-98

In the 17th, this pearl of an annex of the Ballon des Ternes consists of a curved mosaic counter with only 14 stools (and no reservations) where clients perch and partake of "magnificent seafood" and other briny treats, ordered à la carte or by the platter; strangers quickly become friends thanks to the "convivial" ambiance – though "you need to speak French to fit in."

BAM bar à manger **☒** *Bistro*   - | - | - | I

1ᵉʳ | 13, rue des Lavandières-Ste-Opportune (Châtelet) | 01-42-21-01-72 | www.baramanger.canalblog.com

Les Halles' hip little bistro pulls a food-loving young crowd with a contemporary French menu, sometimes spiked with Asian spices, that changes regularly but remains deliciously affordable; stone walls, dark-stained tables and chairs and a shiny zinc-topped bar convey a casual attitude, augmented by a few tables out front for sidewalk dining in good weather.

Bamboche (Le) *New French*

19	18	19	€66

7ᵉ | 15, rue de Babylone (Sèvres-Babylone) | 01-45-49-14-40

The pair of chefs who took over this "small, romantic" New French "away from the crowds, despite its [proximity] to the Bon Marché" emporium, have hit cruising speed, and fans praise their "inventive flavors" and servers whose "suggestions are right on the mark"; still, not all are convinced the place is worth "the relatively high prices."

Banyan ● *Thai*

19	12	16	€38

15ᵉ | 24, pl Etienne Pernet (Félix Faure) | 01-40-60-09-31

This "little corner in the 15th" might be an "unexpected location" for a "culinary adventure", especially given the "plain" surroundings; but epicurean explorers know they'll find "a large variety" of "succulent", "original" Thai dishes prepared with "a bit of flair" by an alumnus of the Blue Elephant; the service is "serene" and the ambiance "relaxing", though some do get hot and bothered by the "expensive" cost for "derisory portions."

Bar à Huîtres (Le) ● *Seafood*

17	14	14	€41

3ᵉ | 33, bd Beaumarchais (Bastille) | 01-48-87-98-92
5ᵉ | 33, rue St-Jacques (Cluny La Sorbonne) | 01-44-07-27-37
14ᵉ | 112, bd du Montparnasse (Raspail/Vavin) | 01-43-20-71-01
17ᵉ | 69, av de Wagram (Ternes) | 01-43-80-63-54
www.lebarahuitres.fr

The "eponymous [oyster] is the best thing" at this school of seafooders "with kitschy, shells-plastered-all-over-the-walls" decor by Jacques Garcia; they're a tad "touristy" and "factorylike" (while "cordial", the staff's "happy to have you finish fast"), but they're "reliable for a quick, late supper"; do stick to playing the shell game, however, as "they don't know how to cook fish."

Baratin (Le) ●🚫Ⓜ *Wine Bar/Bistro*

16	11	12	€33

20ᵉ | 3, rue Jouye-Rouve (Belleville) | 01-43-49-39-70

This "good little" Belleville *bistrot à vins* packs them in with "an original, reasonably priced wine list" and a short daily menu of "market-fresh", "copious", "original" French dishes; but the real appeal of this "unpretentious" hole-in-the-wall is its "remarkable ambiance for an evening among friends" – even if some sense "the owner saves his smile for the regulars."

Bar des Théâtres ● *Bistro*

15	10	15	€44

8ᵉ | 6, av Montaigne (Alma Marceau) | 01-47-23-34-63

For over 60 years, this "classic" bistro "facing the Théâtre des Champs-Elysées" has been "a rendezvous before or after the theater", "a place to stop if shopping on the Avenue Montaigne" or a "great perch for people-watching" the performers who often patronize it; if the "steak tartare is *magnifique*, the rest" of the menu is barely "adequate" – as is the service – and even the aura's "not what it was" since this vet "lost most of its dining rooms" to construction.

Barlotti ● *Italian*

15 | 22 | 15 | €50

1er | 35, pl du Marché St-Honoré (Pyramides/Tuileries) | 01-44-86-97-97 | www.buddhabar.com

"It's all about the decor" at this "modern Italian" in the midst of the furiously "trendy" Place du Marché Saint-Honoré – and yes, the setting's "superb", a two-story atrium with soaring glass windows, parquet floors and jewel-toned seats; but the "disappointed" declare if you're looking for "authentic cuisine" that's not "overpriced", you should walk right on past; as for the staffers, they're quite "caring . . . about their tip."

Baron Rouge (Le) Ⓜ *Wine Bar/Bistro*

– | – | – | M

12^e | 1, rue Théophile Roussel (Ledru-Rollin) | 01-43-43-14-32

"Just off the Marché d'Aligre", this "really pleasant" *bar à vins* – a neighborhood "institution" – is a must for "amazing oysters" (a weekend tradition) or cheese and charcuterie plates; of course, "it's mostly about the wine", which you can consume "standing up" *sur place* or bring home, in "decanters filled right from the barrel."

Barrio Latino ● *Pan-Latin*

▽ 12 | 21 | 14 | €39

12^e | 46-48, rue du Faubourg St-Antoine (Bastille) | 01-55-78-84-75 | www.buddhabar.com

Salsaholics "head downstairs to work off dinner with a little Latin dance" in this four-story nightclub near the Bastille that's "always crowded, always a scene" with "pulsing music" making temperatures rise around the Gustave Eiffel–designed staircase and "great" Hispanic decor; though the kitchen seems like an afterthought with its "bland" Pan-Latin cuisine, it doesn't much matter, for the fiesta is "so much fun."

Bartolo ⓧ Ⓜ ⌀ *Pizza*

17 | 11 | 12 | €40

6^e | 7, rue des Canettes (St-Germain-des-Prés) | 01-43-26-27-08

What's "probably the best pizza in town – the way they do it in Naples", baked in a wood-burning beehive-shaped oven – has kept 'em coming for nearly 60 years to this Italian in Saint-Germain; however, its notoriously "nasty" service, tacky 1950s-vintage decor (complete with Bay of Naples vistas) and "pricey" tabs that you "must pay with cash" cause many to murmur it's "for masochists" only.

Bar Vendôme ● *Classic French*

23 | 26 | 25 | €71

1er | Hôtel Ritz | 15, pl Vendôme (Concorde/Opéra) | 01-43-16-33-63 | www.ritzparis.com

"Drop your Hermès purse by your Manolo-clad feet nestled by all those shopping bags" and enjoy a "great glass of champagne" while celebrity-spotting at this "chic, sophisticated" bar at the Ritz; it's always "a good refuge" for a Classic French "light lunch", tea or happy-hour drinks, whether in the "elaborate" interior or in "the peaceful garden, with birds chirping"; and if you squawk "ouch after you see the bill" – well, just "charge it to the room."

	FOOD	DECOR	SERVICE	COST

Bascou (Au) ☒ *Basque*

20 | 14 | 20 | €43

3ᵉ | 38, rue Réaumur (Arts et Métiers) | 01-42-72-69-25 | www.au-bascou.fr

"A touch of French Basque country right at the center of Paris" flourishes at this establishment in the 3rd; the chef-owner (a Lucas Carton alum) is "talented" in preparing Southwestern cuisine, supplemented by a "good selection of regional wines"; "this is the kind of place you tell no one about, so it remains uncrowded" – and its prices "fair"; N.B. a recent redo may outdate the above Decor score.

Basilic (Le) *Basque*

15 | 13 | 16 | €50

7ᵉ | 2, rue Casimir Périer (Invalides/Solférino) | 01-44-18-94-64

Possessing a "lovely terrace" "away from traffic and overlooking the park" that surrounds the Basilique Sainte-Clothilde ("hence, the play on basilica" in the name), this establishment in the silk-stocking 7th can be "charming for a Sunday evening" admirers attest; however, some sermonize that the Basque–Classic French cooking is "pleasant without prompting any gastronomic emotion" – even the signature leg of lamb is "uninteresting" – and there's almost "no service to speak of."

Bastide Odéon (La) ☒Ⓜ *Provence*

22 | 18 | 20 | €55

6ᵉ | 7, rue Corneille (Odéon) | 01-43-26-03-65 | www.bastide-odeon.com

This "contemporary" bistro in the 6th is popular with Americans in-the-know, so much so, they "tend to be seated together" – some say it's to ensure we have an English-speaking server, while a cynic might surmise we're being hidden from the locals"; tables aside, voters split over this Southern French: fans find the cuisine and "pleasant atmosphere" in the red-and-yellow rooms are "almost as good as a trip to Provence", but others shrug it's "a standby, not a destination."

Bath's ☒ *Auvergne/New French*

20 | 19 | 19 | €56

17ᵉ | 25, rue Bayen (Etoile) | 01-45-74-74-74 | www.baths.fr

Everybody's back into the bath after the "elegant launching" of this father/son-run table, moved from the exclusive 8th to the more egalitarian 17th and offering a younger, more "relaxed" (and less expensive) experience; there's still "delicious" Auvergnat cuisine "with Spanish-inflected dishes", wine recommendations from the lengthy list that are "spot on" and "warm service"; in short, "a real jewel."

Beaujolais d'Auteuil (Le) *Classic French*

17 | 14 | 14 | €44

16ᵉ | 99, bd de Montmorency (Porte d'Auteuil) | 01-47-43-03-56 | www.beaujolaisdauteuil16.com

Open every day, this "classic at the edge of the 16th" "holds no surprises", which explains its "elbow-to-elbow" occupancy – regulars know they can count on the "bistro ambiance", "friendly enough" service and "quality", "typical French food" in "sufficient quantity"; while "prices have increased", they're "still honest"; N.B. the Decor score doesn't reflect a recent gray-hued redo of the premises.

	FOOD	DECOR	SERVICE	COST

BE Boulangépicier 🎟 *Sandwiches* | 19 | 11 | 14 | €23 |

8ᵉ | 73, bd de Courcelles (Courcelles/Ternes) | 01-46-22-20-20
9ᵉ | Printemps | 64, bd Haussmann, 3rd fl. (Havre-Caumartin) |
01-42-82-67-17
www.boulangepicier.com

"Eating on the run" becomes a gastronomic experience at this "new-concept" bakery with branches in the 8th and 9th, owned by superstar chef Alain Ducasse; the "best baguettes ever" envelop haute sandwiches, alongside "excellent soups and salads", and though some find it "really overpriced", "only in Paris would you find food this extraordinary in a setting so completely ordinary."

Bel Canto *Italian* | 13 | 15 | 17 | €56 |

4ᵉ | 72, quai de l'Hôtel de Ville (Hôtel-de-Ville/Pont-Marie) |
01-42-78-30-18
Neuilly-sur-Seine | 6, rue du Commandant Pilot (Les Sablons) |
01-47-47-19-94 🎟 Ⓜ
www.lebelcanto.com

The staff literally hits the high note of this "original" duo in the 4th and Neuilly – opera *artistes* all, they deliver arias along with traditional dishes from the land of Puccini, and their "talented singing more than makes up for any serving faux pas"; culinary critics pan the meals as "mediocre", especially given how "expensive" they are – though no more so than two on the aisle at the Opéra Bastille.

Bellini 🎟 *Italian* | ▽ 24 | 21 | 23 | €56 |

16ᵉ | 28, rue Le Sueur (Argentine) | 01-45-00-54-20 |
www.restaurantbellini.com

There's something "about pasta and cheese that's very comforting" sigh surveyors about this "cozy" Italian near L'Etoile, whose "wonderful" noodles include tagliatelle in a flambéed Parmesan wheel; *paesani* also praise the "relaxed, yet formal service" and "tranquil ambiance" of the terra-cotta-colored room.

Bellota-Bellota 🎟 Ⓜ *Spanish* | ▽ 19 | 15 | 19 | €50 |

7ᵉ | 18, rue Jean-Nicot (La Tour-Maubourg) | 01-53-59-96-96 |
www.bellota-bellota.com

"If there were a Nobel prize for ham", they'd win it at this *jamon*-and-wine bar in the 7th, which attracts with an "awesome" array of the cured pork, plus Spanish cheeses, wines and bread from the bakery next door; "amiable service" and modest but "pretty decor" of azulejo tiles explain why the place is so "popular with the locals", though even they lament the "expensive" cost of hamming it up.

Benkay *Japanese* | ▽ 24 | 21 | 19 | €94 |

15ᵉ | Hôtel Novotel Tour Eiffel | 61, quai de Grenelle (Bir-Hakeim/Charles Michels) | 01-40-58-21-26 | www.novotel.com

Political bigwigs are often spotted at Seine-side tables with a "great view" that only adds to the "high-end" experience of this hotel eatery many call the city's "best" for "authentic" Japanese cuisine; patrons choose between the teppanyaki grill with its accompanying spectacle and classic plates, including sushi and sashimi, served by an "attentive", kimono-clad staff; be advised, though, that "you pay for what you get" (a lunchtime prix fixe diminishes the damage).

☑ Benoît *Lyon*

| 24 | 21 | 22 | €77 |

4ᵉ | 20, rue St-Martin (Châtelet-Les Halles/Hôtel de Ville) | 01-42-72-25-76 | www.benoit-paris.com

"Step into 1912" at this "elegant" "Paris classic" in the 4th that has "kept its charm" after being "dusted off" by chef-restaurateurs Alain Ducasse and Thierry de la Brosse; while "prices have gone up", the "authentic" "high-quality Lyonnais bistro food" "tastes as good as it looks", and "the service is friendly, if variable"; really, "the only negative is the number of tourists", even if they're often "shunted" to "English-speakers' Siberia in the back room."

Berkeley (Le) ◑ *Eclectic*

| 14 | 16 | 14 | €60 |

8ᵉ | 7, av Matignon (Champs-Elysées-Clémenceau/Franklin D. Roosevelt) | 01-42-25-72-25 | www.leberkeley.com

It may have "a great location" just off the Champs-Elysées, but the "indifferent", "expensive-for-what-you-get" Classic French–Eclectic eats and "cool – make that frozen – service" at this *brasserie de luxe* leave most surveyors cold; still, some supporters smile at the striped-tented ceiling, the most noticeable feature of the decor, and "the great terrace out front", "a fantastic spot to see everyone who's anyone pass by."

Beurre Noisette (Le) ☒Ⓜ *Bistro*

| ▽ 23 | 13 | 19 | €44 |

15ᵉ | 68, rue Vasco de Gama (Lourmel/Porte de Versailles) | 01-48-56-82-49

Easy to overlook, this "neighborhood bistro" in the faraway 15th has a following among food lovers and off-duty chefs, thanks to chef-owner Thierry Blanqui's "refined", "inventive" French cuisine that's especially "great for the price", plus an equally "approachable wine list"; the "laid-back but professional service" helps make for "a lovely, relaxed" experience, one "good for rubbing elbows with the locals (because there isn't much room!)."

Biche au Bois (A la) ☒ *Bistro*

| 20 | 12 | 17 | €42 |

12ᵉ | 45, av Ledru-Rollin (Gare de Lyon) | 01-43-43-34-38

Lovers of wildlife – on their plate – hunt no further than this "convivial" bistro near the Gare de Lyon that's known for "excellent" game in autumn, and "massive portions" of "succulent" French "home cooking" (followed by an "awesome cheese plate") the rest of the year, all "smilingly" served in an "old-fashioned" brown-hued interior that reminds some of the forest; "no-stress" prices ensure the place is always "hopping."

Bigarrade (La) ☒ *New French*

| - | - | - | VE |

17ᵉ | 106, rue Nollet (Brochant) | 01-42-26-01-02 | www.bigarrade.fr

Working in a tiny shop front–cum–chef's atelier in the quiet Batignolles neighborhood, chef Christophe Pelé (ex the defunct Le Jardin) puts on one of the best new shows in Paris as he cooks two set New French tasting menus daily in an open, compact, stainless-steel galley kitchen; the small, simple white-and-lime-green dining room with pendant lights pulls in a stylish crowd that doesn't seem to mind paying the high prices.

BIOArt ⊠ New French

-	-	-	M

13^e | 3, quai François Mauriac (Bibliothèque François Mitterrand/ Quai de la Gare) | 01-45-85-66-88 | www.bioart.fr
Resetting the clock on 1960s hippie-ish health food, this spacious, contemporary dining room – self-styled as the largest organic restaurant in Paris – uses "excellent-quality produce" to create "light, refined" New French dishes (bass with steamed veggies, chocolate-orange terrine); the "hinting toward the healthy" orientation extends to the environs, an ecological building with glass-wall views of the Seine and the area around the Bibliothèque François Mitterrand.

Bis du Severo (Le) Bistro

-	-	-	M

14^e | 16, rue des Plantes (Mouton-Duvernet/Pernety) | 01-40-44-73-09
When the popular Le Severo "is bursting at the seams", the Montparnasse "neighborhood crowd" heads down the street to its "relaxed" annex with a Japanese chef and a "good *quartier* vibe"; like its big brother, it has a meat-heavy traditional French menu – though they serve fish too – and connoisseurs claim the "quality of the food is exactly the same"; the wine list is heavy on organic labels.

Bistral (Le) ⊠ Ⓜ Bistro

19	10	15	€48

17^e | 80, rue Lemercier (Brochant) | 01-42-63-59-61 | www.lebistral.com
Boosters believe this Batignolles bastion of the 'bistronomic' scene (young chefs serving "serious gourmet" fare in a "bistro setting") is "worth the trek" for "ambitious", "highly creative cuisine paired with great organic wines", even if the "small" room's slightly "banal" decor "is not its strong point"; but some sigh that "prices – particularly of the wine – are creeping up."

Bistro 121 Ⓜ Bistro

-	-	-	M

15^e | 121, rue de la Convention (Boucicaut) | 01-45-57-52-90
The "exceptionally warm welcome" at this long-standing neighborhood bistro in the 15th reminds surveyors why they "love the French"; and this place with its 1970s-era decor has built up a loyal clientele with its time-honored, "classic cooking" that keeps it "crowded and noisy" seven days a week; N.B. so far, chef-owner Eric Corailler, who assumed command post-Survey, hasn't tampered with tradition.

Bistro de Breteuil (Le) Bistro

16	16	15	€40

7^e | 3, pl de Breteuil (Duroc) | 01-45-67-07-27 | www.bistrocie.fr
"A real bargain of a prix fixe that includes three courses and a bottle of wine" keeps this "stuff-yourself" bistro "popular with the locals" of the 7th; admittedly, the Classic French fare "ain't no Haute Cuisine" and the pace makes for rather "mechanical service", but "there's plenty to choose from on the regularly changing menu", "tables are decently spaced" and there's a "great terrace in summer", so why carp?

	FOOD	DECOR	SERVICE	COST

Bistro de l'Olivier (Le) ⊠ *Provence* | 18 | 14 | 17 | €43

8ᵉ | 13, rue Quentin-Bauchart (George V) | 01-47-20-78-63
Parisians dreaming of Provence get "a whiff of vacation" at this "typically southern" French table that's a "reasonably priced", "welcome find" in the business-oriented 8th; diners taste "a bit of sunshine" in the "fresh and flavorful" dishes, soak in the "warmth" of the "simple" setting with olive trees and appreciate the "charming service" – though its "slow" rhythm is also "authentic" of the rush-free region.

Bistro des Deux Théâtres (Le) ●⊠ *Bistro* | 14 | 14 | 13 | €41

9ᵉ | 18, rue Blanche (Trinité) | 01-45-26-41-43 | www.bistrocie.fr
Featuring "three courses and a bottle of wine", "the prix fixe is a fabulous value" at this veteran in the 9th that's part of the "same chain as Bistro Melrose"; however, it's clearly the cheap eats that keep this production running, since most "find it average" foodwise, and the "theatrical, red-curtained" decor is "aging"; but at least the "hurried service" makes it "good for [pre- and] post-theater meals."

Bistro d'Hubert (Le) ⊠ *Classic/New French* | ▽ 22 | 19 | 21 | €47

15ᵉ | 41, bd Pasteur (Pasteur) | 01-47-34-15-50 | www.bistrodhubert.com
Surveyors say you'll feel "more like a relative than a client" at this "homey", "unpretentious" Montparnasse bistro, whose "country-style" look belies a menu that "takes traditional French cuisine to a new level" with "unusual spicing" from various corners of the globe and "good Basque" wines; add in "affordable" prices and a "delightful staff" and it's a "pleasant place" all around.

Bistro du 17ème (Le) *Bistro* | 18 | 16 | 16 | €36

17ᵉ | 108, av de Villiers (Péreire) | 01-47-63-32-77 | www.bistrocie.fr
Part of Willy Dorr's Bistro & Cie group of low-priced places, this "neighborhood crowd-pleaser" ensures that residents of the 17th are well-fed with a "solid bargain" prix fixe of Classic French fare (including wine) that's "not overly imaginative" but "always a little better than you expect"; though "slow", the staff's "kind to kids", and the "convivial setting" is particularly appealing during "summer-terrace season."

Bistro Melrose ●⊠ *Bistro* | - | - | - | M

17ᵉ | 5, pl de Clichy (Place de Clichy) | 01-42-93-61-34 | www.bistrocie.fr
This Place de Clichy standby, part of the Willy Dorr group of budget-friendly bistros, is "always crowded" with locals who can't resist what they call "the best buy in Paris", a fixed-price menu of serviceable French faves comprising two or three courses, wine and *café*, served until midnight; the typically Parisian interior features red banquettes and a ceiling cupola.

Bistro Poulbot ⊠Ⅿ *Bistro* | - | - | - | M

18ᵉ | 39, rue Lamarck (Lamarck-Caulaincourt) | 01-46-06-86-00
Up in a quiet corner of Montmartre, this twentysomething bistro now boasts fresh management and chef (acclaimed French

Polynesian toque Véronique Melloul), but the cuisine remains "as always – classic with sly innovations"; in fact, the entire scene is "superb", from the "helpful service" to the "non-touristy" clientele to the cozy dining room decorated with prints by illustrator Francisque Poulbot, who once lived on this street.

Bistro St. Ferdinand ◐ *Bistro* | 14 | 12 | 13 | €36 |

17ᵉ | 275, bd Péreire (Porte Maillot) | 01-45-74-33-32 | www.bistrocie.fr
This Porte Maillot bistro is a lifesaver for locals when they just "don't feel like cooking", since the "all-inclusive" prix fixe menu might be "unoriginal" – even a tad "industrial" – but it's "good enough", and there are "no disagreeable surprises" when the bill comes; the "modern" decor with its varying rooms leaves most diners indifferent, though the courtyard remains a favorite when the weather's fine.

Bistrot à Vins Mélac ⌧ Ⓜ *Wine Bar/Bistro* | 14 | 12 | 13 | €34 |

11ᵉ | 42, rue Léon Frot (Charonne) | 01-43-70-59-27 | www.melac.fr
"The principal attraction is the wine" at this "cheap and cheerful" 11th-arrondissement *bistrot à vins* where the "quality and large choice" of vintages, especially from the Languedoc, make up for the limited menu of Auvergnat "dishes like *grand-mère* made"; the mustachioed Monsieur Mélac is a "character" who reigns over the "convivial ambiance", but the staffers can be "brusque" – especially "if you ask for water"; N.B. the Decor score doesn't reflect a post-Survey redo, which includes a giant automated Bacchus in the window.

Bistrot d'à Côté ⌧ *Bistro* | 21 | 16 | 18 | €51 |

17ᵉ | 10, rue Gustave Flaubert (Péreire/Ternes) | 01-42-67-05-81
Neuilly-sur-Seine | 4, rue Boutard (Pont-de-Neuilly) | 01-47-45-34-55
www.michelrostang.com
"Favorites with the bustling advertising and PR crowd", chef-owner Michel Rostang's "intimate" baby bistros in the 17th and Neuilly serve "solid", "simple" Classic French cuisine that seems "always the same" – that is, "consistently delicious"; "service is variable" – "friendly" vs. "snotty" – and the fare can be "too expensive for what you get"; "but with excellent ingredients and attentive preparation", "the quality is there"; P.S. "the old-grocery decor is nice" in the Rue Gustave Flaubert branch.

Bistrot d'André (Le) ⌧ *Bistro* | - | - | - | I |

15ᵉ | 232, rue St-Charles (Balard) | 01-45-57-89-14
With an "atmosphere reflecting the long-gone Citroën factory" across the street, this bistro named for the carmaker coasts on the memory of the 1920s when it was a company canteen; the kitchen still turns out dishes workers might have eaten, "traditional French cuisine that's unexceptional but fine", and modern motorists appreciate the "inexpensive" prices.

⌧ Bistrot de l'Oulette ◐⌧ *Southwest* | 26 | 16 | 21 | €40 |

4ᵉ | 38, rue des Tournelles (Bastille) | 01-42-71-43-33 | www.l-oulette.com
Once known as Bistrot Baracane, this "intimate" favorite near the Bastille now has a different name, a fresh chef and updated decor,

but the "same ownership" – and, most important, the "satisfying experience" hasn't changed, to the relief of those (including "many tourists") who call it a must; its "wonderful" menu of "serious Southwestern cooking" now has a few more "inventive twists", but the price is still "terrific" and the service "just super."

Bistrot de Marius (Le) *Seafood*   21 | 14 | 16 | €51

8e | 6, av George V (Alma Marceau) | 01-40-70-11-76 | www.bistrotdemarius.com

The "ultra-high-rent district known as the Triangle d'Or" can be a Bermuda Triangle for the wallet, so cost-conscious consumers set sail for this "bustling" seafooder that serves "well-prepared" "fresh fish" at "lower prices" than the "mother ship, Marius et Janette, next door"; clients are "squeezed together" like sardines in the "cramped interior", so if possible, "eat outside and enjoy people-watching on Avenue George V" – or check out the covered terrace.

Bistrot de Paris (Le) ◑🗷Ⓜ *Bistro*   16 | 16 | 16 | €42

7e | 33, rue de Lille (Rue du Bac/St-Germain-des-Prés) | 01-42-61-16-83

Those "nostalgic for Paris of the [early] 1900s" time travel in this 106-year-old institution with an "authentic" "old" bistro interior that formerly welcomed André Gide and now draws a "busy lunch crowd including members of the French Senate" nearby; the "traditional dishes" are admittedly "unoriginal", but they're of "good quality", and besides, "at these prices you can't expect the moon."

Bistrot des Dames (Le) 🗷 *Bistro*   ▽ 14 | 17 | 14 | €30

17e | Hôtel El Dorado | 18, rue des Dames (Place de Clichy) | 01-45-22-13-42 | www.eldoradohotel.fr

"Go in summer for the garden" and "wonderful terrace" at this edgy, stylish little bistro in the ever-trendier Batignolles neighborhood; the "menu's unchanging, but suitable", and it's a "great place for friends and drinks", especially when the prices are as easygoing as the crowd.

Bistrot des Vignes (Le) *Bistro*   ▽ 17 | 13 | 20 | €37

16e | 1, rue Jean Bologne (La Muette/Passy) | 01-45-27-76-64 | www.bistrotdesvignes.fr

"When you're looking for a casual, comfortable meal without spending too much" (after your shopping jag on the Rue de Passy nearby), this "atmospheric" yet "unpretentious little neighborhood bistro" open seven days a week is "appreciated by tourists and locals alike" for its "attentive" service, "very good" basic French cuisine, children's menu and "simple" decor done up in cheery colors.

Bistrot d'Henri (Le) ◑ *Bistro*   20 | 15 | 21 | €35

6e | 16, rue Princesse (Mabillon/St-Germain-des-Prés) | 01-46-33-51-12 | www.bistro-dhenri.com

"You won't go wrong" at this "busy, bustling and atmospheric" Saint-Germain spot, which is why it's been going strong for nearly 30 years; the "service is friendly" and "prices are terrific" for "large portions" of "excellent" "authentic" bistro cuisine ("oh, those potatoes!"), and though the "tables are so close you can eat from your neighbor's plate", habitués claim they "wouldn't want it any other way."

Bistrot du Cap (Le) *Seafood*   - | - | - | M

15ᵉ | 30, rue Peclet (Convention/Vaugirard) | 01-40-43-02-18
Residents of this low-key corner of the 15th dock at this family-run, recently redecorated bistro "for the owner's smile, the tranquility of the site" and especially "for the [teak] terrace in the summer"; though the inexpensive prix fixe of mostly fish dishes (plus some recently added meat specialties) is "good for the 'hood", it's probably "not worth a trip" across town.

Bistrot du Dôme (Le) *Seafood*   21 | 19 | 20 | €47

14ᵉ | 1, rue Delambre (Vavin) | 01-43-35-32-00

Dôme Bastille (Le) *Seafood*

4ᵉ | 2, rue de la Bastille (Bastille) | 01-48-04-88-44
"Simpler and less expensive than their parent, Le Dôme", these seafood siblings at Bastille and Montparnasse offer "oysters and more oysters", plus a "wide variety" of *poissons* ("meat eaters should look elsewhere" for sustenance); though the "fish are smaller [here], they're just as tasty" and "wonderfully fresh", and served "without any fuss" amid a "homey atmosphere."

Bistrot du Passage ☒ *Bistro*   - | - | - | I

17ᵉ | 14, passage Geffroy Didelot (Villiers) | 01-43-87-28-10
Near the Parc Monceau in a quiet covered passage in the residential 17th arrondissement, this congenial little contemporary bistro for locals and tourists makes an affordable everyday option; creative specials of the day are served by friendly staffers in low-key environs, which feature parquet floors, wood tables and chairs and a few stools at the bar.

Bistrot du Peintre (Le) ● *Bistro*   ▽ 18 | 18 | 18 | €46

11ᵉ | 116, av Ledru-Rollin (Bastille/Ledru-Rollin) | 01-47-00-34-39
This "hip" Bastille bistro is "where the bobos go" for a "seriously funky", art nouveau–styled scene; the "standard fare" comes in "generous portions", but the real reason people "love it" is because it's a "friendly", "lovely place to dine on the sidewalk and watch the world go by."

Bistrot du Sommelier ☒ *Wine Bar/Bistro*   18 | 16 | 19 | €58

8ᵉ | 97, bd Haussmann (St-Augustin) | 01-42-65-24-85 |
www.bistrotdusommelier.com
"A charming sommelier encourages you to guess the wine before he identifies it" at this bacchanalian bistro known for "selected pairings with each course" of "succulent", "inventive" fare; situated in a well-heeled business quarter of the 8th, it can get "very dear", but "sometimes you just have to offer yourself a good time."

Bistrot Niel ☒ *Bistro*   - | - | - | M

17ᵉ | 75, av Niel (Péreire) | 01-42-27-88-44 | www.bistrotniel.fr
The decor, staff and ownership changed not too long ago at this "comfortable" contemporary bistro with a prestigious location near

	FOOD	DECOR	SERVICE	COST

the Etoile and a sidewalk terrace that has always been a hit; most seem pleased by the exotic touches added to the "comfortable" interior, and the "surprisingly good" New French food by a chef who worked with Alain Dutournier; N.B. closed weekends.

Bistrot Papillon (Le) 🅢 *Bistro* — 14 | 13 | 17 | €44

9ᵉ | 6, rue Papillon (Cadet/Poissonnière) | 01-47-70-90-03
Natives of the 9th "feel at home" in this "neighborhood" hangout with its "smiling personnel", "bustling interior" and "solid" bistro food that, if "uninspired", remains "consistently above average"; what's more, it's "affordable."

Bistrot Paul Bert (Le) 🅢Ⓜ *Bistro* — 23 | 14 | 17 | €41

11ᵉ | 18, rue Paul Bert (Faidherbe-Chaligny) | 01-43-72-24-01
Just thinking of the "cozy atmosphere and excellent steak frites" makes lovers of this "good-value" bistro "feel all warm and fuzzy inside", and the flush spreads further when they add in the "extraordinary wine list"; it's "off the beaten path" in the 11th but "reservations are a must", since tables are tight – but "be squished and be happy" knowing this place offers "one of the best evenings out."

Bistrot Vivienne 🅢 *Bistro* — 18 | 17 | 16 | €40

2ᵉ | 4, rue des Petits-Champs (Bourse/Palais Royal-Musée du Louvre) | 01-49-27-00-50
"Best for a quick lunch" with friends decrees the "young crowd" that frequents this "well-located" "little bistro"; it's got "average food, but great ambiance", especially if you "obtain a table" outside "in the fabulous Galerie Vivienne."

NEW Bistro Volnay 🅢 *Wine Bar/Bistro* — - | - | - | M

2ᵉ | 8, rue Volney (Opéra) | 01-42-61-06-65 | www.bistrovolnay.fr
This hip-but-friendly *bistrot à vins* not far from the Place Vendome pours a terrific selection of wines by the glass, pulling a young professional crowd at noon and international types at dinner; its chalkboard menu changes often but runs to classic Gallic comfort food like pig's foot terrine and *gratin de morue,* with reasonable prices (for central Paris) and the welcoming service of proprietresses Delphine and Magali as added incentives.

Bizan *Japanese* — - | - | - | E

2ᵉ | 56, rue St-Anne (Quatre-Septembre) | 01-42-96-67-76 | www.isse-et-cie.fr/bizan
Japanese chef Koshi Shindo's elegant, minimalist restaurant in the Little Tokyo that's grown up in and around the Rue Sainte-Anne is a standout for the quality of its sushi and sashimi, plus cooked dishes like miso soup with baby clams and caramelized eel; the eight-compartment bento box meals are popular with regulars, who include many Japanese expats and French fashion industry types.

Black Calavados ◑🅢Ⓜ *Eclectic* — - | - | - | E

8ᵉ | 40, av Pierre 1er de Serbie (George V) | 01-47-20-77-77
"If you can get in" to this *très* "exclusive" joint co-owned by rocker Chris Cornell and frequented by "Euro hipsters" (both "aging" and

not), you'll find it lives up to its name, an "all-black lacquered box" that "can be fun" when it's not "claustrophobic"; as for the Eclectic menu, it's always "pricey" and sometimes "less than average", but patrons point out this is "more like a nightclub" anyway, a "great place to see and be seen . . . after you dine somewhere else."

Blue Elephant ● *Thai* | 20 | 22 | 19 | €51 |

11ᵉ | 43-45, rue de la Roquette (Bastille/Voltaire) | 01-47-00-42-00 | www.blueelephant.com

While it's "more theme park than restaurant, with jungle sounds, waterfalls and bamboo thickets", the "whimsical" food is a "pleasant surprise" at what the "transported" term one of the "top Thais" in town; "service is friendly although a bit automated", and "on nights with lots of groups" the place is "like a Dantesque version of Trader Vic's" – and it's "overpriced" ("you mainly pay for the decor"); still, most esteem this "Bangkok escapade" close to Bastille.

NEW Bob's Kitchen ≠ *Vegetarian* | - | - | - | I |

3ᵉ | 74, rue des Gravilliers (Arts et Métiers) | 09-52-55-11-66 | www.bobsjuicebar.com

American Mark Grossman has a hit on his hands with this snug-but-friendly table d'hôte restaurant in the 3rd serving freshly squeezed juices and original, well-made vegetarian soups, salads and sandwiches; Sunday brunch is popular with bobos from this gentrifying part of town, and the cash-only tabs are moderate.

Bocconi ⬛ *Italian* | 20 | 11 | 17 | €43 |

8ᵉ | 10 bis, rue d'Artois (St-Philippe-du-Roule) | 01-53-76-44-44 | www.trattoria-bocconi.fr

You might see actress Monica Bellucci tucking into "excellent" pasta at this "business-district" venue in the 8th that serves "true Italian food" from various regions and "seasonal specialties" with the "good humor" typical of The Boot; Neapolitan chef-owner Ciro Polge used to work at Il Cortile, and though some "might find the bill high" for a trattoria, they also note many "nice surprises" on the menu.

Boeuf Couronné (Au) ● *Classic French* | 16 | 13 | 12 | €49 |

19ᵉ | 188, av Jean Jaurès (Porte de Pantin) | 01-42-39-44-44 | www.rest-gj.com

"The French answer to American steakhouses", this "old-fashioned" carnivores' cave in a distant corner of the 19th (where the city's slaughterhouses once were) specializes in "excellent meat"; the remainder of the menu's "nothing exceptional", but patrons applaud the "patient staff", and the once-"dated" decor has recently gotten a refurb (not reflected in the Decor score).

Boeuf sur le Toit (Le) ●⬛ *Brasserie* | 18 | 19 | 18 | €56 |

8ᵉ | 34, rue du Colisée (Franklin D. Roosevelt/St-Philippe-du-Roule) | 01-53-93-65-55 | www.boeufsurletoit.com

"Seafood brimming over crates of ice" marks the entrance of this art deco "landmark" off the Champs that attracts herds of customers for "average" but "acceptable" brasserie fare ("best to go for the *fruits de mer*, which they can't ruin"); "the waiters are attentive but harried" and "the bar area can get festive", but that "craziness" is what makes it "great for last-minute, late-night, large-group dining."

☒ Bofinger ● *Brasserie* `20` `24` `19` `€54`

4ᵉ | 5, rue de la Bastille (Bastille) | 01-42-72-87-82 | www.bofingerparis.com

This "old standby" at the Bastille offers a "perfect last act to the opera" (especially when "the tenor is at the next table"), with a "lively crowd" and a "sumptuous fin de siècle setting" featuring a "glorious glass dome"; but if the decor's "a feast for the eyes", the "standard" Alsatian-accented brasserie fare is somewhat less "exciting" (aside from the "reliable" "shellfish extravaganza"); also, the "still-authentic" ambiance suffers slightly when the "neighboring accents come from Brooklyn and Battersea" as often as Bretagne.

Bon *Asian* `-` `21` `13` `E`

16ᵉ | 25, rue de la Pompe (La Muette) | 01-40-72-70-00 | www.restaurantbon.fr

"Go if you are a Starckanatic" suggest surveyors of this spot in the 16th, redesigned by Philippe Starck to show off four different styles, from cozy library to ski lodge (which may outdate the Decor score); the menu has also gotten a revamp, and now features such Asian-inspired offerings as lobster rolls, bream in a banana leaf and rose panna cotta in lychee sauce.

☒ Bon Accueil (Au) ☒ *Bistro* `24` `19` `22` `€56`

7ᵉ | 14, rue de Monttessuy (Alma Marceau/Ecole Militaire) | 01-47-05-46-11

"At the base of the Eiffel Tower" (and boasting a "sensational" sidewalk view of same), this veteran bistro delights visitors who depend on its "terrific" Classic French cuisine, based on what's "seasonally available" and "prepared with panache"; "stylish service" adds to the *accueil* ('welcome'), and while it's "no longer the amazing bargain it used to be", it "continues to be wonderful."

Bon Saint Pourçain (Le) ☒⊘ *Classic French* `18` `14` `20` `€43`

6ᵉ | 10 bis, rue Servandoni (Odéon/St-Sulpice) | 01-43-54-93-63

"In the shadow of Saint-Sulpice", this "idiosyncratic" bistro makes you "feel like you've come home, even though you've never lived in France", with "friendly atmosphere" provided by its father-and-daughter team; the "small" menu offers "simple French fare prepared by Papa", who shares his "thoughts on everything"; and while the Vieux Paris decor is somewhat "bereft", it doesn't make this place any less "beloved by tourists."

Bons Crus (Aux) ☒ *Wine Bar/Bistro* `-` `-` `-` `M`

1ᵉʳ | 7, rue des Petits-Champs (Bourse/Palais Royal-Musée du Louvre) | 01-42-60-06-45

More than one bon vivant has been known to "pleasantly lose an afternoon" at this "delightful" 100-year-old wine bar behind the Palais-Royal; "perfect for a cold day" with some "filling" bistro dishes, cheese and charcuterie, it's "very French and very warm", especially after a few glasses of red.

Boucherie Roulière ●🌙Ⓜ *Bistro*

-	-	-	M

6ᵉ | 24, rue des Canettes (St-Sulpice) | 01-43-26-25-70
Meat lovers steak out a table and sit "elbow-to-elbow" in the long, skinny, simply decorated room of this "tiny" eatery near Saint-Sulpice, co-owned by a butcher and a native of the Auvergne, home of the famous Salers cattle; grilled "huge steaks" are the main attraction here, though the beef-averse will also find alternate bistro options, "reasonably priced" for dependably "copious" portions.

Boudoir (Le) ●🌙Ⓩ *Classic/New French*

-	-	-	M

8ᵉ | 25, rue du Colisée (Franklin D. Roosevelt) | 01-43-59-25-29 | www.brasserieleboudoir.com
Though relatively new, this plushly decorated venue has a distinguished heritage: owner Alice Bardet is the daughter of famous Tours toque Jean Bardet; her husband, Olivier Loise, helps man the stoves, turning out a mix of Classic and New French fare – from coddled eggs and deviled kidneys to various vegetable-based dishes, backed by a Touraine region–oriented wine list; situated just off the Champs, it boasts a red facade to beckon passersby, while late hours make it ideal for after-theater.

Bouillon Racine Ⓩ *Brasserie*

16	25	19	€39

6ᵉ | 3, rue Racine (Cluny La Sorbonne/Odéon) | 01-44-32-15-60 | www.bouillonracine.com
The "remarkable" "mirrored art nouveau room" is "the principal reason to dine" at this brasserie near the Sorbonne; supplemented by "excellent Belgian beers", the "cooking's not noted for its finesse", but at least it's "a solid meal, not one that looks like plate decoration", and the staff has actually become "accommodating."

Boulangerie (La) Ⓩ *Bistro*

▽ 23	17	20	€32

20ᵉ | 15, rue des Panoyaux (Ménilmontant) | 01-43-58-45-45
There's nothing half-baked about this "darn good" bistro in a former bakery in the funky, multiethnic Ménilmontant neighborhood; the kitchen turns out traditional dishes with a "touch of modernity" and "consistent" quality, the wine list is "excellent" and the "pleasant surprise" only gets better with the bill – a "great bang for your euro."

Boulangerie
Eric Kayser Ⓩ *Bakery/Sandwiches*

16	12	12	€22

NEW 1ᵉʳ | 33, rue Danielle Casanova (Opéra) | 01-42-97-59-29
8ᵉ | 85, bd Malesherbes (St-Augustin) | 01-45-22-70-30
www.maison-kayser.com
Master baker Eric Kayser's boulangeries "set a new standard for bread" and pastries all over town, but these locations in the 8th and in the 1st also serve as restaurants (albeit pretty casual ones) where a "*speedé*" staff slings "beautiful, freshly prepared salads, pretty sandwiches" and "star tarts" to the morning and midday crowds; a

few "expected better of the decor" and it's "a little dear for a lunch break" – but then "you can't put a price on quality."

Boule Rouge (La) ◑⊠ *African* | - | - | - | M |

9ᵉ | 1, rue de la Boule-Rouge (Grands Boulevards) | 01-47-70-43-90

Few surveyors know this large North African in the 9th, but those who do commend the couscous (especially the "excellent" Friday special with spinach); prices are as easygoing as the warm service, and the atmosphere is nostalgic, since the decor reminds expats of the Tunisian eateries they left for the City of Light.

Bound ◑ *Japanese/New French* | - | - | - | E |

8ᵉ | 49-51, av George V (George V) | 01-53-67-84-60 | www.buddhabar.com

Golden Triangle–bound hipsters know this address as the old Barfly, now revamped with "complicated" pink decor – an eye-popping megabar, plasma screens, glossy mock-croc chairs and lighting effects – while a DJ plays "loud music" nightly; as expected, it's "not cheap", but the Japanese–New French food's "a cut above" what one finds in such "cool-vibe" venues; the same goes for the "efficient" staff.

☒ Bouquinistes (Les) ⊠ *New French* | 23 | 19 | 21 | €62 |

6ᵉ | 53, quai des Grands-Augustins (St-Michel) | 01-43-25-45-94 | www.lesbouquinistes.com

"After all these years", this "casually sophisticated" baby bistro from Guy Savoy is still "consistently excellent" (though much "pricier"), offering New French flavors that "excite the tongue" in a "modern, somewhat cool setting" with quayside "views of the Seine"; the crowd combines the Left Bank "literary set" with a "heavy tourist" contingent, and the servers are "professional" (despite a tendency to "rush you through your meal"); in sum, "a great second choice, for those who can't afford the full-blown Savoy restaurant experience."

Bourguignon du Marais (Au) ⊠ *Wine Bar/Bistro* | 23 | 18 | 20 | €51 |

4ᵉ | 52, rue François Miron (Pont-Marie/St-Paul) | 01-48-87-15-40

"Modern but cozy, with a warm French feel", this Marais *bistrot à vins* offers "quite good food" that "pairs really well with the wines" ("if you love Burgundies, this is the place"); though it can be "one of the best deals in Paris", beware – "the bill has a way of zipping upward" with all those "delicious" vinos by the glass.

☒ Braisière (La) ⊠ *Gascony* | 27 | 19 | 23 | €70 |

17ᵉ | 54, rue Cardinet (Malesherbes) | 01-47-63-40-37

The "quiet contented murmurings" attest to the "masterful" cuisine found in this "hidden gem" for "imaginative" Gascon gastronomy in the 17th, with connoisseurs claiming it offers "more value for the money than the better-knowns"; despite "neutral"-toned decor, the ambiance is "cozy" and "down-to-earth", while the "relaxed service encourages you to linger over your meal and savor every bite."

☑ Brasserie Balzar ● *Brasserie* | 19 | 20 | 19 | €44

5ᵉ | 49, rue des Ecoles (Cluny La Sorbonne/St-Michel) | 01-43-54-13-67 | www.brasseriebalzar.com

"A traditional haunt" for tourists, late-nighters and "Left Bank intellectuals" from the nearby Sorbonne, this "quintessential brasserie" "oozes charm" with its "glorious fin de siècle ambiance", "tasty, simple" classic fare and "very French waiters" (right down to "the gentleman with handlebar moustache"); while some old-timers are "wistful for the pre–Groupe Flo days", non-nostalgists claim "nothing's changed" – it may "feel like a cliché, but it's authentic."

Brasserie de l'Ile St. Louis ● *Brasserie* | 17 | 16 | 17 | €37

4ᵉ | 55, quai de Bourbon (Cité/Pont-Marie) | 01-43-54-02-59

"An institution on the Ile Saint-Louis" "facing Notre Dame", this "atmospheric" brasserie is blessed with decor of "1890s-vintage advertising posters" on dark-wood walls – a "tavernlike" setting for "solid Alsatian" eats, served by "slightly wry waiters"; and if a Food score drop supports skeptics who say "yes, Virginia, you can get a bad meal in Paris", at least the place is "not part of a chain."

Brasserie du Louvre *Brasserie* | 16 | 17 | 16 | €42

1ᵉʳ | Hôtel du Louvre | Place André Malraux (Palais Royal-Musée du Louvre) | 01-42-96-27-98 | www.hoteldulouvre.com

"Across the street from the Louvre in the hotel of the same name", this wood-banqueted brasserie offers "great people-watching" from an outdoor terrace; it's "been better in the past", but the "sublime" location means it "can be forgiven a lot of sins"; N.B. a new chef arrived mid-Survey, moving the cuisine from traditional to trendy.

Brasserie Flo ● *Brasserie* | 18 | 20 | 18 | €54

10ᵉ | 7, cour des Petites-Ecuries (Château d'Eau) | 01-47-70-13-59 | www.flobrasseries.com

It may be a bit "grimy" in this patch of the 10th, but the decor of sinuous molding and mirrors "speaks of the belle epoque" at this brasserie that's "part of the Groupe Flo"; possessing the "feeling of a Toulouse-Lautrec painting", it's a fine place "to take tourists", but with the food no more than "acceptable", most suggest you "keep to the conservative side of the menu and chew on the ambiance."

Brasserie Julien ● *Brasserie* | 19 | 26 | 19 | €59

10ᵉ | 16, rue du Faubourg St-Denis (Strasbourg-St-Denis) | 01-47-70-12-06 | www.flobrasseries.com

This "art nouveau gem" glitters "in a seedy neighborhood" in the 10th, where clients "step off of one of Paris' least attractive streets" and into a "magical" setting with wood and mirrors, "waiters in long white aprons" and "large parties" who create the "pleasantly noisy" "action" within; it serves "typical", "reliable" brasserie food seven days a week until 1 AM, but no matter what time you arrive, "don't miss the profiteroles" with a "teapot full of chocolate sauce."

	FOOD	DECOR	SERVICE	COST

Brasserie La Lorraine ⚫ *Brasserie* ` 17 | 17 | 16 | €63 `
8ᵉ | 2, pl des Ternes (Ternes) | 01-56-21-22-00 |
www.brasserielalorraine.com

Though it was overhauled in 2004, many find the "makeover disappointing" at this "typical large brasserie" in the 8th; "the place looks brighter", but it's "a bit too Vegas" now, the formalized service "has become chilly" and while the food's "good" ("of course you must order the quiche"), "the prices, always high, have skyrocketed"; still, this "neighborhood standby" "definitely has an upbeat atmosphere"; N.B. don't ignore the *voiturier*, or you may be mysteriously towed away in the night.

Brasserie L'Européen ⚫ *Brasserie* ` - | - | - | M `
12ᵉ | 21 bis, bd Diderot (Gare de Lyon) | 01-43-43-99-70 |
www.brasserie-leuropeen.fr

One of the city's last independent brasseries, this veteran near the Gare de Lyon joined the Joulie group in 2006, which may be why foes feel the fare "has become very common" of late – though stalwarts insist the seafood choucroute continues to be among the "best in Paris"; the '70s Slavik decor is charmingly retro with mirrors and Chesterfield banquettes, but if you have a train to catch be forewarned: the clock runs backwards.

☑ Brasserie Lipp ⚫🅰 *Brasserie* ` 17 | 20 | 16 | €51 `
6ᵉ | 151, bd St-Germain (St-Germain-des-Prés) | 01-45-48-53-91 |
www.brasserie-lipp.fr

"Parisian and international celebrities greet each other warmly" at this "stalwart" in Saint-Germain, a brasserie frequented by so many regulars "it's like a club", and where insiders say it's "imperative to be seated on the ground floor" for "priceless people-watching" amid art nouveau decor (upstairs is "where they stick the American rubes"); "the food isn't as interesting as the clientele" – keep to the "good old classics" – and since the service "depends on who you are", know that many "pay to be sneered at or ignored."

Brasserie Lutétia 🅰 *Brasserie* ` 18 | 19 | 18 | €58 `
6ᵉ | Hôtel Lutétia | 23, rue de Sèvres (Sèvres-Babylone) | 01-49-54-46-76 |
www.lutetia-paris.com

"Not bad for a hotel restaurant", this "plush and stylish" brasserie with art deco-style decor by Sonia Rykiel is "perfect" for "lunch while shopping" (though "service is slow" sometimes); it's a "lovely place for a seafood platter", but otherwise there are "no real surprises here", including the 6th-arrondissement-"expensive" bills.

Brasserie Mollard ⚫🅰 *Brasserie* ` ∇ 19 | 24 | 16 | €47 `
8ᵉ | 115, rue St-Lazare (St-Lazare) | 01-43-87-50-22 |
www.mollard.fr

The mosaic "tiles alone are worth a visit" to this classified historic monument with its "extraordinary" art nouveau interior near the Gare Saint-Lazare; but while "the decor is always nice, the bill is hefty for traditional brasserie food" wallet-watchers wail (aside from the "succulent" seafood selection).

	FOOD	DECOR	SERVICE	COST

Brasserie Printemps *Classic French* 11 | 15 | 10 | €32

9e | Printemps | 64, bd Haussmann (Auber/Havre-Caumartin) |
01-42-82-58-84 | www.printemps.com

"One never tires of looking at the cupola" overhead, like a 1923 "gigantic stained-glass globe" – the highlight of the "hip" interior of the
packed canteen of the "legendary department store" Printemps;
hélas, the Classic French menu "doesn't shine" like the decor, even if
shoppers say it's "passable quality for a quick lunch" – or perhaps a
slow one, since patrons must put up with "long waits" for everything
from "being seated to paying"; N.B. dinner Thursdays only.

Breakfast in America *American* 15 | 17 | 19 | €18

4e | 4, rue Mahler (St-Paul) | 01-42-72-40-21
5e | 17, rue des Ecoles (Cardinal Lemoine/Jussieu) | 01-43-54-50-28
www.breakfast-in-america.com

From "those round red twirly stools at the soda counter" to the
"burgers, omelets, fries" and shakes on the menu, "this diner could
be from an episode of *Happy Days*"; with branches in the Latin
Quarter and the Marais, it's "a perfect remedy" for "homesick
Americans" on either side of the Seine (and there are many, judging
by the "interminable weekend waits"), who confess "it's a crazy
thing to do in Paris" – but it's authentic "down to the bad coffee."

Breizh Café Ⓜ *Brittany* - | - | - | I

3e | 109, rue Vieille du Temple (Filles du Calvaire/St-Paul) |
01-42-72-13-77 | www.breizhcafe.com

An offshoot of a crêperie in Brittany and Tokyo, this "chic" place in the
upper Marais offers some "surprising" menu items, including organic
buckwheat galettes with smoked herring, dessert crêpes with salted
butter caramel and rare Tzarskaya oysters from the Bay of Cancale
("an exceptional treat"); wash it all down with 20 kinds of cider.

Briciola (La) Ⓩ *Pizza* - | - | - | I

3e | 64, rue Charlot (Filles du Calvaire/République) | 01-42-77-34-10
Located in the ever-trendier northern Marais, this groovy pizzeria
with shabby-chic decor throws a party as good as its pies; the regulars
usually start with a perfect insalata caprese (tomatoes, mozzarella,
basil) before moving on to the mains, topped with such favorites as
bresoala (air-dried beef) and Gorgonzola.

Ⓩ Bristol (Le) *Haute Cuisine* 27 | 28 | 27 | €145

8e | Hôtel Le Bristol | 112, rue du Faubourg St-Honoré (Miromesnil) |
01-53-43-43-40 | www.lebristolparis.com

When an "extravagant experience" is in order, this "special-night-
out kind of place" in the 8th is "close to perfect", with "two separate
dining rooms, depending upon the season": an oak-paneled, "sumptuous circular room" in winter and an "exquisite" garden in summertime; chef Eric Frechon's "phenomenal", "cutting-edge" Haute
Cuisine is worth the "ooh-la-la" prices, "particularly for those who
like strong tastes in original combinations", while the "exceptional"
service extends to "a silver tray of cleaning items" in case a customer should splash gravy on his recommended jacket.

	FOOD	DECOR	SERVICE	COST

ⓩ Buddha Bar ● *Asian* | 16 | 25 | 15 | €67 |

8ᵉ | 8, rue Boissy-d'Anglas (Concorde) | 01-53-05-90-00 |
www.buddhabar.com

This "legendary" "flashy-trashy-fabulous" nightclub/eatery in the
8th is still "a scene" where the Buddha statue–dominated "digs are
cool and the music is bumping", the "lychee martinis are to die for"
and the Asian cuisine is "surprisingly good for a trendy bar" – even
if the monastic portions amount to "finger foods at fistful prices";
protesting it's "past its heyday", nonbelievers call it "understaffed"
and "overrun with tourists" (expect a "very long wait for a table"),
but for fervent followers this "sexy" spot remains nirvana.

Buffalo Grill   *Steak* | 10 | 10 | 13 | €30 |

3ᵉ | 15, pl de la République (République) | 01-40-29-94-98
9ᵉ | 3, pl Blanche (Blanche) | 01-40-16-42-51
10ᵉ | 9, bd Denain (Gare du Nord) | 01-40-16-47-81
13ᵉ | 2, rue Raymond Aron (Quai de la Gare) | 01-45-86-76-71
14ᵉ | 117, av du Général Leclerc (Porte d'Orléans) | 01-45-40-09-72
17ᵉ | 6, pl du Maréchal Juin (Péreire) | 01-40-54-73-75
19ᵉ | 29, av Corentin Cariou (Porte de la Villette) | 01-40-36-21-41
www.buffalo-grill.fr

Like a "surreal take on an American steakhouse", this "popular faux-
cowboy chain" serves up a mishmash of Yank eats (ribs, beef,
Buffalo wings) in an "imitation Wild West" setting, complete with
"Indian statues standing guard at the swinging saloon doors"; foes
gun it down, calling "the pictures on the menu more appetizing than
the food" itself and the "cowgirl"-clad staff "disagreeable"; "the only
reason to go – they're kid-friendly", and the "affordable" eats are
"better than a gas station's."

Buisson Ardent (Le) ⓩ *Bistro* | 19 | 16 | 17 | €38 |

5ᵉ | 25, rue Jussieu (Jussieu) | 01-43-54-93-02 |
www.lebuissonardent.fr

Its clientele of 5th-arrondissement academics creates a "calm" ambiance at this neighborhood "staple", giving high marks to the "frequently changing", "good-value" prix fixe menu featuring bistro
cooking with a few "innovative" touches; the interior includes a
"retro"-looking area with 1925 frescoes and "lots of old wood";
N.B. a new chef arrived post-Survey.

Ca d'Oro   *Italian* | ▽ 18 | 16 | 17 | €43 |

1ᵉʳ | 54, rue de l'Arbre-Sec (Louvre-Rivoli) | 01-40-20-97-79

A "favorite nobody-goes-there restaurant", this little location "overlooking the Louvre" offers "consistently good" "light Northern
Italian food", plus some mighty "prime pasta"; "friendly waiters"
add to the "relaxing atmosphere" of the place.

Café Beaubourg ● *Classic French* | 16 | 20 | 15 | €34 |

4ᵉ | 100, rue St-Martin (Châtelet-Les Halles/Rambuteau) |
01-48-87-63-96

"The beautiful people are still, well, beautiful" at this "aging" but
"hip cafe run by the Costes brothers" that "sits right in the face of the

Centre Pompidou"; such a "great location" "makes it a good spot to meet friends" and offers some of the "best people-watching in Paris", within or without the "interesting", "plush", "podlike interior"; however, the "updated French classics menu" is typical of the *frères'* cuisine (that is, "not too creative"), and the service is "often negligent."

Café Burq ●🗷 *Wine Bar/Bistro*   - | - | - | M

18ᵉ | 6, rue Burq (Abbesses/Blanche) | 01-42-52-81-27

There's a "bohemian arty feel" at this "rocking" Montmartre wine bistro that's eternally "packed with local hipsters" and "pretty girls" who dig the "delightful" food (the "remarkable honey-roasted Camembert is a must"); with slim pickings in this "extremely touristic neighborhood", it's little surprise this "true find" is "always full."

🆕 Café Cartouche 🗷 *Bistro*   - | - | - | M

12ᵉ | 4, rue de Bercy (Bercy/Cour St-Emilion) | 01-40-19-09-95

The Bercy neighborhood of renovated brick wine warehouses in the 12th is still off the beaten track for most visitors to Paris, but some discover it while visiting the Frank Gehry–designed Cinémathèque de Paris; before or after a flick, this easygoing neighborhood bistro run by the former maître d'hôtel of Le Repaire de Cartouche serves good-quality traditional French fare, e.g. *pâté en croûte*, sausage with white beans and fruit tart, at moderate prices.

Café Charbon ● *Classic French*   15 | 16 | 14 | €29

11ᵉ | 109, rue Oberkampf (Parmentier/Rue St-Maur) | 01-43-57-55-13

"Up-and-coming models, actors and many would-be writers and artist/philosophers" "linger" over an espresso" or a mojito "waiting for the next concert at the [adjacent] Nouveau Casino to begin" in this "dark and dingy" "bohemian" bar on the "lively" Rue Oberkampf; some stay for a "casual" Classic French dinner, which is pretty "average", but "who knows? – the next Audrey Tautou or Vincent Perez could be the waiter who ignores you for 20 minutes, before taking another 15 to bring you your drink."

Café Constant 🗷M *Bistro*   24 | 14 | 19 | €39

7ᵉ | 139, rue St-Dominique (Ecole Militaire) | 01-47-53-73-34 | www.cafeconstant.com

"When you're not up to the big stars", chef-owner Christian Constant's "cozy" (or "tight") "second restaurant" makes a "nice substitute for its posh parent", Le Violon d'Ingres; "no reservations, but it's worth the wait" for "classic (if not classy) bistro food" "prepared with love" at "prices among the most reasonable in the whole 7th"; the "decor's old and tired and that rubs off on the waiters" critics carp, but converts call it "charming", as long as you "get a table on the main floor."

Café d'Angel (Le) 🗷 *Bistro*   - | - | - | M

17ᵉ | 16, rue Brey (Charles de Gaulle-Etoile/Ternes) | 01-47-54-03-33

This divine spot in the 17th arrondissement is a "perfect Paris bistro" with "excellent" dishes typical of the genre and - as tradition dictates – a daily blackboard special, plus "gracious service" and a prix fixe at angelic prices.

Z Café de Flore ◑▣ *Classic French*   15 | 20 | 15 | €36

6ᵉ | 172, bd St-Germain (St-Germain-des-Prés) | 01-45-48-55-26 | www.cafe-de-flore.com

"More than a cafe, this is a historic monument" in Saint-Germain – made "famous" by literary lions – and it's still "equally loved by locals and tourists" (the former "on the terrace, the poets upstairs") who "subscribe to all the expected clichés with gusto"; so while the "simple Classic French food" is "serviceable", the service "diffident" and prices "ridiculously expensive", it remains the "consummately Parisian" place for "watching the world go by" – and "to think that Hemingway once did the same makes it that much sweeter."

Café de la Musique ◑ *Classic French*   ▽ 15 | 21 | 17 | €31

19ᵉ | Cité de la Musique | 213, av Jean Jaurès (Porte de Pantin) | 01-48-03-15-91 | www.cite-musique.fr

While its Classic French menu is "limited", this La Villette cafe plays enough tunes to please customers, who go "to meet people passionate about music" (it's part of a cultural complex), for "brunch outside", a "late-night meal" or just to "collapse with drinks and some hors d'oeuvres after a day at the Cité des Sciences with a child."

Café de la Paix ◑ *Classic French*   19 | 22 | 18 | €61

9ᵉ | InterContinental Le Grand Hôtel | 12, bd des Capucines (Auber/ Opéra) | 01-40-07-36-36 | www.cafedelapaix.fr

Following a "magnificent renovation" a while back, this famous cafe across from the Opéra Garnier remains generally "touristy but reliable"; surveyors clash over the Classic French cuisine, with warriors wailing it's "mediocre and overpriced" and peacemongers positing "it's not what it was when I was younger, but then neither am I"; certainly, the Napoleon III decor retains all its "past glories", as does its "great location" for "watching the passing parade."

Café de l'Esplanade (Le) ◑▣ *Classic/New French*   16 | 21 | 15 | €58

7ᵉ | 52, rue Fabert (Invalides/La Tour-Maubourg) | 01-47-05-38-80

Kitty-cornered to Les Invalides is this "trendy canteen", and "if you look at the menu and think you've seen it before, you're right – it's another one in the Costes brothers' series", a sampler of "decent" Classic and New French fare; you might also recognize the same "haughty" but "pretty waitresses and crowd wearing black and sporting sunglasses, darling", even when occupying the "ultimate-in-hip" interior.

Café de l'Industrie ◑ *Bistro*   12 | 14 | 11 | €29

11ᵉ | 15-17, rue St-Sabin (Bastille/Bréguet-Sabin) | 01-47-00-13-53

"You go more for the atmosphere and to be cool than for the food" at this "buzzy" "super-crowded" "find in the 11th"; still, the bistro fare is "generously served" by staffers that are "polite if often overwhelmed"; many deem the "old-fashioned"-but-"updated" decor "cute."

	FOOD	DECOR	SERVICE	COST

Café de Mars ❶ *Bistro*

| | 17 | 13 | 16 | €35 |

7ᵉ | 11, rue Augereau (Ecole Militaire) | 01-47-05-05-91 |
www.cafe-de-mars.fr

Near the Rue Clerc, this "typical little French bistro" ("it looks like
where they'd shoot a scene establishing this is Paris") has "charming decor" of tiles and mosaics; "the staff dotes on all" the "neighborhood residents" and "unobtrusive tourists" who consume the
cuisine with some Eclectic "innovative" touches; "prices are very fair
for this level."

Café des Musées *Bistro*

| | - | - | - | M |

3ᵉ | 49, rue de Turenne (Chemin-Vert/St-Paul) | 01-42-72-96-17

This bistro offshoot of Le Dôme du Marais in the 3rd has become a
genuine hit with its generously served, carefully prepared grandmotherly French comfort food like smoked garlic soup and parmentier de
pintade (a shepherd's pie–like dish made with guinea hen); the vibe
is rustic, service brisk but friendly and prices easy to swallow.

Café du Commerce (Le) ❶ *Bistro*

| | 16 | 20 | 15 | €36 |

15ᵉ | 51, rue du Commerce (Emile Zola) | 01-45-75-03-27 |
www.lecafeducommerce.com

Ever since it opened in 1921 as an auto workers' canteen, this "bustling" "neighborhood eatery" "well-located near Motte-Picquet" has
drawn hordes for its "reasonably priced", "dependable", "basic
French food", even if "those in a hurry" wish the staff would step on
the gas; but the real attraction in this "multilevel" art deco bistro is
the "retractable" skylight that makes it a "destination" "in the summer when it's topless (the roof, not the servers)."

Café du Passage (Le) ❶ *Wine Bar/Bistro*

| | - | - | - | M |

11ᵉ | 12, rue de Charonne (Bastille/Ledru-Rollin) | 01-49-29-97-64

With "an owner who's passionate about wine and whiskey" (including some 80 single-malt scotches), this *bistrot à vins* in the 11th has
"a fantastic selection, much of which is served by the glass" and accompanied by "excellent small plates" with an Italian edge; the "old-
world" decor makes it "worth a visit."

Café Etienne Marcel ❶ *Eclectic*

| | ∇ 18 | 21 | 18 | €38 |

2ᵉ | 34, rue Etienne Marcel (Etienne Marcel) | 01-45-08-01-03

"Champagne McDonald's is the best way to describe" this Costes
brothers outpost on the northern edge of Les Halles that features
much of their "locked-in formula" but is still "just sort of average",
from the Eclectic eats to the "slightly kitschy" "*A Clockwork Orange*-
style decor" to the "wannabe-hip crowd from the suburbs"; "the
prices are pretty high given the quality of the food and service, but
that's typical of fashion restaurants."

Café Faubourg *Classic French*

| | 22 | 20 | 21 | €61 |

8ᵉ | Sofitel Le Faubourg | 11 bis, rue Boissy-d'Anglas (Concorde/
Madeleine) | 01-44-94-14-24 | www.sofitel.com

In the heart of the 8th yet "far from the madding crowd", this "hidden secret" in the Sofitel turns out "surprisingly good food for a ho-

tel" from a Classic French menu that reflects the talents and Southwestern tastes of consulting chef Alain Dutournier (Carré des Feuillants); the "serene view of a courtyard garden" is another reason "everyone smiles" here.

Café Guitry ⓩ *Classic French* | - | - | - | M |

9ᵉ | Théâtre Edouard VII | 10, pl Edouard VII (Auber/Opéra) | 01-40-07-00-77 | www.cafeguitry.com

Inside the Edouard VII theater, this "quite handsome place" offers soigné, red-and-chestnut-toned comfort and "soft armchairs"; the Classic French cooking's "not bad for cafe fare", and given the location, you can't beat it for a pre- or post-curtain bite when you might "come across actors and directors kissing each other"; P.S. "special mention for the beautiful terrace overlooking the pedestrian square."

Café la Jatte *Eclectic* | 14 | 16 | 12 | €44 |

Neuilly-sur-Seine | 60, bd Vital-Bouhot (Pont-de-Levallois) | 01-47-45-04-20 | www.cafelajatte.com

An "enormous" fake skeleton hanging from the ceiling shows the "cavernous" scale of this Ile de la Jatte eatery, a "trendy", "crowded" hangout for Neuilly's smart set who sit indoors or out on a "lovely" terrace; the servers are "not particularly nice or competent" and the Eclectic cooking "is mediocre at best", but these flaws pale compared to the oyster bar, "lovely" terrace, child-friendly Sunday brunch and "agreeable" setting "away from the tourists."

Café Lenôtre (Le) *New French* | 18 | 21 | 16 | €47 |

8ᵉ | Pavillon Elysée | 10, av des Champs-Elysées (Champs-Elysées-Clémenceau) | 01-42-65-97-71 | www.lenotre.fr

With a "charming, simply charming" setting in the Pavillon Elysée, this Italian-accented New French from the Lenôtre caterers is "great on a sunny day" when you can sit on "one of the nicest terraces in Paris"; the "finely displayed foods" are "good", if "limited", and foes find "prices high" for what's essentially "gourmet sandwich fare"; but all ends on a sweet note, since everyone loves the "beautiful pastries."

Café Le Petit Pont ● *Classic French* | 14 | 14 | 16 | €36 |

5ᵉ | 1, rue du Petit Pont (St-Michel) | 01-43-54-23-81

"It all feels so Paris" at this "busy cafe": a "killer" Latin Quarter location, "stunning view of Notre Dame" and "good jazz" live nightly; so *c'est dommage* the traditional French fare falls between "bad and mediocre" ("luckily it's not very expensive") and "service is slow"; small wonder "the French seem to avoid" this "touristy" place.

ⓩ Café Les Deux Magots ● *Classic French* | 16 | 20 | 16 | €38 |

6ᵉ | 6, pl St-Germain-des-Prés (St-Germain-des-Prés) | 01-45-48-55-25 | www.lesdeuxmagots.fr

"Wear glasses and order in French and you'll feel at home" at this "chapter in Parisian history" that's "a must-do for tourists who have read their Sartre and Beauvoir"; though it's "full of foreigners", the ambiance still "lives up to the hype" and the "window onto the

Boulevard Saint-Germain" offers "people-watching supreme"; true, "the viewing beats the chewing", especially given the extraordinary prices for "ordinary" Classic French fare served by "arrogant waiters", so have a drink or at most "a quick bite" and "save dinner for a real restaurant."

Café M 🗷 *New French* ▽ 19 | 19 | 23 | €48

8ᵉ | Hôtel Hyatt | 24, bd Malesherbes (Madeleine/St-Augustin) | 01-55-27-12-34 | www.paris.madeleine.hyatt.com

Guests at the 8th-arrondissement Hyatt hail "the usual professional restaurant" on the premises, this one appointed in black and gold by architect Pascal Desprez; the "good" New French food, served at lunch only, is equally "modern" and casually "upscale", while "attentive service" keeps everything moving right along; N.B. it's a champagne bar in the evening.

🗷 Café Marly ⏺ *Classic/New French* 16 | 24 | 14 | €44

1ᵉʳ | 93, rue de Rivoli (Palais Royal-Musée du Louvre) | 01-49-26-06-60

When the Louvre has done you in, this on-site eatery is "the finest place to recover from museum fatigue" say fans of the "chic" Empire-style setting and "stellar" views of I.M. Pei's pyramid and the sculpture gallery; the "overpriced" Classic–New French food is "predictable if unspectacular" and the "waiters treat you more like trespassers than customers" – "but who cares?" devotees "would endure any rudeness to sit on this terrace" overlooking the "breathtaking" courtyard.

Café Moderne 🗷 *Bistro* 21 | 16 | 17 | €41

2ᵉ | 40, rue Notre-Dame-des-Victoires (Bourse) | 01-53-40-84-10 | www.cafemoderne.fr

"You quickly feel like a regular" at this "endearing" bistro where "a sophisticated, Pan-European clientele", including brokers from the nearby Bourse, comes for "excellent cuisine mixing tradition and innovation", plus a "good choice of wines"; the "tastefully done", "long narrow space" has modern art exhibits and big windows onto a courtyard, creating a "comfortably trendy atmosphere."

Café Pleyel 🗷 *New French* - | - | - | M

8ᵉ | 252, rue du Faubourg Saint-Honoré (Ternes) | 01-53-75-28-44 | www.cafesallepleyel.com

Innovative restaurateur Hélène Samuel, who founded the now defunct Delicabar, plays another tune with this stylish, spacious venue in Paris' renowned concert hall, the Salle Pleyel; the eclectic New French menu changes constantly – there's a new chef each season – but hungry culture vultures can only dine on concert nights (lunch is served every weekday).

Café Rouge *Classic French/Eclectic* - | - | - | M

3ᵉ | 32, rue de Picardie (République/Temple) | 01-44-54-20-60

Young and trendy (but friendly), this eatery in the northern Marais occupies a duplex space with a cozy mezzanine and predominantly *rouge* color scheme; the policy of BYO from the wine bar next door allows for penny-wise drinking and adds to the affordability of the Classic French–Eclectic dishes like the signature tuna millefeuille and veal medallions with honey.

Café Ruc ● *Bistro*

| 15 | 16 | 14 | €42 |

1er | 159, rue St-Honoré (Palais Royal-Musée du Louvre) | 01-42-60-97-54
"Yet another Costes" address, this bistro in "a critical tourist location" "close to the Louvre" works "for a quick bite with style" – but only if "you're hip and French" opponents opine; otherwise, the "beautiful" but "moody staff" "often seems preoccupied elsewhere", and when they "finally get around to your order, you'll receive" "standard fare" that's "a pretty bad buy for the buck"; but for "excellent views of Paris' human delicacies" amid a "Robert Palmer video" ambiance, it's "unbeatable."

Café Terminus *Classic French*

| - | - | - | M |

8e | Hôtel Concorde St-Lazare | 108, rue St-Lazare (St-Lazare) | 01-40-08-43-30 | www.concordestlazare-paris.com
There's "a whiff of old Paris" in this hotel cafe, whose decor represents fashion designer Sonia Rykiel's take on the belle epoque (the building dates from the 1880s); the "calm" atmosphere might be a result of its off-the-beaten-track location near Gare Saint-Lazare, while its Classic French cuisine (including "typical shellfish platters") is "refined" if "not outstanding."

NEW Caffé dei Cioppi ⌧ *Italian*

| - | - | - | M |

11e | 159, rue du Faubourg St-Antoine (Ledru-Rollin) | 01-43-46-10-14
With housemade pasta, buffalo mozzarella salad, homemade fruit tart and such, this *piccolo* Italiano in a passage not far from the Bastille offers a taste of Trastevere for anyone craving a transalpine meal; booking is essential and opening hours vary, but the service is charming, and a side bonus is surprisingly good people-watching (it's a favorite of the French film community).

Caffé Toscano ⌧ *Italian*

| ∇ 19 | 17 | 18 | €36 |

7e | 34, rue des Sts-Pères (St-Germain-des-Prés) | 01-42-84-28-95
It's not easy to find a good, moderately priced meal in the 7th, so this casual Tuscan in the gallery district is a popular spot for antiques dealers and other Left Bankers, with "low-key hospitality" and a wood/terra-cotta interior; the "tasty pasta dishes" are a "welcome Italian diversion from heavy bistro food", since many are made with ingredients like lemon and arugula.

Cagouille (La) *Seafood*

| 25 | 16 | 18 | €55 |

14e | 10, pl Constantin Brancusi (Gaîté/Montparnasse-Bienvenüe) | 01-43-22-09-01 | www.la-cagouille.fr
Some come here for "perfectly prepared" fish they claim is "the freshest you'll get in Paris", others for the "great" cognac collection comprising "some 200 different varieties"; either way, this meat-free eatery near Montparnasse is a definite "find" (if "difficult to locate"); what stands out most in the slightly "sterile surroundings" is the chalkboard menu that changes "depending on today's market."

	FOOD	DECOR	SERVICE	COST

Cailloux (Les) *Italian* | - | - | - | M

13ᵉ | 58, rue des Cinq-Diamants (Corvisart/Place d'Italie) | 01-45-80-15-08
"Worth a trip" "as much for the ambiance as for the pasta" attest advocates of this "decent" Italian "in the heart of Buttes aux Cailles"; though humble, the woody decor is "pleasant", and it's "a good buy" to boot – if "not as economical" since it's been discovered by a "young, attractive crowd."

Caïus ⌧ *New French* | ▽ 19 | 13 | 16 | €50

17ᵉ | 6, rue d'Armaillé (Charles de Gaulle-Etoile) | 01-42-27-19-20
Chef-owner Jean Marc Notelet developed his "original" style at L'Espérance (in Vézelay) and Boyer (Reims), and his "inspired use of spices and unusual ingredients" makes his New French in the 17th a perpetual surprise, especially since the menu changes daily; diners declare the decor is just "ok", but that's easy to forgive when one considers the "great-value" menu and "extensive" wine list.

Caméléon (Le) ⌧ Ⓜ *Bistro* | 20 | 15 | 19 | €49

6ᵉ | 6, rue de Chevreuse (Vavin) | 01-43-27-43-27
This "Montparnasse classic" changed owners a while back, and, chameleonlike, they're "trying to turn it into a chic place"; the decor's still "ordinary" and the attitude "a bit too Rive Droite" for a Left Bank address, "but the bistro food is better", showing "some creativity" at the hands of young chef David Angelot (ex the late Jamin), who works *sans* camouflage in an open kitchen.

Camélia (Le) ⌧ Ⓜ *New French* | 20 | 16 | 20 | €62

Bougival | 7, quai Georges Clémenceau (La Défense RER) | 01-39-18-36-06 | www.lecamelia.com
The 19th-century *auberge* where Alexandre Dumas (*fils*) met the woman who inspired *The Lady of the Camellias* is now "an oasis of refinement in the culinary desert" of Bougival, where chef-owner Thierry Conte creates "high-level" New French cuisine in a *sympathique* ambiance that owes much to the "extremely nice" service and "carefully contemplated" decor in ochre and yellow with columns and flowered-print banquettes.

Camille ⬤ *Bistro* | 16 | 15 | 16 | €38

3ᵉ | 24, rue des Francs-Bourgeois (St-Paul) | 01-42-72-20-50
"Small" yet "charming", this Marais minx is a dependable "neighborhood spot" serving "unpretentious" bistro fare that's "reasonably priced", seven days a week (for breakfast too); a "great place for lunch after a visit to the Picasso Museum" or browsing the boutiques, it gets "crowded and noisy", with the sidewalk terrace particularly coveted come summer.

Cantine de Quentin (La) Ⓜ *Wine Bar/Bistro* | - | - | - | I

10ᵉ | 52, rue Bichat (Jacques Bonsergent/République) | 01-42-02-40-32
With its hand-painted sign on the facade, this "tiny", "lovely" spot is highly recommended for lunch or brunch when cruising the funky Canal Saint-Martin area; a chef who was formerly at Guy Savoy makes "inexpensive" bistro fare, plus a boutique "full of good

things" – artisanal foods and modestly priced wines that can be consumed on-site for a small corking fee.

Cantine du Troquet (La) 🗷 *Basque/Bistro* | - | - | - | M |

14ᵉ | 101, rue de l'Ouest (Pernety)

The only drawback to Le Troquet chef Christian Etchebest's tremen-
dously popular bistro not far from the Gare Montparnasse is that it
doesn't take reservations; still, most people don't mind the wait for
a go at the delicious Basque-accented bistro menu, especially the
roast Landes chicken and pork breast Ibaiona; service sometimes
gets overwhelmed but the price is right, especially for such good-
quality fare; N.B. closed weekends.

Cap Seguin (Le) 🗷 *Classic French* | - | - | - | M |

Boulogne-Billancourt | Face au 27, quai le Gallo (Pont-de-Sèvres) |
01-46-05-06-07 | www.capseguin.com

Boulogne-area "advertising and media types come in droves" to this
barge "facing the Seine", with a riverside terrace and yacht-club ambiance; the "Classic/New French cuisine is agreeable", even if the "service is embarrassingly slow" (though "less pathetic than before");
overall, though, this is "a nice place to be when the sun is shining."

🗹 Carré des Feuillants 🗷 *Haute Cuisine* | 26 | 23 | 25 | €126 |

1ᵉʳ | 14, rue de Castiglione (Concorde/Tuileries) | 01-42-86-82-82 |
www.carredesfeuillants.fr

"One of the great ones", this Haute Cuisine table "adjacent to the
Place Vendôme" "deserves more recognition" than it gets, since "inventive veteran" Alain Dutournier prepares "divine", "classical"
food with Southwestern flavors, plus, in autumn, "the best game
menu in Paris", accompanied by a "wine list that's tops" and service
that's almost "at the level of the food"; while "elegant", "the decor
reminds one of the Ice Queen's palace", but overall, the experience
is "memorable", so "order with abandon if your wallet can afford it."

Carr's *Irish* | - | - | - | M |

1ᵉʳ | 1, rue du Mont-Thabor (Tuileries) | 01-42-60-60-26 |
www.carrsparis.com

Though "Irish food is not an obvious choice" in Paris, they give
"great brunch" on weekends at this bit o' "the Emerald Isle" near the
Tuileries; it's "always convivial", with "cordial hosts that look like
they stepped out of Dickens", and has gotten to be quite a singles
venue with the Anglophile-meets-French crowd, even if some of
them "go for the beer" (Guinness, of course) rather than the eats.

Carte Blanche 🗷 *Bistro/New French* | - | - | - | M |

9ᵉ | 6, rue Lamartine (Cadet) | 01-48-78-12-20 |
www.restaurantcarteblanche.com

"Not your father's Paris restaurant", this bistro in the 9th offers "an
unusual, witty mix of French ingredients and Asian flavors" on an
oft-changing chalkboard menu that ensures you probably won't "eat
the same thing twice"; converts call its "creative" cuisine a "dream",
and what's more, there's no rude awakening when the bill arrives.

Cartes Postales (Les) ⊠ *New French*

	FOOD	DECOR	SERVICE	COST
	▽ 24	10	16	€48

1ᵉʳ | 7, rue Gomboust (Opéra/Pyramides) | 01-42-61-02-93

Worth writing home about, this table "the size of a postcard" behind the Place du Marché Saint-Honoré has long been a "sure bet" for "an interesting, successful blend of Japanese and French cuisine", prepared by an Asian chef-owner who "was one of the first to start doing this"; the room is slightly "sterile", but the "reasonable prices" please, and correspondents concur it's "a fine idea to offer half-portions."

Casa Bini *Italian*

FOOD	DECOR	SERVICE	COST
21	13	17	€47

6ᵉ | 36, rue Grégoire de Tours (Odéon) | 01-46-34-05-60

"This is the place" for a "real Italian" experience, "from the chef to the staff" say surveyors of this *casa* "in the heart of the 6th"; "service and food can be erratic", leading to a "was-it-worth-that-price feeling", but most are delighted with the "delicious" dishes and wines from the northern part of The Boot; P.S. one sometimes "sees French stars dining here."

Casa Olympe ⊠ *New French/Provence*

FOOD	DECOR	SERVICE	COST
24	15	20	€62

9ᵉ | 48, rue St-Georges (Notre-Dame-de-Lorette/St-Georges) | 01-42-85-26-01 | www.casaolympe.com

Chef-owner Olympe Versini "is a pioneer who has been on the Paris scene for over 30 years", the last 17 running this neighborhood bistro in the 9th, where a "genial crowd" comes for "hearty" New French–Provençal food that's "cooked to perfection" and served with "unobtrusive" efficiency; it can be "difficult to make a reservation" even though "they pack you in", but "since the restaurant is teensy, you don't have to look hard to find someone to bring you a check."

Casa Tina ◗ *Spanish*

FOOD	DECOR	SERVICE	COST
-	-	-	M

16ᵉ | 18, rue Lauriston (Kléber) | 01-40-67-19-24 | www.casa-tina.net

Flamenco music and bullfighting posters leave no doubt that Spanish blood courses through the veins of this "basic", "cozy" eatery close to the Etoile, where a "fun" ambiance goes hand in hand with "decent" tapas, plus more substantial fare such as paella; the nearby annex, Casa Paco, picks up the overflow when this "tiny place" is full.

Casier à Vin (Le) ⊠ *Bistro/Mediterranean*

FOOD	DECOR	SERVICE	COST
-	-	-	I

15ᵉ | 51-53, rue Olivier de Serres (Convention/Porte de Versailles) | 01-45-33-36-80 | www.izaguyot.com

The recognized culinary talents of chef Iza Guyot combine spices from her native Morocco and the Mediterranean with traditional French recipes, attracting tourists and foodies alike to this cozy enclave of the far-fetched 15th arrondissement near Porte de Versailles; daily specials include artfully rendered creations such as tagine with pickled lemons or duck pot roast featuring quality products sourced directly from small producers, matched with an amazing selection of local wines chosen from the wine racks *casiers* along the wall – and best of all, prices are remarkably easygoing.

	FOOD	DECOR	SERVICE	COST

Caveau du Palais (Le) *Classic French*
| 19 | 17 | 17 | €50 |

1er | 17-19, pl Dauphine (Cité/Pont-Neuf) | 01-43-26-04-28
On the "tranquil" Place Dauphine, in a "quiet 17th-century court-yard", this "lovely secret spot" is "definitely worth the visit" for its "consistent, delicious food" in the Classic French vein; at lunch the service tends to be "rushed" due to "all the lawyers and judges" from the Palais de Justice nearby, but "on a summer evening, it makes you forget you're in the heart of Paris", especially since your "romantic dinner will not break the bank."

Cave de l'Os à Moëlle M *Wine Bar/Bistro*
| 22 | 18 | 19 | €34 |

15^e | 181, rue de Lourmel (Lourmel) | 01-45-57-28-28
"Diners eat at communal tables" at this hangout "deep in the 15th", a stone wine cellar that is "informal in the extreme" – you help yourself from "a pot in the back" and the "all-you-can-eat dessert buffet", and "pick your wines (at retail prices) off the wall" (the "genuinely nice staff" opens the bottles); "the self-serve approach can make for commotion at times", but the bistro fare's "simple yet delicious"; so "fill up with joyful satisfaction and learn to love your neighbors."

Cave Gourmande (La) – le Restaurant de Mark Singer *Bistro*
| ▽ 25 | 13 | 21 | €49 |

19^e | 10, rue du Général Brunet (Botzaris/Danube) | 01-40-40-03-30
"Maybe it's a bit out of the way for the average tourist", but gour-mands gush it's "well worth the Homeric effort to find" this bistro in the far reaches of the 19th, thanks to the "splendid market-driven", "inventive" cuisine concocted "with much thought to taste, texture and presentation" by chef-owner Mark Singer, an "American in Paris"; "efficient service" and an "affordable, sharp wine list" make up for the "modest setting."

Caves Pétrissans *Wine Bar/Bistro*
| ▽ 19 | 15 | 17 | €46 |

17^e | 30 bis, av Niel (Péreire/Ternes) | 01-42-27-52-03
The same family has owned this "classic, timeless bistro" in the 17th "for a very long time" – more than a century, in fact – and "not much of the decor has changed since WWII"; "warmth and welcome" await customers who cram into "tight quarters", then dig into Classic French specialties "like nobody makes anymore"; but the biggest "attraction here is the wine list", sold from the "attached boutique" at retail plus a corkage fee.

Caviar Kaspia ● *Russian*
| 25 | 19 | 22 | €121 |

8^e | 17, pl de la Madeleine (Madeleine) | 01-42-65-33-32 | www.caviarkaspia.com
"If you have a lust for caviar", this "tsarist-decorated" Russian "landmark" is "the perfect place" to satisfy it, preferably at "a table for two in a window overlooking the Place de la Madeleine"; the "young servers are easy on the eyes" and the "truly wealthy" "cus-tomers are a show by themselves"; but the "star" here is the "divine" black gold, backed by the "best blini and smoked fish" – a "light meal", perhaps, but a worthy "sky's-the-limit" "splurge."

	FOOD	DECOR	SERVICE	COST

Cazaudehore
La Forestière M *Haute Cuisine* — 22 | 22 | 20 | €67

Saint-Germain-en-Laye | 1, av Kennedy (St-Germain-en-Laye RER) |
01-30-61-64-64 | www.cazaudehore.fr

Attached to a Relais & Chateaux hotel in Saint-Germain-en-Laye,
this "venerable house" is an "easy getaway from the city" for
Southwestern-influenced, "exquisite" Haute Cuisine *"en terrace"*
overseen by "gracious hosts"; the "lovely" setting with a "great view
of gardens" is "wonderful on a sunny Sunday for lunch, but late autumn by the fireplace can be even better."

Céladon (Le) *Classic French* — 21 | 21 | 22 | €81

2ᵉ | Hôtel Westminster | 15, rue Daunou (Opéra) | 01-47-03-40-42 |
www.leceladon.com

In the majestic Hôtel Westminster, this "elegant" table is "like dining
in the home of a refined friend" – or even your stereotypical "wealthy
aunt's parlor", with "luscious" Classic French cuisine and "fancy"
service; a few feel it's "a bit too old-fashioned", fretting "substantial
price increases aren't reflected in the quality of the cuisine", but on
weekends it becomes more relaxed, with different decor and a fixed-
price menu that may be "the best gourmet deal in Paris"; P.S. "be
sure to drop by the Duke's Bar" after dinner.

153 Grenelle Ⓢ M *Haute Cuisine* — - | - | - | E

7ᵉ | 153, rue de Grenelle (La Tour-Maubourg) | 01-45-51-54-12

One of the rising stars of the 1980s, chef Jean-Jacques Jouteux
makes his Parisian comeback (he'd most recently been on the
Côte d'Azur) at this little dove-gray dining room in the 7th; his
charming sister supervises the well-mannered, rather formal service, which – along with the brief but innovative Haute Cuisine
menu – has already made the place popular with UNESCO bigwigs
and bourgeois couples alike.

Ⓩ 144 Petrossian (Le) Ⓢ M *Seafood* — 25 | 21 | 22 | €84

7ᵉ | 18, bd de la Tour-Maubourg (Invalides/La Tour-Maubourg) |
01-44-11-32-32 | www.petrossian.fr

Fish egg lovers roe their boats to this caviarteria in the swanky 7th
for the "sublime indulgence" of beluga's best; though if black gold is
"the highlight" here, the "outstanding" menu also shows "good
depth" with products from the depths (the Food score's climbed under chef Rougui Dia); other pluses include the "elegant" decor and
"attentive", unobtrusive service, but "if you have to think of price,
best not to go" (or else opt for the lunch prix fixe).

Cerisaie (La) Ⓢ *Southwest* — 21 | 11 | 18 | €43

14ᵉ | 70, bd Edgar Quinet (Edgar Quinet/Montparnasse-Bienvenüe) |
01-43-20-98-98

A "young chef" and his "charming" wife run this venue that has a
"neighborhood feel" despite its location "within sight of the Tour
Montparnasse"; the "intelligent" Southwestern menu features
"wonderful combinations", so "reservations are a must" for a "jam-
packed table" in the "tiny room."

Chai 33 ● *Wine Bar/Bistro*

FOOD	DECOR	SERVICE	COST
14	16	12	€41

12e | 33, Cour St-Emilion (Cour St-Emilion) | 01-53-44-01-01 | www.chai33.com

"Walls of windows, large staircases", "unpolished concrete" surfaces and two terraces have turned the "vast open space" of an old Bercy wine warehouse into this "chic", "original" *bistrot à vins*; "spend the night sampling wines from the cellar" of 300 labels, while you nibble on "trendy", albeit "banal" bistro dishes, served by a *très chic*, if often "busy", staff.

Chalet (Le) *Alpine/Classic French*

-	-	-	M

Neuilly-sur-Seine | 14, rue du Commandant Pilot (Les Sablons/ Porte Maillot) | 01-46-24-03-11 | www.lechaletdeneuilly.com

The rustic, mountain-inn decor "transports you to the Alps without being overdone" ("no one's yodeling, luckily") at this Neuilly venue; but if the wooden interior isn't cheesy, the food is – *fondue savoyarde* and other "simple" but "well-prepared", "authentic" Montagnarde specialties that have habitués hiking in for an "out-of-the-ordinary" experience; N.B. in summertime, the menu switches to lighter Classic French cuisine.

Chalet de l'Oasis (Le) *Bistro*

-	-	-	I

Boulogne-Billancourt | Parc de St-Cloud (Pont-de-Sèvres) | 01-49-66-12-83 | www.chalet-oasis.fr

Opened by the Dumant brothers (Auberge Bressane and Paris Seize) in the bucolic, historic Parc de Saint-Cloud, this joyful terrace is one of the best warm-weather spots to enjoy simple, traditional bistro fare such as saucisson, eggs mayonnaise or steak frites with a bottle of fresh rosé or white wine; while access is a little difficult unless you go by car or taxi, the panoramic view of Paris, easygoing ambiance and gentle tabs make it really worthwhile; N.B. open April–October only.

Chalet des Iles (Le) *Classic French*

FOOD	DECOR	SERVICE	COST
14	24	14	€57

16e | Lac Inférieur du Bois de Boulogne (La Muette/La Pompe) | 01-42-88-04-69 | www.chaletdesiles.net

Sunday afternooners feel like "the subject of a Seurat painting" as they "approach by little boat this charming restaurant" on an "enchanting island" in the Bois de Boulogne; "it's a real pity the Classic French cuisine is not at a level this place deserves" – in fact, "it would be banal" without the "paradisiacal" premises that make it "one of the most romantic in Paris."

Chamarré Montmartre *New French*

-	-	-	E

18e | 52, rue Lamarck (Lamarck-Caulaincourt) | 01-42-55-05-42 | www.chamarre-montmartre.com

For years, this Montmartre address was the setting for Beauvilliers, one of the grander beau monde tables in town; now Mauritian chef Antoine Heerah (of the old, original Chamarré in the 7th) has given it a dramatic makeover with sea-green walls, art-glass light fixtures and an open kitchen; the New French menu features his personal take on the cooking of Mauritius, an intriguing Indian Ocean hybrid of African, Indian, Gallic and Chinese cuisines – hence, dishes like chicken cooked with fresh curry leaves and hare in cocoa sauce; young, friendly service compensates for the substantial prices.

Chantairelle ⓧ *Auvergne*
- | - | - | M

5ᵉ | 17, rue Laplace (Maubert-Mutualité) | 01-46-33-18-59 | www.chantairelle.com

Recorded bird calls, stone walls, a woodsy scent and a forest – or at least a garden – make this "small, friendly" spot "near the Panthéon" like "a trip to the Auvergne", for a discovery of the mountainous region's "fantastic", "hearty" fare ("order the stuffed cabbage") along with "basic and reasonable" wines; surveyors "love the owner", the "cozy terrace", Monsieur Maurice the resident cat and the fact that it's all so comfortably "predictable."

Chardenoux (Le) *Bistro*
∇ 19 | 15 | 15 | €51

11ᵉ | 1, rue Jules Vallès (Charonne/Faidherbe-Chaligny) | 01-43-71-49-52

"After a low period it's back at the expected level" laud lovers of this century-old bistro, "one of the best of its type in Paris"; the menu is a "reference" for "classic offerings", and the building with its original belle epoque interior is a classified historic monument, "worth the trip by métro" to the 11th – and a postcard from the past; N.B. scores don't reflect its acquisition by TV chef Cyril Lignac (Le Quinzième).

Charlot – Roi des Coquillages ❶ *Brasserie*
15 | 13 | 14 | €54

9ᵉ | 12, pl de Clichy (Place de Clichy) | 01-53-20-48-00 | www.charlot-paris.com

Reflecting the improving demographics of the once "dodgy" Place de Clichy neighborhood, sleek decor has replaced the kitschy look of this veteran brasserie; menuwise, you can still "always count on the fresh shellfish", and if some find it "hard on the wallet", "order a *plateau* for a group, and it's surprisingly reasonable."

Charpentiers (Aux) ❶ *Bistro*
18 | 16 | 19 | €43

6ᵉ | 10, rue Mabillon (Mabillon/St-Germain-des-Prés) | 01-43-26-30-05

"Linked to the Carpenter's Guild, this solid landmark of French culinary history" – established 1856 – still serves "no-frills bistro" comestibles in a "comfortable", collegial setting ("your new best friend is at the next table"); the "unmovable menu" and "oh-so-typical *garçons*" suggest that "it's never changed and, we suspect, never will."

Chartier *Classic French*
(aka Bouillon Chartier)
13 | 21 | 14 | €24

9ᵉ | 7, rue Faubourg Montmartre (Grands Boulevards) | 01-47-70-86-29 | www.restaurant-chartier.com

"Tucked away off the Grands Boulevards", "one of the last classic dining halls" of Paris makes you "feel like you're stepping back in time" to an era of "no-frills" Classic French food, "rushed waiters" and communal tables in a "barn"-sized "beautiful building"; the food is "incredibly cheap" – but most jeer you get "the quality you pay for", plus often you "have to wait next to the garbage cans"; but that doesn't stop "both natives and tourists" lining up for the "lively" ambiance.

Chateaubriand (Le) 🚫Ⓜ *New French*   22 | 15 | 16 | €48

11ᵉ | 129, av Parmentier (Goncourt/Parmentier) | 01-43-57-45-95

Serving up nothing less than "the future of bistro cuisine", according to its acolytes, this dinner-only eatery adds to the "buzz of the Oberkampf area" with "surprising and explosive" New French cooking by "young Basque" chef Inaki Aizpitarte; there's "a real bobo atmosphere" in the minimalist interior with its "casual" service, "high" noise level and handwritten blackboard menu, but though this place might be "terribly à la mode", it's also "s-o-o-o good."

NEW Chateau Poivre (Le) *Bistro*   - | - | - | M

14ᵉ | 145, rue du Château (Mouton-Duvernet/Pernety) | 01-43-22-03-68 | www.chateaupoivre.com

Not far from the Gare Montparnasse is this friendly new bistro run by a former maître d'hôtel at Le Troquet and a chef who trained with Robuchon and Ducasse; mirrors on the walls lend some breathing room to its cozy, white-and-gray space, and the chef puts an haute spin on good-value contemporary French bistro fare along the lines of potato galette with sautéed foie gras and wild mushrooms or saddle of rabbit stuffed with figs.

Chen Soleil d'Est 🚫 *Chinese*   - | - | - | VE

15ᵉ | 15, rue du Théâtre (Charles Michels) | 01-45-79-34-34

"Even if the chef passed away a [few] years ago, it's still the best Chinese restaurant in Paris" (certainly, it's one of the most "pricey") declare defiant devotees of this table; in the midst of a somewhat bleak, "out-of-the-way location" in the 15th, it's "a haven" for "divine Peking duck" dinners, "elegantly presented" and made with "French products" – as are the "serious wines."

Cherche Midi (Le) ● *Italian*   19 | 15 | 17 | €41

6ᵉ | 22, rue du Cherche-Midi (Sèvres-Babylone/St-Sulpice) | 01-45-48-27-44

"On a lovely quiet street near Saint-Sulpice", this "hole-in-the-wall is an insider's favorite" for "reliably good Italian cuisine" that's often served with "tongue-in-cheek commentary from the waiter"; "ideal for celebrity-spotting", it's usually "crowded and noisy", due to the "elbow-to-elbow seating", so you "better reserve or be a habitué" (who heads straight for the coveted "seats on the sidewalk terrace").

Chéri Bibi ● *Bistro*   - | - | - | M

18ᵉ | 15, rue André-del-Sarte (Anvers/Château Rouge) | 01-42-54-88-96

Bobos from the Butte are making tracks for this "hip spot on the eastern side" of Montmartre, open late and co-owned by Yannig Samot (La Famille, Le Réfectoire), where "1950s flea-market furnishings" set the scene for an "excellent-value" meal consisting of "simple", "classic" bistro recipes in "copious" portions and "well-chosen wines"; perhaps "the service is nicer for habitués than for others", but nevertheless this place is "ever full."

Chez André ● *Bistro* | 20 | 15 | 18 | €51 |

8ᵉ | 12, rue Marbeuf (Franklin D. Roosevelt) | 01-47-20-59-57
"Just a block from the hustle and bustle" of the Champs sits this "epitome of bistros", complete with "oyster shucker outside"; seems as if "nothing here has changed since before World War II", when it opened: neither the "simple and oh-so-good" cuisine nor the "classic environment" nor the "grandmotherly" waitresses, "all dressed in black with white aprons"; however, "if you don't like [sitting] close to strangers, this is not the place for you."

Chez Catherine 🗷 *New French* | 23 | 19 | 22 | €71 |

8ᵉ | 3, rue Berryer (George V/St-Philippe-du-Roule) | 01-40-76-01-40
While its side-street address in the 8th is "a tad off the beaten track", it's worth "studying your map" to find this New French, with "pricey" but "interesting", "inventive" cuisine offered amid "lovely", gray-toned decor; the "warm, welcoming service" is led by Franck Paget, who recently (post-Survey) took over from the namesake founding chef, and who trained at the likes of La Grand Cascade and Le Jules Vernes.

Chez Cécile | - | - | - | M |
(La Ferme des Mathurins) 🗷 *Classic French*

8ᵉ | 17, rue Vignon (Madeleine) | 01-42-66-46-39 | www.chezcecile.com
Owner Cécile de Sintel provides a "terrific evening" at this "excellent-value" table in the 8th, where "a hardworking chef in a tiny kitchen" turns out "truly outstanding" Classic French food with "inventive presentations and flavors", plus "consistently whimsical service"; music lovers sing that the "live jazz on Thursday nights" is "a blast"; N.B. a recent renovation added a new bar and red-and-taupe color scheme.

Chez Clément ● *Classic French* | 15 | 17 | 16 | €35 |

2ᵉ | 17, bd des Capucines (Opéra) | 01-53-43-82-00
4ᵉ | 19, rue Beaumarchais (Bastille) | 01-40-29-17-00
4ᵉ | 21, bd Beaumarchais (Bastille/Chemin-Vert) | 01-40-29-17-00
6ᵉ | 9, pl St-André-des-Arts (St-Michel) | 01-56-81-32-00
8ᵉ | 123, av des Champs-Elysées (Charles de Gaulle-Etoile) | 01-40-73-87-00
8ᵉ | 19, rue Marbeuf (Franklin D. Roosevelt/George V) | 01-53-23-90-00
14ᵉ | 106, bd du Montparnasse (Vavin) | 01-44-10-54-00
15ᵉ | 407, rue de Vaugirard (Porte de Versailles) | 01-53-68-94-00
17ᵉ | 47, av de Wagram (Charles de Gaulle-Etoile/Ternes) | 01-53-81-97-00
17ᵉ | 99, bd Gouvion-St-Cyr (Porte Maillot) | 01-45-72-93-00
www.chezclement.com
Additional locations throughout Paris

"Everything is average" at this "country-style chain with lots of copper decor" ("kitschy, but not bad") and "standard" Classic French cuisine; still, it's a "popular spot for tour groups", "cheap reunions" or "a quick meal before or after a movie."

	FOOD	DECOR	SERVICE	COST

Chez Denise - La Tour de Montlhéry ● 🗷 *Bistro*

| | 24 | 18 | 18 | €47 |

1ᵉʳ | 5, rue des Prouvaires (Châtelet-Les Halles) | 01-42-36-21-82

"Every night's a party" (one that runs all night) at this "wonderful old-style bistro that has survived for years" in the old Les Halles ("you'll expect Hemingway to be seated next to you any minute"); cuisine "doesn't come more traditionally Parisian" than the "delicious", "hearty portions" of "French rustic food", including "many animal parts that may seem strange to city folk", "served with humor that takes your mind off the noise level" and the fact "you're sitting in your neighbor's lap."

Chez Francis ● *Brasserie*

| | 17 | 19 | 16 | €58 |

8ᵉ | 7, pl de l'Alma (Alma Marceau) | 01-47-20-86-83

"At the very end of the chic Avenue Montaigne", this "stalwart" boasts perhaps "the best view from a restaurant in all of Paris", and throughout the day, shoppers, business-lunchers and theatergoers vie to "grab an outdoor table" with "a straight shot at the Eiffel Tower", or to sit inside for "a taste of the belle epoque"; surveyors say the "honest" brasserie cuisine has "improved" since the arrival of a different chef ("have the fish") – but frankly, the fare's "not the point, *n'est-ce pas?*"

Chez Françoise ● *Classic French*

| | 17 | 14 | 17 | €55 |

7ᵉ | Aérogare des Invalides (Invalides) | 01-47-05-49-03 | www.chezfrancoise.com

Located inside the Invalides *aérogare* ("don't let this scare you away"), this is a "favorite place for French politicians" from the nearby National Assembly who ignore the "air-terminal ambiance" and concentrate on the "quite acceptable" Classic French cuisine; it's ideal for a business meal, especially as the staff is "efficient and diplomatic."

Chez Fred 🗷 *Lyon*

| | – | – | – | M |

17ᵉ | 190 bis, bd Péreire (Péreire/Porte Maillot) | 01-45-74-20-48

"Staunch Lyonnais cooking" is the specialty of this *bouchon* (a bistro-style restaurant from the Rhône city), which makes it "a good place to know near Porte Maillot" when you hanker for hearty favorites like *côte de boeuf* or the inimitable *andouillette* (tripe sausage); surveyors smile at its slightly "wacky" side, wondering what other venue is "decorated with snapshots of customers and staff, yet offers valet parking"?

Chez Gégène 🅼 *Classic French*

| | – | – | – | M |

Joinville-le-Pont | 162 bis, quai de Polangis (Joinville-le-Pont RER) | 01-48-83-29-43 | www.chez-gegene.fr

"If you want to have a feel for the '20s around Paris", this century-old *guinguette* in Joinville-le-Pont, along the Marne River, is "a step back into another epoch, especially on the weekends" when people come to dance; just remember that the "fun" here is all about the *fête* – waltzers whisper "avoid at all costs" the Classic French food; N.B. closed January–March, open weekends only October–December.

	FOOD	DECOR	SERVICE	COST

⧈ Chez Georges ⧆ *Bistro* | 24 | 19 | 21 | €60 |

2ᵉ | 1, rue du Mail (Bourse) | 01-42-60-07-11

"A mix of traditional and hip diners" "makes a beeline" to this bistro, a "charming slice of old Paris life" near the Palais-Royal and belonging to "the same family" for several generations; "tradition abounds" here, from the red banquettes to the "motherly waitresses" to the "classic" "comfort" "food of great distinction" – and a higher Food score; even the "raucous crowd" seated "elbow-to-elbow" is "as French as it gets."

Chez Georges-Porte Maillot ● *Brasserie* | ▽ 18 | 16 | 18 | €55 |

17ᵉ | 273, bd Péreire (Porte Maillot) | 01-45-74-31-00 | www.chez-georges.com

Residents of the upscale Porte Maillot area appreciate this "always predictable" institution that's "traditional but not tired"; "famous for its meats", the kitchen turns out "good solid" brasserie food in "huge portions", and the "solicitous" (though sometimes "spotty") service adds to the "classy ambiance"; P.S. "open Sunday night."

Chez Gérard ⧆ *Auvergne* | ▽ 19 | 16 | 18 | €36 |

Neuilly-sur-Seine | 10, rue Montrosier (Porte Maillot) | 01-46-24-86-37

The "menu hasn't changed for 10 years" (even if the chef has) in this "traditional" Neuilly bistro with "refined", "delicious" food from the Auvergne; "but why should it when it is as good" as this shrug surveyors who "feel like they're at home" thanks to the "relaxed atmosphere", "affordable" prices and "service with a smile."

Chez Géraud ⧆ *Classic French* | 20 | 15 | 18 | €56 |

16ᵉ | 31, rue Vital (La Muette) | 01-45-20-33-00

"In a quiet area" of the 16th, this "simple" standby treats even first-timers "like regulars" and is considered by loyal locals to be "one of the best bistros" around, with classic, "old-style bourgeois cooking" using "seasonal or regional delicacies" (including "wow"-worthy game in the fall) and a small but "perfect choice of wines" that spurs oenophiles to cry "break out the Burgundy!"

NEW Chez Grenouille ⧆ *Bistro* | - | - | - | M |

9ᵉ | 52, rue Blanche (Blanche/Trinité) | 01-42-81-34-07 | www.chezgrenouille.com

Equidistant to the Place Blanche and the Eglise de la Trinité, this simple neighborhood bistro has quickly won a following among food-loving local bobos for the generously served, often long-simmered traditional French dishes of chef Alexis Blanchard (ex L'Auberge Bressane), who has a particular love of offal, including pig's feet terrine and tripe dishes; friendly service compensates for the simple, brightly lit white stucco setting.

Chez Grisette ⧆ *Wine Bar/Bistro* | - | - | - | M |

18ᵉ | 14, rue Houdon (Abbesses/Pigalle) | 01-42-62-04-80 | www.chez-grisette.fr

"There's no putting on airs" in this Montmartre wine bistro where the "charming *patronne*", Grisette, creates a "warm and friendly" ambiance and serves "simple but savory" classic cooking (including "excellent blood sausage") accompanied by "great" bottles from "small independent producers", stacked up on the wall as part of the decor; N.B. wine and foie gras available for takeout.

Chez Janou ◐ *Provence*   23 | 19 | 18 | €36

3e | 2, rue Roger Verlomme (Bastille/Chemin-Vert) | 01-42-72-28-41 | www.chezjanou.com

"Oh, you just want to hate" this place "next to the Place des Vosges" "for being so cute, trendy and touristy – but it delivers" with "divinely fresh", "sun-drenched" Provençal cuisine, including fish "that tastes like the water is down the hill", at least "80-plus [kinds of] pastis" and a "bottomless chocolate mousse "like no other"; but "they really pack 'em in tight" at this "boisterous", "buzzing" spot, so "even with a reservation, you'll probably have to wait for your table."

Chez Jenny ◐ *Alsace*   19 | 18 | 19 | €44

3e | 39, bd du Temple (République) | 01-44-54-39-00 | www.chezjenny.com

Alsace admirers "always enjoy" this "choucroute paradise" opened in 1932 by a Strasbourg native in the 3rd (now owned by the Frères Blanc chain); a "traditional brasserie", it's "great" "on a cold night" or late in the evening with a "large group", and though critics call it "more fun than delicious", the "rushed atmosphere", "amiable service" and old-fashioned decor take patrons back to "a bygone time."

Chez Julien *Bistro*   19 | 22 | 18 | €49

4e | 1, rue du Point-Louis-Philippe (Hôtel-de-Ville/Pont-Marie) | 01-42-78-31-64

The "fabulous" Empire decor has long been the selling point of this "cozy", "romantic" bistro located Seine-side in the Marais, and with its takeover by Thierry Costes, the "old-school dining" deserves a second look – though a few deem the cuisine "a bit of a disappointment"; even so, it's "not bad for a quick bite", the "staff's sincere" and in the summer, there's a "lovely outdoor seating area overlooking the Ile Saint-Louis" and the "beautiful old church" Saint-Gervais.

Chez L'Ami Jean ◐⊠Ⓜ *Basque/Bistro*   24 | 16 | 19 | €49

7e | 27, rue Malar (Invalides/La Tour-Maubourg) | 01-47-05-86-89

Chef Stéphane Jego, "the Basque king of Paris", is basking in compliments nowadays, which explains why his "high-energy" bistro a short walk from Les Invalides is "always packed with fun-loving gourmands"; in fact, it's "too crowded to be comfortable", but few care since his "fabulous" *nouveau*-Southwestern cuisine, served by a "helpful staff", could be the "best value in town."

Chez la Vieille ⊠ *Bistro*   ▽ 16 | 13 | 15 | €47

1er | 1, rue Bailleul (Louvre-Rivoli) | 01-42-60-15-78

Peripatetic chef Michel del Burgo (ex La Bristol, Taillevent, Le Negresco) has taken over the kitchen (post-Survey) at this small, two-story bistro with a 1950s interior near Les Halles, and he's serving up a regularly changing menu of impressive French cuisine bourgeoise; if some regulars miss the trencherman's fare that made this place famous, they can take comfort in the sepia-toned atmosphere that hasn't changed a bit.

Chez Léna et Mimile *Bistro*   ∇ 15 | 22 | 16 | €42

5ᵉ | 32, rue Tournefort (Censier-Daubenton/Place Monge) | 01-47-07-72-47 | www.chezlenaetmimile.com

Boasting "one of the nicest terraces around", above a trickling fountain "on a tiny, quiet square off the usually hectic Rue Mouffetard", this traditional '30s bistro is "a treasure" for locals who laud the "well-priced" Classic French menu; but dissidents declare "it's a shame the food is mediocre when the setting is so exceptional."

Chez Léon 🅢 *Bistro*   13 | 11 | 13 | €36

17ᵉ | 32, rue Legendre (Villiers) | 01-42-27-06-82

This "lively" 1930s bistro in the 17th (not to be confused with the mussels chain with a similar name) reopened a few years ago under different ownership with an "engaging staff" and a "lovely" redo all adding to the "convivial" feel; the "freshness of the cuisine matches the varnish on the place", while the "refined" traditional dishes have a "satisfying" flavor "like you rarely find"; N.B. closed weekends.

Chez Les Anges 🅢 *Brasserie*   23 | 19 | 19 | €61

7ᵉ | 54, bd de la Tour-Maubourg (La Tour-Maubourg) | 01-47-05-89-86 | www.chezlesanges.com

Owners Jacques and Catherine Lacipiere have returned this 7th-arrondissement address "back to the old" name, yet this time the angels have a "hip", primarily white abode; opinions are more harmonious regarding the "affordable" market-based fare featuring "creative", "careful" preparations of "traditional" brasserie dishes, plus an "excellent wine list" with some heaven-sent Burgundies.

Chez Livio *Italian*   13 | 11 | 11 | €40

Neuilly-sur-Seine | 6, rue de Longchamp (Pont-de-Neuilly) | 01-46-24-81-32

A family-run "institution" for over 50 years, Neuilly's "popular" trattoria serves up a wide array of Italian eats; detractors dis the "mediocre" "small portions" and "interminable waits", "particularly on the weekends", but it's "an excellent choice for families with kids" – especially "when they open up the roof on a hot summer day."

Chez Ly ☾ *Chinese/Thai*   - | - | - | M

17ᵉ | 95, av Niel (Péreire) | 01-40-53-88-38

"Yes, Madame Ly exists", and "for those who enjoy Cantonese cooking", her place in the 17th – the family's third in Paris – is "a must" with "wonderful ambiance", exotic woods and Chinese porcelain, and "diverse", "tasty" dishes from Hong Kong and Thailand, plus original offerings such as sake-marinated foie gras studded with lotus.

Chez Maître Paul 🅢 *Alsace*   21 | 18 | 19 | €48

6ᵉ | 12, rue Monsieur-le-Prince (Odéon) | 01-43-54-74-59 | www.chezmaitrepaul.fr

"Every foodie loves coming to this bistro" for an insider's take on "utterly delicious" "cuisine from the Jura" mountains (their signature "chicken in yellow wine with morels is heavenly"); it's served "with a welcoming smile" in a "small, cozy and classy" space near Odéon.

Chez Marcel 🗵 *Lyon* | - | - | - | M |

6ᵉ | 7, rue Stanislas (Notre-Dame-des-Champs) | 01-45-48-29-94

It's "like going to dinner at someone's grandparents'" at this "very small", "quirky", "family-run restaurant" in the 6th, where patrons find the "historic look" – complete with lace curtains and "faded rose wallpaper" – totally "charming", while the staff is "solicitous" and the "classic" Lyonnais cuisine is both "excellent" and "dependable"; "end your meal with an Armagnac, which [owner] Jean-Bernard Daumail retrieves from a hidden cellar under his bar."

Chez Marianne *Mideastern* | 18 | 13 | 14 | €23 |

4ᵉ | 2, rue des Hospitalières St-Gervais (St-Paul) | 01-42-72-18-86

"Even if you're broke" you can come to this haven in the historical "heart of the Marais" for a "great variety" of "tasty", "solid Middle Eastern" and Eastern European food; but service is "irregular" and "getting a table in the dining room can be a struggle, especially on weekends", as it's "very crowded even by Paris standards"; hence, "if it's nice weather, eating outside is recommended."

NEW Chez Marie-Louise 🗵 Ⓜ *Bistro* | - | - | - | M |

10ᵉ | 11, rue Marie-et-Louise (Goncourt/Jacques Bonsergent) | 01-53-19-02-04

Located not far from the Canal Saint-Martin, this funky little bistro is popular with media-business hipsters and other arty types who've brought this corner of the 10th back to life; the menu runs to modern takes on bistro classics, including dishes like stuffed saddle of rabbit and langoustine-filled ravioli, with flea-market decor and tame tariffs to boost the appeal.

Chez Michel ❶🗵 *Brittany/New French* | 24 | 16 | 20 | €46 |

10ᵉ | 10, rue de Belzunce (Gare du Nord/Poissonnière) | 01-44-53-06-20

With this "tiny shrine" to the food of Brittany "off the beaten path", "aptly named" chef Thierry Breton has "helped redefine midpriced Parisian dining"; converts claim his prix fixe of "homey but sophisticated" New French cooking is "one of the best bargains" in town, especially "in game season" (though some grouse that "many dishes require a supplement"); "be sure to reserve and reconfirm" before trekking to the 10th, and try not to be "relegated to the basement."

Chez Nénesse 🗵 *Classic French* | - | - | - | I |

3ᵉ | 17, rue de Saintonge (Filles du Calvaire/République) | 01-42-78-46-49

In the happening northern Marais, this family-run, old-style bistro with a heating stove in the middle of the room is "one of the very few" of its kind left, offering "inexpensive" Classic French food such as *tête de veau* along with "friendly service" in a "homey atmosphere."

Chez Omar ❶⊄ *Moroccan* | 21 | 14 | 17 | €32 |

3ᵉ | 47, rue de Bretagne (République/Temple) | 01-42-72-36-26

For "couscous at its most trendy", check out this "casual" "fashion-industry favorite" in the 3rd, where plates are "piled high" with "pleasant" Moroccan morsels, the "jovial" owner makes "you feel like a local on your first" visit and the "waiters never stop joking around"; they "don't take reservations", but "don't be turned off by the line that often extends out the door" – it's "worth the wait."

Chez Papa ❶ Southwest

17 | 14 | 15 | €25

8ᵉ | 29, rue de l'Arcade (Madeleine/St-Lazare) | 01-42-65-43-68
10ᵉ | 206, rue la Fayette (Louis Blanc) | 01-42-09-53-87
14ᵉ | 6, rue Gassendi (Denfert-Rochereau/Raspail) | 01-43-22-41-19
15ᵉ | 101, rue de la Croix Nivert (Commerce/Félix Faure) | 01-48-28-31-88
www.chezpapa.fr

"Cheap and nourishing", this chain is "aimed toward students" and "young, underpaid office workers" with its "huge portions" of "typically Southwestern fare" ("meaning heavy and full of fat"); "the food is not tops", "the decor's pretty lowbrow" and the servers are geared toward turning over tables, but "if you're hungry, this is the place to go"; P.S. the "salade Boyarde with fried potatoes, Cantal and blue cheese, ham and lettuce is by far the best choice on the menu."

Chez Paul ❶ Bistro

21 | 18 | 19 | €39

11ᵉ | 13, rue de Charonne (Bastille/Ledru-Rollin) | 01-47-00-34-57 | www.chezpaul.com

There's a "good scent of tradition" at this "always-packed" Bastille bistro that's been around since 1945 and still has a "great neighborhood vibe" for "post-Opéra" suppers; "tables are sardined" with eaters enjoying "generous portions" of "Classic French fare done simply and well", plus "plenty of red wines at reasonable prices to help wash it all down"; however, the "meaty" menu and "homemade desserts to die for" are definitely "not for dieters."

Chez Paul ❶ Bistro

16 | 12 | 13 | €35

13ᵉ | 22, rue de la Butte aux Cailles (Corvisart/Place d'Italie) | 01-45-89-22-11

"Eat like a Parisian" on grandmotherly cooking ("the baked figs in autumn are the stuff dreams are made of") at this bistro "off the tourist beat" in the 13th arrondissement; the decor's "not original" and the service is "up and down", but "the energy level is high", fueled by the "affordable prices."

Chez Prune ❶ Eclectic

∇ 18 | 19 | 16 | €26

10ᵉ | 36, rue Beaurepaire (Jacques Bonsergent/République) | 01-42-41-30-47

A cool clique frequents this "casual" eatery with a "lovely view of the Canal Saint-Martin", particularly from a "coveted table outside"; "rather rude" waiters serve "pretty good" Eclectic eats, seven days a week from morning till late at night, though many come just for "a drink and to hang with the beautiful crowd."

Chez Ramona Ⓜ Spanish

- | - | - | M

20ᵉ | 17, rue Ramponneau (Belleville/Couronne) | 01-46-36-83-55

The warm Iberian welcome from chef-owner Ramona and her daughter, Cucu, plus their excellent tapas and other Spanish dishes, have trendy young types charging for this affordable bodega in bohemian Belleville; the simple, charming decor re-creates an old-fashioned grocery store, and prices are as friendly as the atmosphere.

Chez Ramulaud ●🗷 Bistro
	FOOD	DECOR	SERVICE	COST
	16	13	17	€37

11ᵉ | 269, rue du Faubourg St-Antoine (Faidherbe-Chaligny/Nation) | 01-43-72-23-29 | www.chez-ramulaud.fr
A faithful "neighborhood clientele" fills up this "cool" "hangout" not far from Place de la Nation, where, despite management changes, the dishes remain an "original" mix of "exotic" and "classic" bistro cuisine, studded with "lots of unfamiliar things" that are "worth trying"; the "wine list is interesting", the staff readily "available" and the cost a "good value", all reasons why this place "never lets you down."

Chez René 🗷Ⓜ Lyon
	21	17	21	€47

5ᵉ | 14, bd St-Germain (Maubert-Mutualité) | 01-43-54-30-23
"Think Paris in the '20s and '30s and you'll get the idea" confide clients of this "old-style, old-world, old-charm" institution in the 5th, where the waiters wear aprons and "nothing ever changes", even after the retirement of the beloved longtime owner; its regulars, businessmen and politicians claim the "mainly Lyonnaise cuisine is unequalled" – "this is the kind of restaurant that gives French food a good name."

Chez Savy 🗷 Aveyron
	18	15	17	€45

8ᵉ | 23, rue Bayard (Franklin D. Roosevelt) | 01-47-23-46-98
Savvy diners looking for the "most affordable pleasure" near the "chic Avenue Montaigne boutiques" hit this "efficient and filling" bistro where "ancient mirrors" give the setting "timeworn cachet" and the kitchen turns out "solid" Aveyronnaise cuisine, including "shirred eggs with Roquefort worth the four hours of walking to burn off."

Chez Vincent ●🗷 Italian
	-	-	-	E

19ᵉ | Parc des Buttes Chaumont (Botzaris/Buttes Chaumont) | 01-42-02-22-45
Vincent Cozzoli's fans have followed their favorite chef-owner to this location in the Parc des Buttes Chaumont for "a fix of good Italian food" served in "huge portions" that help make up for the fact it's "not inexpensive"; the "theatrical" personality of the *proprietario* makes for interesting – and sometimes even "overwhelming" – service.

Chez Vong ●🗷 Chinese
	21	20	19	€54

1ᵉʳ | 10, rue de la Grande Truanderie (Etienne Marcel) | 01-40-26-09-36 | www.chez-vong.com
"Chef Vai Kuan Vong came to Paris over 25 years ago", and what he cooks is "as close to Haute Chinese cuisine as you can get" converts claim – though purists pout that the "overpriced", "Frenchified cooking lacks authenticity"; still, in a shabby part of Les Halles, the decor of this "upscale" Asian offers a "mysterious atmosphere with its old stone dining rooms dotted with Buddhas, parasols and bamboo", and the "service is adorable."

	FOOD	DECOR	SERVICE	COST

Chiberta (Le) ⌧ New French
22 | 21 | 22 | €101

8ᵉ | 3, rue Arsène Houssaye (Charles de Gaulle-Etoile) | 01-53-53-42-00 | www.lechiberta.com

Now "one of Guy Savoy's stable", this venue in the 8th gets mixed responses: scores side with those who find the "inventive" New French fare "wonderful", the "modern decor" "elegant" and the "service fine"; but dissenters deem the digs "dark" ("wear a miner's helmet in the restrooms if you want to see") and the "rather simple" cuisine "much too dear for what it is", making this site do-able "only for business lunches."

Chieng Mai ⌧ Thai
16 | 13 | 13 | €32

5ᵉ | 12, rue Frédéric Sauton (Maubert-Mutualité) | 01-43-25-45-45

"Run in an old-fashioned way", this "authentic Thai" in the 5th arrondissement "near Notre Dame" "is like taking a mini-vacation from Paris"; but while the "multicourse meals are an adventure, it's too bad the rooms are so plain"; luckily service is *un peu* more "pleasant", as are the prices.

Chien qui Fume (Au) ● Brasserie
18 | 18 | 17 | €42

1ᵉʳ | 33, rue du Pont-Neuf (Châtelet-Les Halles) | 01-42-36-07-42 | www.au-chien-qui-fume.com

At "the edge of the Les Halles garden", this "standard brasserie" decorated with "original" images of "dogs smoking" provides "a good deal for what you get" – namely, competent Classic French dishes; some growl that it's "living off its history and its name" – in particular, the staff, "although witty, is ineffective" – but you gotta "keep it in perspective: it's about fun, not Haute Cuisine" or service here.

Christine (Le) ● Bistro
23 | 20 | 21 | €55

6ᵉ | 1, rue Christine (Odéon/St-Michel) | 01-40-51-71-64 | www.restaurantlechristine.com

"Tucked away" on a "charming" street in Saint-Germain, this "welcoming", "romantic" spot with "rustic"-chic decor of stone walls and "quirky art" serves "creative", "well-crafted" bistro cuisine; it fulfills the dream of "what Americans imagine a great French restaurant should be", which explains why it's "often filled" with them, especially in the front room; locals ask for a table in the back, where "French doors open onto a courtyard."

Christophe Bistro
- | - | - | M

5ᵉ | 8, rue Descartes (Cardinal Lemoine) | 01-43-26-72-49

After training under Eric Briffard at the Plaza Athénée and Anne-Sophie Pic in Valence, young chef Christophe Philippe goes solo with this tiny, casually upscale bistro in a "really nice section" of the Latin Quarter; the chalkboard menu offers "very good quality for the price", with excellent regional meats, fish from the Poissonnerie du Dôme and wines from De Vinis Illustribus, one of the city's finest suppliers, located conveniently a few doors away; N.B. closed Wednesdays and Thursdays.

Cibus ☒ *Italian*

–	–	–	M

1er | 5, rue Molière (Palais Royal-Musée du Louvre/Pyramides) | 01-42-61-50-19

Close to the Palais-Royal, this Italian is a little-known address, and with only 20 seats it's probably better that way; there's no menu – the server tells you what the chef-owner has on offer that day – but regulars know they can count on "perfectly al dente" pastas and other dishes made with organic ingredients, plus homemade liqueurs and "nice wines by the glass" from Italia.

Cigale Récamier (La) ☒ *Classic French*

21	18	20	€53

7e | 4, rue Récamier (Sèvres-Babylone) | 01-45-48-86-58

"Lots of neighborhood regulars" gather at this Classic French in a cul-de-sac near the Bon Marché store (it's "lovely dining outside without cars buzzing in your face"); "they really know how to make soufflés", which are "varied and wonderful" – though critics caution "choosing anything else will leave you deflated"; even though "the staff is sometimes overwhelmed", it's "still nice."

☑ Cinq (Le) *Haute Cuisine*

28	29	28	€178

8e | Four Seasons George V | 31, av George V (Alma Marceau/George V) | 01-49-52-71-54 | www.fourseasons.com/paris

"Come here for the meal of your life" swoon sated surveyors who say this Haute Cuisine table in the 8th, voted Tops in Decor and Service, is "perfect in every way", from the "delectable", "adventurous" menu to the "exquisite" classic decor with "vases of flowers everywhere" to the "surprisingly friendly service", "as personal as it is professional" (even offering "a box of reading glasses" to far-sighted diners); yes, this "splendid splurge" "will rob you of every last euro", but "the experience is so wonderful, somehow one doesn't mind"; N.B. the Food score doesn't reflect the arrival of Eric Briffard (ex Les Elysées).

Cinq Mars ☒ *Bistro*

▽ 19	17	19	€44

7e | 51, rue de Verneuil (Rue du Bac/Solférino) | 01-45-44-69-13

"Chic BCBG locals in tweeds" make this "upbeat" spot "tucked away behind the Musée d'Orsay" their neighborhood canteen, for its retro-"relaxed" interior, "informal but thoughtful" staff and "simple, consistently well-prepared" bistro cuisine, including "great eat-per-your-discretion choices, in particular the chocolate mousse", served family-style.

Citrus Etoile ☒ *Classic/New French*

20	19	18	€80

8e | 6, rue Arsène Houssaye (Etoile) | 01-42-89-15-51 | www.citrusetoile.fr

"Owned by a talented chef" (who spent a decade at L'Orangerie Beverly Hills) and his Californian wife, this "contemporary" table near the Etoile offers "quality" New French cuisine (plus some classics) that's "imaginative" without ever being "fussy", in a "sober, modern", gray-and-orange setting with well-spaced tables; if the "relaxed service" has a slight LA vibe, diners just deem that the "perfect antidote to a hectic day"; N.B. closed weekends.

	FOOD	DECOR	SERVICE	COST

NEW Claude Colliot *Bistro/New French*   - | - | - | M

4e | 40, rue des Blancs Manteaux (Hôtel-de-Ville) | 01-42-71-55-45 |
www.claudecolliot.com

After being unsuccessfully cast as a hotel-restaurant chef near the
Porte Maillot, Claude Colliot, who first won his reputation for inventive contemporary French cooking when he opened Le Bamboche in
the 7th, is back with an art gallery–like space in the Marais; exposed
stone walls, suspension lamps, bare wood tables and leaf-green
chairs create a mellow mood, while friendly, well-drilled staffers offer helpful commentary as they serve Colliot's latest, often minimalist and deconstructed creations.

Cloche des Halles (La) Ⓢ *Wine Bar/Bistro*   - | - | - | M

1er | 28, rue Coquillière (Les Halles/Louvre-Rivoli) |
01-42-36-93-89

There's "a lot of history" in this "truly Parisian" wine bar named
for the bell that signaled the opening and closing of the now-
defunct Les Halles market; nostalgic clients can reminisce while
munching "excellent", "fairly priced" "light" fare, like cold meat and
cheese platters, washed down with "great Beaujolais"; the cozy ambiance is "especially warm and welcoming when the weather is
cold and damp."

Clos des Gourmets (Le) Ⓢ Ⓜ *New French*   25 | 20 | 21 | €51

7e | 16, av Rapp (Alma Marceau/Ecole Militaire) | 01-45-51-75-61 |
www.closdesgourmets.com

Converts "cannot recommend this place enough", as it offers a
chance to dine on "fine cuisine" "in the shade of the Eiffel Tower
for a fraction of the usual upscale prices"; the owner's "inspired"
New French cooking appears "wholly understated – and then
wow" – while the "warm", recently renovated (post-Survey) dining
room is particularly "pleasant", thanks to service so friendly it "ruins
Paris' arrogant reputation."

Closerie des Lilas (La) ⬤ *Classic French*   18 | 23 | 19 | €63

6e | 171, bd du Montparnasse (Port Royal/Vavin) | 01-40-51-34-50 |
www.closeriedeslilas.fr

This Montparnasse "mythical place" "has a great reputation to live
up to" and how well it succeeds depends on which part you patronize; "the brasserie is an experience" – "even though Hemingway is
long gone, the oysters and drinks are still fine", and in the "charming
bar" the piano-playing and people-watching are "divine"; but "the
restaurant is formal and stuffy" with merely "reliable" Classic
French cuisine that "can get very expensive"; "all in all, this historical
landmark is worth a visit", though.

Clos Morillons (Le) Ⓢ Ⓜ *New French*   - | - | - | M

15e | 50, rue des Morillons (Porte de Vanves) | 01-48-28-04-37

The chef-owner at this long standing table "in an offbeat location" in
the 15th runs a "competent kitchen", and locals say his New French
cuisine flavored with exotic spices makes it "a reliable and pleasant
place to eat", especially in the evening by candlelight.

	FOOD	DECOR	SERVICE	COST

Clou (Le) 🗷 *Bistro* ▽ 19 | 15 | 19 | €40

17ᵉ | 132, rue Cardinet (Malesherbes) | 01-42-27-36-78 |
www.restaurant-leclou.fr

"Helpful service" headed up by chef-owner Christian Leclou
(ex Ledoyen and Drouant) makes this Batignolles bistro a bastion
for locals, with "consistently excellent" Classic French dishes, a
"nice wine list" and daily market-fresh specials; the "low-key, comfortable setting" may be "nothing special", but the "good-value"
price for this "quality" certainly is.

Clovis (Le) 🗷 *New French* - | - | - | E

8ᵉ | Sofitel Arc de Triomphe | 14, rue Beaujon (Charles de Gaulle-Etoile) |
01-53-89-50-53 | www.sofitel.com

"A couple of steps from the Arc de Triomphe", this New French in the
Sofitel provides "refined", "inventive" dishes in a "calm", "agreeable" setting; if critics cavil "it should be better, given the price",
expense-account holders hail it as just right "for business lunches."

Clown Bar ●🗷Ⓜ⌐ *Wine Bar/Bistro* 17 | 17 | 17 | €38

11ᵉ | 114, rue Amelot (Filles du Calvaire) | 01-43-55-87-35 |
www.clown-bar.fr

Its "clown-laden setting" with "colorful" art nouveau Sarreguemines
tiles – a reference to the nearby Cirque d'Hiver – makes this wine bar
a "cute" corner to curl up in; "fortunately the food is more serious" –
"simple but delicious" bistro fare – but even so, it may not justify going "out of your way" unless you're jammed into a Volkswagen with
a red-nosed crowd; N.B. Wednesday–Saturday only.

Coco & Co. Ⓜ *Classic French* - | - | - | E

6ᵉ | 11, rue Bernard Palissy (St-Germain-des-Prés/Sèvres-Babylone) |
01-45-44-02-52

Tucked away in the heart of Saint-Germain, this farmhouse-gray bistro, decorated à la chicken coop, is literally egg-ceptional, with a
Classic French menu that features 'em 30 different ways – scrambled,
fried, coddled, poached; it's a popular light-lunch spot for Left Bank
shoppers and brunchers (offered all week long), though when the
check comes, you may wonder if those eggs in the dishes were golden.

Coco de Mer ●🗷 *Seychelles* - | - | - | M

5ᵉ | 34, bd St-Marcel (Les Gobelins/St-Marcel) | 01-47-07-06-64 |
www.cocodemer.fr

In the 5th, this "second embassy of the Seychelles" serves "very good
cuisine that allows you to travel with your feet in the sand" sprinkled
across the entrance; the prix fixe offers "excellent fish" at "reasonable
prices"; don't be surprised if "coming out, you'll feel like taking off
for Mahé, La Digue or another of the archipelago's islands."

Cocottes (Les) 🗷 *New French* ▽ 21 | 18 | 20 | €35

7ᵉ | 135, rue St-Dominique (Ecole Militaire/Les Invalides) |
01-45-50-10-31 | www.leviolondingres.com

Christian Constant is at his "simple, affordable best" in this "con-
ceptual restaurant" where the "delicious, healthy" New French

dishes are served in "individual casseroles" (made by Staub) at a "long, communal counter"; even if "service is friendly but slow", this "gastronomic fast-food" joint (the wine is "poured from cardboard boxes") is an "amusing" address "in the posh 7th."

Coffee Parisien ●🛇 *American*

16 | 13 | 13 | €28

6ᵉ | 4, rue Princesse (Mabillon) | 01-43-54-18-18
16ᵉ | 7, rue Gustave Courbet (Trocadéro/Victor Hugo) | 01-45-53-17-17
Neuilly-sur-Seine | 46, rue de Sablonville (Les Sablons) | 01-46-37-13-13

"Surprisingly filled with" "trendy Gallic teens", this trio of "crammed" Yankee-style coffee shops offers a "French take on diner food" ("real pancakes, eggs Benedict, club sandwiches, hamburgers, etc."); critics claim that though it's among "the best American fare" in town, it's still "not great", and abhor the "amateurish service"; but "excited expats" aver "if you've the patience to wait a long time" ("particularly on weekends"), you'll feel "just like back home."

Coin des Gourmets

22 | 14 | 19 | €35

(Au) *Cambodian/Vietnamese*

1ᵉʳ | 38, rue du Mont-Thabor (Concorde) | 01-42-60-79-79 🛇
5ᵉ | 5, rue Dante (Cluny La Sorbonne/Maubert-Mutualité) | 01-43-26-12-92

"When you need an Asian food fix" in Paris but don't feel like making the trip to far-flung *quartiers,* delve into this "delightful" duo that draws a crowd with "well-executed", "home-cooked" dishes from Cambodia and Vietnam that are "decent" value, particularly "at lunch"; some feel the branch in the 1st (formerly known as Indochine) boasts a "more agreeable" setting than the "indifferent"-looking Latin Quarter address, though a post-Survey redo of the latter might change that view.

Comédiens (Les) ●🛇 *Classic French*

- | - | - | M

9ᵉ | 7, rue Blanche (Trinité) | 01-40-82-95-95

Two steps from the Trinité church in the 9th, showbiz denizens and theatergoers congregate at this Classic French with exposed-brick walls, a zinc bar and posters galore; amid the boisterous ambiance, it's "fun to watch everything going on in the open kitchen"; the "superb" service is swift, and the specials on the chalkboard menu are "always different."

Comptoir (Le) ●🛇 *Eclectic/Moroccan*

21 | 18 | 19 | €53

1ᵉʳ | 37, rue Berger (Les Halles/Louvre-Rivoli) | 01-40-26-26-66 | www.comptoirparis.com

Inveterate travelers congregate in this "relaxed" table with neo-Moroccan decor in Les Halles, serving real and invented dishes from around the world, with an emphasis on North Africa ("very good tagine and mint tea"); roamers report the food's "not exceptional" but it is "original", plus it's a fine "option at lunch", with "ample platters" and a terrace where you can "sit outside and people-watch" the Parisians of the 1st.

☑ Comptoir du Relais (Le) *Bistro/Brasserie* `26` `14` `19` `€50`

6ᵉ | Hôtel Relais Saint-Germain | 9, carrefour de l'Odéon (Odéon) | 01-44-27-07-97

It's practically "impossible" "to get into this place" in the 6th – dinner reservations are "the element unobtainium" "unless you're staying at the hotel", while lunch means "standing in line" – but determined foodies overcome the odds for Yves Camdeborde's "brilliant twist on French bistro fare" with "super brasserie" offerings at noon and a "no-choices" evening prix fixe, both a "tremendous value"; admirers admit the space is "small and cramped" ("was that really a table for four or for one?") and the "efficient" staff is "prissy", but if they could, they'd "eat every meal there."

Comte de Gascogne (Au) 🖾 *Gascony* `-` `-` `-` `VE`

Boulogne-Billancourt | 89, av Jean-Baptiste Clément (Pont-de-St-Cloud) | 01-46-03-47-27 | www.aucomtedegascogne.com

Like a tropical greenhouse, with tree branches waving under a lofty ceiling, this formal restaurant with "magic decor" in the suburb of Boulogne offers "traditional but savory" Gascon cuisine, starring various types of foie gras; the "perfect service" starts with chef-owner Henri Charvet, who was born in Bourgogne, ran Marius et Janette in Paris and developed a passion for palm trees while at the restaurant Lafayette in Martinique.

Congrès Maillot (Le) ❶ *Brasserie* `▽` `18` `15` `14` `€54`

17ᵉ | 80, av de la Grande-Armée (Porte Maillot) | 01-45-74-17-24

Oyster lovers can slurp 'em down until 2 AM, seven days a week, at this "typical brasserie" near the Palais des Congrès, part of the Gérard Joulie chain; discordant elements complain the "tables are cramped, the service rushed" and the traditional fare "too expensive" for what it is, but all agree you can't go wrong when you order "a seafood platter paired with a Chablis"; N.B. they serve breakfast too.

Copenhague 🖾 *Danish* `18` `17` `16` `€75`

8ᵉ | 142, av des Champs-Elysées (Charles de Gaulle-Etoile/George V) | 01-44-13-86-26 | www.floradanica-paris.com

Everything's copasetic at this Copenhagen import where little has changed despite a takeover by the Frères Blanc chain; known as an "institution" for "good Nordic" cuisine (and a "nice view of the Champs-Elysées"), clients "are never disappointed by the freshness of the fish", saying the "quality of the food" justifies the "expensive" prices; alas, the "sober" Danish decor lacks "a bit of warmth", while the servers have become downright "cold."

Cordonnerie (La) 🖾 *Classic French* `-` `-` `-` `M`

1ᵉʳ | 20, rue St-Roch (Pyramides/Tuileries) | 01-42-60-17-42 | www.restaurantlacordonnerie.com

"What a charming place" enthuse patrons of this 17th-century "old house" just off the Rue Saint-Honoré, where the chef-owner, Hugo Wolfer, "inherited his talent and the restaurant from his classically trained father" (who opened it in 1964); he and wife Valérie provide a "delightful" experience – diners can "sit right in front of the kitchen" and watch him prepare the "savory" traditional French fare.

Cosi *Sandwiches*

19	9	13	€14

6ᵉ | 54, rue de Seine (Mabillon/Odéon) | 01-46-33-35-36

"You like sandwiches and music?" they merge in this eat-in or take-out "trendy" Saint-Germain shop, a "student hangout gone yuppie" with "delicious combinations of meats, cheese and veggies" on "fresh-from-the-oven breads" as well as "real salads"; a "cool staff and laid-back atmosphere, with Vivaldi playing, complete the experience."

Cosi (Le) 🅇 *Corsica*

16	15	12	€33

5ᵉ | 9, rue Cujas (Cluny La Sorbonne/Luxembourg) | 01-43-29-20-20 | www.le-cosi.com

This Latin Quarter purveyor of *stufatu* (macaroni casserole), *brocciu* (sheep's milk cheese) and other specialties of the Maquis has earned a reputation as "one of the best Corsican restaurants in Paris", with a chef who creates "original", "heartwarming" and inexpensive plates using "fresh products" from the island in a "cozy", "stylish" room with jazzy music and book-filled library shelves.

Costes ◗ *Eclectic*

18	25	15	€72

1ᵉʳ | Hôtel Costes | 239, rue St-Honoré (Concorde/Tuileries) | 01-42-44-50-25 | www.hotelcostes.com

Just being in this "über-hip" eatery in the Hôtel Costes "raises your cool factor by 10", as you join the "jet set", "old men with younger women" and "caricatures of beautiful people" who gather like moths to the flame in a "sexy", "dark brothellike setting" (in the summer, there's "no more glamorous place to have a casual dinner" than the courtyard); insiders report the "expensive" Eclectic food is "reasonably good" while the service is "woefully inefficient" ("failed models do not make as good a staff as failed actors") – but who cares? "the scene is the only thing that matters here."

Cotolettes (Les) 🅇 Ⓜ *Bistro*

–	–	–	M

4ᵉ | 4, impasse Guéménée (Bastille) | 01-42-72-08-45

In the heart of the Marais, the exposed-stone walls of a former 17th century convent give this friendly bistro the relaxingly rustic feel of a country auberge, and the menu follows suits with traditional Gallic favorites like brandade of yellow pollack and andouillette; a diverse neighborhood crowd of young fashion types and older academics appreciates the attentives service and moderate tabs.

Cottage Marcadet (Le) 🅇 Ⓜ *New French*

–	–	–	E

18ᵉ | 151 bis, rue Marcadet (Lamarck-Caulaincourt) | 01-42-57-71-22 | www.cottagemarcadet.com

Behind Montmartre, this most elegant cottage has streamlined Louis XVI decor with white tablecloths and silver candlestick holders on each table, a "pleasant" ambiance "perfect for intimate, romantic dining" and a young chef-owner whose "creative" New French food inspires "overwhelming enthusiasm" among his disciples; the "professional but relaxed" staff remains "attentive", "even if your French is not so great."

Cotte Roti (Le) 🗷Ⓜ *Bistro* — | — | — | M

12ᵉ | 1, rue de Cotte (Gare de Lyon/Ledru-Rollin) | 01-43-45-06-37
Just across from the lively Marché d'Aligre, chef Michel Nicholas, who's worked under Bernard Pacaud at L'Ambroisie, has turned this corner cafe into a popular contemporary French bistro with a moderately priced market-driven menu that runs to dishes like tuna tartare with ginger, braised lamb with potato purée and poached quince with a berry coulis; the red-and-gray decor doesn't amount to much, but service is warm and well drilled.

Coude Fou (Le) ❶ *Wine Bar/Bistro* 19 | 14 | 19 | €34

4ᵉ | 12, rue du Bourg-Tibourg (Hôtel-de-Ville) | 01-42-77-15-16 | www.lecoudefou.com
Oenophiles opine this is "the most pleasant wine bar in the neighborhood" behind the Hôtel de Ville; even if the small room offers "not much in terms of decor" (despite native frescoes and tile floors), it's a "good basic place for a nice bite" of "comforting" bistro dishes; "tables are tight, so if you tend to get hot, you won't have a good time", but the staff "is fine with Americans, of which there are multitudes."

Cou de la Girafe (Le) 🗷 *New French* 15 | 15 | 15 | €44

8ᵉ | 7, rue Paul Baudry (Franklin D. Roosevelt/St-Philippe-du-Roule) | 01-56-88-29-55 | www.lecoudelagirafe.com
A "business and shopping crowd" flees the jungle of the Champs at this "trendy" "escape" with an ambiance that's both "convivial" and "intimate", thanks to lounge music and "soft lighting" (not to mention "elbow-to-elbow seating"); the "warm-colored" decor is a good match for the "original, exotic" New French cuisine, and though service can seem "amateurish", prices are relatively "affordable for the area."

Couleurs de Vigne 🗷 *Wine Bar/Bistro* — | — | — | I

15ᵉ | 2, rue Marmontel (Convention/Vaugirard) | 01-45-33-32-96
This "sweet" "intimate *bar à vins* is worth seeking out" in a remote part of the 15th, with 300 types of "wines that are well chosen" and wrapped up in a "typically French ambiance"; a little while back a new owner installed a fresh menu of hearty fare (cassoulet, game in season, coq au vin), but kept one custom: your accompanying bottle can be taken home if you don't finish it at table.

Coupe-Chou (Le) ❶ *Classic French* 23 | 25 | 22 | €54

5ᵉ | 9-11, rue de Lanneau (Maubert-Mutualité) | 01-46-33-68-69 | www.lecoupechou.com
"Who can resist an open fireplace" sigh lovers of this "rustic" restaurant in a "cozy little alley in the heart of the Latin Quarter", where a "warren" of 17th-century rooms breathes "charm, history and romance" with numerous candles and hearths "ablaze"; unsurprisingly, this is "not the place to come if you're seeking culinary innovation", but classicists concur the ambiance and "excellent, tra-

ditional fare" make dining here a "very French experience" – even if it's "frequented by many tourists."

Coupe Gorge (Le) ◑ *Bistro*

-	-	-	M

4e | 2, rue de la Coutellerie (Hôtel-de-Ville) | 01-48-04-79-24 | www.coupegorge.com

"Good" traditional bistro cuisine that's pleasingly "underpriced" makes it easy to overlook the "mediocre setting" of this century-old standard behind Hôtel de Ville, though the red-banquette-and-wooden-table decor does evolve every couple of months with different art exhibits on the walls.

☑ Coupole (La) ◑ *Brasserie*

19	23	18	€55

14e | 102, bd du Montparnasse (Vavin) | 01-43-20-14-20 | www.flobrasseries.com/coupoleparis

"The mother of all brasseries" in Montparnasse is an "enduring charmer" with a "huge", "gorgeously appointed art deco" interior and "tremendous ambiance" provided by a "boisterous" crowd and "bustling, efficient waiters with lots of personality"; perhaps this Groupe Flo member is "not quite what it once was" – certainly "the food doesn't live up to the magic of the place", unless you "stick to the seafood platter" – but go anyway, cuz "you haven't been to Paris until you've been here."

Crémerie (La) 🗷Ⓜ *Wine Bar/Bistro*

-	-	-	M

6e | 9, rue des Quatre-Vents (Odéon) | 01-43-54-99-30 | www.lacremerie.fr

A wine-loving architect has taken over this pocket-size wine bar/shop in the 6th, keeping the decorative ceiling and marble counter of the original 1880 dairy; fine palates find it a "place to stop your watch and snack on cold cuts" with prestigious provenances, from a rare Italian Burrata cheese to Spanish Bellota ham, plus "good" natural vintages by the glass.

Crêperie de Josselin (La) ◑Ⓜ⇅ *Brittany*

22	14	18	€19

14e | 67, rue du Montparnasse (Edgar Quinet/Montparnasse-Bienvenüe) | 01-43-20-93-50

On a "street filled with 'em in Montparnasse", what's "maybe the most famous crêperie in Paris" wins praise for a pancake filled with "both novel combinations and traditional flavors" that's "so enormous the plate's incapable of containing it"; given the "snug" surrounds, "you'll get to know your neighbors even if you don't want to", but rest assured, this Breton's "crêpes are worth the crowding" (and "service is fast" too).

Cristal de Sel 🗷Ⓜ *New French*

-	-	-	E

15e | 13, rue Mademoiselle (Commerce/Félix Faure) | 01-42-50-35-29 | www.lecristaldesel.fr

It's becoming increasingly difficult to snag a reservation at this table near the Place du Commerce, where a "great team" is headed up by chef and co-owner Karil Lopez, who spent five years at Eric Frechon's side at the Bristol; unmissable with his tall white toque in a semi-open kitchen, he turns out sophisticated New French cuisine that contrasts with the chalkboard menus and the gray-and-white interior.

☑ Cristal Room ⌧ *New French*

| 17 | 28 | 18 | €91 |

16ᵉ | Baccarat | 11, pl des Etats-Unis (Boissière/Iéna) | 01-40-22-11-10 | www.baccarat.fr

"In the former palace of the Countess of Noailles" in the 16th (now Baccarat's HQ), the dining room has been turned into a restaurant composed of an "enchanting" "splendid combination" of exposed brick, wood paneling and chandeliers, reflecting Philippe Starck's design and some of the world's finest crystal; but while this glass house is "quite special", critics throw stones at the "sometimes haughty service" and a "greedy" policy of "tiny portions and huge tabs" for merely "correct" New French food – though that sentiment, along with the score, doesn't reflect the arrival of a chef trained by Guy Martin (Le Grand Véfour) to the kitchen.

Crudus ⌧ *Italian/Wine Bar*

| – | – | – | M |

1ᵉʳ | 21, rue St-Roch (Pyramides/Tuileries) | 01-42-60-90-29

Featuring over 70 different wines and a daily changing menu prepared almost entirely with organic produce, this Italian *bistrot à vins* is popular with fashion execs, bankers and pasta-loving vinophiles – not to mention worldly types in the 1st who prefer staying close to home for dinner, attracted by the reasonable prices and warm atmosphere; N.B. closed weekends.

NEW Cru Rollin (Le) ⌧ Ⓜ *Wine Bar/Bistro*

| – | – | – | M |

11ᵉ | 156, av Ledru-Rollin (Ledru-Rollin/Voltaire) | 01-43-72-73-20 | www.lecrurollin.fr

With brown leatherette–upholstered banquettes, a big wooden service bar and white walls decorated with flea-market finds, this *bistrot à vins* in the 11th pulls a crowd of local bobos with its chalkboard menu of generously served contemporary French dishes like a tart of carmelized onions and *tête de veau* with a sauce gribiche; prices are easygoing, and service is relaxed and friendly.

Crus de Bourgogne (Aux) ⌧ *Bistro*

| ▽ 17 | 16 | 15 | €41 |

2ᵉ | 3, rue Bachaumont (Les Halles/Sentier) | 01-42-33-48-24

There's "not a trendy item on the old-fashioned menu" of this "charming" century-old bistro on an "unexpected side street of *le quartier Montorgueil*"; detractors mutter the food and service "never fail to disappoint", but it remains a "great place to take out-of-towners for that Frenchy feel."

Cuisine (La) *New French*

| ▽ 25 | 21 | 27 | €65 |

7ᵉ | 14, bd de la Tour-Maubourg (Invalides/La Tour-Maubourg) | 01-44-18-36-32

A "perfect gem" proclaim pleased patrons of this posh address near Les Invalides, whose "chic", "*haute-bourgeois* atmosphere" – including a contemporary art deco–style interior, porcelain dishes and well-spaced tables – makes it all the more surprising to find such "solicitous service" ("I'd go back just for the lack of attitude") and prices that range from "low to escalating"; compliments also abound for the New French cooking – "a little slice of culinary magic"; P.S. "they are open on Sunday."

Cuizine (La) 🗷 Ⓜ *Bistro*

	FOOD	DECOR	SERVICE	COST
	-	-	-	M

11e | 73, rue Amelot (Chemin-Vert) | 01-43-14-27-00 | www.lacuizine.fr

Occupying the long, skinny space once inhabited by Les Jumeaux, this kitchen on a quiet street in the 11th is attracting the attention of trendy young locals, thanks to a chef-owner from Chez Paul, colorful modern decor with baroque touches and contemporary bistro fare (rabbit pâté, Creole baba au rhum) on an ever-changing menu.

Cul de Poule 🗷 *Bistro*

	-	-	-	M

9e | 53, rue des Martyrs (Pigalle) | 01-53-16-13-07

Located in the heart of trendy Bobo-land (the 9th), the latest table from restaurateur Yannig Samot (Chéri Bibi, La Famille) has the same signature flea-market furniture as his other bistros, but the Basque-influenced menu is a perfect short-list of the comfort foods the chic thirtysomething craves – squash soup, squid with pistou sauce, roast Bresse chicken and *faisselle* (fresh white cheese) with red fruits coulis or honey are typical; easygoing prices and a see-and-be-seen scene mean reservations are always necessary.

Curieux Spaghetti Bar (Le) ◐ *Italian*

	-	-	-	M

4e | 14, rue St-Merri (Hôtel-de-Ville/Rambuteau) | 01-42-72-75-97 | www.curieuxspag.com

"Even spaghetti can be fun" discover diners at this "funky and eclectic", "one-of-a-kind" noodle bar behind the Beaubourg that combines "really good pasta" (served with a bib) and disco atmosphere ("don't expect to have too much conversation, as the music is very loud"); nobody comes here in search of *haute gastronomie,* but rather for the "incredible ambiance", right down to the colorful psychedelic decor, long counter, chandeliers and periodically changing wallpaper.

Dali (Le) *Classic French*

	-	-	-	E

1er | Hôtel Meurice | 228, rue de Rivoli (Concorde/Tuileries) | 01-44-58-10-44 | www.lemeurice.com

Following Philippe Starck's slick redesign of the Meurice's public spaces, the old winter-garden room has morphed into an Egyptian-inspired palace, complete with a huge painted canvas-tent ceiling and silver winged armchairs; named for one of the hotel's famed guests (and with his surreal details in the furnishings), it showcases house toque Yannick Alléno in a more casual, Classic French mode at – slightly – more relaxed prices than in the main dining room.

Dalloyau *Dessert/Tearoom*

	23	18	18	€32

4e | 5, bd Beaumarchais (Bastille) | 01-48-87-89-88
6e | 2, pl Edmond Rostand (Cluny La Sorbonne/Odéon) | 01-43-29-31-10
8e | 101, rue du Faubourg St-Honoré (Miromesnil/St-Philippe-du-Roule) | 01-42-99-90-00
15e | 69, rue de la Convention (Boucicaut) | 01-45-77-84-27

(continued)

Dalloyau

Boulogne-Billancourt | 67, av J.B. Clément (Boulogne-Jean Jaurès) | 01-46-05-06-78
www.dalloyau.fr

"Magnificent éclairs, stupendous tarts and fabulous macaroons" are among the "sweet-tooth satisfiers" offered at these "calm", "high-class" *salons de thé* "all over Paris" – you could "have breakfast at the one on Faubourg Saint-Honoré, then afternoon tea on the terrace across from the Luxembourg Gardens" and finally "before the Opéra Bastille", a light dinner on "something savory to justify a few desserts"; they're also "wonderful" for takeout – in fact, even "flight attendants get their picnics for the plane, and eat better than anyone!"

Dalva ⌧ *New French*

| – | – | – | M |

2ᵉ | 48, rue d'Argout (Louvre-Rivoli/Sentier) | 01-42-36-02-11 | www.dalvarestaurant.fr

There's "stellar karma" in this lovely little New French with a mod but homey interior and a sidewalk terrace on what's perhaps the "hippest street in Paris"; ingredients for the "fresh, inventive fare" come from the nearby Montorgueil market and are whipped into shape by a chef who earned his chops at L'Arpège and Taillevent, while the entire affordable menu is overseen by Bruno Schaeffer, chef-owner of the late L'Argenteuil.

Dame Tartine *Sandwiches*

| 14 | 15 | 13 | €27 |

4ᵉ | 2, rue Brisemiche (Hôtel-de-Ville) | 01-42-77-32-22

"Right next to the Stravinsky Fountain near the Beaubourg", this "unpretentious" *sandwicherie* stands out for tasty *tartines* that, if "not revolutionary", are "always respectable" and quite "affordable"; being able to "eat outdoors makes for good decor."

Da Mimmo ●⌧Ⓜ *Italian*

| – | – | – | M |

10ᵉ | 39, bd de Magenta (Gare de l'Est/Jacques Bonsergent) | 01-42-06-44-47 | www.damimmo.fr

Da pizza enjoys a reputation as "the best" in town at this Neapolitan-style trattoria, a "hangout for the young who's who" of Paris; while fans willingly part with their dough for the "expensive" pies, others feel you can get "better food served by nicer people" elsewhere – though a renovation has at least altered the "Scorcese movie"-looking interior.

Da Rosa *Classic French*

| ▽ 19 | 15 | 15 | €33 |

6ᵉ | 62, rue de Seine (Mabillon/Odéon) | 01-40-51-00-09 | www.darosa.fr

"Perfect for watching the shoppers" in Saint-Germain, "this small restaurant" in a "gourmet grocery store" serves up "delicious" Classic French light bites made with "Spanish Bellota ham, cheeses" and other nonpareil products – plus some "wines of the same caliber" – that owner José Da Rosa seeks out and supplies to many chefs around town; some sniff there's "no real cuisine" here, but since they serve continuously from 11 AM to 11 PM, it's "good when everything else is closed."

	FOOD	DECOR	SERVICE	COST

Daru ☒ *Russian* — — — M

8ᵉ | 19, rue Daru (Courcelles/Ternes) | 01-42-27-23-60 | www.daru.fr
"Real Russians who attend the Orthodox church down the block" faithfully frequent this "idiosyncratic" but "charming" 8th-arrondissement institution created in 1918 by an officer of the Czar; supporters swear it has "some of the best" Soviet fare – from smoked salmon to beef stroganoff – and the service is "simple but warm", while prices exhibit a policy of "containment" that's rare; P.S. the "iced vodka in all varieties is a must."

Davé *Chinese/Vietnamese* — 18 | 14 | 19 | €54

1ᵉʳ | 12, rue de Richelieu (Palais Royal-Musée du Louvre) | 01-42-61-49-48
"An institution for fashion-world [types] when they're in Paris" ("Marc Jacobs has parties here"), this "cool", compact Chinese-Vietnamese in the 1st "boasts images of the celebrities who've dined" and been doted on by the namesake owner, who is something of "a legend" himself; lesser mortals call the place "overrated, over-priced, just plain over" – but they're overridden by devotees who declare "eccentric service is what makes this place charming."

D'Chez Eux ☒ *Bistro/Southwest* — 25 | 19 | 25 | €68

7ᵉ | 2, av Lowendal (Ecole Militaire) | 01-47-05-52-55 | www.chezeux.com
"Come hungry" to this "old-school neighborhood bistro" "two steps from Les Invalides", where "sturdy", "stunning" Southwestern "comfort" food is served in "copious" portions ("huge baskets of charcuterie", an "all-you-can-eat dessert trolley") "perfect for American appetites"; the "convivial" setting owes much to "happy" waiters making clients feel as "relaxed" as if they "were in the owner's home" or, as the French say, *chez eux*.

Délices d'Aphrodite (Les) *Greek* — ▽ 18 | 15 | 17 | €38

5ᵉ | 4, rue Candolle (Censier-Daubenton) | 01-43-31-40-39 | www.mavrommatis.fr
A "simpler, no-fuss version of its big brother, Mavrommatis", also in the 5th, this Grecian goddess attracts a good many followers, so "the staff sometimes is overwhelmed" – especially on summer evenings when the "agreeable" sidewalk seats fill up quickly.

Dell Orto ❶ ☒ Ⓜ *Italian* — — — E

9ᵉ | 45, rue St-Georges (St-Georges) | 01-48-78-40-30
Its name is Italian for 'from the garden', but there's nothing garden-variety about this 9th-arrondissement address that *amici* applaud as "one of the city's tops" for "a multitude of inventive fresh pasta" and other Tuscan dishes; "a warm neighborhood welcome" comes from the owner, a French filmmaker.

NEW Derrière ❶ *New French* — — — M

3ᵉ | 69, rue des Gravilliers (Arts et Métiers) | 01-44-61-91-95
Tucked away in a courtyard behind their two other very successful restaurants (Andy Wahloo and Le 404), Momo and Kaim Mazouz's

latest arrival is this duplex with a funky loft feel – think Ping-Pong tables, armchairs, couches, mismatched tables and chairs – that enchants the hip twenty- and thirtysomethings who've made it a see-and-be-seen scene; the eclectic contemporary French menu runs to grilled veggies with pesto sauce and roast chicken with potato purée.

Des Gars dans la Cuisine Ⓜ Bistro

–	–	–	M

3ᵉ | 72, rue Vieille du Temple (Hôtel-de-Ville) | 01-42-74-88-26 | www.desgarsdanslacuisine.com

A cross-section of locals and bar-crawlers – typical Marais mavens – mixes it up in the cozy dining room of this hip canteen; the moderately priced menu runs from burgers to bistro classics, but specializes in seafood, such as squid flambéed in pastis; all's brought to table by laid-back servers.

Dessirier ⬤ Seafood

20	16	19	€75

17ᵉ | 9, pl du Maréchal Juin (Péreire) | 01-42-27-82-14 | www.michelrostang.com

Near the Place Péreire, this "well-mannered" Michel Rostang–run "grand fish specialist" serves "delicious seafood", which makes it a bull's-eye for business dining – though even the executive clientele goes ballistic over the "breathtaking prices"; malcontents are mollified, however, by the "pleasant service" and an "excellent wine list."

Deux Abeilles (Les) Ⓩ Dessert/Tearoom

▽ 21	17	16	€41

7ᵉ | 189, rue de l'Université (Alma Marceau) | 01-45-55-64-04

"Ladies who lunch" buzz into this "cozy" spot run by a "welcoming mother and daughter" behind the Musée Branly with a "quiet", "English tearoom" ambiance that's particularly inviting "on a rainy day", plus "delicious" salads and "homemade pastries" including a "lemon meringue pie to die for"; when the weather's fine, "bring grand-mère" for a view of the Eiffel Tower from sidewalk tables.

Deux Canards (Aux) Ⓩ Classic French

18	17	17	€46

10ᵉ | 8, rue du Faubourg Poissonnière (Bonne Nouvelle) | 01-47-70-03-23 | www.lesdeuxcanards.com

Fans say you'd have to be a quack not to love this offbeat Classic French in the 10th, where "chatty" owner Gérard Faesch "makes you feel like part of his family"; "his narration of the chalkboard menu is priceless" too, and "obviously the duck is a must"; some find the decor, adorned with "jars of oranges in various states of fermentation", "a little overwrought" but most say it's "warm" and "rustic."

2 Pieces Cuisine Ⓩ Bistro

–	–	–	M

18ᵉ | 65, rue du Ruisseau (Jules Joffrin) | 01-42-23-31-23 | www.2pieces-cuisine.com

It's a "nice neighborhood place – no more, no less" declare the few that have found this casual bistro tucked away in a gentrifying corner of Montmartre; within its warm-toned premises, it feeds the starving artists of today with a good-value Classic French dinner prix fixe that changes every two months.

	FOOD	DECOR	SERVICE	COST

Devèz (Le) ● _Steak_   ▽ 16 | 10 | 12 | €47

8ᵉ | 5, pl de l'Alma (Alma Marceau) | 01-53-67-97-53 |
www.devezparis.com

"Before going to see a show", beef eaters come to sink their teeth
into "superb steaks", meaty tapas or a "delicious mac'Aubrac"
burger – all made from one of the finest races of French cattle, and
washed down with a full-bodied red from "a serious wine list"; the
ambiance is cozy in the winter, while in summer clients stake out a
place on the "large outdoor terrace on Place de l'Alma."

Diamantaires (Les) _Armenian/Greek_   - | - | - | M

9ᵉ | 60, rue La Fayette (Cadet/Le Peletier) | 01-47-70-78-14 |
www.lesdiamantaires.com

Founded in 1929 and aptly located in the 9th, the neighborhood long
known as New Athens, this "old Greco-Armenian address" still
serves the same standards: meze, souvlaki, kebabs and grilled lamb,
while live musicians give wannabe Zorbas the chance to dance the
sirtaki Thursday–Sunday nights.

Diapason (Le) 🗷 _Southwest_   - | - | - | E

18ᵉ | Terrass Hôtel | 12-14, rue Joseph de Maistre (Abbesses/
Place de Clichy) | 01-44-92-34-00 | www.terrass-hotel.com

It's all about eating alfresco at this Montmartre hotel venue that
boasts "one of the best views in Paris" from its seventh-floor terrace
(open May through September); it actually serves Southwestern
fare year-round, in a neutral-toned Asian interior, but most feel the
"food and service seem automatically better" "on summer evenings,
when there is no more romantic" place in town.

Diep ●🗷 _Asian_   21 | 17 | 18 | €59

8ᵉ | 55, rue Pierre Charron (George V) | 01-45-63-52-76 |
www.diep.fr

"Good but expensive" – the latter "due to the location" in a pricey
part of the 8th arrondissement – is the majority read on this "jet-
setty" Asian; "it's not a place to recommend for a romantic dinner",
given the galloping service of "waiters who are in a hurry for you to
leave, bringing the check before you ask" and the "ok, not extraordinary" Oriental decor; on the other hand, the victuals are
"among the best Chinese-Thai-Vietnamese in Paris" and – for those
who care about such things – it's "an indispensable [site] for seeing
and being seen."

Divellec (Le) 🗷 _Seafood_   24 | 20 | 21 | €132

7ᵉ | 107, rue de l'Université (Invalides) | 01-45-51-91-96 |
www.le-divellec.com

"Conservative but sound" sums up this "traditional French seafooder" on the Esplanade des Invalides that nets "local bigwigs"
with "excellent" fish (including the "legendary pressed lobster") and
"attentive but unintrusive service"; while the decor's now "handsome", some still sniff over the "stiff atmosphere" – folks "speaking
softly as if in church" – and the "sky-high prices" are "not for everyday"; "but from time to time, it's worth it" to splurge.

	FOOD	DECOR	SERVICE	COST

☑ 1728 ☒ *New French* — 19 | 27 | 17 | €73

8ᵉ | 8, rue d'Anjou (Concorde/Madeleine) | 01-40-17-04-77 |
www.restaurant-1728.com

Boasting "gorgeous", "regal" decor, paintings (for sale) on the walls and "private salons for intimate dinners", "the setting alone is worth the trip" to this 18th-century manse just off the Faubourg Saint-Honoré, Lafayette's final home; while it "doesn't live up to" the surrounds, the New French fare with a soupçon of "Sino sophistication" is "unusual" and at times "delightful"; and if that's not your cup of tea, it's also open afternoons for a "perfect" pot of chamomile and "great pastries" by dessert deity Pierre Hermé.

Dix Vins (Le) ☒ *Wine Bar/Bistro* — - | - | - | M

15ᵉ | 57, rue Falguière (Pasteur) | 01-43-20-91-77

This "nice neighborhood place" in the 15th has gained a following with fresh, inexpensive bistro food, including game in season, and an ever-changing *carte des vins*; the small, informal space with oil lamps on the tables works equally well "for a tête-à-tête or a group."

Djakarta Bali *Indonesian* — 20 | 18 | 18 | €41

1ᵉʳ | 9, rue Vauvilliers (Châtelet-Les Halles/Louvre-Rivoli) |
01-45-08-83-11 | www.djakarta-bali.com

A "serene ambiance" reigns at this Indonesian table next to Les Halles run by a brother/sister team, offering "refined", "authentic" cooking filled with "exotic flavors" from the archipelago; "stress-free" service and traditional decor almost make patrons "believe they are over there" – especially on Friday nights, when dancers from Bali take to the floor.

Domaine de Lintillac ☒ *Southwest* — ▽ 18 | 13 | 18 | €28

2ᵉ | 10, rue St-Augustin (Quatre-Septembre) | 01-40-20-96-27 |
www.lintillac-paris.com
7ᵉ | 20, rue Rousselet (Duroc) | 01-45-66-88-23 |
www.restaurantdomainedelintillac.com Ⓜ
9ᵉ | 54, rue Blanche (Blanche/Trinité) | 01-48-74-84-36 |
www.lintillac-paris.com ●

"Lovers of duck in all its varieties" migrate to this trio of tables where the "tasty Southwestern" cuisine is "cheap and plentiful", from the foie gras to the "must-have" confit de canard that come straight from the Périgord "producer to the consumer"; it's rustic, "casual" and "fast", so it's easy to fill up "and waddle home."

Dôme (Le) ● *Seafood* — 22 | 23 | 21 | €70

14ᵉ | 108, bd du Montparnasse (Vavin) | 01-43-35-25-81

This "lovely, luxurious" seafooder with "a rich literary" heritage has a "traditional atmosphere with overstuffed booths and large floral arrangements filling nooks and crannies"; "you can spend an afternoon just sampling the oyster selection" and "the best bouillabaisse" ("we so obviously enjoyed it, they offered us seconds"); "service is precise", if "in a hurry", and while the "expensive" prices make some mourn its bohemian brasserie past, for most it's "worth a visit to Montparnasse."

	FOOD	DECOR	SERVICE	COST

Dôme du Marais (Le) 🗷Ⓜ *New French*   22 | 22 | 20 | €47

4ᵉ | 53 bis, rue des Francs-Bourgeois (Hôtel-de-Ville/Rambuteau) |
01-42-74-54-17

True to its name, this "spacious" place in the Marais boasts courtyard dining under "a magnificent dome" in a "beautifully restored
space that was once Paris' official pawn shop"; but while this
"unique" address is "historical", the "tasty, imaginative" cuisine is
New French, with a "good-value" quotient that extends to the kiddie
menu, priced according to each child's age.

❷ Dominique Bouchet 🗷 *Haute Cuisine*   27 | 21 | 24 | €86

8ᵉ | 11, rue Treilhard (Miromesnil) | 01-45-61-09-46 |
www.dominique-bouchet.com

Although it's "hidden" in the upper 8th arrondissement, those who
find this Haute Cuisine haven declare it "delivers 100% on the promise of greatness reflected in Bouchet's résumé", which includes Les
Ambassadeurs; a "joy of a man", the chef-owner makes "creative
preparations" of French classics while steering clear of trendy
"foams and froths"; converts also compliment the "modern but
warm interior" and "polite, attentive service from English-speaking
waiters"; so, travelers, take note: "this is the food that you went
to Paris for."

Drouant ● *Classic French*   22 | 21 | 20 | €82

2ᵉ | 16-18, pl Gaillon (Opéra/Quatre-Septembre) | 01-42-65-15-16 |
www.drouant.com

The "revelation of the year" roar reviewers about chef-owner
Antoine Westermann's "superb reinvention" of this "historical" table near the Opéra Garnier; architect Pascal Desprez's "magnificent" update of the original decor is the backdrop for "stunning"
"small bites" of Classic French cuisine (starters, sides and "desserts
come in groups of four") that "allow elegant tastings of a variety of
dishes without culinary overload"; only a heretical handful hiss that
the results are "disappointing", given the "high prices."

Duc (Le) 🗷Ⓜ *Seafood*   23 | 15 | 20 | €81

14ᵉ | 243, bd Raspail (Raspail) | 01-43-20-96-30

Ah, but life is good when you're seated in front of "a buttery sole
meunière served in a room resembling a ship of the French line" –
which is the situation at this "sedate" but "sublime" seafooder in
Montparnasse; after more than 40 years, perhaps the "tired" hull
needs overhauling, but "watching waiters fillet the fish is great
fun", so plenty are pleased to put into port at "one of the top" *poisson*
palaces in Paris.

Duc de Richelieu (Le) ●🗷 *Lyon*   - | - | - | M

12ᵉ | 5, rue Parrot (Gare de Lyon) | 01-43-43-05-64

"Cooking from the heart" is what draws people to this Lyonnais-
like bistro near, naturally, the Gare de Lyon; "even if the decor is
unremarkable", this place pleases with "chatty, ultraefficient"
service and "fabulous wine choices" to back up the "terrific value"
of a menu.

	FOOD	DECOR	SERVICE	COST

Durand Dupont Drugstore ◑ *Eclectic* | - | - | - | M |
Neuilly-sur-Seine | 14, pl du Marché (Les Sablons) | 01-41-92-93-00 | www.duranddupont.com

It may be "trendy, but don't expect more" of this Eclectic brasserie frequently "frequented by families in Neuilly" (especially for brunch on the "agreeable terrace"); the "disappointingly inconsistent menu and service make every visit hit-or-miss", and given that risk-reward ratio, it's "too expensive."

Ebauchoir (L') ⌷ *Bistro* | - | - | - | M |
12ᵉ | 43-45, rue de Citeaux (Faidherbe-Chaligny) | 01-43-42-49-31 | www.lebauchoir.com

With its "old-style" decor in red and yellow (it's even been "used as a movie set"), this "typical neighborhood place" quickly fills up with a young, cool crowd from the funky area between Bastille and Nation; the inventive bistro cooking "never disappoints" ("the rice pudding alone is worth the trip"), and it's "good value for the price" - especially the "wine *au compteur*", where you only pay for what you drink.

Ebouillanté (L') *Classic French/Tearoom* | - | - | - | I |
4ᵉ | 6, rue des Barres (St-Paul) | 01-42-71-09-69 | www.restaurant-ebouillante.com

On a quiet, cobblestone pedestrian lane in the 4th, this small *salon de thé* enjoys an exceptional location for its light meals such as stuffed pastry *briques* (Tunisian crêpes) and salads; the terrace is irresistible when the weather's fine - if only you can find a free table.

Ecaille de la Fontaine (L') ⌷ *Shellfish* | - | - | - | M |
2ᵉ | 15, rue Gaillon (Opéra) | 01-47-42-02-99 | www.la-fontaine-gaillon.com

Don't be surprised if you bump into Gérard Depardieu here, since he owns this "intimate seafooder that shares a kitchen with a more expensive place across the street" (La Fontaine Gaillon); located in a "lovely neighborhood" near the Opéra Garnier, it's a "great pick before a show" with a choice selection of French shellfish, plus "nice outdoor seating" in the summer - and if you don't see the celebrity patron, you can always admire the photos of his life that line the walls; N.B. closed on weekends.

Ecailler du Bistrot (L') ⌷Ⓜ *Seafood* | ▽ 19 | 15 | 19 | €49 |
11ᵉ | 20-22, rue Paul Bert (Faidherbe-Chaligny) | 01-43-72-76-77
Birthed by the "mother house next door", the Bistrot Paul Bert, this spawn specializes in "seafood, seafood, seafood" that utilizes the "freshest" shellfish around, including "little guys you've never seen before"; though "sometimes the oyster opener is a little clumsy", it's "worth the trip" to the 11th because it's a terrific catch "for the buck."

Eclaireur (L') ⌷ *New French* | - | - | - | VE |
8ᵉ | 10, rue Boissy d'Anglas (Concorde) | 01-53-43-09-99 | www.leclaireur.com

An avant-garde, eternally chic chain of boutiques branches out into food with a fashionable lounge/eatery attached to the address in the

8th; the decor, conceived with Barnaba Fornasetti (son of Piero, whose 1950s dishes are sold in the store), is a fabulous mix of his father's baroque and surrealism, the bar concocts creative cocktails and the chef prepares New French food served by an unexpectedly friendly staff against a soundscape of cool tunes.

Ecluse (L') ● *Wine Bar/Bistro*   16 | 13 | 18 | €35

1er | 34, pl du Marché St-Honoré (Pyramides/Tuileries) | 01-42-96-10-18
6e | 15, quai des Grands-Augustins (St-Michel) | 01-46-33-58-74
8e | 15, pl de la Madeleine (Madeleine) | 01-42-65-34-69
8e | 64, rue François 1er (George V) | 01-47-20-77-09
17e | 1, rue d'Armaillé (Charles de Gaulle-Etoile) | 01-47-63-88-29
www.leclusebaravin.com

"A chain but a good one" oenophiles opine about these rustic wine bars around town, offering an especially "great selection of Bordeaux by the glass"; clearly the Classic French "food is secondary", "but you do have to eat something with the wine", and since "the staff knows" its stuff, a "reasonably priced", "pleasant experience is guaranteed."

Ecume Saint-Honoré (L') 🄯🄼 *Shellfish*   – | – | – | M

1er | 6, rue du Marché St-Honoré (Pyramides/Tuileries) | 01-42-61-93-87
Steps from the Marché Saint-Honoré, this popular oyster bar shucks briny bivalves from Brittany and Normandy for the professional types who fill its bare wooden tables and grin at the tongue-in-cheek soundtrack of seagull cries; service is brisk, and they pour a good variety of white wines by the glass.

Editeurs (Les) ● *Brasserie*   14 | 20 | 15 | €38

6e | 4, carrefour de l'Odéon (Odéon) | 01-43-26-67-76 | www.lesediteurs.fr
Rapidly becoming the "cornerstone of the square" around the Odéon, this "sophisticated rendezvous" is renowned for its "congenial" "library decor", with "comfortable chairs and shelves filled with books you can take down and actually read"; it's the "great setting that makes it a busy place all day – you don't come here for the food" ("solid but overpriced" brasserie eats) or the somewhat "slow service"; indeed, the bookish believe it's "best just for drinks and snacks."

El Mansour 🄯 *Moroccan*   17 | 17 | 17 | €52

8e | 7, rue de la Trémoille (Alma Marceau) | 01-47-23-88-18 | www.elmansour.fr

"Morocco is close enough to touch" at this "refined" table in the 8th; the menu is "an invitation to travel" with "slightly industrial" but "good couscous and tagine", and the exotic decor "fits perfectly with the meal"; "though not friendly at first, the service warms up as the night progresses."

El Palenque 🄯🄼🀿 *Argentinean*   19 | 10 | 12 | €34

5e | 5, rue de la Montagne Ste-Geneviève (Maubert-Mutualité) | 01-43-54-08-99

"Heaven for homesick Argentines", this pint-sized patch of the pampas in the Latin Quarter is a *"bueno, bueno"* address for "delicious meat", along with "typical dishes, including dulce de leche and wonderful wines"; "a student-y atmosphere" and "friendly service from the Latin American waiters" ensure it's "excellent value for the money."

Elysées (Les) *Haute Cuisine*

| 23 | 24 | 25 | €126 |

8ᵉ | Hôtel Vernet | 25, rue Vernet (Charles de Gaulle-Etoile/George V) | 01-44-31-98-98 | www.hotelvernet.com

This perpetual sleeper in the Hôtel Vernet holds a place on many foodies' lists for its "delightful" Haute Cuisine – although its toque, the "great Eric Briffard", has moved to Le Cinq post-Survey (Gérald Barthélémy is his successor); however, the "magnificent room" still features a "beautiful stained-glass ceiling" and a "not-snobby", "unusually friendly atmosphere"; what's more, it's "not as expensive as many other grand palaces (and the chef is actually in the kitchen!)."

Elysées Hong Kong *Chinese*

| - | - | - | M |

16ᵉ | 80, rue Michel-Ange (Exelmans) | 01-46-51-60-99

Chinese food is not the City of Light's specialty, yet for 40 years this space in the silk-stocking 16th has pulled in a soigné crowd of regulars, including French showbiz types, with "consistently excellent" classics; maybe the food is "Westernized", but most find it suits them to a tea, especially since prices are moderate.

Emporio Armani Caffé ☒ *Italian*

| 19 | 19 | 16 | €57 |

6ᵉ | 149, bd St-Germain (St-Germain-des-Prés) | 01-45-48-62-15 | www.emporiocaffe.fr

"As you would expect", "a fab fashion attitude – dramatic decor, beautiful people galore and a staff straight off a catwalk" – dominates this "sooo chic" cafe "on the second floor of the Emporio Armani"; but "surprisingly, there's actually decent food to go with the design", a "light" but "true taste of Northern Italy"; yes, those pretty servers can be "haughty", and many moan the "model-sized portions for exorbitant prices" appeal to "Armani, not the appetite"; most, though, are "impressed."

NEW Enfants Terribles (Les) ☒ *Classic French*

| - | - | - | E |

8ᵉ | 3-5, rue Balzac (George V) | 01-53-89-90-91 | www.enfantsterribles-paris.com

Known for the keen decorating talent that's made her Les Fermes de Marie hotel in Megève a regular subject in French shelter magazines, Jocelyne Sibuet has created this stylish urban auberge just off the Champs-Elysées with a relaxing aura of Alpine freshness, modern art, parquet floors and comfy velvet club chairs; it offers traditional French comfort food (marinated leeks, sole meunière, roast chicken), with many dishes served in half-portions in deference to the fashionable, calorie-conscious clientele.

Enoteca (L') ❂ *Italian/Wine Bar*

| 20 | 16 | 17 | €44 |

4ᵉ | 25, rue Charles V (St-Paul/Sully Morland) | 01-42-78-91-44 | www.enoteca.fr

"In pasta e vino veritas" declare devotees of this "intimate" Italian vino bar in a centuries-old Marais house; massive beams overhead create a "romantic" but "low-key" setting in which to sample possibly the "best list of wines from The Boot" (with the "good by-the-glass selection changing weekly") and "unfussy", "well-cooked" *cucina*; surveyors also salute "the staff that knows its stuff", even though some warn they grow "distant if you refuse their expensive suggestions."

Entêtée (L') 🖼️Ⓜ️ *Bistro*

- | - | - | M

14ᵉ | 4, rue Danville (Denfert-Rochereau) | 01-40-47-56-81 | www.myspace.com/entetee

Dominated by a big clock face, this cozy bistro with bare wood floors and simple gray tables has a happy young vibe – the secret to its success in this residential corner of the 14th; the chalkboard menu changes monthly but runs to fresh, imaginative dishes like endives braised in red wine, sautéed scallops with Creole-spiced potato purée and a white chocolate crème brûlée; service is relaxed, and the lunch and dinner prix fixes offer great bang for the buck.

Entoto *Ethiopian*

- | - | - | I

13ᵉ | 143-145, rue L.M. Nordmann (Glacière) | 01-45-87-08-51

"If you've never eaten Ethiopian food, you are in for a treat" confide clients of this "simple" though "friendly" venue in the 13th, where "flavorful" dishes with "interesting seasonings" include *wot*, a platter of meat and vegetables eaten by hand with injera bread; but this East African offers more than just a cultural adventure – "it's a bargain" too.

Entracte (L')
(Chez Sonia et Carlos) *Bistro*

- | - | - | E

18ᵉ | 44, rue d'Orsel (Abbesses/Anvers) | 01-46-06-93-41

"A favorite with the locals" and "colorful" types from the "theater across the street", this traditional "treasure" in the 18th also attracts trekkers "on the way up the hill to Sacré Coeur", who are drawn by the "beautiful flowers that brighten the decor", the "wonderful atmosphere" and the "warm welcome" of the owner, whose functions also include greeter, bartender and chef; his "exquisitely prepared" bistro food is "served with justifiable pride."

Entredgeu (L') 🖼️Ⓜ️ *Bistro*

17 | 9 | 13 | €42

17ᵉ | 83, rue Laugier (Porte de Champerret) | 01-40-54-97-24

"Jammed and jamming", this "quirky bistro at the top end of the 17th" is run by a pleasant couple: the chef prepares an "imaginative" menu that "changes with the market" while his wife oversees the room; alas, while "affordable", it's "awfully average" according to antagonists, while sensitive souls shrink from the "surly service" – but at least "they've installed air-conditioning."

Enzo 🖼️ *Italian*

- | - | - | M

14ᵉ | 72, rue Daguerre (Denfert-Rochereau/Gaîté) | 01-43-21-66-66 | www.pizzaenzo.fr

Eponymous chef-owner Enzo Camerino earns kudos for what many consider the "best pizza in town", thin-crusted and always freshly made, plus pastas and "good vegetarian options" at this tiny trattoria in the 14th; but it's all just pie in the sky for those who show up too late to claim one of the 30 "less than comfortable", but coveted, seats.

Epicure 108 🆑 *Alsace/Asian*   - | - | - | M

17ᵉ | 108, rue Cardinet (Malesherbes) | 01-47-63-50-91

"Unjustly overlooked due to the lack of tourist traffic in the area", this intriguing and thoroughly original table in the 17th offers an "Alsatian menu from an Asian chef-owner"; happily, his efforts such as fish choucroute and green tea crème brûlée avoid "crazy fusion", showing instead the delicious results of a "respectful interaction between two traditions."

Epi d'Or (L') 🆑 *Bistro*   16 | 15 | 17 | €41

1ᵉʳ | 25, rue Jean-Jacques Rousseau (Louvre-Rivoli) | 01-42-36-38-12

It's "small and not fancy", "but everyone here is serious about the food" at this "authentic" bistro near the Bourse, with a "moody old interior" that dates back to 1935 and a "warm welcome" for all; malcontents mutter "there was a time when it was better" (and indeed, the Food score's slipped), but since this old-fashioned type of "good-value" place is "getting harder and harder to find", disciples deem it "worth the detour."

🆉 Epi Dupin (L') 🆑 *Bistro*   24 | 14 | 19 | €51

6ᵉ | 11, rue Dupin (Sèvres-Babylone) | 01-42-22-64-56 | www.epidupin.com

There's "good reason" this "bubbly" bistro near the Bon Marché is "always packed" exclaim "gobsmacked" gastronomes who guarantee the "inspired", "innovative" prix fixe is such "great value" it's practically "a giveaway" – overriding serenity-seekers shuddering it's "not worth the cattle-car experience" (though a post-Survey modernized decor may alleviate matters); the staff is "rushed", but "nice"; P.S. you "must book" one of the two nightly seatings, remembering that the tourist-heavy early one feels like "eating in the States."

Epigramme (L') 🆑🅼 *Bistro*   - | - | - | M

6ᵉ | 9, rue de l'Eperon (Odéon/St-Michel) | 01-44-41-00-09

It can be surprisingly tough to find good ol' French food in Saint-Germain, site of so many Italian eateries, which explains why fans have been writing epigrams about this "sparkling" little bistro; exposed-stone walls create a warm country-house type atmosphere in which to enjoy the good-value chalkboard menu that runs to dishes like cauliflower soup, grilled veal breast with pumpkin purée and Campari-flavored orange and grapefruit gelée.

Erawan 🆑 *Thai*   17 | 10 | 12 | €41

15ᵉ | 76, rue de la Fédération (La Motte-Picquet-Grenelle) | 01-47-83-55-67

Bangkok buffs affirm that this intimate spot near Ecole Militaire offers "authentic" Thai food, "not the watered-down French version" – indeed, this is "one of the few places where you can ask for *prig nam pla* (a condiment with chiles in fermented fish sauce) and actually get it"; the personnel is "affable", and despite "uninteresting decor", it still manages to conjure a "lovely atmosphere."

	FOOD	DECOR	SERVICE	COST

Escale du Liban (L') ● *Lebanese*

| | - | - | - | I |

4ᵉ | 1, rue Ferdinand Duval (St-Paul) | 01-42-74-55-70

This Lebanese port of call in a 17th-century building in the Marais was taken over by a different chef-owner last year, but nothing has changed, from the busy take-out counter to the tables on two floors above, where patrons sit and graze on meze and sticky-sweet pastries.

Escargot Montorgueil (L') *Bistro*

| | 21 | 22 | 21 | €62 |

1ᵉʳ | 38, rue Montorgueil (Les Halles) | 01-42-36-83-51 | www.escargot-montorgueil.com

The golden snail over the door of this "unique old" "ornate" bistro is an unmistakable sign that this is "a must-stop if you love escargot", served in sauces as disparate as "traditional, curry and Roquefort", or "crêpes suzette made tableside" (another star of a menu "that couldn't be more Classic" French); located near Les Halles since 1832, this place still has decor "straight out of the 19th century", although "it's easy to overspend" given the 21st-century prices.

☒ Espadon (L') *Classic French*

| | 26 | 27 | 28 | €149 |

1ᵉʳ | Hôtel Ritz | 15, pl Vendôme (Opéra/Tuileries) | 01-43-16-30-80 | www.ritzparis.com

It's "like being invited to dinner by Louis XVI" at this "over-the-top" table in the Hôtel Ritz with "sublime" formal surroundings, a "beautiful summer patio" and "royal treatment" from "surprisingly friendly" servers; most marvel at chef Michel Roth's "lovely", "perfectly executed" Classic French cuisine – even if a few subjects sigh it doesn't merit "prices that register on the ridiculous scale."

Etc. ●☒ *New French*

| | - | - | - | VE |

16ᵉ | 2, rue La Pérouse (Kléber) | 01-49-52-10-10

Not far from the Arc de Triomphe in the 16th is this luxury bistro owned by top toque Christian Le Squer of Pavillon Ledoyen; he's installed his Ledoyen sous-chef, Bernard Pinaud, to oversee a frequently changing New French menu that runs to dishes like steak lacquered with soy sauce; the high-ceilinged setting with Scandinavian modern furnishings appeals to local power-broker types looking to relax in a casual, but correct, venue.

Etoile Marocaine (L') *Moroccan*

| | - | - | - | M |

8ᵉ | 56, rue Galilée (George V) | 01-47-20-44-43 | www.etoilemarocaine.com

"It's not fancy and the service can be slow", but this place serves some of "the most delicious and authentic Moroccan food in town"; intricately painted and glazed "tiled walls and small fountains" create "nice ambiance", and prices are "reasonable" for the pricey 8th.

Eugène ☒ *Eclectic*

| | - | - | - | M |

8ᵉ | 166, bd Haussmann (St-Philippe-du-Roule) | 01-42-89-00-13

Just steps from the charming Musée Jacquemart-André lies this "decent neighborhood bistro with Eclectic furnishings and menu"; the former features warm orange-and-brown colors and a big picture window (designed by Gustave Eiffel) and long pewter bar, while the latter offers market-fresh fish and lamb; a 23.5€ prix fixe makes it a particularly "nice place to have lunch."

Fables de La Fontaine (Les) *Seafood*   24 | – | 21 | €54

7e | 131, rue St-Dominique (Ecole Militaire) | 01-44-18-37-55

"Overlooking a cute traffic-free" square in the 7th, this "wonderful fish restaurant" founded by chef Christian Constant is now being helmed by two of his protégés, alums of the master's Le Violon d'Ingres, who have instituted dark-wood and warm-toned decor but kept the focus on "fresh, simple and outstanding" catch-of-the-day items; service is "prompt and friendly" and prices are "reasonable" for such "transcendent seafood", so "the only thing it needs is more tables."

Fakhr el Dine ● *Lebanese*   ▽ 24 | 20 | 18 | €49

16e | 30, rue de Longchamp (Trocadéro) | 01-47-27-90-00 | www.fakhreldine.com

"Less showy than others on the Right Bank", this elegant Lebanese offers "a range of interesting tagines" and other "excellent, abundant dishes"; the shawarma-warm milieu is "pleasant to linger in", but also good "for a quick lunch."

Famille (La) 🗷 🖩 *New French*   19 | 15 | 17 | €49

18e | 41, rue des Trois-Frères (Abbesses/Anvers) | 01-42-52-11-12

This "convivial", loftlike space on a tiny cobbled street in Montmartre pulls a hip, younger crowd with an inventive New French menu that changes every 15 days; if fans find the food "delicious", foes feel it's "expensive for such small portions" – but then, "you always have to be patient with your family", *n'est-ce pas?*; N.B. the Decor score doesn't reflect its post-Survey look: white walls adorned with photos and graffiti murals.

Fellini *Italian*   21 | 14 | 17 | €51

1er | 47, rue de l'Arbre-Sec (Louvre-Rivoli) | 01-42-60-90-66

15e | 58, rue de la Croix Nivert (Commerce/Emile Zola) | 01-45-77-40-77 🗷

Spearheaded by "good-humored", "personable service", a "warmly welcoming atmosphere" pervades this pair of pasta purveyors in the 1st (with "mellow stone walls" and a Sardinian slant) and 15th (with Neopolitan cuisine); patrons also are "pleased" by the "appetizing *plats*" and the "well-selected list of wines"; some say it seems "a little expensive" for spaghetti, but most shrug "that's the price you pay" for "a trip to Italy in the course of an evening."

Ferdi ● *Eclectic*   – | – | – | E

1er | 32, rue du Mont-Thabor (Concorde) | 01-42-60-82-52

Fashionistas of the world unite at this insider's address in the heart of the 1st, run by a sister of the founder of Maria-Luisa, a trendsetting women's boutique nearby; the Eclectic menu takes inspiration from points as varied as Venezuela (homeland of the chef's madre), Thailand, Russia and the U.S.; N.B. be sure to book.

	FOOD	DECOR	SERVICE	COST

Ferme (La) *Sandwiches*
| - | - | - | I |

1er | 55-57, rue St-Roch (Opéra/Pyramides) | 01-40-20-12-12

This rustic, wood-paneled *sandwicherie* was one of the first in the 1st to challenge the traditional city-center steak-frites lunch with mostly organic, "good, healthy food, reasonably priced whether it's a salad, a yogurt or a cookie"; it's self-service, but the "help is nice", and while "handy for lunch on the run", it's also a "good place for breakfast."

Ferme St-Simon (La) ☒ *Classic French*
| 23 | 22 | 23 | €62 |

7e | 6, rue de St-Simon (Rue du Bac/Solférino) | 01-45-48-35-74 | www.fermestsimon.com

The "charming", "cozy" decor of exposed beams and etched glass "makes for a pretty fancy" farm at this "old-world hangout"; it's the "place to see how French politicians dine" – the Assemblée Nationale's nearby – as you enjoy the "luscious" "Classic French dishes served by classy pros"; and if upstarts say it's "older-style dining", "lots of regulars" revel in the level of "luxury and calm that hasn't faltered over the last 20 years", despite management changes a while back.

Fermette Marbeuf 1900
| 18 | 24 | 18 | €56 |
(La) ◐☒ *Classic French*

8e | 5, rue Marbeuf (Alma Marceau) | 01-53-23-08-00 | www.fermettemarbeuf.com

"A jewel of art nouveau" declare those who "love the stained-glass ceiling" and "walls of mirrors and gold" at this Classic French just off the Champs-Elysées in the 8th; such "a shame", then, that the "food is good, but nothing special" and the servers swing from "disinterested" to "friendly"; of course, one option is to "ogle the place and leave."

Ferrandaise (La) ☒ *Bistro*
| 21 | 16 | 21 | €50 |

6e | 8, rue de Vaugirard (Odéon/Cluny/Luxembourg RER) | 01-43-26-36-36 | www.laferrandaise.com

Just across from the Luxembourg Gardens, this "charming neighborhood bistro serves delicious hearty dishes, including Ferrandaise beef from the Auvergne"; some cavil there's "not much in the way of ambiance" – the decor's mostly "pictures of cows lining the rustic walls" – but the "service is friendly" and the prix fixe "a great buy."

Findi ◐ *Italian*
| 16 | 16 | 16 | €55 |

8e | 24, av George V (Alma Marceau/George V) | 01-47-20-14-78 | www.findi.net

"You'd think you were in a smart home" – provided home was an "à la mode" "Italian palazzo" – at this "upscale date place"; the food is almost as "smart", especially the "good, fresh homemade pastas", and "the waiters really try to please"; costs seem "reasonable, given the prestigious location" on the swank Avenue George V.

Fines Gueules (Les) ◐ *Wine Bar/Bistro*
| - | - | - | M |

1er | 43, rue Croix-des-Petits-Champs (Bourse/Palais Royal-Musée du Louvre) | 01-42-61-35-41 | www.lesfinesgueules.fr

Those intrepid few who have discovered this "hip wine bar" just off the Place des Victoires in the 1st praise its "good selection" of vinos and its daily changing bistro menu that includes the best ingredients, including meat from star butcher Hugo Desnoyer; the stylish interior includes exposed-stone walls and a waxed cement floor.

Fins Gourmets (Aux) 🗷 *Southwest*   19 | 16 | 16 | €53

7ᵉ | 213, bd St-Germain (Rue du Bac) | 01-42-22-06-57

Breathe "the atmosphere of eternal Paris" at "one of the last of the old bistros" in Saint-Germain, where "pleasant personnel" serve "carefully prepared" Southwestern specialties in a "typical, traditional" room; true, the setting seems "tired" at times, but "you eat well and you don't pay too much", so if it apparently "hasn't changed" since 1959, many "hope it never does."

Finzi *Italian*   ▽ 13 | 8 | 15 | €46

8ᵉ | 182, bd Haussmann (St-Philippe-du-Roule) | 01-45-62-88-68

"Always lively", this long-running "neighborhoodlike" Italian serves "refined cuisine" suited to this business-y part of the 8th; even so, a fallen Food score suggests many now find it pasta prime, saying "everything's going downhill here except the prices."

Firmin le Barbier 🅼 *Bistro*   - | - | - | M

7ᵉ | 20, rue de Monttessuy (Alma Marceau/Ecole Militaire) | 01-45-51-21-55

Launched by a former surgeon, this stylish bistro with exposed-stone walls and sleek modern lighting fixtures has quickly become a favorite with the well-heeled locals of the 7th; the kitchen specializes in traditional French bistro dishes like pan-fried foie gras, rack of lamb with baby vegetables and apple tart, all served by a charming staff for reasonable prices.

First (Le) *New French*   18 | 21 | 17 | €72

1ᵉʳ | Westin Hotel | 234, rue de Rivoli (Concorde) | 01-44-77-10-40 | www.lefirstrestaurant.com

With its low-lit, supper-club/"boudoir" feel, designer Jacques Garcia's decor for the Westin's New French is just the ticket "if you like cozy places where purple is the dominant color"; "but the food and service have a lot of catching up to do": the staff can be "a little bit stuffy" and the menu, while "sophisticated", is "not good value for the money."

🔽 Fish La Boissonnerie 🅼 *Provence*   22 | 15 | 19 | €40

6ᵉ | 69, rue de Seine (Mabillon/Odéon) | 01-43-54-34-69

"In overpriced, touristy Saint-Germain", this "hectic but friendly" old *poissonnerie* serves "remarkably good" food – dishes prepared with "a taste of Southern France", with "fish the obvious specialty", plus "exceptional wines supplied by co-owner Juan Sanchez, who has a shop around the corner"; at times service seems "overburdened and untrained", and as a virtual "home for the American expat", the room rings with "noisy", English-speaking voices.

Flandrin (Le) ● *Brasserie*   15 | 14 | 14 | €62

16ᵉ | 80, av Henri Martin (Rue de la Pompe) | 01-45-04-34-69

"A golden girl/boy staple", "this old train station–turned-brasserie" is "the place to be seen in the posh" 16th, particularly the "sunny patio"; but "unless you want to show off your Ferrari" (the car-watching is as big as the people-watching here), many moan it's "not worth going", since it's "expensive for no real reason" – certainly not the "mediocre dishes" or the servers "only interested in the regulars."

Floors ●Ⓜ *American/Burgers* | - | - | - | M |

18ᵉ | 100, rue Myrha (Chateau Rouge) | 01-42-62-08-08

Occupying a three-story former printing press on the southwestern slopes of Montmartre, this all-white homage to a '50s diner is Paris' own burger heaven; aside from the classic toppings (cheese, bacon, etc.), it also offers some decidedly Gallic garnishes, including foie gras and truffles; but with French's mustard on the table and Philadelphia Cream Cheese cake for dessert, the menu's definitely more American than Franco.

Flora Danica *Classic French/Danish* | 19 | 18 | 16 | €58 |

8ᵉ | 142, av des Champs-Elysées (Charles de Gaulle-Etoile/George V) | 01-44-13-86-26 | www.restaurantfloradanica.com

Amid "a neighborhood filled with tourist traps", this "ultimate Nordic experience in the heart of the Champs" is "the place to go if you want to eat salmon" or herring (plus some Classic French favorites); there's a "beautiful courtyard for summer dining", which many prefer to the "noisy", Danish "modern" dining room; prices are "reasonable" compared to Copenhague, its "expensive upstairs brother."

Flore en l'Ile (Le) ● *Classic French* | 18 | 19 | 18 | €30 |

4ᵉ | 42, quai d'Orléans (Cité/Pont-Marie) | 01-43-29-88-27 | www.lefloreenlile.com

Boasting a "strategic location on the tip of the Ile Saint-Louis", this busy "neighborhood place" has "great views" of Notre Dame to enhance its "consistent and appealing" Classic French meals, including "brunch, lunch, tea" and "late-night Berthillion" ice cream; if several find it "overpriced", most say "it's worth whatever they charge" for that "movie-set" setting, despite "impersonal" service.

Florimond (Le) 🅢 *Classic French* | 24 | 19 | 26 | €50 |

7ᵉ | 19, av de la Motte-Picquet (Ecole Militaire/La Tour-Maubourg) | 01-45-55-40-38

"What a find!" crows the crowd over this "delightful" Classic French where a staff that's "so kind and helpful" and "effortlessly attentive" delivers "delicious" dishes ("the incredible stuffed cabbage" is a real *chou*-in), supervised by the "warm, friendly owner"; the "small storefront space" may not be much to look at, but who cares when the tab is "reasonable", given the "pricey neighborhood" near Les Invalides.

Fogón ●Ⓜ *Spanish* | 21 | 15 | 18 | €53 |

6ᵉ | 45, quai des Grands-Augustins (Odéon/St-Michel) | 01-43-54-31-33 | www.fogon.fr

"It's pricey for paella, but this is Paris' only Spanish restaurant worthy of the name" aver amigos of this Seine-side site in Saint-Germain ("dynamite location"); whether devouring "interesting, unique tapas" or items on the "super-inventive tasting menu", the "crowd is young and fun", which – along with "kind and *muy* professional" staffers – creates a "good atmosphere" amid the "original modern decor."

☑ Fontaine de Mars (La) *Southwest* | 21 | 19 | 21 | €50 |

7ᵉ | 129, rue St-Dominique (Ecole Militaire) | 01-47-05-46-44 | www.lafontainedemars.com

Now famous as the site of a quiet repast for Barack and Michelle Obama, this century-old stalwart in "the shadow of the Eiffel Tower" is deemed exactly what a "typical bistro should be", with "charming owners" and staff, "huge checked" linens, moleskin banquettes and traditional, "memorable" Southwestern cuisine; even if it's getting "a little on the pricey side", it "never fails to make you happy" – especially in summer when you can "opt for a table outside near the fountain."

Fontaine Gaillon (La) ●⑤ *Classic French* | 22 | 22 | 20 | €75 |

2ᵉ | 1, pl Gaillon (Opéra/Quatre-Septembre) | 01-42-65-87-04 | www.la-fontaine-gaillon.com

Best-known for playing Cyrano, actor Gérard "Depardieu demonstrates his panache", providing "a visual and culinary delight" with this celebrity-studded Classic French in the 2nd; the "food can be delicious" – especially the "fresh fish" – and the "surroundings are beautifully appointed", particularly if you sit outside "next to the [namesake] fountain"; while "the staff appears a bit haughty at first, that goes away", making this "pleasant" place "worth the price"; N.B. closed weekends.

Fontaines (Les) *Bistro* | 17 | 11 | 15 | €37 |

5ᵉ | 9, rue Soufflot (Cluny La Sorbonne/Luxembourg) | 01-43-26-42-80

"A lively choice by the Panthéon" ("the sidewalk tables offer great views"), "this bistro has all the typical" dishes in such "huge portions" that one "serving is enough for a family"; the "decor's pretty pitiful", and the "staff is available, without much else", but overall, the place is "tasty, unpretentious" and relatively "cheap."

Fontanarosa *Italian* | - | - | - | E |

15ᵉ | 28, bd Garibaldi (Cambronne/Ségur) | 01-45-66-97-84 | www.fontanarosa-ristorante.eu

"Fantastic Sardinian food", "convivial service" (perhaps including a chat with English-speaking owner Flavio Mascia) and "an impressive wine list, including a fair bit of juice from Sardinia, keep 'em coming back" to this Italian with an "enjoyable patio" in the 15th; sole regret: it "has become really expensive."

Foujita *Japanese* | - | - | - | M |

1ᵉʳ | 41, rue St-Roch (Pyramides) | 01-42-61-42-93 ⑤
1ᵉʳ | 7, rue 29 Juillet (Tuileries) | 01-49-26-07-70

There are almost "no amenities" at this sushi-purveying pair in the 1st; but if you need a fix of "stark, fresh" fish, at "great quality for the price", they're "the best."

| | FOOD | DECOR | SERVICE | COST |

Fouquet's (Le) ☾ *Classic French*
18 | 21 | 17 | €67

8ᵉ | 99, av des Champs-Elysées (George V) | 01-40-69-60-50 | www.lucienbarriere.com

"It's all about the view and the history" at this "Parisian landmark" on the Champs-Elysées, with its "tourist magnet" of a terrace without and a "charming boudoir atmosphere" (all "old-line red velvet") within; be prepared to spend "*beaucoup d'* euros" for what most call "distinctly average" Classic French fare, and be aware that "ego has crept into" the staff attitude; still, you too can "feel like someone famous here" – and that makes it "worth sampling, at least once."

NEW Fourchette du Printemps (La) ☒ *Bistro*
- | - | - | M

17ᵉ | 30, rue du Printemps (Wagram) | 01-42-27-26-97

Though in a challenging location on the northern edges of the 17th, this friendly, modern bistro with simple decor (red upholstered chairs, hanging lamps) rewards the effort of travel with its creative, high-quality contemporary French bistro cooking; the chalkboard menu changes regularly but often includes dishes like foie gras-stuffed terrine wrapped in leeks and deconstructed tarte Tatin, with excellent-value prices ensuring it's already a local favorite.

Fous d'en Face (Les) ☾ *Bistro*
- | - | - | M

4ᵉ | 3, rue du Bourg-Tibourg (Hôtel-de-Ville) | 01-48-87-03-75

Overlooking a pretty square in the 4th arrondissement ("good for people-watching"), this traditional bistro offers "nicely prepared" "solid country French" food, including a "great" pot-au-feu; owner Philippe Llorca is a "gregarious guy who wants you to have a nice experience."

Frégate (La) ☒ *Seafood*
∇ 24 | 17 | 21 | €38

12ᵉ | 30, av Ledru-Rollin (Gare de Lyon/Quai de la Rapée) | 01-43-43-90-32 | www.lafregate-ledrurollin.fr

Located "right on the *quai*" in the 12th (its name means 'frigate'), this "elegant" seafooder is "an enchanted island" that's featured "fabulous food, full of intense flavors" in "a nice, quiet" setting for the last 40 years; "the clientele tends to be businesspeople and/or the middle-aged" who savor "service so attentive, you feel like a private guest"; N.B. the above Decor score does not reflect a post-Survey redo that ushered in a new mango-hued look.

NEW Frenchie *Bistro*
- | - | - | M

2ᵉ | 5, rue du Nil (Sentier) | 01-40-39-96-19 | www.frenchie-restaurant.com

After stints with Jamie Oliver in London and at New York's Gramercy Tavern, young Frenchman Gregory Marchand returned home and hung out a shingle for his own tiny, charming contemporary French bistro in a film noir–like lane in the rapidly gentrifying Sentier, where the short, nearly daily changing market menu reflects his Anglo-American trajectory and nervy culinary imagination; the space's exposed-brick walls and industrial suspension lamps create a Soho groove matched by the stylish young customers.

	FOOD	DECOR	SERVICE	COST

Fumoir (Le) ● *Eclectic* | 17 | 21 | 18 | €43 |

1er | 6, rue de l'Amiral de Coligny (Louvre-Rivoli) | 01-42-92-00-24 | www.lefumoir.com

Since its main drawback – having to "endure the smoke" – is now history, there's nothing to impede one's enjoyment of this "ineffably cool", "*très* NYC" "meet-for-a-drink spot" "facing the Louvre"; it's "always packed" with a "seriously hip" crowd soaking up "the warm ambiance of the library room", the "nice strong cocktails" and the "reliable" Eclectic fare (though, truthfully, "you'll be so busy checking out the people checking you out that you won't notice what you're eating").

Gaigne (Le) 🗷Ⓜ *New French* | - | - | - | M |

4e | 12, rue Pecquay (Hôtel-de-Ville/Rambuteau) | 01-44-59-86-72 | www.restaurantlegaigne.fr

This tiny shopfront space with cyclamen-colored walls in the Marais has a major talent in chef Mickaël Gaignon, who previously cooked at Gaya before going out on his own; his New French menu runs to precisely cooked, vividly flavored dishes like artichoke soup with cockles and yellow pollack en papillotte (fish is a specialty, though there's a wicked herb-stuffed roast lamb as well); Gaignon's charming wife, Aurélie, negotiates the narrow environs with balletic grace.

Gallopin ●🗷 *Brasserie* | 16 | 20 | 17 | €47 |

2e | 40, rue Notre-Dame-des-Victoires (Bourse/Grands Boulevards) | 01-42-36-45-38 | www.brasseriegallopin.com

"Big, busy and [blessed] with belle epoque decor" sums up this "classic brasserie" with an "inviting bar" behind the Bourse in the 2nd; "it's a pity that the cuisine isn't up to" the environs, and that the gallopin' waiters, "garbed in long aprons", tend to be "impersonal"; still, this veteran works as "a really reliable standby."

Gare (La) ● *Classic French* | 14 | 21 | 15 | €46 |

16e | 19, Chaussée de la Muette (La Muette) | 01-42-15-15-31 | www.restaurantlagare.com

If you're one of the 16th's "golden youth" (entry "forbidden to those over 18" some jest) you go to this "chic" Classic French "for the setting" – "a great renovation of an old railway station", complete with plasma TVs and mirrors – and "for the really pleasant terrace"; unchanged, though, are criticisms of the cooking – which ranges from "culinary disaster" to "very ordinary" – and the staff, which is a bit too "casual" for comfort.

Garnier *Brasserie/Seafood* | 22 | 18 | 18 | €82 |

8e | 111, rue St-Lazare (St-Lazare) | 01-43-87-50-40

Things go swimmingly at this brasserie just across the street from the Gare Saint-Lazare, "an area with few good restaurants"; not only does it serve some of the "best seafood in Paris" – "there's shellfish, and then there's Garnier's shellfish" – it also offers a setting that somewhat "surrealistically" blends aquariums with Lalique lamps and mirrors; however, dissidents deride the "disorganized" staff (confirmed by a Service score drop).

Gauloise (La) ⓩ *Bistro* — ▽ 15 | 16 | 13 | €40

15ᵉ | 59, av de la Motte-Picquet (La Motte-Picquet-Grenelle) | 01-47-34-11-64

Searchers for some "reasonably priced class" declare this traditional bistro in the 15th fills the bill with "jovial atmosphere" and "quite adequate cooking"; however, the circa-1900 "decor's aging" a bit, and the "service is "accommodating – for locals."

Gavroche (Le) ◕ⓩ *Bistro* — 17 | 14 | 16 | €48

2ᵉ | 19, rue St-Marc (Bourse/Richelieu-Drouot) | 01-42-96-89-70

"Carnivores rejoice" to taste *côte de boeuf at its best*" at this traditional bistro in the 2nd that's "worth a trip to see what Paris was really like before World War II"; despite the "atmosphere of camaraderie", however, some sigh it costs "such a lot of euros", given the "gritty" digs, "slow service" and general sense – supported by sliding scores – that it's "gone downhill of late."

Gaya ⓩ *Seafood* — 23 | 16 | 19 | €79

7ᵉ | 44, rue du Bac (Rue du Bac) | 01-45-44-73-73 | www.pierre-gagnaire.com

"Even more chic" since baroque toque Pierre Gagnaire acquired it, this vintage Left Bank fish house is now a cutting-edge catch-of-the-day place; his "alchemic concoctions" (tandoori-style monkfish, red pepper iced parfait) are served in a Corian table and stainless-steel setting that strikes some as "almost as cold as the room that the fish is kept in"; "it was always excellent and pricey – since the takeover, it's excellent, pricey – and hard to get a reservation."

Gazzetta (La) ⓩⓜ *Mediterranean/New French* — – | – | – | M

12ᵉ | 29, rue de Cotte (Ledru-Rollin) | 01-43-47-47-05 | www.lagazzetta.fr

Those who discover this venue in the 12th call it a pleasant "surprise", featuring a New French–Med menu from Swedish chef Peter Nilsson (ex Troisgros, in the Rhône Valley) that changes daily, but runs to "excellent" unusual dishes, like lamb with pickled lemons and honey, or banana terrine; equally "remarkable" is the decor featuring a crazy quilt tiled floor and framed antique posters, as well as the "impeccable welcome."

ⓩ Georges ◕ *Eclectic* — 18 | 25 | 15 | €62

4ᵉ | Centre Georges Pompidou | 19, rue Beaubourg (Hôtel-de-Ville/ Rambuteau) | 01-44-78-47-99

"God, what a scene" it is, as "beautiful people" (they "turn away the unfashionable") mix it up with "visiting housewives from Dallas" amid the "smashing" "space-age" decor of this "glamorous" Costes brothers venue on the roof of the Pompidou Center – "one of the most gorgeous views in Paris"; also offering an eyeful are the "snooty", "modellike waitresses in micro-minis" "carrying big heavy trays that weigh more than they do"; the Eclectic fare "is too expensive for the quality", but who cares – "even a McDonald's up here would warrant a visit"; N.B. closed Tuesdays.

	FOOD	DECOR	SERVICE	COST

Georgette 🚫Ⓜ *Bistro*   ▽ 22 | 13 | 21 | €40

9ᵉ | 29, rue Saint-Georges (Notre-Dame-de-Lorette) | 01-42-80-39-13

"Exactly the kind of place that makes eating out in Paris so charming", this contemporary bistro in the 9th boasts an owner who is "both delightful and delighted to explain" the New French menu of "simple" foods that "mix well with the homestyle service and diner-like decor"; admittedly, the latter's "a bit '60s, with brightly colored Formica tables", but overall, this is "an entire pleasure"; N.B. open Tuesday–Friday only.

Ⓩ Gérard Besson 🚫 *Classic French*   25 | 21 | 24 | €121

1ᵉʳ | 5, rue du Coq-Héron (Louvre-Rivoli/Palais Royal-Musée du Louvre) | 01-42-33-14-74 | www.gerardbesson.com

"Small, intimate and semi-formal", and "much frequented" by foreigners, this carved-wood-and-velvet veteran in the 1st pleases with "retro" "food to be relished", especially by "those who like game in season", and with service that's "polite" "without being condescending"; "perhaps it's hurt a bit by not adhering to fashionisms, but if you want great Classic French fare, this is one of the best."

Gitane (La) 🚫 *Classic French*   - | - | - | M

15ᵉ | 53 bis, av de la Motte-Picquet (La Motte-Picquet-Grenelle) | 01-47-34-62-92 | www.la-gitane.com

When media exec Olivier Mayeras and his wife, Corinne (both ex Condé Nast), took over this old-timer in the bustling La Motte-Picquet Grenelle district, they gave it a major overhaul, installing a mosaic-tiled floor and well-spaced tables with linen cloths and oil paintings; today, this elegant, rejuvenated gypsy (*gitane*) offers updated French bourgeois cuisine in the true sense of the term – just as when the middle class ate their meals *à la maison* – to a clientele of locals, politicians and tourists who enjoy sitting out on the small terrace in summer.

Giulio Rebellato *Italian*   ▽ 20 | 14 | 20 | €59

16ᵉ | 136, rue de la Pompe (Victor Hugo) | 01-47-27-50-26

"In a *quartier* that's frequented by the chic clique" of the 16th, this "small", "low-key" Italian offers Venetian victuals that are "very good" but "very dear" as well; a "nice welcome" accompanies the "well-prepared" fare, though a few fear it's somewhat Frenchified.

Gli Angeli ●🚫 *Italian*   18 | 14 | 15 | €40

3ᵉ | 5, rue St-Gilles (Chemin-Vert/St-Paul) | 01-42-71-05-80

When the "Italians who live in Paris eat there", you know you have "a great place for pasta", and that's why "a reservation is a must" at this trattoria near the Place des Vosges; though "service can be a bit rude", the "authentic" "affordable" eats are absolutely angelic.

Glou *Bistro*   - | - | - | M

3ᵉ | 101, rue Vieille du Temple (Filles du Calvaire/Rambuteau) | 01-42-74-44-32 | www.glou-resto.blogspot.com

Backed by Julien Fouin, the former editor-in-chief of French food magazine *Regal*, this hipster hangout in the northern Marais serves a short, regularly changing bistro menu of traditional and contemporary dishes made with the highest quality, often-organic, produce; the stone-and-brick interior has a slightly clubby atmosphere, but the table d'hôte is a good place for chance encounters, provided you *parlez français*.

Gordon Ramsay au Trianon 🅂🅼 *Haute Cuisine*

-	-	-	VE

Versailles | Trianon Palace | 1, bd de la Reine (Versailles-Rive Droite RER) | 01-30-84-55-55 | www.gordonramsay.com

British celeb chef Gordon Ramsay made his French debut in a high-profile way within the storied dining room at the Trianon Palace hotel – a belle epoque beauty in lush gardens across from the park in Versailles; the ornate setting of yellow chairs, patterned floor and contemporary chandeliers makes a fitting backdrop for his refined, cautiously inventive Haute Cuisine dishes such as scallops with snail ragoût, and roast pigeon with marjoram seasoned cabbage, which, *naturellement,* command a king's ransom; N.B. Ramsay also runs the hotel's more casual Veranda restaurant complete with titular terrace.

Gorille Blanc (Le) 🅂 *Bistro*

▽ 21	14	20	€41

7ᵉ | 11 bis, rue Chomel (Sèvres-Babylone/St-Sulpice) | 01-45-49-04-54

"Just steps away from the bustle of the Bon Marché" department store in the 7th, this "cozy little box" of a bistro pulls a stylish crowd with "delightful" cuisine that swings from "creative" to "classic"; whether French or foreign, "guests are well served", and the pretty room is a perfect place to "relax after a long day of shopping in Saint-Germain."

Goumard *Seafood*

24	22	23	€94

1ᵉʳ | 9, rue Duphot (Madeleine) | 01-42-60-36-07 | www.goumard.fr

At this "magic address" near the Madeleine, "terrific seafood" – from "flavorful, succulent oysters" to "excellent sea bass" – reels in compliments from surveyors, who also salute service that's "polite without being snooty" and the "maple-paneled dining room" with Lalique inserts that "makes you feel like you're on a '30s oceanliner like the Normandie" (don't miss the "belle epoque toilets" and art deco–style lounge either); "prices are nose-bleed", so unless "a rich uncle wants to treat you to dinner", check out the (relatively) "bargain lunch."

Gourmand (Au) 🅂 *Classic/New French*

20	17	19	€47

1ᵉʳ | 17, rue Molière (Palais Royal-Musée du Louvre/Pyramides) | 01-42-96-22-19 | www.augourmand.fr

"Moving from the 6th" to the 1st has caused a "great rebirth of this fine place"; the French "food is creative, yet nods to the past", with a produce-only prix fixe that's "ideal for vegetarians"; the "warm colors" of the trompe l'oeil theatrical decor and equally "warm, well-paced service" make reviewers vow "I will return."

	FOOD	DECOR	SERVICE	COST

Gourmets des Ternes (Les) ⊠ *Bistro* ▽ 19 | 14 | 15 | €45

8ᵉ | 87, bd de Courcelles (Ternes) | 01-42-27-43-04 |
www.lesgourmetsdesternes.com

"Politically incorrect and unabashedly so", this "down-and-dirty
meat-and-potatoes" bistro near the Place des Ternes is "cramped
and loud – but hey, it's been like that for decades" shrug supporters
who still line up for the "steak lover's dream" of a menu; a score rise
confirms the service "standard is way up" ("the snootiness is just
shtick"); even so, several say "you can do better elsewhere."

Graindorge ⊠ *Belgian/Northern French* 22 | 18 | 19 | €55

17ᵉ | 15, rue de l'Arc-de-Triomphe (Charles de Gaulle-Etoile) |
01-47-54-00-28

"Notoriously great for beers", this north star near the Etoile also offers
"fine Belgian and Northern French food", "original", "meticulously
prepared" and presented by "immaculate servers" in "homey" digs.

Grand Café (Le) ● *Brasserie* 13 | 15 | 12 | €45

9ᵉ | 4, bd des Capucines (Opéra) | 01-43-12-19-00 | www.legrandcafe.com
"Right near the opera house" in the 9th, this "huge, classic" brasserie is "definitely a tourist-type place", with "very pretty" belle
epoque decor and prices "too high for what they serve" ("*le grand
médiocre*"); the service is rather variable ("professional when it's by
one of the 'old guys', amateurish when not"), but at least they sling
the "fresh shellfish" and other staples into the wee hours.

Grand Colbert (Le) ● *Brasserie* 19 | 24 | 20 | €54

2ᵉ | 2, rue Vivienne (Bourse/Palais Royal-Musée du Louvre) |
01-42-86-87-88 | www.legrandcolbert.com
Typifying the "glorious belle epoque", "the decor remains the draw"
of this "boisterous" brasserie tucked away in the Passage Vivienne –
that, "and nostalgia for the scene from a Diane Keaton movie shot
here"; cynics sniff "*Something's Got to Give* with the bland food" and
attitude ("they're a little high on themselves after the film"), but
fans find the "old standbys competently executed" and the staff "as
warm and inviting as ever"; P.S. tip: "go late to avoid Americans."

Grande Armée (La) ● *Classic French* 15 | 15 | 15 | €46

16ᵉ | 3, av de la Grande-Armée (Charles de Gaulle-Etoile) | 01-45-00-24-77
"Simple but chic" – think striped canvas walls in military-tent
mode – this Classic French is "pleasant" "if you like Napoleonic
memorabilia" and want to be part of the well-heeled young folk of
the 16th; if foes assault it on gastronomic grounds ("nothing
good, nothing bad"), fans battle back, citing the "varied menu";
at least the service sparks a ceasefire, since everyone likes
the "efficient waiters."

⊠ Grande Cascade (La) *Haute Cuisine* 25 | 29 | 26 | €137

16ᵉ | Bois de Boulogne | Allée de Longchamp (Porte Maillot) |
01-45-27-33-51 | www.grandecascade.com
"Feel like royalty for an evening" or afternoon when you visit this
Second Empire pavilion; it's always had an "ultraromantic setting" in

the Bois de Boulogne ("spectacular" in summer, while in winter "the glass walls bring the outside in"), but after the advent of "creative" chef Frédéric Robert, the Haute Cuisine has "definitely improved to excellent", and so has the staff – "unobtrusive, but always anticipating one's needs"; some swoon at the "hysterical, are-you-kidding-me prices", but overall, this "over-the-top" experience is "a step back in time that's worth the trip."

Grand Louvre (Le) *Classic French*   18 | 18 | 15 | €41

1er | Musée du Louvre | below the Pyramide (Palais Royal-Musée du Louvre) | 01-40-20-53-41 | www.eliancemusee.com

"A huge flower arrangement greets you at the entrance" to this Classic French with "a wonderful location on the courtyard of the Louvre" ("under the I.M. Pei glass pyramid") and "sleek and sophisticated" decor by Jean-Michel Wilmotte; ok, "so it's not great cuisine", but it's "not bad for a museum restaurant", either – and besides, it's "a boon for tired feet" and "perfect for a quick bite" "while the gargoyles stare down at you"; N.B. closed Tuesday; dinner Wednesday and Friday only.

Grand Pan (Le) ☒ *Bistro*   - | - | - | M

15e | 20, rue Rosenwald (Convention/Plaisance) | 01-42-50-02-50

In a quiet corner of the 15th, young chef-owner Benoît Gauthier's "excellent bistro" is a great destination for anyone who wants to sample Gallic grill skills, since the short and simple chalkboard menu offers up various *viandes* (pork, beef, etc.), served with homemade frites and a green salad; the small space gets noisy with a diverse crowd that appreciates the huge, shareable portions and good wines by the carafe; N.B. closed weekends.

☒ Grand Véfour (Le) ☒ *Haute Cuisine*   28 | 29 | 28 | €157

1er | Palais Royal | 17, rue de Beaujolais (Palais Royal-Musée du Louvre) | 01-42-96-56-27 | www.grand-vefour.com

Chef Guy Martin's "exquisite" Haute Cuisine offers a "glorious feast for the senses in the midst of old-world luxury" at this "mythic address" in the 1st; "dripping with atmosphere", the "exceptional setting" – a gilded box of a room with a painted ceiling and brass plaques engraved with the names of its celebrated clientele (Colette, Maria Callas) – is animated by a staff that's "professional and welcoming"; true, such "royal treatment needs a royal treasury" when the bill comes – but "it meets each and every expectation"; N.B. closed weekends.

Grand Venise (Le) ☒Ⓜ *Italian*   ▽ 25 | 20 | 23 | €88

15e | 171, rue de la Convention (Convention) | 01-45-32-49-71

Tucked way in the 15th arrondissement, "one of the very best Italian restaurants in Paris" offers up a "warm welcome", "spectacular flower arrangements" and leisurely served *cucina* with "superb flavors from a loving mama"; however, some say you may want to "fast for a week before" going, since portions are "gigantic" and it's "expensive."

	FOOD	DECOR	SERVICE	COST

Grille (La) ⦻ *Bistro*   17 | 14 | 15 | €40

10ᵉ | 80, rue du Faubourg Poissonnière (Poissonnière) | 01-47-70-89-73 | www.lagrille.abemadi.com

"The grilled turbot for two is so fresh it jumps off your plate", and it's made the reputation of this "small, authentic" "old-fashioned neighborhood bistro" in the 10th, which is also known for its "eccentric" decor of lace, dolls and gewgaws; N.B. a post-Survey change of ownership may outdate the above ratings.

Grille St-Germain (La) ◑ *Bistro*   ∇ 17 | 17 | 17 | €44

6ᵉ | 14, rue Mabillon (Mabillon) | 01-43-54-16-87

With "Bordeaux-colored velvet curtains at the door and beautiful celebrity photos on the wall", a "pleasant" feeling prevails at this "comfy joint" in Saint-Germain; the "solid bistro food" pleases most, since "the kitchen works with quality produce", and if "service can be a little slow", few mind when "it's such a good buy for the money."

Guilo-Guilo Ⓜ *Japanese*   - | - | - | E

18ᵉ | 8, rue Garreau (Abbesses) | 01-42-54-23-92 | www.guiloguilo.com

The horseshoe-shaped bar presided over by genial chef Eiichi Edakuni, one of Kyoto's most famous toques, is the centerpiece of a hit in Montmartre; diners sit on stools in the sleek, dark-brown space and watch the master prepare the suite of small plates that compose his ever-changing tasting menu; most dishes are of Japanese inspiration, but a few betray a fusion touch, as seen in his popular foie-gras sushi.

Guinguette de Neuilly (La) *Classic French*   - | - | - | M

Neuilly-sur-Seine | 12, bd Georges Seurat (Pont-de-Levallois) | 01-46-24-25-04 | www.laguinguette.net

This "old-fashioned *guinguette*" on the Ile de la Jatte is a "pleasant" place to paddle down memory lane, since it serves the same blowsy vibe that made these waterside dance halls so popular a century ago; "you could say it's living off its reputation and Seine-side setting", but the Classic French fare is "reliable", even "agreeable in summer."

Guirlande de Julie (La) *Classic French*   15 | 16 | 15 | €46

3ᵉ | 25, pl des Vosges (Bastille/St-Paul) | 01-48-87-94-07 | www.latourdargent.com

In "an elegant location under the arches of the Place des Vosges", this Classic French comes trailing "garlands of taste, sophistication and cachet" (it's owned by La Tour d'Argent's Terrail family); if the fare is "just so-so", at least the "sympathetic" servers create a "convivial" atmosphere in the rosy-toned dining room – as does the good wine list, composed by the sommelier from the mother ship; N.B. a decor revamp by Hubert de Givenchy is in the works.

🄯 Guy Savoy, Restaurant ⦻Ⓜ *Haute Cuisine*   28 | 25 | 27 | €179

17ᵉ | 18, rue Troyon (Charles de Gaulle-Etoile) | 01-43-80-40-61 | www.guysavoy.com

Clearly, his ventures in Las Vegas "haven't distracted" chef-owner Guy Savoy – his "modern", "elegantly understated" Rue Troyon flagship remains "consistently superior in every way"; the "innovative" cooking "brings Haute Cuisine as close to art as it can come", the "formal but friendly" service hits a "high watermark" ("the staff all but spoon-fed us") "and – unusual for a big-name chef – M. Savoy often is actually at the restaurant"; yes, they charge "ridiculous prices", but since "you can't take it with you, leave some of it here."

Hangar (Le) ● ⬚⬚⬚⬚ *Classic French*   18 | 12 | 15 | €46

3ᵉ | 12, impasse Berthaud (Rambuteau) | 01-42-74-55-44
There's "hardly any decor" at this "pleasantly casual" "little bistro" around the corner from the Pompidou, but "the atmosphere's cozy" and the Classic French food "delicious" (especially "the magnificent seared foie gras"), if "not always original"; "they don't take credit cards – pretty annoying", but it keeps the prices "reasonable."

ⓩ Hélène   25 | 22 | 22 | €122
Darroze ⬚⬚ *New French/Southwest*

6ᵉ | 4, rue d'Assas (Rennes/Sèvres-Babylone) | 01-42-22-00-11 | www.helenedarroze.com
"La belle Hélène" is one of "the best female chefs in France", and her "innovative" New French–Southwestern creations, served in a "striking" room with parquet floors and plum accents in the 6th, are "exquisite"; but even *amis* admit they're "priced way above what they should be", especially given that they only arrive "after an in-terminable wait" despite the "cordial" staff; one tip: "eat in the ground-floor tapas bar – it's the same cooking, small-plates-style, at lower prices"; P.S. "the Armagnacs are worth the splurge."

Hide (Le) ⬚ *Bistro*   - | - | - | M

17ᵉ | 10, rue du Général Lanrezac (Charles de Gaulle-Etoile) | 01-45-74-15-81 | www.lehide.fr
The high quality – and low prices – of Japanese-born chef Hide Kobayashi's traditional French bistro menu have made this small spot near l'Etoile a big hit with a business crowd at noon and locals and tourists in the evening; the pair of lively waitresses who animate the room creates a happy atmosphere too.

Hier & Aujourd'hui ⬚ *New French*   - | - | - | M

17ᵉ | 145, rue de Saussure (Perreire) | 01-42-27-35-55 | resto.hieraujourdhui.free.fr
"Good food, friendly people" and an "excellent value/quality ratio" make it "worth going" to this gray-toned bistro, "a bit lost at the top of the 17th"; the few who've found it deem it "a welcome addition" to their culinary list, since the daily changing New French fare comes courtesy of a chef who cooked with Guy Savoy; warm service from wife/co-owner/fellow Savoy alum Karin is part of the bargain too.

Higuma *Japanese*   15 | 5 | 11 | €19

1ᵉʳ | 163, rue St-Honoré (Palais Royal-Musée du Louvre) | 01-58-62-49-22
1ᵉʳ | 32 bis, rue Ste-Anne (Pyramides) | 01-47-03-38-59
Providing a "perfect" gyoza/noodle fix, these Asian "canteens" offer "huge, delicious" plates of "authentic" fare (as borne out by "their

popularity with the Paris Japanese community"); neither looks great (though the younger one "near the Palais-Royal has nicer decor than its Rue Sainte-Anne cousin"), but at least you're "served immediately."

Hippopotamus ● *Steak* | 11 | 11 | 12 | €28

1er | 29, rue Berger (Les Halles) | 01-45-08-00-29
2e | 1, bd des Capucines (Opéra) | 01-47-42-75-70
4e | 1, bd Beaumarchais (Bastille) | 01-44-61-90-40
5e | 9, rue Lagrange (Maubert-Mutualité) | 01-43-54-13-99
6e | 119, bd du Montparnasse (Vavin) | 01-43-20-37-04
8e | 20, rue Quentin-Bauchart (George V) | 01-47-20-30-14
10e | 8, bd St-Denis (Strasbourg-St-Denis) | 01-53-38-80-28
12e | 145 bis, av Daumesnil (Daumesnil) | 01-53-02-40-40
14e | 80, av du Général Leclerc (Alésia) | 01-53-90-31-20
15e | 12, av du Maine (Duroc/Montparnasse-Bienvenüe) | 01-42-22-36-75
www.hippopotamus.fr
Additional locations throughout Paris

"Curiously, the quality and the service vary from one restaurant to another" at this "factory chain" – sort of a "TGI Friday's of France" – "catering to conventioneers, students and tourists" with steak "filets and frites"; but overall, the bar's pretty low ("who says you can't get a bad meal in Paris?") – even though parents proclaim "if you're traveling with kids, the place will save your sanity."

☑ Hiramatsu Ⓢ *Haute Cuisine/New French* | 26 | 25 | 26 | €122

16e | 52, rue de Longchamp (Boissière/Trocadéro) | 01-56-81-08-80 | www.hiramatsu.co.jp

The "meticulous attention to detail, immaculate presentation, and delicate sauces and flavors" offer a "spectacular experience" at this Haute Cuisine destination owned by chef Hiroyuki Hiramatsu in the 16th; though it's "becoming more Frenchified", the "inventive" fare still offers "an uncanny union of Gallic complexity and Japanese elegance", while waiters who are "responsive, helpful and elegant without being stuffy" warm the slightly "cold", if "refined", dining room; most are "just waiting to go back", even though it's "sooo expensive."

Hotaru Ⓢ Ⓜ *Japanese* | - | - | - | E

9e | 18, rue Rodier (Notre-Dame-de-Lorette/Cadet) | 01-48-78-33-74

Though vaunted by Parisian food critics, this vest-pocket Japanese near the Place Saint-Georges remains an insider's address for impeccably prepared, traditional dishes such as seaweed salad and sushi; adding to the authenticity is a drinks list that includes sake and shochu, and a Zen-like interior adorned mainly with Asian knickknacks.

Hôtel Amour ● *New French* | ▽ 8 | 18 | 9 | €46

9e | Hôtel Amour | 8, rue Navarin (St-Georges) | 01-48-78-31-80 | www.hotelamour.com

Co-owned by a sprig of the Costes brothers tree, this eclectically decorated restaurant/lounge in the "very hip" Hôtel Amour has "good music" and a "nice" garden patio; but there's not much *amour* for the New French fare ("nothing great on your plate") or the "disappointing service", both of which, says one reviewer, "reminds me of my college days (the prices less so)."

	FOOD	DECOR	SERVICE	COST

Huîtrerie Régis ●Ⓜ *Shellfish* — ▽ 22 | 14 | 19 | €43

6ᵉ | 3, rue de Montfaucon (Mabillon) | 01-44-41-10-07 |
www.huiterieregis.com

"World-class oysters", along with a "wonderful owner", make
this Saint-German raw bar a pearl of a place; "it's a little
cramped for space", but "everyone eating here knows exactly
what they're here for and they're rarely disappointed"; P.S. "go early
or be willing to wait."

Huîtrier (L') Ⓜ *Seafood* — 20 | 12 | 15 | €47

17ᵉ | 16, rue Saussier-Leroy (Ternes) | 01-40-54-83-44

The crustaceans may "cost their weight in gold" and some find the
vintage '70s decor "dubious", but this maritime-themed seafooder
in the 17th "offers a great selection" of shellfish, plus a few cooked
dishes ("great deep-fried calamari"); "everything's so amazingly
fresh", and the "really nice" crew assures smooth sailing too.

I Golosi Ⓩ *Italian* — 17 | 11 | 17 | €48

9ᵉ | 6, rue de la Grange-Batelière (Grands Boulevards/Richelieu-Drouot) |
01-48-24-18-63 | www.igolosi.com

This "convivial" spot with a "convenient location" in the 9th remains
a "preferred place" for its "original dishes from different Italian regions" on a "menu that changes constantly"; "the tabs can get a little hefty" and the "decor's a bit basic", but for most "this is a secret
address to guard jealously."

Il Barone ●Ⓩ *Italian* — ▽ 21 | 11 | 18 | €38

14ᵉ | 5, rue Léopold Robert (Raspail/Vavin) | 01-43-20-87-14

"Finding a good Italian restaurant in Paris can be difficult", but this
"real trattoria" in Montparnasse is a "charming experience", starring homemade pasta, robustly flavored and served by a staff that's
as "friendly as an Italian crew usually is"; "don't sweat the lack of decor", but do "avoid the hallwaylike front room" (strictly for tourists).

Ile (L') ● *Classic/New French* — 18 | 21 | 15 | €51

Issy-les-Moulineaux | Parc de l'Ile St-Germain | 170, quai de Stalingrad
(Issy-Val de Seine RER) | 01-41-09-99-99 | www.restaurant-lile.com

Prices are "high, but justified" by the "leafy", "exceptionally agreeable" waterside setting on the Ile Saint-Germain that's won this
"stylish site" a loyal following, despite the "undistinguished", if "decent" Classic–New French cuisine; one tip is to "go early – afterwards, it's a factory" with correspondingly "industrialized service."

Il Etait une Oie dans le Sud-Ouest Ⓩ *Southwest* — - | - | - | M

17ᵉ | 8, rue Gustave Flaubert (Courcelles/Ternes) |
01-43-80-18-30

"Foie gras heaven" awaits at this plum-toned Southwestern French
in the 17th, where delights like duck, puréed potatoes and the afore-
mentioned liver may amount to "heart attack on a stick, but worth
the near-death experience"; you'd have to be quackers to pass this
place up, especially given the reasonable prices.

	FOOD	DECOR	SERVICE	COST

Ilot Vache (L') ● *Classic French*

| 18 | 18 | 16 | €48 |

4ᵉ | 35, rue St-Louis-en-l'Ile (Pont-Marie) | 01-46-33-55-16 |
www.ilotvache.fr

"With a kitschy cow theme, this little spot on the Ile Saint-Louis" is
"recommended" for Classic French cuisine ("the chocolate mousse
is moo-licious"); some malcontents mutter that the food's fallen to
"mediocre" levels of late, but most feel it remains "ideal for tourists
wishing to discover traditional *gastronomie française*" (and indeed,
"there will be Americans at every meal").

Il Viccolo ☒ *Italian*

| - | - | - | E |

6ᵉ | 34, rue Mazarine (Odéon) | 01-43-25-01-11

A chic crowd of pasta lovers, including the occasional well-known
face, camps out at this "genuinely Italian" spot in Saint-Germain;
the "food is good, if not high-end", the "service almost shockingly
friendly" and, with a glassed-in sidewalk space, it "feels cozy, despite its modern-leaning decor"; however, "prices are a bit high" for
what's essentially a "neighborhood place."

Il Vino ● *Classic French/Mediterranean*

| - | - | - | VE |

7ᵉ | 13, bd de la Tour-Maubourg (Invalides) | 01-44-11-72-00 |
www.ilvinobyenricobernardo.com

An award-winning former sommelier at Le Cinq, Italian-born Enrico
Bernardo is the owner of this unique eatery near Les Invalides that
exalts the art of pairing wines with its Classic French–Med cuisine
(from chefs who were formerly at George V and Brittany's
Roellinger, respectively); politicians, editors and oenophiles pack its
sleek dining room with cobalt-blue carpet and modern art on the
walls, in search of the benefits of Bacchus.

Inagiku *Japanese*

| 18 | 14 | 12 | €45 |

5ᵉ | 14, rue de Pontoise (Maubert-Mutualité) | 01-43-54-70-07

"Chefs who cook meat, fish and veggie on a teppanyaki table" "before
your eyes" is the "original" – for Paris, anyway – concept of this Latin
Quarter Japanese; however, surveyors split over the service ("polite,
but they don't talk much") and decor ("very Zen"), adding that, aside
from "the Benihana-style show", it's "expensive for what you get."

Indiana Café ● *Tex-Mex*

| 7 | 8 | 8 | €26 |

3ᵉ | 1, pl de la République (République) | 01-48-87-82-35
6ᵉ | 130, bd St-Germain (Odéon) | 01-46-34-66-31
8ᵉ | 235-237, rue du Faubourg St-Honoré (Ternes) | 01-44-09-80-00
9ᵉ | 79, bd de Clichy (Place de Clichy) | 01-48-74-42-61
10ᵉ | 42 bis, bd de Bonne Nouvelle (Bonne Nouvelle) | 01-45-23-01-77
11ᵉ | 14, pl de la Bastille (Bastille) | 01-44-75-79-80
14ᵉ | 1, av du Général Leclerc (Denfert-Rochereau) | 01-40-47-60-41
14ᵉ | 72, bd du Montparnasse (Montparnasse-Bienvenüe) |
01-43-35-36-28
14ᵉ | 77, av du Maine (Gaîté) | 01-43-22-50-46
www.indiana-cafe.fr

"So touristy you'd think you actually were in Indiana", this "noisy"
"mass-market version of a French idea of a Western-themed restau-

rant" serves a "tired attempt at Tex-Mex" food (if the "forgetful waitresses" remember how, that is); it'll do "when you're craving a greasy burger and beer" perhaps – "the happy-hour prices are a good deal" – otherwise, leave it "for your concierge's kids."

Indra 🗷 *Indian*

| - | - | - | M |

8ᵉ | 10, rue du Commandant Rivière (St-Philippe-du-Roule) | 01-43-59-46-40 | www.restaurant-indra.com

One of the oldest subcontinental eateries in Paris (established 1976) occupies a primo spot just off the Champs; it serves all the classics – tandoori meats, naan, kulfi – in a traditional, warm-hued setting; but heat-seekers say "the spices they use don't seem as interesting", advising "if it's good Indian food you're after, take the Chunnel train to London."

Isami 🗷🅼 *Japanese*

| 25 | 14 | 16 | €62 |

4ᵉ | 4, quai d'Orléans (Pont-Marie) | 01-40-46-06-97 | www.isami.abemadi.com

"The best sushi in Paris" is the draw at this small (some say "cramped"), "simple" Japanese "with a nice Seine view" of the Ile Saint-Louis; if a few things seem fishy – the "haughty service" and "extremely expensive" tabs – the "good selection of cold sakes" erases any unease; but "come only if you're a serious sushi aficionado, because there's almost nothing else on the menu."

Issé 🗷 *Japanese*

| ▽ 23 | 16 | 22 | €42 |

1ᵉʳ | 45, rue de Richelieu (Palais Royal-Musée du Louvre/Pyramides) | 01-42-96-26-60

From "old favorites" ("possibly the best tempura ever") to "inventive ice creams", the small-plates menu offers "a delectable journey through Japanese cuisine" at this "unusual" Asian in the 1st; "the minimalist Zen decor may leave something to be desired for some, but others will like its clean lines."

Itinéraires 🗷🅼 *Bistro*

| - | - | - | M |

5ᵉ | 5, rue de Pontoise (Maubert-Mutualité) | 01-46-33-60-11

Young chef Sylvain Sendra, who previously cooked at the tiny Le Temps au Temps, has spread his wings since moving to this handsome, ecru-hued spot in the Latin Quarter; Sendra's wife, Sarah, explains the contemporary French bistro menu, which changes almost daily but runs to dishes like beef cheeks poached in red wine and white-chocolate ganache; a very stylish Left Bank crowd of media and fashion types have already added it to their dining itineraries.

🆉 Jacques Cagna 🗷 *Haute Cuisine*

| 26 | 23 | 25 | €107 |

6ᵉ | 14, rue des Grands-Augustins (Odéon/St-Michel) | 01-43-26-49-39 | www.jacques-cagna.com

"Civilized, old-world charm and delicious", classic "Haute Cuisine par excellence" – no wonder "it's like stepping back in time" to visit this "elegant" Saint-Germain stalwart adorned with 17th-century artwork and jacket-clad customers; yes, it's "a bit too expensive", the staff's "a tad snooty" and sentimentalists sob "it's not what it was", but chef-owner Cagna and his sister "put you at ease", visiting each table, and overall, "if you want to pamper yourself, this is the place."

Jadis ⑤ *Classic/New French* | - | - | - | M |

15ᵉ | 208, rue de la Croix Nivert (Boucicaut) | 01-45-57-73-20

Translated as 'in times past', the name of this eatery in a remote corner of the 15th is slightly misleading, because chef Guillaume Delage (ex Gaya) surprises with some dazzlingly original New French creations; but never fear, nostalgists – the menu includes many classics too, served in a Bordeaux-and-gray room adorned with antique advertising posters.

NEW Jamin ⑤ *New French* | - | - | - | M |

16ᵉ | 32, rue de Longchamp (Iéna/Trocadéro) | 01-45-53-00-07 | www.restaurant-jamin.com

No, this new contemporary French table with the same name and at the same address as Joël Robuchon's famous restaurant in the 16th isn't a relaunch of the storied original; instead, restaurateur Alain Pras, an alum of Guy Savoy's erstwhile La Butte Chaillot, has created a low-lit chocolate-brown dining room with contemporary art on the walls, where a well-heeled crowd (including lots of business diners) gathers for chef David Legrand's moderately priced French favorites like sea bass with Thai rice and curried coconut sauce.

Jardin des Cygnes *Classic French* | 22 | 23 | 21 | €81 |

8ᵉ | Hôtel Prince de Galles | 33, av George V (George V) | 01-53-23-78-50 | www.luxurycollection.com

"A classic in a tranquil setting" – a courtyard overlooking a "delightful garden" in the 8th – this hotel restaurant is "perfect for that romantic date"; while "the food simply doesn't match" the ambiance, it's still "very good traditional French cuisine" and supplied by a "gracious staff"; prices are somewhat "pretentious", however.

Jardinier (Le) ⑤ *Bistro* | - | - | - | M |

9ᵉ | 5, rue Richer (Bonne Nouvelle) | 01-48-24-79-79

With pretty Napoleon III decor that includes cast-iron columns, an elaborate chandelier and lavish moldings, this relaxed bistro not far from the Folies Bergère is "a fun place" where young chef-owner Stéphane Fumaz serves up "well-priced creative cuisine" with lots of lovely legumes; Fumaz's friendly wife runs the dining room.

Jardins de Bagatelle (Les) *Classic French* | 17 | 18 | 15 | €56 |

16ᵉ | Parc de Bagatelle | Route de Sèvres (Pont-de-Neuilly) | 01-40-67-98-29

"Wander the rose gardens and then have a leisurely lunch [or dinner] under the trees" – "in spring and summer, this is one of the most romantic places in Paris" say believers in this Bois de Boulogne site; given the "wonderful venue", it's understandable the Classic French "food and service are disappointing" in comparison, but you'll hear few complaints from the cosmopolitan "clientele craving greenery"; better "bring your bank book", though.

	FOOD	DECOR	SERVICE	COST

Jarrasse, l'Ecailler de Paris *Seafood*   - | - | - | E

Neuilly-sur-Seine | 4, av de Madrid (Pont-de-Neuilly) | 01-46-24-07-56 |
www.michelrostang.com

Since chef-restaurateur Michel Rostang took it under his wing three
years ago, this Neuilly veteran has become an "excellent suburban
seafooder", with "nice service" and offbeat decor (Japanese-style
cloth lanterns and velvet banquettes) that's "fair enough"; it's "a little expensive" – but then, so is Neuilly.

Jean ⊠ *New French*   19 | 16 | 19 | €56

9ᵉ | 8, rue St-Lazare (Notre-Dame-de-Lorette) | 01-48-78-62-73 |
www.restaurantjean.fr

The ratings may not reflect the recent kitchen changes at this New
French "owned and managed by a former maître d'hôtel at
Taillevent": young Anthony Boucher, whose résumé includes
Pierre Gagnaire, now helms the stove, while an alumna of NYC's
Eleven Madison Park, Alison Johnson, performs pastry chef duties;
unchanged is the presence of patron Jean-Frédéric Guidoni, "a su-
perb host", making the place "an unexpected find in an inglorious
neighborhood" (the 9th).

Jean-Paul Hévin ⊠ *Dessert/Tearoom*   24 | 15 | 16 | €26

1ᵉʳ | 231, rue St-Honoré (Madeleine/Tuileries) | 01-55-35-35-96 |
www.jphevin.com

Upstairs from "*chocolatier extraordinaire*" Jean-Paul Hévin's shop
near the Tuileries Gardens is this "lovely tearoom", aka "hot chocolate heaven"; it's "enough to make you rethink any diet", since
"you'll want to have all of the desserts", maybe preceded by a "quick
[bite of] traditional French fare"; there's some grousing about "inconsistent service" and "faded decor", but for most this is "perfect
for a pick-me-up after a morning of shopping" – and, of course, "a
must for any chocoholic."

Je Thé . . . Me ⊠Ⓜ *Classic French*   - | - | - | M

15ᵉ | 4, rue d'Alleray (Convention/Vaugirard) | 01-48-42-48-30 |
www.jetheme.net

"Probably one of the quaintest restaurants in Paris", this "cozy" (ok,
maybe "a little cramped") venue attracts 15th-arrondissement locals with its landmarked locale in a "quirky" old grocery store full of
mirrors, earthenware jugs and bric-a-brac; the "charming" chef-
owner provides "true Classic French fare" that's "well up to standard –
but it's the overall ambiance that's so good" here.

Jeu de Quilles ⊠Ⓜ *Wine Bar/Bistro*   - | - | - | M

14ᵉ | 45, rue Boulard (Mouton-Duvernet) | 01-53-90-76-22

Located next door to star butcher Hugo Desnoyer, who supplies its
excellent meat, this friendly white-painted shopfront *bistrot à vins*
deep in the 14th is an agreeable if out-of-the-way place for an excellent lunch (they're only open for dinner on Thursday and Friday); the
menu changes daily, but runs to first-rate seasonal produce simply
prepared – a salad of organic heirloom tomatoes, followed by
chicken *basquaise* and tarte Tatin is a typical meal.

	FOOD	DECOR	SERVICE	COST

J'Go ◐ *Southwest* ▽ 14 | 14 | 13 | €43

6ᵉ | 3, rue Clément (Mabillon) | 01-43-26-19-02
9ᵉ | 4, rue Drouot (Richelieu-Drouot) | 01-40-22-09-09 🅢
www.lejgo.com

"The atmosphere is all rugby and *corrida* (bull fights)", the twin passions of the French Southwest, at this Toulouse-based "temple to lamb and pork" in the 9th (with a *soeur* in the 6th); even if the service can be "middling", "it's perfect for business at noon, and buddies at night", especially as it's reasonably priced – "but be careful, because the native Southwestern products" can cause the bill to charge.

Joe Allen ◐ *American* 13 | 13 | 16 | €40

1ᵉʳ | 30, rue Pierre Lescot (Etienne Marcel) | 01-42-36-70-13 |
www.joeallenparis.com

With "a somber red-brick interior lined with classic [star's] Hollywood photos", it "feels like NYC's theater district" at this "casual" Les Halles veteran, a virtual "American pied-à-terre in Paris" in terms of clientele and cuisine; it's "best to stick with the basic burgers" and brunches, ignoring the servers who often seem to be "having a bad day" – and while perhaps the whole place "needs to be refreshed", fans wonder "why change a formula that's worked for so long?"

Joséphine "Chez Dumonet" 🅢 *Bistro* 23 | 16 | 19 | €63

6ᵉ | 117, rue du Cherche-Midi (Duroc/Falguière) |
01-45-48-52-40

"Like walking into a period-set piece" – full of beveled glass dividers and brass gas jets that are "truly old Paris" – this veteran in the 6th offers "great preparations of bistro classics", from "excellent confit de canard to Grand Marnier soufflé", with the welcome innovation of "huge" half portions for many dishes; supporters don't even mind that "prices have skyrocketed", because there's "not many of these left."

🅩 Jules Verne (Le) *Haute Cuisine* 22 | 26 | 24 | €203

7ᵉ | Tour Eiffel | Ave Gustave Eiffel, Champ de Mars, 2nd level
(Ecole Militaire/Varenne) | 01-45-55-61-44 |
www.lejulesverne-paris.com

Globe-trotting gastronaut "Alain Ducasse had taken over, but hadn't yet put his stamp" on Paris' favorite room-with-a-view when our survey closed; but initial reports praise designer Patrick Jouin's low-lit, "futuristic, yet swank" space done in camel and black, and a staff that's "attentive", "without being condescending (even when my husband mistook the sommelier for the waiter)"; while "certainly good", the updated Classic French food doesn't live up to "the hype" and is "extremely expensive"; "but ultimately, you go for the view" from this Eiffel Tower perch – it's "like floating on a cloud, watching the city unfold in front of you."

Juvéniles 🅢 *Wine Bar/Bistro* 16 | 13 | 19 | €35

1ᵉʳ | 47, rue de Richelieu (Bourse/Palais Royal-Musée du Louvre) |
01-42-97-46-49

"The food is fine, and the wine's divine" at this "scruffy but atmospheric" *bar à vins* in the 1st, where there are just enough

Eclectic eats to provide ballast for the "beautiful selection of bottles from all over the world"; all unfolds under the "watchful eye of the owner", a "quick-quipping" Scot, who supplies samples for all you "sherry aficionados."

Kai 🅱🅼 *Japanese*   - | - | - | E

1er | 18, rue du Louvre (Louvre-Rivoli) | 01-40-15-01-99

"Expensive and classy, this Japanese place" not far from the Louvre remains rather confidential, but those in-the-know say it offers "great food": "from the presentation to the textures, every dish is a little surprise, and the Pierre Hermé desserts are to die for"; the "accommodating service" caters to the "fashion crowd" within the "small space."

Kaïten ●🅱 *Japanese*   - | - | - | E

8e | 63, rue Pierre Charron (Franklin D. Roosevelt) | 01-43-59-78-78 | www.kaiten.fr

Some of "the best sushi we've had in Paris" is on hand at this countertop just off the Champs-Elysées; true, prices veer toward the "expensive", but it's "useful for noonday" lunch, the "staff is quick and efficient", and there's "the all-important conveyor belt to keep the kids amused."

Kambodgia 🅱 *SE Asian*   - | - | - | M

16e | 15, rue de Bassano (Charles de Gaulle-Etoile/George V) | 01-47-20-41-22 | www.kambodgia.com

"Reminiscent of an opium den" in its vaguely louche, "dark" decor, this "beautiful" basement in the 16th arrondissement offers a chance to sample some of "Southeast Asia's best" cuisines, mainly of the Cambodian and Vietnamese variety; some find the prices for the "highbrow" cooking higher than usual, but most just enjoy the "romantic venue."

Karl et Erich 🅱🅼 *New French*   - | - | - | E

17e | 20, rue de Tocqueville (Villiers) | 01-42-27-03-71

The twin brothers – one in the kitchen, the other in the dining room – who ran the late Les Jumeaux have crossed town to the 17th and set up shop in a sleek, very contemporary loftlike space; not many surveyors have made the move with them, but the few who have laud the "inventive" New French fare.

🆕 KGB 🅱🅼 *Bistro/Eclectic*   - | - | - | M

6e | 25, rue des Grands-Augustins (Odéon) | 01-46-33-00-85 | www.zekitchen-galerie.fr

Following on the success of Ze Kitchen Galerie, his world-food bistro, chef William Ledeuil has opened this sleek, gallery-like annex down the street, with a striking almost-all-white interior setting off colored Plexiglas inserts and modern art; the menu is shorter and less expensive than at the mother ship, but the intriguing East-meets-West cooking for which Ledeuil is so popular – dishes like panko-coated shrimp-and-chicken croquettes with piquillo ketchup – has made it an immediate and rather noisy success.

Khun Akorn ⓜ *Thai*

FOOD	DECOR	SERVICE	COST
-	-	-	M

11ᵉ | 8, av de Taillebourg (Nation) | 01-43-56-20-03

"On the edge of the 11th, Bangkok opens its arms to you" at this "authentic" Thai with "pretty", "exotic decor" (regulars "try for the rooftop terrace in summer"); but even those who deem the cuisine "delicious" for its "truly spicy" flavors castigate the servers, who seem so "indifferent" "that we laughed out loud in disbelief."

Kifune ⓩ ⓜ *Japanese*

FOOD	DECOR	SERVICE	COST
-	-	-	E

17ᵉ | 44, rue St-Ferdinand (Porte Maillot) | 01-45-72-11-19

"Tops in tuna", this Japanese in the 17th remains the hidden favorite of fin fans in search of authenticity and "exquisite raw fish"; service can be a bit brusque, and it's not cheap, but you put up with these shortcomings when you've got "one of the capital's best sushi bars."

NEW Kiku ⓩ *Japanese*

FOOD	DECOR	SERVICE	COST
-	-	-	M

9ᵉ | 56, rue Richer (Cadet/Grands Boulevards) | 01-44-83-02-30

After stints in Tokyo, Sydney and London, Japanese chef Kyoichi Kai has opened this Franco-Japanese table not far from the Folies Bergère in the 9th; its little dining room with walls trimmed in finely cut flagstone has found an instant following among office workers at noon and couples out for a good time in the evening, all drawn by the delicate cooking, e.g. salmon carpaccio with sesame oil, yuzu and soy sauce; an environmentally conscious philosophy adds to its appeal.

Kim Anh ⓜ *Vietnamese*

FOOD	DECOR	SERVICE	COST
-	-	-	E

15ᵉ | 51, av Emile Zola (Charles Michels) | 01-45-79-40-96

Its "menu doesn't change", but since the "nice owners" serve "some of the best Vietnamese cuisine in the city, year in and year out", positives "have no problem" with the "refined food" at this 15th-arrondissement "Zen setting for a romantic date"; "however, it is more expensive than expected."

Kinugawa ⓩ *Japanese*

FOOD	DECOR	SERVICE	COST
23	13	19	€73

1ᵉʳ | 9, rue du Mont-Thabor (Tuileries) | 01-42-60-65-07

Hanawa ⓩ *Japanese*

8ᵉ | 26, rue Bayard (Franklin D. Roosevelt) | 01-56-62-70-70
www.kinugawa-hanawa.com

A big Asian clientele persuades many that this duo of sushi slingers, which also delivers delicate dishes from Kyoto and Tokyo, is "almost as good as what you'll find in Japan" – and certainly among "the best in Paris"; both the "sublime" sashimi and the "excellent" cooked fare are "charmingly served"; "but the prices cut like a samurai's sword", and "the Armani/Zen minimalism" of the decor seems "somewhat corporate in feel"; N.B. sibling Hanawa serves more fusion-y fare – e.g. both Toraya and Jean-Paul Hévin pastries in its tea salon.

Kong ⏺ *Eclectic*

FOOD	DECOR	SERVICE	COST
14	25	14	€55

1ᵉʳ | Pont Neuf Bldg. | 1, rue du Pont-Neuf (Pont-Neuf) | 01-40-39-09-00 | www.kong.fr

"The ambiance may be fantastic" and the "Philippe Starck decor second to none" at this double-decker, "glass-domed, trendy restaurant in the sky" in the 1st, but while it's "an excellent, see-and-be-seen place", the Eclectic Franco-Japanese menu is "only passable" and the staff has "an attitude problem", so "go for the drinks" (like Carrie did in *Sex and the City*), enjoy "the spectacular rooftop view" and move on.

	FOOD	DECOR	SERVICE	COST

Lac-Hong ⚫ *Vietnamese* ▽ 20 | 11 | 16 | €51

16ᵉ | 67, rue Lauriston (Boissière/Victor Hugo) | 01-47-55-87-17

Even if the setting is "modest", the "food is wonderful" at this "not-cheap" Vietnamese in the 16th; service varies from "attentive and professional" to "brusque and disinterested", so you go for the "sublime" cooking instead.

⚫ Ladurée *Classic French/Tearoom* 23 | 24 | 17 | €35

6ᵉ | 21, rue Bonaparte (St-Sulpice) | 01-44-07-64-87

8ᵉ | 16, rue Royale (Concorde/Madeleine) | 01-42-60-21-79

8ᵉ | 75, av des Champs-Elysées (George V) | 01-40-75-08-75 ⚫

9ᵉ | Printemps | 52, bd Haussmann (Havre-Caumartin) | 01-42-82-40-10 ⚫

www.laduree.fr

Dating back to 1862, these "tearooms *extraordinaires*" are "a Paris institution for good reason" – namely, the "best macaroons in the world", plus other "orgasmic sweets", "heavenly hot chocolate" and light eats like a "sophisticated club sandwich"; "refined but not snooty" sums up their atmosphere, especially "at the original Rue Royale location (a great Proustian *patisserie*)"; so the only sour note is the somewhat "brisk" staff, but as the "chic Parisiennes" say, "when you go to Ladurée, it feels like everything will be all right."

Ladurée Le Bar ⚫ *Eclectic* - | - | - | M

8ᵉ | 13, rue Lincoln (George V) | 01-40-75-38-25 | www.laduree.com

The historic tearoom branches out with this swanky venue adjacent to its longstanding Champs-Elysées address; dominated by a large, undulating, neon-lit bar with cobweb-backed stools, it serves a day-long menu of Eclectic savories that includes organic egg dishes, blini and salads, along with a wicked choice of cocktails and, of course, a tempting selection of sweets.

Laiterie Sainte Clotilde (La) ⚫⚫ *Bistro* - | - | - | M

7ᵉ | 64, rue de Bellechasse (Solférino) | 01-45-51-74-61

An edgy mix of Science Po students, ministry employees and ladies who lunch have made this reasonably priced canteen a hit; the chalkboard menu – basic bistro with some Med and Asian flourishes – changes daily, but is big on soups and grilled meats; service is relaxed but well mannered, as befits the well-bred 7th.

Languedoc (Le) *Southwest* - | - | - | M

5ᵉ | 64, bd de Port-Royal (Les Gobelins/Glacieres) | 01-47-07-24-47

Apparently "unchanged for 30 years", this "mom-and-pop operation" in the 5th still delights with "dependable" dishes of "authentic Southwestern food", particularly from the namesake region; while the digs are "small enough to have the owner's dog under your legs", the "portions are generous" and the "staff good-humored"; best of all, it's as "reasonable" as it is "reliable."

Lao Lane Xang *Asian*

-	-	-	M

13ᵉ | 102, av d'Ivry (Tolbiac) | 01-58-89-00-00

Coming from a family of restaurateurs, brothers Ken and Do Siackhasone have a hit on their hands with this sleekly designed restaurant that forsakes the Asian decorative clichés common to most in Paris' largest Asian neighborhood for a look that's more Malibu than Indochine; the moderately priced menu covers Thailand, Vietnam, Laos and Cambodia, and the kitchen's compass is authenticity – to wit, spices are not toned down for timid French palates.

Lao Siam ● *Thai*

15	9	11	€26

19ᵉ | 49, rue de Belleville (Belleville/Pyrénées) | 01-40-40-09-68

"For nearly 30 years", this "amusing" Asian has lured believers up to Belleville for "a large choice" of Thai and Laotian dishes; true, the "kitschy" decor "needs some serious refreshing" and the service can be "mediocre, because it's always so crowded"; even so, almost everyone agrees it offers a "great bang for the buck."

Lao Tseu *Chinese*

-	-	-	M

7ᵉ | 209, bd St-Germain (Rue du Bac) | 01-45-48-30-06

When craving "a taste of authentic Chinese in Paris", regulars – including philosopher Bernard-Henri Lévy – make tracks to this tri-level veteran; along with the "thoughtfully prepared" fare, an "atmosphere of neighborhood friendliness" prevails; best of all, it's "reasonably priced, considering the location" in swanky Saint-Germain.

❷ Lapérouse ⊠ *Haute Cuisine*

21	27	24	€108

6ᵉ | 51, quai des Grands-Augustins (Pont-Neuf/St-Michel) | 01-43-26-90-14 | www.restaurantlaperouse.com

"Wonderfully romantic", this Seine-side "Paris landmark" is "a beautiful throwback" to the 18th century, with plush "old-world" decor ("check out the upstairs assignation rooms", private dining salons where the scratches on the mirrors were reportedly made by ladies verifying the veracity of offered gems); the "traditional" Haute Cuisine "has its ups and downs" but is "fine" overall, and – as befits the *amour*-oriented ambiance – the "service is attentive, but not intrusive"; P.S. "the prix fixe lunch is an elegant bargain."

L'Assaggio ⊠ *Italian*
(fka Il Cortile)

23	20	20	€76

1ᵉʳ | Hôtel Castille Paris | 37, rue Cambon (Concorde/Madeleine) | 01-44-58-45-67

Chef Vittorio Beltramelli, a lieutenant of renowned Milanese toque Gualtiero Marchesi, mans this recently redubbed hotel dining room in the 1st, and fans applaud his "delectable", "inventive" Italian cuisine; in summer, "try for the outside courtyard and view the lovely fountain" – it'll distract from the service that swings from "sublime" to "exasperatingly slow"; N.B. closed weekends.

	FOOD	DECOR	SERVICE	COST

☑ **Lasserre** ☒ *Haute Cuisine* — 27 | 28 | 28 | €153

8ᵉ | 17, av Franklin D. Roosevelt (Franklin D. Roosevelt) | 01-43-59-02-13 | www.restaurant-lasserre.com

Experience "elegance personified" at this "old-world" "orchid-filled" establishment in the 8th; combining "great classics with innovations", chef Jean-Louis Nomicos' "brilliant" Haute Cuisine bags bushels of compliments, as does the "flawless" staff, but the real raves are for the "fabulously '60s" technical touches, "from the James Bond entrance by the mini-lift" to the "unique open roof" (it's the "best topless place in town!"); "it all adds up to one magical evening for which you'll pay – but without the sense of being robbed."

☑ **Laurent** ☒ *Haute Cuisine* — 24 | 26 | 23 | €139

8ᵉ | 41, av Gabriel (Champs-Elysées-Clémenceau) | 01-42-25-00-39 | www.le-laurent.com

"If you're looking for a romantic garden in the middle of Paris, this is it" crow converts of this "elegant" pavilion on the edge of the Champs; while the "traditional" Haute Cuisine and service "shine", several say they're "not as good as the prices would indicate"; still, this is "where the movers and shakers have lunch" ("better lunch than dinner") – because "it's tough to beat dining on the patio on a spring" day.

Lavinia ☒ *Classic French* — 17 | 17 | 18 | €39

1ᵉʳ | 3-5, bd de la Madeleine (Madeleine) | 01-42-97-20-20 | www.lavinia.fr

"Just steps from the Madeleine", "plunge into a universe of wine" at this "impressive" store – 6,500 labels, baby – where you can eat "surrounded by gleaming bottles" amid an "atmosphere of wine geeks and social butterflies"; while "good", the Classic French fare is "a little pricey for what it is, considering the wait time before getting served", but "who cares about the food or service – what you care about here is the vino"; best of all, "any bottle in the shop is available in the restaurant at the retail price"; P.S. "lunch only" (sandwiches and charcuterie until 8 PM).

Legrand Filles et Fils ☒ *Wine Bar/Bistro* — - | - | - | M

2ᵉ | Galerie Vivienne | 1, rue de la Banque (Bourse/Palais Royal-Musée du Louvre) | 01-42-60-07-12 | www.caves-legrand.com

"Don't tell everyone – this is still a reasonably well-kept secret" plead patrons of this *bar à vins*, "a great little place for a quick snack and a glass of one of the outstanding wines served by the legendary shop" Caves Legrand; "sitting at this casual spot, you know you are in Paris" – "atmospheric Old Paris" to be exact – since it's located "in one of the city's most beautiful" arcades, the glass-roofed Galerie Vivienne.

Lei *Italian* — ▽ 21 | 24 | 18 | €49

7ᵉ | 17, av de la Motte-Pìcquet (Ecole Militaire/La Tour-Maubourg) | 01-47-05-07-37

"A hit with the fashion crowd in the 7th", this "modern Italian" with sleek, stone-paneled decor "has made a lot of progress" since it opened seven years ago; some aspects can be "a bit expensive", but "stick to the tagliata and you'll never go wrong."

	FOOD	DECOR	SERVICE	COST

Léon de Bruxelles *Belgian*
| 16 | 10 | 14 | €29 |

1er | 120, rue Rambuteau (Les Halles) | 01-42-36-18-50
4^e | 3, bd Beaumarchais (Bastille) | 01-42-71-75-55 ☾
6^e | 131, bd St-Germain (Mabillon/Odéon) | 01-43-26-45-95 ☾
8^e | 63, av des Champs-Elysées (Franklin D. Roosevelt/George V) |
01-42-25-96-16 ☾
9^e | 8, pl de Clichy (Place de Clichy) | 01-48-74-00-43 ☾
11^e | 8, pl de la République (République) | 01-43-38-28-69 ☾
14^e | 82 bis, bd du Montparnasse (Edgar Quinet/
Montparnasse-Bienvenüe) | 01-43-21-66-62 ☾
17^e | 95, bd Gouvion-St-Cyr (Porte Maillot) | 01-55-37-95-30 ☾
www.leon-de-bruxelles.fr

"All mussels, all the time" is the mantra at this "bustling" bevy of Belgians that bring out bucketfuls of bivalves, "lots of beer" and "all-you-can-eat frites"; "the service is indifferent and the decor far from inspiring" (unless you like that "plastic-y" "family restaurant look"), but "for what it is, a cheap chain with a theme, it's not bad at all."

Lescure ⓩ *Bistro*
| 17 | 12 | 16 | €37 |

1er | 7, rue de Mondovi (Concorde) | 01-42-60-18-91
Unless "you're shy, it's impossible not to enjoy yourself with a variety of strangers, both local and tourist, when you're packed in family-style" at this 1st-arrondissement "hole-in-the-wall" with rustic decor (is that "garlic and onions hanging from the ceiling"?); it's been serving the same "tried-and-trusted French bistro fare" since 1919 at a "remarkable value"; yes, it's "too small, too loud and the food's average – but it's absolutely charming" anyway.

Libre Sens ☽ *Classic French*
| - | - | - | E |

8^e | 33, rue Marbeuf (Franklin D. Roosevelt/George V) | 01-53-96-00-72 |
www.groupe-bertrand.com

Perhaps the "trendy decor", including an Op Art '70s cognac bar and a room with a red velvet bed for supine supping, is more of a hit than the Classic French fare at this "happening place" just off the Champs; still, fans praise the "compose-your-own salad" menu, and while some say it's "just for lunch", it gets "quite busy late in the evening" too.

Lina's *Sandwiches*
| 16 | 10 | 12 | €16 |

2^e | 50, rue Etienne Marcel (Bourse/Etienne Marcel) | 01-42-21-16-14 ☒
7^e | 22, rue des Sts-Pères (St-Germain-des-Prés) | 01-40-20-42-78 ☒
8^e | 61, rue Pierre Charron (Franklin D. Roosevelt/George V) |
01-45-63-70-20 ☒
8^e | 8, rue Marbeuf (Alma Marceau) | 01-46-23-04-63 ☒
9^e | 30, bd des Italiens (Opéra/Richelieu-Drouot) | 01-42-46-02-06 ☒
12^e | 102, rue de Bercy (Bercy) | 01-43-40-42-42 ☒
16^e | 116, av Kléber (Trocadéro) | 01-47-27-28-28
17^e | 23, av de Wagram (Charles de Gaulle-Etoile/Ternes) |
01-45-74-76-76 ☒
Neuilly-sur-Seine | 156, av Charles de Gaulle (Pont-de-Neuilly) |
01-47-45-60-60 ☒
www.linascafe.fr

"While shopping and schlepping", this string of "American-style sandwich/salad shops" makes a "good pit stop", offering "simple, dependable" "fast food with a human face"; but cynics say it's "not super-exciting" and warn "watch out – all of the extras add up", so that a seemingly "affordable" meal can turn "surprisingly expensive."

Liza *Lebanese*
24 | 24 | 20 | €45

2ᵉ | 14, rue de la Banque (Bourse) | 01-55-35-00-66 | www.restaurant-liza.com

"What a nice surprise", a place that "looks, tastes and sounds like modern Lebanon" enthuse the many fans of "charming" Liza Soughayar's "amazing restaurant" on a "quiet street" in the 2nd; the decor is "stunning", the food "interesting and original" – think "Lebanese nouvelle cuisine" – and the service is "good", and best of all the prices are reasonable, aside from the "expensive wines."

Loir dans la Théière (Le) *Dessert/Tearoom*
16 | 15 | 13 | €24

4ᵉ | 3, rue des Rosiers (St-Paul) | 01-42-72-90-61

"Ideal for brunch and snacks", this tearoom in the Marais is "warm and cozy", with a bobo vibe – "like the edgy arty neighborhoods in New York" – and has "nice, if inefficient", service; given all this, plus the "affordable" tabs, you'll have to "get past the crowds to bag a table."

Lô Sushi ● *Japanese*
15 | 13 | 12 | €40

8ᵉ | 8, rue de Berri (Franklin D. Roosevelt/George V) | 01-45-62-01-00 | www.losushi.com

Fans of "sushi on the fly" can "watch the chefs preparing dishes and sending them down the conveyor belt along the edge of the counter-top seating" at this "temple of techno-Zen" in the 8th, which boasts "TVs to keep you entertained"; while "inventive", the rolls are only "remotely Japanese", and "expensive", given they're "not the best"; still, they're "quite popular, especially with the lunch crowd."

Louchebem (Le) ●🅱 *Steak*
15 | 12 | 12 | €37

1ᵉʳ | 31, rue Berger (Châtelet-Les Halles) | 01-42-33-12-99 | www.le-louchebem.fr

With "a pretty view of the church of Saint-Eustache" (focus on that, because "the interior is design-challenged"), this "butcher's shop-turned-restaurant" "is a place to go for grills and [old] Les Halles ambiance"; "fine dining it ain't, but if you're not too proud to queue for a table, there's nothing pretentious about the excellent-value steaks."

Louis Vin (Le) ⌿ *Wine Bar/Bistro*
19 | 16 | 17 | €47

5ᵉ | 9, rue de la Montagne Ste-Genevieve (Maubert-Mutualité) | 01-43-29-12-12 | www.fifi.fr

Reviewers raise a toast to this "reliable *bistrot à vins*, with an ever-changing menu" of "traditional French" fare and – *bien sûr* – a "good selection of wines"; "service can be uneven", but "the owner likes chatting with his patrons, which is always pleasant"; P.S. "FYI: cash only."

Lozère (La) 🅱Ⓜ *Auvergne*
▽ 18 | 11 | 19 | €27

6ᵉ | 4, rue Hautefeuille (St-Michel) | 01-43-54-26-64 | www.lozere-a-paris.com

"Simple", "delicious cuisine from a lesser-known region" – Lozère in the south – delights reviewers who are into "robust" eats and "rustic" scenes; "now that everyone knows about it", its "narrow" quarters get "crowded" ("reservations are a must") but it's "in a convenient location" in the 6th, and "what's more, it's not expensive"; P.S. "the Thursday night special is a great treat" – a creamy, cheesy mashed potato dish, *aligot*.

Luna (La) ☒ *Seafood*

17	13	13	€56

8ᵉ | 69, rue du Rocher (Europe/Villiers) | 01-42-93-77-61 | www.restaurant-laluna.fr

Surveyors split over this veteran seafooder hidden in a small street behind the Gare Saint-Lazare: though stalwarts insist it "deserves its reputation as one of the best fish places in Paris", a Food score slide supports a sense of "drop in quality" – or perhaps the place just seems "overpriced" given that "the physical characteristics are pretty ordinary" and the "service leaves something to be desired"; still, few deny the dishes are "delicate and original", with "wonderfully fresh" catch.

Lup (Le) ●☒☒☒ *Eclectic*

–	–	–	E

6ᵉ | 2-4, rue Sabot (St-Germain-des-Prés) | 01-45-48-86-47 | www.lelup.com

Tucked away in a tiny street, this after-hours venue renews the famous nightlife vibe of Saint-Germain, with late hours, nightly entertainment, exotic cocktails and an Eclectic, offbeat snacking menu that runs from risotto with shrimp to crab and mango salad, served up in a mirrored, bordello-red setting.

☒ Lyonnais (Aux) ☒☒ *Lyon*

21	19	19	€57

2ᵉ | 32, rue St-Marc (Bourse/Richelieu-Drouot) | 01-42-96-65-04 | www.alain-ducasse.com

Sure, the "Alain Ducasse name brings in the crowds" to this veteran in the 2nd – but they stay for the "subtle twists on classic Lyonnais cooking", like "a delicious pig's foot and foie gras starter", and the "wonderful atmosphere" of the tiled 1900-vintage dining room; cynics say "it's become a victim of its own success" (other bistros "are half the price and better foodwise"), but positives proclaim "it's a perfect Lyon *bouchon*" – "cramped" conditions, "surly servers" and all.

Ma Bourgogne ●☒⇗ *Burgundy*

18	18	16	€40

4ᵉ | 19, pl des Vosges (Bastille/St-Paul) | 01-42-78-44-64 | www.mabourgogne.com

"Even by Paris standards, the setting under the arches of the Place des Vosges is unique", which is why this "bistro is a must" "on beautiful days"; be advised, though, that the "service is brusque" and the "simply good, not exceptional" Burgundian–Classic French "food is heavy in the warmer months" (the key time to go); so some say it's "best for a coffee and croissant" before "the crowds make it crazy."

Macéo ☒ *Classic/New French*

23	21	21	€64

1ᵉʳ | 15, rue des Petits-Champs (Bourse/Palais Royal-Musée du Louvre) | 01-42-97-53-85 | www.maceorestaurant.com

"Run by Mark Williamson of Willi's Wine Bar", this more formal eatery behind the Palais-Royal offers an "agreeable", "interesting" combination of Classic and New French flavors, plus a "good vege-tarian menu for those looking" and, of course, a "handpicked wine list that can't be beat"; "happy, helpful waiters" wander the wood-paneled, "bright, spacious" setting, with "tables set apart enough for real conversation."

Magnolias (Les) 🗷 Ⓜ *New French*

▽ 25 | 21 | 21 | €72

Perreux-sur-Marne | 48, av de Bry (Nogent-le-Perreux RER) | 01-48-72-47-43 | www.lesmagnolias.com

The "astonishing creativity" of chef-owner Jean Chauvel makes it "well worth the cab ride" to suburban Perreux-sur-Marne and his "magical" New French establishment, a parquet-floored dining room with "pretty decorations" and well-spaced tables; occasion-ally the food gets "a bit too out there (we couldn't even figure out how to consume one amuse-bouche)" – but most surveyors salute this "superb address", with "rather reasonable prices for such" "brilliantly presented" eats.

Maharajah (Le) ◐ *Indian*

▽ 17 | 12 | 18 | €29

5ᵉ | 72, bd St-Germain (Maubert-Mutualité/St-Michel) | 01-43-54-26-07 | www.maharajah.fr

"One of the first Indian restaurants in Paris", this Latin Quarter stalwart curries mixed sentiments from surveyors; some find their northern regional fare "delicious", while skeptics say sari, it's just "ordinary"; but there's no denying "it's one of the best, value-for-money–wise."

Mai Do Ⓜ *Vietnamese*

– | – | – | M

6ᵉ | 23, bd du Montparnasse (Duroc) | 01-45-48-54-60

With a stylish new look that surprises anyone who remembers it as a nondescript Indochinese hole-in-the-wall, this small, friendly, modestly priced Vietnamese veteran not far from the Gare Montparnasse has become a Left Bank word-of-mouth favorite among fans of pho, green papaya and beef salad, carmelized pork and other Viet specialties.

Main d'Or (La) ◐🗷 *Corsica*

– | – | – | M

11ᵉ | 133, rue du Faubourg St-Antoine (Ledru-Rollin) | 01-44-68-04-68

"A pleasant surprise in an out-of-the-way spot" sums up this "spicily marvelous", "genuine Corsican" near the Bastille; the personnel's "very solicititous" too, so that even if this millstone-and-wrought-iron dining room is a little spartan, a meal here is a guaranteed good time, especially given the "fair prices."

Maison Blanche ◐ *New French*

20 | 24 | 18 | €102

8ᵉ | 15, av Montaigne (Alma Marceau) | 01-47-23-55-99 | www.maison-blanche.fr

Though its "cutting-edge" menu was designed by "two brothers with excellent culinary" credentials (the Pourcel twins of Montpellier's acclaimed Le Jardin des Sens), it's the "wonderful location" atop Avenue Montaigne, with "fantastic" Eiffel Tower views, that makes this "white-on-white" New French "an amazing place to [see and] be seen" for fashionistas and "terminally trendy" types; *hélas,* cynics snap that a sense of "style over substance" applies to everything else, from the "variable" food to the "uninvolved" servers.

Maison Courtine (La) ☒ *Southwest*   ▽ 24 | 16 | 21 | €57

14ᵉ | 157, av du Maine (Mouton-Duvernet) | 01-45-43-08-04 | www.lamaisoncourtine.com

There's no ducking the fact that the Southwestern French food – including "a *magret de canard* for an army" – can be "really excellent" at this "modern" mainstay in Montparnasse; "gracious service", a "pleasant setting" and relatively "reasonable prices" (given the quality of the cuisine) add up to "a winner" say the few who have found it.

Maison de l'Amérique   ▽ 18 | 28 | 18 | €75
Latine ☒ *Classic French*

7ᵉ | 217, bd St-Germain (Solférino) | 01-49-54-75-10 | www.mal217.org

With "a great garden in a great location", this "lively" Classic French in a 7th-arrondissement mansion is a fine choice when a breath of fresh air is essential; the cuisine's "good, if not exciting" and the interior "lacks personality", so "go mostly for the setting and sit" outdoors; N.B. dinner May–September only.

Maison du Caviar (La) ● *Russian*   ▽ 22 | 14 | 19 | €109

8ᵉ | 21, rue Quentin-Bauchart (George V) | 01-47-23-53-43 | www.caviar-volga.com

"Good caviar and even better vodka" make an unbeatable combination at this luxurious Russian in the silk-stocking 8th arrondissement; it's a "bustling scene with global socialites" dining on "decadent meals" that include Soviet specialties and an "excellent crab salad"; perhaps the vaguely art deco decor could use "rethinking", but ambiance enough is provided by all the beautiful "people putting on a show"; as to price – well, that depends "on how much caviar you consume."

Maison du Jardin (La) ☒ *Bistro*   24 | 19 | 23 | €43

6ᵉ | 27, rue de Vaugirard (Rennes/St-Placide) | 01-45-48-22-31

This "true gem" "near the Luxembourg Gardens" is a "favorite little" bistro for "remarkable" New French food served by "dedicated", "personable" people in a "cozy" dining room; the fact that it offers "excellent value for money" also makes it "one to recommend", even if many beg to "keep it secret."

Maison Prunier ☒ *Seafood*   21 | 20 | 19 | €77

16ᵉ | 16, av Victor Hugo (Charles de Gaulle-Etoile) | 01-44-17-35-85 | www.prunier.com

"Landmarked for its decor" – "gorgeous art deco rooms" below and a "lavish" Russian salon above – this long-running seafooder in the 16th is "still a treasure" for its "classic" but "irreproachable" *fruits de mer,* smoked salmon and caviar and service that's "professional", if *un peu* "pompous"; and while many mutter it's "too expensive" given the increasingly limited offerings, it's still "cheaper than a round trip to the seaside."

Mama Shelter ● *Brasserie*

	-	-	-	E

20ᵉ | Mama Shelter | 109, rue de Bagnolet (Gambetta/Porte de Bagnolet) | 01-43-48-48-48 | www.mamashelter.com

Those seeking shelter of a chic variety might well find it in this off-the-beaten-path hotel restaurant, fashioned out of a 20th-arrondissement parking garage by Philippe Starck; the self-styled 'urban kibbutz' decor boasts several witty touches, from black Eiffel Tower end-table lamps to curtains printed with photos of smiling faces, while the eclectic French brasserie menu is designed by chef Alain Senderens; as the involvement of such boldface names suggest, the final tab will not come cheap.

Mandalay (Le) ⊠ *Eclectic*

	-	-	-	M

Levallois-Perret | 35, rue Carnot (Anatole France/Louise Michel) | 01-47-57-68-69

Chef-owner Guy Guenego's Eclectic "exotic cuisine, full of flavors and fragrances" from around the world, makes this modest place worth the trek to quiet suburban Levallois-Perret; the tables are a tad "tight" in the colorful dining room with African-Asian "ethnic decor", but the "welcome is warm" and the prices are reasonable.

Mansouria ⊠ *Moroccan*

	22	18	20	€42

11ᵉ | 11, rue Faidherbe (Faidherbe-Chaligny) | 01-43-71-00-16

One of "the top Moroccans in Paris – and it shows" say surveyors of this "wonderful" eatery with a "well-priced, lengthy menu" and "fun waiters"; "in between the food and decor, it transports you straight to North Africa" – doubtless a better place to be than its "lost location" near the Bastille.

Marée (La) *Seafood*

	23	19	21	€110

8ᵉ | 1, rue Daru (Courcelles/Ternes) | 01-43-80-20-00 | www.lamaree.fr

For nearly 50 years this "haute" seafooder in the 8th has hooked politicians and other big *poissons* with "fish of the highest quality", prepared in both classic and "inventive" ways, not to mention "incredible desserts" and "professional service"; there are a few who feel that "it's no longer the world-class experience it used to be", but they should know that it recently changed owners (post-Survey) and its "classical" decor with mirrors and tapestries has been revamped.

Marée Denfert (La) *Seafood*

	-	-	-	E

14ᵉ | 83, av Denfert-Rochereau (Denfert-Rochereau) | 01-43-54-99-86

Marée Passy (La) *Seafood*

16ᵉ | 71, av Paul Doumer (La Muette/Trocadéro) | 01-45-04-12-81 www.lamareepassy.com

Fearless fish lovers wade deep into the 14th or 16th for a first-rate feed at these trendy, "pricey but excellent" seafooders; decked out with bright-red furnishings and nautical artifacts, they're landing an arty crowd with its catch-of-the-day menu, friendly staff and seven-days-a-week service; "don't miss the baba au rhum dessert."

Marée de Versailles (La) 🗷 Ⓜ *Seafood*   19 | 18 | 18 | €44

Versailles | 22, rue au Pain (Versailles-Rive Droite RER) | 01-30-21-73-73 |
www.restaurantlamaree.com

It's always high tide at this Versailles seafooder, which keeps its
many fans aboard its yachtlike, wood-paneled dining room with
the "very freshest", luxe fish (lobster, etc.) used in "creative recipes"; a "warm welcome" and "lovely" terrace also make this a
great place to drop anchor, and if it's not cheap, at least "you get
your money's worth."

Mariage Frères   *Dessert/Tearoom*   21 | 22 | 20 | €31

4ᵉ | 30, rue du Bourg-Tibourg (Hôtel-de-Ville) | 01-42-72-28-11
6ᵉ | 13, rue des Grands-Augustins (St-Michel) | 01-40-51-82-50
8ᵉ | 260, rue du Faubourg St-Honoré (Ternes) | 01-46-22-18-54
www.mariagefreres.com

A "temple of tea" with three "shrines" in the city, this "divine time
warp" has a "colonial ambiance" "straight out of the movie *Indochine*" –
right down to the "solicitous" waiters "in spotless white jackets";
even the "couture prices" don't deter the lines at the door for "refined" lunches and brunch, "heavenly" cakes and an "extraordinary
selection" of brews "from the far reaches of the world" with "heady
aromas" and "names that make you dream."

Marius 🗷 *Seafood*   18 | 13 | 17 | €57

16ᵉ | 82, bd Murat (Porte de St-Cloud) | 01-46-51-67-80

The "regular" clientele of "locals" from the 16th ensures this "classic" seafooder is "always almost full"; for more than two decades it's
reeled 'em in with "delicious" shellfish of "exceptional freshness"
and a whale of a bouillabaisse; customers also commend the "affordable" prices and "agreeable terrace in summer."

Marius et Janette ● *Seafood*   25 | 18 | 20 | €96

8ᵉ | 4, av George V (Alma Marceau) | 01-47-23-84-36 |
www.mariusetjanette.com

Maybe it's "way too expensive" ("bring your banker – you'll need
him"), and the "extreme nautical decor" is a bit much, but "the
fish is superbly prepared" at this old-timer, "one of the better seafood houses" in Paris; if the clientele's "slightly snobbish" (reflecting the stylish address in the 8th), the service is "surprisingly
warm"; however, it does get "crowded and noisy", so try to snag a
terrace table in summer, with its enviable "view of the Eiffel Tower"
across the Seine.

Market ● *Eclectic*   22 | 23 | 19 | €74

8ᵉ | 15, av Matignon (Champs-Elysées-Clémenceau) | 01-56-43-40-90 |
www.jean-georges.com

"Hip and happening", chef-restaurateur Jean-Georges Vongerichten's
Paris outpost has "cool, modern" "Manhattan-like" decor (a bit
"me-too minimalist" some snipe) and an equally "chic" "Asian-
inspired" Eclectic menu; if "not his best", it's still "high-quality", and
highly "popular with the young and trendy, and businesspeople"
"who don't want to get fat"; it's "not cheap, but you can't expect a

bargain, considering the location" "just off the Champs"; P.S. while "often reported as cold", the service "flows with grace" – and upward, as a higher score attests.

Marlotte (La) *Classic French*

| 16 | 12 | 15 | €44 |

6ᵉ | 55, rue du Cherche-Midi (Sèvres-Babylone/St-Placide) | 01-45-48-86-79 | www.lamarlotte.com

Ratings may not fully reflect that a team from La Bastide Odéon has taken over this long-running "neighborhood place" near the Bon Marché; the freshened digs host basically the same "unoriginal" but "fine traditional French food" ("don't miss the lentil salad") brought by "slow" but "sociable" servers; prices continue to be "affordable."

Martel (Le) ● ☒ *Classic French/Moroccan*

| – | – | – | M |

10ᵉ | 3, rue Martel (Château d'Eau) | 01-47-70-67-56

"Hang with the fashionistas" at the "hippest couscous joint in the city", where owner Mehdi Gana, ex-waiter at Chez Omar, has created a hideaway "for non-dieting Parisians with a sense of style" in the shabby-chic 10th; the menu includes Moroccan mainstays, Classic French fare and "a dessert tray that'll kill you", while the "cool" ambiance includes 1900-era bistro decor, soft lighting "and Coleman Hawkins music"; if few know this place, that suits fans just fine – "it's too good to be publicized."

Marty *Brasserie*

| 16 | 17 | 15 | €53 |

5ᵉ | 20, av des Gobelins (Les Gobelins) | 01-43-31-39-51 | www.marty-restaurant.com

"Finally, a brasserie that's a little different" say patrons of this "jovial" family business, opened in the 5th in 1913 and now run by the founders' granddaughter; she's created a "chic" art deco setting where reproductions of works by Picasso and Erté hang on the walls, and her chef creates "flavorful" dishes to accompany the seafood; however, hostiles hiss at the "highish prices" for "smallish portions."

Mascotte (La) ● *Auvergne*

| – | – | – | M |

18ᵉ | 52, rue des Abbesses (Abbesses/Blanche) | 01-46-06-28-15 | www.la-mascotte-montmartre.com

Surveyors seeking a "typical Montmartre place" ("back when Montmartre was the place to be") find it at this "old institution", a family-owned brasserie where locals dig into "superlative oysters" and "fine" Auvergnat fare "with appropriate accompanying alcohols"; "ambiance is guaranteed on Sundays", when "an amazing cast of characters, from little old ladies to local drag queens", congregates.

Mathusalem (Le) ☒ *Bistro*

| – | – | – | M |

16ᵉ | 5 bis, bd Exelmans (Exelmans) | 01-42-88-10-73 | www.restaurant-mathusalem.com

Habitués raise a glass to this "unpretentious" neighborhood bistro named for a six-liter champagne bottle; a "good pick in the depths of the 16th", at lunch it's "packed with media people" from nearby France Télévision, who call it "one of the best buys in the area" for "typical" "filling" Classic French fare and ever-"smiley service."

Matsuri *Japanese*

FOOD	DECOR	SERVICE	COST
14	13	13	€38

1er | 36, rue de Richelieu (Pyramides) | 01-42-61-05-73 Ⓢ
NEW **7e** | 74, rue du Bac (Rue du Bac) | 01-45-49-19-92
NEW **16e** | 119-121, av Victor-Hugo (Victor Hugo) | 01-47-27-00-59 Ⓢ
16^e | 2-4, rue de Passy (Passy) | 01-42-24-96-85
La Défense | Tour Coeur Défense | 70, Esplanade Charles de Gaulle (La Défense) | 01-49-01-27-09
www.matsuri.fr

"Instant sushi gratification" is on offer 365 days a year at this "convivial" chain where the Japanese specialties constantly circle "on a conveyor belt"; it's "practical at lunch", given the guarantee of "extremely fast service from the parading plates"; but skeptics sneer at the "worn-out gimmick", saying the morsels taste "machine-made."

Maupertu (Le) Ⓢ *Classic French*

FOOD	DECOR	SERVICE	COST
21	19	25	€46

7^e | 94, bd de la Tour-Maubourg (Ecole Militaire/La Tour-Maubourg) | 01-45-51-37-96 | www.restaurant-maupertu-paris.com

"With its fantastic view of Les Invalides", it's no wonder tourists and locals alike love this "wonderful neighborhood place"; "to add to the lovely atmosphere", there's an "extremely warm welcome from the gracious, bilingual owner" and staff, who serve "expertly prepared" Classic French fare "at a reasonable price."

Mauzac (Le) *Wine Bar/Bistro*

FOOD	DECOR	SERVICE	COST
-	-	-	M

5^e | 7, rue de l'Abbé de l'Epée (Luxembourg) | 01-46-33-75-22 | www.lemauzac.com

Since the "welcome is warm" and "the wine selection robust", don't let "the awful '70s decor" put you off this "pleasant neighborhood hangout" "on an arbored street" in the Latin Quarter; in between sips, you can "stuff yourself with an assortment of pâté" and other bistro bites; the "small sidewalk terrace is a real plus in nice weather."

Mavrommatis Ⓢ Ⓜ *Greek*

FOOD	DECOR	SERVICE	COST
19	14	16	€48

5^e | 42, rue Daubenton (Censier-Daubenton) | 01-43-31-17-17 | www.mavrommatis.fr

Fans would sail the wine-dark sea to eat at this Hellenic haven, the "best in Paris" for its "traditional Greek food with Cypriot influences" "updated to the 21st century"; the fare's "beautifully presented" in a space that "feels like an old Athenian home" in the 5th; and while the tab strikes some as "above average", most feel it's "justified."

Maxan (Le) Ⓢ *New French*

FOOD	DECOR	SERVICE	COST
-	-	-	E

8^e | 37, rue de Miromesnil (Miromesnil) | 01-42-65-78-60 | www.rest-maxan.com

Young chef Laurent Zajac, who sharpened his skills in several Haute Cuisine havens, goes it alone at this small insider's address "in a ritzy neighborhood" near the Faubourg Saint-Honoré; the funky-"chic" decor – felt strips hanging from the ceiling, plaster dots on the walls – acts as backdrop to the "surprisingly good", inventive New French fare that is "expensive, but a treat" to a clientele ranging from cabinet ministers to fashion designers.

	FOOD	DECOR	SERVICE	COST

Maxim's 🏷🅼 Classic French

`18` `25` `20` `€106`

8ᵉ | 3, rue Royale (Concorde/Madeleine) | 01-42-65-27-94 |
www.maxims-de-paris.com

This Rue Royale venue may be the most "famous French" restaurant
in the world, site of scenes in *Gigi* and countless other films, plays and
books set in belle epoque Paris; *hélas,* "fantasy decor" can't compensate for Classic French "dishes that lack magic", leading most to
moan "the only thing maxim here these days are the prices" ("I
never knew that a $150 green salad existed on God's green earth un-
til I ate here"); at least the "waiters look spiffy" – as you'd better too:
"men are required to wear jacket and tie"; N.B. the arrival of former
Goumard chef Olivier Guyon may outdate the above Food rating.

NEW MBC 🏷 New French

`-` `-` `-` `M`

17ᵉ | 4, rue du Débarcadère (Argentine/Porte Maillot) | 01-45-72-22-55 |
www.gilleschoukroun.com

After closing Angl'Opera, inventive chef Gilles Choukroun remains in
fine form with this herb-loving – the name is short for *'menthe, basil-*
ique, coriandre' – contemporary French arrival with a sleek, loungelike look created with metal mesh room dividers and high stools at a
table d'hôte; its location near the Porte Maillot means it pulls a
business crowd at noon, but in the evening a lively scene unfolds
featuring stylish young locals who turn out for Choukroun's creative
cosmopolitan cooking, e.g. mushroom ravioli in miso broth.

Meating 🏷 Steak

`▽ 17` `11` `14` `€62`

17ᵉ | 122, av de Villiers (Péreire) | 01-43-80-10-10

If "you're hunkering for a big piece of meat [broiled] to perfection",
this Franco-American steakhouse in the 17th is a good steer; however, the traditional Gallic side of the menu is "mediocre" (though
that view doesn't reflect the arrival of an ex-Taillevent chef post-
Survey), and some "arrogant" servers are admonished "don't
forget – the client is king."

Méditerranée (La) Seafood

`21` `21` `19` `€59`

6ᵉ | 2, pl de l'Odéon (Odéon) | 01-43-26-02-30 | www.la-mediterranee.com

"The charming decor with Cocteau drawings" is a big draw at this
"bustling" sixtysomething Classic French "located on a lively inter-
section" in the 6th; while the old-time "dash is gone", it "still serves
good seafood" (don't miss the "real bouillabaisse"), and if the service can be "sullen" sometimes, the "sunny, bright" setting will leave
you "very relaxed" – at least, until you get the check.

Memère Paulette 🏷🅼 Bistro

`-` `-` `-` `M`

2ᵉ | 3, rue Paul Lelong (Bourse) | 01-40-26-12-36

Lavish portions of old-fashioned French bistro food and friendly service characterize this retro venue in the 2nd, decorated with kitschy
advertising plaques and Vichy-print oil tablecloths; the prix fixe is
an exceptionally good deal, especially since many dishes are easily
shared by the clientele, which runs to bargain-hunting bankers at
noon and a cosmopolitan crowd at night.

	FOOD	DECOR	SERVICE	COST

Mesturet (Le) 🛡 *Southwest* | - | - | - | M |

2ᵉ | 77, rue de Richelieu (Bourse) | 01-42-97-40-68 | www.lemesturet.com
"A zoo at lunch", this "casual restaurant" with a "great owner"
(Alain Fontaine, founder of the former Bistrot Baracane) near the
old Bourse is "delightful at night" for "foot-weary tourists" in search
of "a nice dinner" of Southwestern "food that combines finesse with
bistro cooking" for "not a lot of euros."

☑ Meurice (Le) 🛡 *Haute Cuisine* | 27 | 28 | 27 | €153 |

1ᵉʳ | Hôtel Meurice | 228, rue de Rivoli (Concorde/Tuileries) |
01-44-58-10-55 | www.meuricehotel.com
"One of the great French chefs in one of Paris' prettiest dining rooms"
sums up "the Haute Cuisine experience" at the Hôtel Meurice; loaded
with luxe items like truffles and caviar, "culinary wizard" Yannick
Alléno's "food is just exquisite", and matched by the "balletlike" service "gliding" within the "grand, gorgeous" and "gilded" space done
up with Philippe Starck's silver chairs and abstract glass sculpture;
"yes, it's expensive" – but "the experience is magnificent."

☑ Michel Rostang 🛡 *Classic French* | 27 | 24 | 27 | €150 |

17ᵉ | 20, rue Rennequin (Péreire/Ternes) | 01-47-63-40-77 |
www.michelrostang.com
"Where charm and sophistication intersect", you find chef-owner
Michel Rostang's "chic" table in the 17th, whose "every detail is perfect", from the "superb" cuisine ("rich, rich" "but delicious") to the
"charming maître d'" and "flawless staff" to the "wood-paneled
beauty" of the decor; yes, it's "a bit too pricey" – but after 30-plus
years, this is "still among the best of the Classic French" establish-
ments; P.S. "in season, ask to be truffled for the entire meal."

Mirama *Chinese* | 20 | 6 | 12 | €28 |

5ᵉ | 17, rue St-Jacques (Maubert-Mutualité/St-Michel) | 01-43-54-71-77
"If you really crave Chinese while in Paris", this Latin Quarter "dive"
with smoked ducks hanging in the front window is perfect for "authentic Cantonese" cooking, including "wonderful shrimp dumpling
soup" and "killer roast pork"; there's "not much decor" or service,
but since the "food's always good" and the prices low, the academic
and arty regulars don't much mind.

Miroir Ⓜ *Bistro* | - | - | - | M |

18ᵉ | 94, rue des Martyrs (Abbesses) | 01-46-06-50-73
The young hipsters of Montmartre's Abbesses quarter have adopted
this contemporary bistro as a hangout; ranging from shellfish salad
to roast lamb, the market-driven menu changes often but is always
reasonable, adding to the convivial feel of the comfortable room
adorned with – what else? – many mirrors.

Moissonnier 🛡Ⓜ *Lyon* | 19 | 13 | 19 | €49 |

5ᵉ | 28, rue des Fossés St-Bernard (Cardinal Lemoine/Jussieu) |
01-43-29-87-65
This "long-standing" Latin Quarter Lyonnais is so "reliable", "there's
doubt you'd find any better in Lyon" itself – or so believe boosters of

this bistro and its "efficient but discreet servers"; the "unpretentious" "decor doesn't detract" from the "impeccably prepared traditional cuisine", some of whose specialties (such as tripe) are admittedly "an acquired taste – but worth acquiring."

NEW Mon Oncle ●⊅ *Bistro* - | - | - | M

18ᵉ | 3, rue Durantin (Abbesses) | 01-42-51-21-48 | www.mon-oncle.fr

Located in Montmartre's hip Abbesses quarter, this '50s-vintage bistro has been given some sizzle with black, gray and white-checked tile and red-painted walls, a sassy backdrop for the groovy young media and film types who've become regulars; though the feel is rather clubby, it's a lively place, and the kitchen keeps pace with affordable bistro classics that run to wild-boar terrine and duck breast with figs.

Monsieur Lapin Ⓜ *Classic French* 18 | 16 | 17 | €46

14ᵉ | 11, rue Raymond Losserand (Gaîté/Pernety) | 01-43-20-21-39 | www.monsieurlapin.fr

"Less rabbit-fixated since the change in ownership", this "charming" little Classic French in the 14th still has "bunny love on full display, from the seven-course, rabbit-only chef's menu to the absolutely delightful wall dioramas that depict French life with the bunnies standing in for their human counterparts"; "deft service" and "great bang for the buck" prices make this an address worth hightailing it to.

Montagnards (Les) Ⓩ *Alpine* - | - | - | M

1ᵉʳ | 58, rue Jean-Jacques Rousseau (Les Halles) | 01-40-26-68-75 | lesmontagnardsparis.fr

Looking like a miniature Savoyard chalet, this friendly venue – carved out of an old Les Halles butchery – offers a quality run of Alpine classics, including tartiflette, raclette and several varieties of fondue; modest prices and good-humored service make it a popular choice with dating couples and groups of friends on a night out.

Montalembert (Le) *New French* 19 | 21 | 18 | €61

7ᵉ | Hôtel Montalembert | 3, rue de Montalembert (Rue du Bac) | 01-45-49-68-03 | www.montalembert.com

The "trendy interior" of this "small" "slick-looking" eatery in the 7th "attracts businessmen and -women for the ideal power breakfast" or lunch of "modern" French fare; although it offers "better-than-average hotel dining", this "calm" spot is "expensive for what it is", especially given the "nice" but "relaxed service (you have to wait to be noticed)."

Mont Liban (Le) *Lebanese* - | - | - | M

17ᵉ | 42, bd des Batignolles (Rome) | 01-45-22-35-01 | www.montliban.fr

Meze maniacs find "delicious" morsels "at bargain prices" in this casual, modern Lebanese on a busy boulevard near the Place de Clichy; a "nice kofta kebab or chiche taouk sandwich" can be washed down with a shot of anise-flavored arak; N.B. takeout also available.

	FOOD	DECOR	SERVICE	COST

Montparnasse 25 (Le) 🔁 *New French* | 16 | 14 | 15 | €60 |

14ᵉ | Le Méridien Montparnasse | 19, rue du Commandant René Mouchotte (Montparnasse-Bienvenüe) | 01-44-36-44-25 | www.m25.fr

Maybe because it's tucked away upstairs at the Méridien Montparnasse hotel, this "intimate" black-and-silver dining room "remains too little-known"; among the knowledgeable, however, it's "celebrated for its cheese selection and art deco–style ambiance" and chef Christian Moine's "classy" New French cuisine; since this venue is most popular for business dining, service is "polite" and prices are "slightly high."

⚡ Mon Vieil Ami Ⓜ *Bistro* | 24 | 20 | 21 | €55 |

4ᵉ | 69, rue St-Louis-en-l'Ile (Pont-Marie) | 01-40-46-01-35 | www.mon-vieil-ami.com

Tucked away on the "charming Ile Saint-Louis", chef-owner Antoine Westermann's "wonderful bistro" serves "innovative" "modern Alsatian food" ("this chef truly knows how to make vegetables sing") and French country classics in an "intimate" – ok, "cramped" – dining room with black, half-timbered walls; it's "always packed, often with Americans", and some find it "overhyped", but given the "accommodating staff", it's a "good gathering place for a group" of *amis,* either *vieils* or new; P.S. "beware – they have two seatings, and if you choose the first one, you'll be rushed through dinner."

Mood (Le) ◑ *Asian Fusion* | - | - | - | M |

8ᵉ | 114, av de Champs-Elysées (George V) | 01-42-89-98-89 | www.mood-paris.fr

Right on the Champs, this split-level space with low-lit, red-hued decor by fashionable Parisian decorator Didier Gomez is "good for a quick business lunch", while "the bar's big selection of cocktails" gets a "trendy" crowd in the mood at night; the Franco-Asian "fusion food" is "nothing special", but a decent deal given this expensive area.

Mori Venice Bar ◑🔁 *Italian* | 17 | 16 | 16 | €69 |

2ᵉ | 2, rue du Quatre Septembre (Bourse) | 01-44-55-51-55 | www.mori-venicebar.com

Near the old Bourse, "this flashy Italian" grabs a "glamorous" crowd with its "original", rather baroque decor; while many find the Venetian fare "a nice surprise", the mori-ose mutter you should walk pasta this "overrated" place; perhaps you need to be one of the "famous faces" – "you're treated better if the maitre d' knows you."

Moulin à Vent (Au) 🔁Ⓜ *Bistro* | 19 | 13 | 17 | €45 |

5ᵉ | 20, rue des Fossés St-Bernard (Cardinal Lemoine/Jussieu) | 01-43-54-99-37 | www.au-moulinavent.com

This "longtime favorite" in the Latin Quarter pulls "a great mix of locals and tourists" who love the "traditional" ambiance and bistro cuisine, with carnivores clamoring for the "Châteaubriand and crispy potatoes (yes, cooked in duck fat!)"; given the "crowded" conditions, the "service is not quite as attentive" as it used to be, but at least "you get to know your neighbors."

	FOOD	DECOR	SERVICE	COST

Moulin de la Galette (Le) *Classic French* — 15 | 15 | 14 | €45

18ᵉ | 83, rue Lepic (Abbesses/Lamarck-Caulaincourt) | 01-46-06-84-77 | www.moulindelagalette.fr

Immortalized in Renoir's paintings, this famous former dance hall in an old Montmartre windmill is now the "original" setting for a "dynamic team" – Antoine Heerah and Jerome Bodereau, formerly of Le Chamarré; they're trying hard to dispel the place's "touristy" reputation via "delicious" Classic French fare with a Mauritian touch (e.g. suckling pig with dark muscavado sugar); however, many lament that "light" portions make the prices seem "onerous."

Mousson (La) ☒ *Cambodian* — - | - | - | M

1ᵉʳ | 9, rue Therese (Pyramides) | 01-42-60-59-46

Connoisseurs of Khmer cuisine head to this "delightful Cambodian" near the Palais-Royal for classic dishes from the Mekong Delta, including "divine loc lac beef"; true, the room's "too tiny", but the prices are just right.

Murano (Le) ☽ *New French* — 16 | 21 | 15 | €62

3ᵉ | Murano Urban Resort | 13, bd du Temple (Filles du Calvaire/République) | 01-42-71-20-00 | www.muranoresort.com

"Hip" habitués and hotel guests frequent this "fabulous" watering hole in the northern Marais, where the mega-white, "magnificent contemporary" decor is accented with "spectacular" colored lighting; trendoids tuck into "inventive" New French food that's "minimalist" in style (and content), then head to the bar for "very good cocktails" and 164 brands of vodka; P.S. "the inner courtyard is lovely in summer."

Murat (Le) ☽ *Classic French* — ∇ 13 | 17 | 12 | €50

16ᵉ | 1, bd Murat (Porte d'Auteuil) | 01-46-51-33-17

In a setting rich with red velvet, Paris Hilton wannabes, Maserati drivers and "advertising/media types at play" "vie for the attention of the beautiful staff" at this "trendy" Classic French near the Porte d'Auteuil; but "there's no chance of that, so just sit back and soak up the atmosphere."

Muscade ☒ *Eclectic/Tearoom* — - | - | - | M

1ᵉʳ | 36, rue Montpensier (Palais Royal-Musée du Louvre/Pyramides) | 01-42-97-51-36 | www.muscadepalaisroyal.fr

"Sitting surrounded by the Palais-Royal makes for a perfect lunch" or "afternoon tea pick-me-up" at this "nice little spot" that offers "huge salads" and other Eclectic fare; dinner is also served – in summer, tables overlooking the historical gardens are prime real estate – but do reserve in winter, to ensure they'll be open.

Musichall ☽ *New French* — 15 | 19 | 12 | €62

8ᵉ | 63, av Franklin D. Roosevelt (St-Philippe-du-Roule) | 01-45-61-03-63 | www.music-hallparis.com

It's a never-ending spectacle at this "lively" club/eatery off the Champs that keeps jumping until 4 AM on weekends; the decor is "as kitsch as it could be", with "all-white" walls bathed by "continually changing" colored lights and "tight tables" so low they're "practically on the floor"; cynics sneer "the action's all on the walls, not on the plates", but defenders declare the New French cuisine is "better than you would expect" for such a "trendy" spot, with special mention for the "remarkable" desserts.

Nabulione ● *Asian/Eclectic* | - | - | - | E |

7^e | 40, av Duquesne (St-François-Xavier) | 01-53-86-09-09 | www.nabulione.com

Replacing a long-running Chinese, this self-consciously stylish spot in the 7th serves an Asian-inflected Eclectic menu to a diverse crowd of press attachés, politicos and poodle-walkers, plus a footballer or two; the soundtrack is lively and the decor Milanese modish, down to the giant white floor lamps on the sidewalk terrace (one of the largest and prettiest in Paris).

Natacha ●⊠ *Classic French* | - | - | - | M |

14^e | 17 bis, rue Campagne-Première (Raspail) | 01-43-20-79-27

Fresh "chef-owners are settling in" to this veteran Montparnasse bistro, leaving unchanged the warm-toned, "artistic setting" with contemporary paintings, and ensuring the Classic French cuisine is "still good"; though "few of the [old] movie-star-and-celebrity clientele are now seen", it remains a "premier street restaurant", so insiders advise "don't accept a table in the cellar – the action (if any) is on the first floor."

Nemrod (Le) ● *Auvergne* | 16 | 12 | 16 | €32 |

6^e | 51, rue du Cherche-Midi (Sèvres-Babylone/St-Placide) | 01-45-48-17-05 | www.lenemrod.fr

Shoppers "take a break from the Bon Marché" and other boutiques in the 6th arrondissement for the "hustle and bustle" of this "hopping" Auvergnat cafe, serving "hearty portions" of "authentic cooking", plus "huge salads"; it's "old-fashioned fun" with "good terrace seating" and "people-watching", despite the "pure craziness" of lunch hour.

New Jawad ● *Indian/Pakistani* | ▽ 18 | 15 | 18 | €38 |

7^e | 12, av Rapp (Alma Marceau) | 01-47-05-91-37 | www.newjawad.com

When struck by sudden Sunday night subcontinental cravings, residents of the posh 7th head to this "spacious" Indo-Pakistani that, while "not extraordinary", is a "good standby when you don't want to leave the neighborhood for 'ethnic' food"; "helpful staffers" "will serve it spicy when asked."

New Nioullaville ● *Chinese* | ▽ 16 | 11 | 12 | €28 |

11^e | 32-34, rue de l'Orillon (Belleville) | 01-40-21-96-18

"Without a doubt one of the most authentic Chinese in Paris" (though it also offers "Pan-Asian cooking from five different kitchens"), this busy Belleville site seems "just like Hong Kong" with a "gigantic menu" and "waitresses coming through with steam carts" full of "delicious dim sum" delicacies; the "impersonal" decor doesn't amount to much, but then neither does the bill.

	FOOD	DECOR	SERVICE	COST

Noces de Jeannette (Les) *Bistro* — | — | — | M

2ᵉ | 14, rue Favart (Richelieu-Drouot) | 01-42-96-36-89 |
www.lesnocesdejeannette.com

With its central location off the Grands Boulevards and five salons
decorated in a range of styles, this "tourist-group destination" for
traditional bistro fare is often "crowded" with foreigners, who find
the food "uneven" (some suspect the caliber "depends on the price
of your tour"); "the staff allows plenty of time for people-watching."

Nos Ancêtres
les Gaulois (A) 🕐 *Classic French* 13 | 20 | 15 | €40

4ᵉ | 39, rue St-Louis-en-l'Ile (Pont-Marie) | 01-46-33-66-07 |
www.nosancetreslesgaulois.com

Ok, so this Ancient Gaul–themed restaurant on the Ile Saint-Louis
"won't check your gourmet-meal box" – it's "very touristy", with
"below-average" Classic French food and service that runs to "wan-
dering warriors banging their staffs on your table"; even so, in between the strolling minstrels, the singing and the "all-you-can-eat
crudités and charcuterie and red wine", it manages to be "as much
fun as you can have in Paris with your clothes on."

No Stress Café 🕐 Ⓜ *Eclectic* — | — | — | M

9ᵉ | 2, pl Gustave Toudouze (St-Georges) | 01-48-78-00-27

"In a quiet part of the 9th", touchy-feely types come to this "popular" place for its "cool laid-back atmosphere", Med-inspired setting and hands-on service, including the option of a "massage
before, during or after your meal"; while the oft-changing Eclectic
menu is mostly "mediocre", there's a "great terrace" for hanging
loose on the square Gustave Toudouze; N.B. it's no stress – and
no reservations either.

Noura *Lebanese* 19 | 14 | 16 | €40

2ᵉ | 29, bd des Italiens (Chaussée d'Antin/Opéra) | 01-53-43-00-53 🕐
6ᵉ | 121, bd du Montparnasse (Vavin) | 01-43-20-19-19 🕐
16ᵉ | 21, av Marceau (Alma Marceau/George V) |
01-47-20-33-33 🕐 🔲
16ᵉ | 27, av Marceau (Alma Marceau/George V) | 01-47-03-02-20
www.noura.fr

There's almost always a Noura nearby when a hankering for hummus
hits; true, "the decor is plain" and the staff "could try harder", but
it's "a safe choice for Lebanese fare" – hence, this "high-quality chain"
is "constantly crowded"; P.S. "for more chic quarters and refined
service, choose the Pavilion" at 21 Avenue Marceau.

Nouveau Village Tao-Tao 🕐 *Chinese/Thai* ▽ 18 | 16 | 16 | €30

13ᵉ | 159, bd Vincent Auriol (Nationale) | 01-45-86-40-08

Though this Asian in the 13th is "big" enough to feed a village, its
popularity means reservations are required if you want to taste traditional dishes from China and Thailand; the experience can be akin
to eating at a "large factory" foes find; yet advocates argue it's "always a sure value" for the "real" thing, including an "especially
good" Peking duck.

	FOOD	DECOR	SERVICE	COST

Obé (L') *Classic French*
(fka L'Obélisque)

| | 23 | 21 | 22 | €77 |

8e | Hôtel de Crillon | 10, pl de la Concorde (Concorde) | 01-44-71-15-15 | www.crillon.com

In the Crillon's recently (post-Survey) revamped and renamed "second restaurant", diners now enjoy a lighter take on Classic French cuisine amid more modern environs; however, its chief allure may still be the promise of what's "truly an affordable lunch for such a prestigious place."

Oeillade (L') Ⓢ *Bistro*

| | ▽ 14 | 11 | 13 | €47 |

7e | 10, rue de St-Simon (Rue du Bac/Solférino) | 01-42-22-01-60
"Tucked away" in the posh 7th, this bistro for the bourgeoisie serves up a "true Gallic meal" from a "limited menu" that is "good if uninspired" fans find; but the less-forgiving declare it downright "lackluster", adding that this restaurant's decor "needs a redo" too.

Office (L') Ⓢ Ⓜ *Bistro/New French*

| | - | - | - | M |

9e | 3, rue Richer (Bonne Nouvelle/Cadet) | 01-47-70-67-31
With a sleek modern interior featuring '70s lighting fixtures and a very short contemporary French menu reflecting Italian and Alsatian influences, this bistro in the 9th feeds briefcase-toting types at noon and a theater crowd in the evenings; the kitchen follows the seasons, so the chalkboard offerings change regularly, but often include inventive dishes like roasted beets with smoked mozzarella and gnocchi with braised beef, at fair prices that ensure it's always full.

Olivades (Les) Ⓢ *Provence*
(aka Bruno Deligne-Les Olivades)

| | 17 | 14 | 16 | €47 |

7e | 41, av de Ségur (Ségur/St-François-Xavier) | 01-47-83-70-09 | www.deligne-lesolivades.fr.tc

You can almost "hear the grasshoppers singing" at this "charming, easy bistro" in the 7th arrondissement, where the Provençal-accented menu runs to "well-presented and conceived dishes", which "often include olives"; though "plain", the dining room also has a southern French allure, and if a sagging Food score suggests it's "less special" than before, you still get "good prices for the quality of the food."

Ⓩ Ombres (Les) *New French*

| | 18 | 27 | 15 | €79 |

7e | Musée du Quai Branly | 27, quai Branly, Portail Debilly (Alma Marceau) | 01-47-53-68-00 | www.elior.com

This "spectacular", all-glass Jean Nouvel–designed dining room in the Musée du Quai Branly "defies the stereotype that great views and fine food are rarely found together": while the star here is clearly the "to-die-for" panorama of Paris, the New French fare is "interesting and tasty, if not outstanding"; yes, the "staff manages to be rushed and slow at the same time", and it's "too expensive", but it's still worth dining in this "enormous, dramatic stage" of a space; besides, "what's not to like with the Eiffel Tower as your dining companion?"

	FOOD	DECOR	SERVICE	COST

Opportun (L') ●🅩 *Lyon* | 15 | 11 | 17 | €47 |

14ᵉ | 64, bd Edgar Quinet (Edgar Quinet) | 01-43-20-26-89
"Surrounded by locals", a meal at this "convivial" bistro in the 14th
is "like eating at home" "as much for the personality of the owner"
as for the "typical Lyonnais bistro cuisine", featuring "perfectly
cooked sweetbreads"; but malcontents moan the meaty menu's
"lacking in imagination" and dismiss the "imitation retro decor."

Orient-Extrême ●🅩 *Japanese* | 18 | 17 | 17 | €47 |

6ᵉ | 4, rue Bernard Palissy (St-Germain-des-Prés) | 01-45-48-92-27
Sashimi-philes would swim miles to get to this "fashionable" Saint-
Germain site serving with a "wider selection than the run-of-the-
mill" Japanese joints; "among the best in Paris", it's also "the place
to go if you want celebrity with your sushi" – so while the "service is
spotty" (unless "you're known"), it's rarely a raw deal.

🆉 Os à Moëlle (L') ●🅩🅜 *Classic French* | 25 | 16 | 20 | €44 |

15ᵉ | 3, rue Vasco de Gama (Lourmel) | 01-45-57-27-27
Despite its huge popularity, chef-owner and "Crillon alumnus"
Thierry Faucher's "tiny bistro" with "decor of beams and mirrors" in
the 15th arrondissement "still retains its simple charm", wowing the
crowds with a "divine" prix fixe of "market-based" Classic French
dishes (e.g. "lovely cold pea soup, skate in brown butter and floating
island just like *grand-mère* used to make"); it can be "crowded and
noisy", but the staff is "friendly" as it offers up "an incredible meal
for the price."

Ostéria (L') 🅩 *Italian* | 22 | 14 | 17 | €54 |

4ᵉ | 10, rue de Sévigné (St-Paul) | 01-42-71-37-08
"Though it changed hands" a few years ago, this literally "hidden
jewel" – "no sign or street number to identify it" – still serves some of
"the most authentic Italian food" in town ("they cook risotto as it
should be cooked") in "extremely small" Marais quarters; on the
downside, "if you're not a VIP, you get the feeling you're bothering the
bosses", and "prices are now too high" ("sign of the times in Paris").

Oth Sombath 🅩 *Thai* | - | - | - | E |

8ᵉ | 184, rue du Faubourg St-Honoré (St-Philippe-du-Roule) |
01-42-56-55-55 | www.othsombath.com
Chef/co-owner Oth Sombath – who made his name at the Blue
Elephant a decade ago – has settled in swimmingly at this swanky
duplex in the 8th after a stint in Saint Tropez; though technically
Thai, the cuisine bears many a refined French touch, from the langous-
tines with Thai basil to the banana nems in a red-wine sauce, and
the slick white, red and gold-leaf decor by interior designer Patrick
Jouin and the suave servers bear an equally chic Gallic stamp.

Oto-Oto 🅩🚫 *Japanese* | - | - | - | M |

6ᵉ | 6, rue du Sabot (St-Germain-des-Prés/Mabillon) | 01-42-22-21-15 |
www.ramla.net
The setting is *très* Saint-Germain-des-Prés – an ancient house with
exposed beams and cozy white salons – but it's Japanese fare that

has won this restaurant a devoted following among sushi-mad Left Bank locals; quality and authenticity make the prix fixe menus most popular (though you can also order à la carte), and while the offerings change daily, they often include sushi, udon, feather-light tempura, and cooked entrees like grilled eel; N.B. check out the terrific selection of sakes.

Oudino (L') 🖳 *Bistro* — | — | — | M

7ᵉ | 17, rue Oudinot (Duroc) | 01-45-66-05-09 | www.oudino.com

Since it has "a charming staff and an inventive menu", this "intimate bistro tucked away in a quiet backstreet" in the 7th is well worth seeking out for a tasty meal; the '30s-style dining room makes a "nice spot for a casual evening."

Oulette (L') 🖳 *Southwest* 19 | 14 | 17 | €68

12ᵉ | 15, pl Lachambeaudie (Cour St-Emilion/Dugommier) | 01-40-02-02-12 | www.l-oulette.com

"If you can't make it to Southwest France", this site in the 12th is "well worth the métro ride" for cuisine that includes both classic, like a "foie gras confit to die for", and "innovative" dishes (maybe a bit "too modern for me"); even so, sliding scores support the sense it's "not quite what it once was, especially the service" – though the decor has gotten a new, modern look post-Survey.

Oum el Banine 🖳 *Moroccan* — | — | — | E

16ᵉ | 16 bis, rue Dufrenoy (Porte Dauphine/Rue de la Pompe) | 01-45-04-91-22 | www.oumelbanine.com

"Watch your waistline" at this "wonderful neighborhood Moroccan" in the 16th, where the "authentic" tagines and couscous cause "gourmets to cross town for the pure delight"; despite the "rather gloomy" digs, "meticulous" service is guaranteed because the "*patronne* keeps an eye" on everything.

Ourcine (L') 🖳🅜 *Classic/New French* 24 | 14 | 21 | €43

13ᵉ | 92, rue Broca (Glacière/Les Gobelins) | 01-47-07-13-65

"The sign above the door says it all: 'a cook's cuisine, a winemaker's wines'" at this "cozy, new-style bistro" in the 13th, where "really talented" chef-owner Sylvain Danière (ex La Régalade) serves "classic, with a hint of contemporary", French food "at prices that couldn't be gentler" – "32€ buys a three-course menu without a single been-there, done-that option"; the "staff works really hard to complete the experience", but surveyors "hesitate to say" any more: "there are few tables and I want to get one."

Ozu *Japanese* ▽ 23 | 24 | 17 | €69

16ᵉ | 2, av des Nations-Unies (Trocadéro) | 01-40-69-23-90 | www.ozu-paris.com

Perhaps "the samurai decor looks a little Las Vegas", and it's definitely "weird to watch your dinner swimming" around the huge aquarium – but that doesn't stop supporters from taking the plunge at this glass-walled Japanese in the 16th; "sensational sushi" shares the menu with "wonderful fusion dishes"; just be prepared to reel in a big-fin bill.

	FOOD	DECOR	SERVICE	COST

Palanquin (Le) 🗷 *Vietnamese*
| | 18 | 13 | 16 | €39 |

6ᵉ | 12, rue Princesse (Mabillon/St-Germain-des-Prés) | 01-43-29-77-66 |
www.lepalanquin.com

Those looking for "a break from standard French" cooking can savor
a soupçon of Saigon in Saint-Germain at this Vietnamese, which
features "authentic, fresh" favorites like pho soup, *Banh cuon*
(steamed ravioli) and ginger duck; the "cozy setting" displays the
exposed beams and stones of its 18th-century building.

Pamphlet (Le) 🗷 *Basque/Southwest*
| | 23 | 19 | 23 | €50 |

3ᵉ | 38, rue Debelleyme (Filles du Calvaire) | 01-42-72-39-24

"Excellent, "exquisitely prepared" Southwestern French and Basque-
inspired dishes make this "cozy", "casual neighborhood place" in
the Marais "well worth a visit", especially since the prices are so
"reasonable"; the decor of "taupe stone walls and red accents" gets
a thumbs-up too, but the real praise (and higher score) goes to "the
staff – sweet, funny and kinder than kind."

Paolo Petrini 🗷 *Italian*
| | - | - | - | E |

17ᵉ | 6, rue du Débarcadère (Argentine/Porte Maillot) | 01-45-74-25-95 |
www.paolo-petrini.fr

"*Bravissimo!*" bellow fervent fans of this "excellent Italian" near
Porte Maillot, where chef-owner Paolo Petrini's "refined" cooking is inspired "by his memories of teenage experiences in
Tuscany and Venezia"; the dining room may be "modest" but the
decor is "elegant", and the business types who fill the room at noon
and well-heeled locals who come for dinner appreciate the "warm
and enchanting" service.

Papilles (Les) 🗷🅼 *Classic French*
| | 23 | 15 | 20 | €43 |

5ᵉ | 30, rue Gay-Lussac (Luxembourg RER) | 01-43-25-20-79 |
www.lespapilles.com

Patrons' *papilles* (taste buds) are tantalized at this "adorable little
address, something between a gourmet grocery and gastronomic
port of call" near the Panthéon, where "superb wines" "shown,
store-style, on the walls" complement a "one-choice menu" of "consistently flavorful" Classic French food; it's "bright and lively" (some
say "noisy"), so "go with a group, but not on a first date" – especially
since "you'll need a nap after" all that well-priced vino.

Paradis du Fruit (Le) ◑ *Eclectic*
| | 14 | 11 | 12 | €23 |

1ᵉʳ | 4, rue St-Honoré (Les Halles) | 01-40-39-93-99
5ᵉ | 1, rue des Tournelles (Bastille) | 01-40-27-94-79
6ᵉ | 29, quai des Grands-Augustins (St-Michel) | 01-43-54-51-42
8ᵉ | 35, rue Marbeuf (Franklin D. Roosevelt/George V) | 01-45-62-47-22
8ᵉ | 47, av George V (George V) | 01-47-20-74-00
11ᵉ | 12, pl de la Bastille (Bastille) | 01-43-07-82-25
14ᵉ | 21, bd Edgar Quinet (Edgar Quinet) | 01-40-47-53-44
17ᵉ | 32, av de Wagram (Ternes) | 01-44-09-02-02
www.leparadisdufruit.fr

Students sick of spaghetti swarm to this Eclectic chain for a "natural,
fresh" fix from the "fruit-based menu", including "copious" salads

and "delicious", "healthy" smoothies served amid "kitschy" "coconut tree-style" decor; "it's a nice place to refuel", but certainly "not refined", and the "young" servers are often "overwhelmed" by the crowds; in short, while cheaper than spring break in the Caribbean, it's "a bit expensive for the quality."

Paradis Thai ● Thai | ▽ 15 | 20 | 17 | €28 |

13ᵉ | 132, rue de Tolbiac (Tolbiac) | 01-45-83-22-26 | www.paradisthai.com
The "original" "templelike decor within a huge warren of rooms with tropical fish" swimming under a glass floor impresses patrons more than the "decent" dishes at this stylish Thai in the 13th; still, the service is soigné, the "menu enormous" and the prices *petits*.

Parc aux Cerfs (Le) Bistro | ▽ 21 | 18 | 23 | €47 |

6ᵉ | 50, rue Vavin (Notre-Dame-des-Champs/Vavin) | 01-43-54-87-83
Vintage '30s decor channels a Montparnasse frame of mind at this former artists' atelier-turned-bistro with "thoughtfully prepared dishes" both traditional and contemporary (special kudos to "their unique two-cabbage salad"); the "servers go to any lengths to look after you", and the small terrace out back is ideal for dining alfresco.

Paris (Le) ⌧ Haute Cuisine | 20 | 17 | 18 | €83 |

6ᵉ | Hôtel Lutétia | 45, bd Raspail (Sèvres-Babylone) | 01-49-54-46-90 | www.lutetia-paris.com
A "small jewel in the Hôtel Lutétia" in the 6th, this Haute Cuisine table with "classy" if slightly "dated" art deco-style decor by Sonia Rykiel offers "refined" fare "in the grand style"; service is "alert and efficient" if "a little distant", and "prices are high, but justified."

Parisiennes (Les) ⌧ Ⓜ Mediterranean/Moroccan | - | - | - | M |

11ᵉ | 243, rue du Faubourg St-Antoine (Faidherbe) | 01-43-73-37-58 | www.lesparisiennes-leresto.fr
This 11th-arrondissement bistro under the aegis of actor Edouard Baer perfectly catches the laid-back bobo groove of eastern Paris, with its nonchalantly theatrical decor (a red curtain, candles and a piano that patrons are encouraged to play); the place was recently taken over by a new owner, Bob de Marseilles, and now features more Mediterranean dishes, as well as art shows and live music on Thursday nights.

Paris Seize (Le) ⌧ Italian | 18 | 11 | 16 | €40 |

16ᵉ | 18, rue des Belles-Feuilles (Trocadéro) | 01-47-04-56-33
"Noisy, animated" and "always packed with locals" from the upper-crust 16th, this "neighborhood" Italian doles out "generous servings" at "reasonable" prices; but while some cherish the "young atmosphere", others are irate that it's "invaded by trendy rich kids."

Pasco Mediterranean/Southwest | 22 | 21 | 21 | €45 |

7ᵉ | 74, bd de la Tour-Maubourg (La Tour-Maubourg) | 01-44-18-33-26 | www.restaurantpasco.com
"With a cozy setting across from Les Invalides", this "fairly priced" site (run by a pair of pals named Pascal) caters to "a mix of

| | FOOD | DECOR | SERVICE | COST |

Americans and locals" within its "light, modern" confines; there's a Southwestern-"Med tilt to the menu" – many recommend the risotto with Serrano ham – and while it may "need more staff to handle the crowds", it's "excellent for Sunday dinner when many places are closed."

NEW Passage 53 ⑤ *New French* — — — E

2ᵉ | 53, Passage des Panoramas (Grands Boulevards) | 01-42-33-04-35
Hidden away in one of Paris' most charming *passages* (covered arcades), this tiny storefront with a loungelike setup featuring low chairs wows adventurous gastronomes with the light, inventive prix fixe menus of Japanese chef Shinichi Sato; Sato works with pedigreed Parisian produce – meat from Hugo Desnoyer, organic vegetables, Gillardeau oysters – to create unique, Asian-inspired contemporary French cuisine that runs to foie gras with strawberry juice and grilled cod with white radish cream; a fashionable crowd appreciates the amiable service and low lighting.

Passage des Carmagnoles — — — M
(Le) ◑⑤ *Wine Bar/Bistro*

11ᵉ | 18, Passage de la Bonne Graine (Ledru-Rollin) | 01-47-00-73-30
Once upon a time, "the attraction of this charming place was actually the host, Antoine Toubia"; a new owner is in place now, but this popular wine bar in a passage near Bastille still proposes a "superb selection" of bottles and a "well-prepared" menu of meaty Classic French dishes such as andouillette or steak tartare with mint; food for thought as well as stomach is provided by well-lubricated philosophical debates held on the first Thursday of every month.

☑ Passiflore ⑤ *Asian/Classic French* 26 | 20 | 21 | €79

16ᵉ | 33, rue de Longchamp (Boissière/Trocadéro) | 01-47-04-96-81 | www.restaurantpassiflore.com
"East meets West on the Right Bank" – specifically, the 16th – where chef-owner Roland Durand's "über-creative" "Asian-inspired" Classic French fare, such as lobster ravioli in a mulligatawny sauce, is "prepared with finesse"; the decor was revamped recently, ushering in a 'new wave' orchid-and-bamboo look (which may outdate the above Decor score) – this "pricey-all-around" trendsetter continues to "reveal new surprises every trip."

Passy Mandarin *Asian* 20 | 17 | 21 | €49

16ᵉ | 6, rue Bois-le-Vent (La Muette) | 01-42-88-12-18
Passy Mandarin Opéra ◑ *Asian*
2ᵉ | 6, rue d'Antin (Opéra) | 01-42-61-25-52
Reportedly, "this is where Joël Robuchon comes for Peking duck – enough said" proclaim converts who crowd this Asian with two addresses, one out in the 16th with "wonderful" authentic Chinese digs, and the other "close to the Opéra Garnier" whose "decor takes you back to the '70s"; at both, though, you'll enjoy "one authentic flavor after another", served by a staff that's "quick", despite "occasional problems understanding your requests."

	FOOD	DECOR	SERVICE	COST

Pates Vivantes (Les) ⓩ *Chinese* | — | — | — | I |

NEW 5ᵉ | 22, bd St-Germain (Maubert-Mutualité) |
01-40-46-84-33
9ᵉ | 46, rue du Faubourg Montmartre (Le Peletier) |
01-45-23-10-21 ◐

There's always a small crowd gathered at the front window of this
tiny Chinese near the Folies Bergère in the 9th, gazing at the signature noodles being made by hand before they go into big bowls of
soup or other northwestern specialties; cheap and filling, the cuisine compensates for the packed quarters and sometimes grouchy
service; N.B. an offshoot opened rencently in the 5th.

Paul Chêne ●ⓩ *Classic French* | 20 | 17 | 20 | €59 |

16ᵉ | 123, rue Lauriston (Trocadéro) | 01-47-27-63-17 |
www.paulchene.com

"One of the 16th's treasures", this "standby" may be "stuck in a
time warp" but that's what its regulars have come to expect:
"French comfort food at its best" in a "relaxed", "intimate dining
room" where "old-line elegance and service" are assured; it's
"not inexpensive", but it's "perfect for a discreet affair or a
romantic first date."

⛉ Pavillon Ledoyen ⓩ *Haute Cuisine* | 26 | 26 | 26 | €170 |

8ᵉ | 8, av Dutuit (Champs-Elysées-Clémenceau/Concorde) |
01-53-05-10-01

For a "truly elegant" Haute Cuisine experience, head for this "magical" pavilion with "palatial" Napoleon III–style decor by star designer Jacques Grange and a "beautiful setting" under the chestnut
trees at the lower end of the Champs; chef Christian Le Squer's efforts, especially with seafood, are "subtle, brilliant" and brought to
table "by an army of highly trained footmen" ("attentive", though
some seem to "lack the joy of waitering"); "from the portable champagne bar to the choice of sugars with coffee, this is sybaritic dining –
and priced accordingly."

Pavillon Montsouris *Classic French* | ∇ 17 | 23 | 16 | €60 |

14ᵉ | 20, rue Gazan (Porte d'Orléans) | 01-43-13-29-00 |
www.pavillon-montsouris.fr

With an "enchanting", glass-roofed dining room and "exceptional
terrace", it's "like eating in the middle of the park" at this Classic
French that in fact overlooks the Parc Montsouris; the "refined
dishes", well-"spaced" tables and "discreet, attentive" waiters make
this perpetual garden party "perfect" for "grand occasions"; it's
technically "expensive, but good value for the money."

Pelouse (La) *Classic French* | — | — | — | M |

19ᵉ | 86, rue Botzaris (Botzaris) | 01-42-08-45-13

Adjacent to the charming Buttes-Chaumont park and its lovely
pelouses (lawns), this lively bistro pleases the locals with a Classic
French menu that runs to dishes like squid sautéed with shellfish
and duck breast with honey; if some find the service slow, reasonable prices and a friendly atmosphere make most happy.

	FOOD	DECOR	SERVICE	COST

Père Claude (Le) *Classic French*

▽ 17 | 13 | 15 | €51

15e | 51, av de la Motte-Picquet (La Motte-Picquet-Grenelle) | 01-47-34-03-05

At this "institution for those meat-craving moments", this "casual, friendly" rotisserie is where "regulars from the neighborhood" around the Ecole Militaire come to chow on "serious" Classic French grilled goodies; first-timers are struck by the "bustling" "'60s-chic" ambiance – "I felt like I was in a movie by Roger Vadim" (who peddled flesh of a different sort).

Pères et Filles *Bistro*

▽ 16 | 15 | 17 | €36

6e | 81, rue de Seine (Mabillon/Odéon) | 01-43-25-00-28 | www.restaurantpreresetfilles.fr

A "young crowd" appreciates this "convenient" Saint-Germain address that's replete with all the classic bistro trimmings (zinc bar included); still, some say when it comes to the Classic French fare, "the food is better at home"; as for the welcome, you can count on "better service if you are skinny, pretty and 25."

Perraudin (Le) *Bistro*

▽ 13 | 13 | 15 | €37

5e | 157, rue St-Jacques (Cluny La Sorbonne/Luxembourg) | 01-46-33-15-75 | www.restaurant-perraudin.com

Straight "out of the movies, with checkered tablecloths and aged decor", this "classic", "noisy" bistro "near the Sorbonne" is "popular among students" and "many Americans" looking for "a breath of old Paris"; "after more than 100 years, it's still reliable" for "Classic French dishes in a convivial atmosphere"; "arrive early or be sure to reserve" or you'll have to "hang out at the bar, brushing up on your savoir-faire."

Perron (Le) 🗷 *Italian*

18 | 16 | 17 | €52

7e | 6, rue Perronet (St-Germain-des-Prés) | 01-45-44-71-51

On a Saint-Germain side street, this "cozy", clubby and slightly "cave"-like Italian "always fills up" with editors, antiques dealers and other "colorful locals" consuming "good, standard fare" within the "exposed beams and stone walls"; "service is passable, if not exactly on top of things", but "everyone is having a great time" nonetheless.

Pershing, Restaurant ◖ *Eclectic/New French*

17 | 23 | 14 | €72

8e | Hôtel Pershing Hall | 49, rue Pierre Charron (George V) | 01-58-36-58-36 | www.pershinghall.com

"Tremendous decor", with an "amazing [inside] garden wall", makes this hotel eatery in the 8th "rather 'in'"; but critics would "rather stay out" – while the Eclectic–New French "food is improving", it's still "a rip-off", and if the "pretty waitresses make you forget the uninteresting dishes and overpriced wines", they "must be grabbed to speed along the meal"; so unless you like "paying for the scene", maybe "it's most enjoyable just for drinks"; P.S. "don't touch anything in the garden, or you'll get yelled at."

Petit Bofinger *Brasserie*

18 | 18 | 18 | €36

4e | 6, rue de la Bastille (Bastille) | 01-42-72-05-23 ◖🗷
La Défense | 1, pl du Dôme (La Grande Arche) | 01-46-92-46-46 🗷

	FOOD	DECOR	SERVICE	COST

(continued)

Petit Bofinger

Vincennes | 2, av de Paris (Château de Vincennes) | 01-43-28-25-76

These "offshoots" of the original, historic Bofinger are "typical brasseries" serving up "classic" "if unsurprising" fare – including oysters that are "some of the freshest in town" – "without chichi"; operated by Groupe Flo, there's no surprise it has "a bit of a chain restaurant" feeling; the Bastille branch is voted "the best" with "food nearly as good as its mother's across the street", "but cheaper."

Petit Châtelet (Le) *Classic French*   – | – | – | M

5ᵉ | 39, rue de la Bûcherie (St-Michel) | 01-46-33-53-40

"Wedged amongst a bevy of cafes capitalizing on their proximity to Notre Dame", this "cute spot" is a "haven of good Classic French cuisine" "in the midst of a touristy area"; "the food is pleasantly straightforward", the service is so "welcoming" it's "endearing" and if you "eat outside" facing the cathedral "you won't soon forget the view."

Petit Colombier (Le) ⌦ *Classic French*   18 | 16 | 18 | €59

17ᵉ | 42, rue des Acacias (Argentine/Charles de Gaulle-Etoile) | 01-43-80-28-54

The name of the game is game ("the selection is fresh and unique") at this "cozy" "welcoming" auberge with "an old-style country decor" near the Etoile; "solid French classics" round out the rest of the menu, aided by "amiable service", and many find the prices "reasonable" "for a romantic evening out."

Petite Chaise (A la) *Classic French*   19 | 18 | 20 | €43

7ᵉ | 36, rue de Grenelle (Rue du Bac) | 01-42-22-13-35 | www.alapetitechaise.fr

This "1600s Classic French" in the 7th claims to be the "oldest restaurant in Paris", which makes it a big draw for foreigners and an "eccentric university clientele" seduced by the "charming" "retro" ambiance and a "good-value", "old-fashioned" menu of "dependable comfort food" "served with attention"; "try to sit downstairs" since the "top floor is frequently filled with American tour groups."

Petite Cour (La) *New French*   21 | 22 | 21 | €52

6ᵉ | 8, rue Mabillon (Mabillon/St-Germain-des-Prés) | 01-43-26-52-26 | www.la-petitecour.com

In the past the cuisine's "been up and down", but the kitchen seems to have found its footing at this "charming" New French "on a quiet side street [near] Saint-Sulpice Cathedral"; even if it hadn't, the "lovely", "vine-cloaked" "sunken garden patio" would "compensate for all sins", aided by the "sophisticated" service; be warned though, "it's on every concierge's list of places to go" – hence, "lots of Americans."

Petite Sirène de Copenhague (La) ⌦Ⓜ *Danish*   – | – | – | M

9ᵉ | 47, rue Notre-Dame-de-Lorette (St-Georges) | 01-45-26-66-66

Aptly situated in the northern 9th, this bit of "Copenhagen in Paris" is "worth the detour" for fare "with a Scandinavian flair" courtesy of its "charming" Danish chef-owner; his siren song is "remarkable fish", along with "warm" service in a "sober" yet "light-filled" setting.

Petites Sorcières de Ghisaline Arabian (Les) 🛇 Ⓜ Northern French
`- | - | - | M`

14ᵉ | 12, rue Liancourt (Denfert-Rochereau) | 01-43-21-95-68
After a few years off-stage, chef-owner Ghislaine Arabian is back with a cozy little shopfront in the 14th; known for her Northern French and Flemish fare, she feeds the masses with dishes like breaded shrimp croquettes and cod in beer sauce; already the cramped, red-and-beige dining room is getting packed with guests who go for the good-value lunch menu (prices head north at dinner).

Petite Tour (La) 🛇 Classic French
`- | - | - | M`

16ᵉ | 11, rue de la Tour (Passy) | 01-45-20-09-31
"Worth trying if you're in the neighborhood" say surveyors of this "good local" that's been serving Classic French fare to the Passy bourgeoisie for over 20 years; while the owners have spruced up the decor (which "needed some life"), longtimers lament that the menu now "appears to be too ambitious for the chef."

Petit Lutétia (Le) Brasserie
`19 | 20 | 20 | €47`

6ᵉ | 107, rue de Sèvres (Vaneau) | 01-45-48-33-53
"Belle epoque atmosphere and vest-wearing waiters" continue to charm at this "perfect neighborhood brasserie" in a silk-stocking section of the 6th; the "short but ever-changing menu" runs to "yummy mussels", "fresh oysters", "homemade terrines" and "quite good fruits de mer", brought by one of the "happiest staffs in Paris"; in short, a good time is had by all, "365 days a year."

Petit Marché (Le) ● New French
`22 | 17 | 19 | €39`

3ᵉ | 9, rue de Béarn (Bastille/Chemin-Vert) | 01-42-72-06-67
Near the Place des Vosges, this "neighborhood joint" is "jumping with a younger crowd" that comes for "fantastic" New French cuisine with "an Asian twist" at "reasonable" prices; with an open kitchen that keeps humming till midnight and "frenetic but effective" service, it's "perfect for a late-night bite on a hot summer night", especially if you can snag a table on the tiny terrace.

Petit Marguery (Le) Bistro
`21 | 17 | 19 | €48`

13ᵉ | 9, bd de Port-Royal (Les Gobelins) | 01-43-31-58-59 | www.petitmarguery.com
This "eternal" bistro has got game, and "outstanding game" at that, along with "good old-fashioned French cuisine that practically doesn't exist anymore"; boasting "crisp service", a "fine wine list" and "impeccably traditional ambiance", the place in the 13th is "not elegant, not fancy" but quite simply "the real thing."

Petit Niçois (Le) Provence
`16 | 12 | 18 | €42`

7ᵉ | 10, rue Amélie (La Tour-Maubourg) | 01-45-51-83-65 | www.lepetitnicois.com
The "best bouillabaisse in Paris" is the bait at this Provençal venue, a "typical neighborhood place" in the 7th; if the rest of the menu is

"a disappointment", at least "you can get by paying less here for an honest meal than almost anywhere else in the area."

Petit Pascal (Le) 🖼 *Bistro*   - | - | - | M

13ᵉ | 33, rue Pascal (Les Gobelins) | 01-45-35-33-87
Petit but busy, this bistro is always packed with picky penny-pinchers who appreciate the excellent quality and generous portions of the Classic French cooking; quick service and a warm atmosphere explain why it grabs the Gobelins neighborhood set; N.B. closed weekends.

Petit Pergolèse (Le) 🖼 *Bistro*   23 | 16 | 19 | €62

16ᵉ | 38, rue Pergolèse (Argentine/Porte Maillot) | 01-45-00-23-66
Resembling a "neighborhood club that welcomes everyone into the family" – thanks largely to owner Albert Corre, who "greets and moves around, watching everything" – this "sophisticated yet cozy" bistro in the 16th supplies "varied", "creative" New French cuisine and "warm service"; "it's tight and noisy, but that's what makes it so much fun"; N.B. closed weekends.

Petit Pontoise (Le) *Bistro*   22 | 16 | 21 | €44

5ᵉ | 9, rue de Pontoise (Maubert-Mutualité) | 01-43-29-25-20
"Wow" exclaim enthusiasts of this "wonderful, unspoiled Parisian bistro" in the Latin Quarter serving up "classic homestyle comfort food" "at great prices"; a "deserved favorite with Americans" along with professors and students from the Sorbonne, this "small venue with big flavors" is "noisy" and "always full", which can "overburden" the "pleasant staff."

Petit Poucet (Le) *New French*   - | - | - | M

Levallois-Perret | 4, rd-pt Claude Monet (Pont-de-Levallois) |
01-47-38-61-85 | www.le-petitpoucet.net
"See and be seen" "on the banks of the Seine" at this "trendy", spacious Ile de la Jatte New French that caters to "bourgeois families in the evening and advertising types at noon"; wet blankets bark the eats are rather "industrial" but all concur that the "agreeable terrace" is "unbeatable in summer."

Petit Prince de Paris (Le) ☽ *Bistro*   - | - | - | M

5ᵉ | 12, rue de Lanneau (Maubert-Mutualité) | 01-43-54-77-26 |
www.lepetitprincedeparis.fr
"You'll feel like you're on another planet" at this "terrific" table "in an old townhouse by the Sorbonne", "tightly packed" with a "mixed gay-straight crowd", a "funky", "vibrant atmosphere" and the "sassiest" waiters in town; open late, it's perfect either "for couples *en tête-à-tête* or a group of friends", and the bistro menu, "an amazing deal", is as "adventuresome" as the Little Prince himself.

Petit Rétro (Le) 🖼 *Bistro*   16 | 16 | 16 | €38

16ᵉ | 5, rue Mesnil (Victor Hugo) | 01-44-05-06-05 | www.petitretro.fr
Like the name suggests, this "little" venue is "highly appreciated for its super-retro character", created out of "charming" belle epoque tiles and the "perfume of good traditional French dishes"; jaded na-

tives may sneer it's "nothing special", but "if you want a typical bistro", this is "one of the best secrets of the 16th"; N.B. closed weekends.

Petit Riche (Au) ● *Bistro* | 18 | 19 | 16 | €49 |

9e | 25, rue le Peletier (Le Peletier/Richelieu-Drouot) | 01-47-70-68-68 | www.aupetitriche.com

Traditional French bistros are going, going, "mostly gone", but steps from the Drouot auction house in the 9th is this "survivor from the 19th century" serving *très riche* "old-fashioned classics" that inspire a mixed lot of views, from "so-so" to "excellent"; but in any case, "you go here for the ambiance", to sit on red velvet banquettes amid the "authentic" 1880s decor – ideal for a business lunch, entertaining out-of-town guests or "after the theater."

Petit St. Benoît (Le) 🗷 ⌀ *Classic French* | 16 | 14 | 16 | €32 |

6e | 4, rue St-Benoît (St-Germain-des-Prés) | 01-42-60-27-92 | www.petit-st-benoit.fr

"Shoehorn yourself into a table, steel yourself for curt service" and tuck in for a "noisy dinner with the locals" at this Saint-Germain "canteen" that's "been here forever" (or at least 1901); you'll find the same "good old family cooking *à la française* (not that we always liked what *maman* served)", the same setting, which "hasn't been redecorated since about 1929", and almost the same prices, making this one of "the cheapest eats in Paris."

Petit Victor Hugo (Le) ● 🗷 *Classic French* | ▽ 19 | 16 | 15 | €52 |

16e | 143, av Victor Hugo (Rue de la Pompe/Victor Hugo) | 01-45-53-02-68 | www.petitvictorhugo.com

Following "a change in ownership", some say this Classic French in the 16th "isn't what it used to be", but fans insist it remains a pleasant "neighborhood place" with "good food from a varied menu" and "great people-watching" amid "plenty of green foliage."

Petit Zinc (Le) ● *Brasserie* | 18 | 22 | 18 | €56 |

6e | 11, rue St-Benoît (Mabillon/St-Germain-des-Prés) | 01-42-86-61-00 | www.petitzinc.com

"Named for its zinc bar that's been around forever", this "art nouveau-style gem" in Saint-Germain serves brasserie fare ("seafood is the specialty") that's "surprisingly good for such a touristy" area; but nostalgists mutter it was "more fun before it became part of a big French chain", finding the "decor more interesting than the formulaic food" and service that swings from "absentminded" to "attentive."

Pétrelle (Le) 🗷 🅼 *New French* | - | - | - | E |

9e | 34, rue Pétrelle (Anvers) | 01-42-82-11-02 | www.petrelle.fr

"The best restaurant with its own cat in Paris" is tucked away on a cobbled side street in the increasingly bobo 9th arrondissement; the "eclectic decor" of flea-market finds creates a "delightful ambiance" that often attracts a boldface name or two (Christian Lacroix, Madonna), who find the "seasonal menu" of New French dishes is "worth every centime"; however, "one waiter really is no longer enough for the whole place."

Pétrus *Brasserie*
▽ 21 | 18

17e | 12, pl du Maréchal Juin (Péreire) | 01-43-80-15-95

Previously a plush seafood house, this business dining fa[...]
17th has been transformed into "an excellent brasserie s[...]
prepared food, notably fish"; pastel- and taupe-toned, "discreetly
modern decor" and a "friendly staff" make it a good catch, even if it's
"a bit expensive – but you leave with a good memory."

Pharamond M *Classic French*
19 | 20 | 20 | €72

1er | 24, rue de la Grande Truanderie (Etienne Marcel/Les Halles) |
01-40-28-45-18 | www.pharamond.fr

Nobody's talking tripe when they say this "noisy, crowded, simple
place" near Les Halles is "as much a taste of Old France as you can
find today" – and by old, we mean dating back to 1832, when it be-
gan serving tripe *à la mode de Caen*; still on the menu, it will "melt in
your mouth", along with the other classics proffered by "friendly"
servers; though renovated a while back after a management change,
its "genuine" belle epoque decor remains intact, leading some to
quip "new owner, new chef, same old furniture" (seriously, "it's
a lovely place").

Pichet de Paris (Le) ⊠ *Seafood*
16 | 11 | 14 | €59

8e | 68, rue Pierre Charron (Franklin D. Roosevelt) |
01-43-59-50-34

"If you're a tourist, it's a find; if you're a local, you're unhappy all the
tourists have found it" say surveyors about this "unpretentious address" approximately "50 meters from the Champs-Elysées"; the
seafood remains as "solid as it's been" for decades, even if "prices
are a little excessive" given the "unoriginal" decor and service that
varies, "depending on the client and the mood" of the staffer.

Pied de Cochon (Au) ☻ *Brasserie*
18 | 19 | 17 | €49

1er | 6, rue Coquillière (Châtelet-Les Halles) | 01-40-13-77-00 |
www.pieddecochon.com

"Call me Miss Piggy" squeal supporters of this "lively" "remnant of
the old Les Halles", who pork out on "abundant" portions of traditional brasserie fare, including "the pig's feet that give the restaurant its name"; "open nonstop", it can feel rather "factory"-like,
but for foreign visitors, its "archetypal Parisian waiters" and
"kitschy" (even "gaudy") decor make it "a must, at least – but
probably only – once."

Pierre au Palais Royal ☻⊠ *Classic French*
17 | 15 | 15 | €54

1er | 10, rue Richelieu (Palais Royal-Musée du Louvre) |
01-42-96-09-17

Scores may not fully reflect the advent of "owner Eric Sertour and his
chef Pascal Bataillé" to this "delightful little" site "near the Palais-
Royal", but those who know say they're "making marvels" with the
L'Arome alum's Classic French fare, both earthy and elevated, and
"handsome" monochromatic decor; while the hoi polloi might hesitate at the prices, there are "menus of thirtysomething euros, even
in the evening", and a post-theater prix fixe too.

	FOOD	DECOR	SERVICE	COST

Gagnaire ⊠ *Haute Cuisine*

| 28 | 25 | 27 | €194 |

...lzac | 6, rue Balzac (Charles de Gaulle-Etoile/George V) |
...2-50 | www.pierre-gagnaire.com

...enses explore uncharted territory" during a "breathtaking
...al" at this "brilliant", completely "unforgettable" Haute Cuisine
haven in the 8th, serving what many describe as "the most innovative food" in Paris ("Pierre Gagnaire is to gastronomy what Picasso
was to contemporary art"); yes, the master's "science experiment"-
like creations, while "out of this world", are "too out there" for some;
but the "exceptional service" in the discreet dove-gray and blond-
wood dining room makes you "feel like royalty", and to the vast majority, it's "worth every euro (damn dollar!)."

Pinxo *New French*

| 21 | 18 | 19 | €64 |

1er | Renaissance Paris Vendôme | 9, rue d'Alger (Tuileries) |
01-40-20-72-00 | www.pinxo.fr
Owned by "star-studded chef" Alain Dutournier, this "stylish spot"
in the 1st "combines aspects of a traditional tapas bar with those of
a contemporary French restaurant" where "two or three people can
share dishes" of "exotic Basque-influenced cuisine" that are "not copious, but flavorful"; perhaps the best seats in the "sleek minimalist
room" are "at the bar with a view of the open kitchen", but the "noise
level is low" throughout, providing a "Zen-chic" experience.

Pitchi Poï *Jewish/Polish*

| - | - | - | M |

4^e | 7, rue Caron (St-Paul) | 01-42-77-46-15 | www.pitchipoi.com
"Discover Jewish cuisine" with a Polish twist at this "small, lively"
eatery, known for its "scrumptious" blini washed down with a large
selection of vodkas and its highly "hyped", all-you-can-eat Sunday
brunch buffet; even devotees declare "the decor is pretty basic" but
"the courtyard is nice" with its coveted location "on a tranquil
square in the Marais."

Pizza Chic ⊠Ⓜ *Pizza*

| - | - | - | M |

6^e | 13, rue de Mézières (St-Sulpice) | 01-45-48-30-38
The latest Italian from owner Julien Cohen (Lei) is a bling-bling pizza
parlor with baroque black-and-white decor and pricey pies topped
with upmarket garnishes like *lardo di colonnata* (salt-preserved
Tuscan fatback) and artichoke; service is of the wannabe model variety, which fits right in with the smugly see-and-be-seen scene
of the 6th.

Pizzeria d'Auteuil *Italian*

| - | - | - | M |

16^e | 81, rue la Fontaine (Michel-Ange-Auteuil) | 01-42-88-00-86
"Overflowing with regulars" from the ritzy 16th, "this pizzeria is in
fact a real Italian restaurant" – and a "good" one too; "but it's best
not to go hungry" since you'll probably have to wait for service that
"runs the gamut from passable to scandalous"; since "it's always
full", though, clearly the "cool crowd" doesn't care that "the welcome is not their strong suit" and the decor's "uninteresting";
P.S. "you can also order pizzas to go."

	FOOD	DECOR	SERVICE	COST

Pizzetta (La) *Italian*
| - | - | - | M |

9ᵉ | 22, av Trudaine (Anvers/Pigalle) | 01-48-78-14-08 | www.lapizzetta.fr
"Hip and hip-to-hip", Sardinian chef Ricardo Podda's "simple place"
packs 'em in with "great pizzas" and other Italian eats "on the lovely
Avenue Trudaine"; "efficient" servers skillfully negotiate the
Napoleon III–meets-Milanese modern decor.

Ploum 🛇 *Japanese/New French*
| - | - | - | M |

10ᵉ | 20, rue Alibert (Goncourt) | 01-42-00-11-90 | www.ploum.fr
"Yet another example of how the French make delightful dining
seem effortless", this futuristic fusion venue "with huge windows
and raw interiors" – like "a UFO that landed in the middle of nowhere" "near the Canal Saint-Martin" – serves sushi and "simple
dishes" that, though "traditional French-sounding", are "innovative
and exciting"; service is "friendly", and prices reasonable.

Poisson Rouge (Le) *Eclectic/Wine Bar*
| - | - | - | M |

10ᵉ | 112, quai de Jemmapes (Gare de l'Est/République) | 01-40-40-07-11 |
www.le-poisson-rouge.com
Overlooking the Canal Saint-Martin, this trendy *bar à vins* was one
of the first to colonize the 10th, and it remains an ongoing hit with
hip locals who like to wash down the variety of vinos with an equally
Eclectic menu that mixes French, Asian and Moroccan influences;
the red-and-gray decor and wine-bottle light fixtures emphasize the
place's offbeat personality, while *petit* prices ensure it's packed
around the clock.

Polichinelle Cafe *Bistro*
| - | - | - | M |

11ᵉ | 64-66, rue de Charonne (Charonne) | 01-58-30-63-52
Yes, it looks "like a '30s soup kitchen with absolutely no updating
since", but that's part of "the charm of this place", yet another of the
eateries turning the 11th into neo-bistro central; regulars rave about
the relaxed aura and modest prices for modern dishes cooked with loving care; there's live entertainment Sundays in the ever-bustling bar.

Polidor ● *Bistro*
| 17 | 16 | 15 | €30 |

6ᵉ | 41, rue Monsieur-le-Prince (Luxembourg/Odéon) |
01-43-26-95-34
"Steeped in history", this "old bistro" (circa 1845) near the
Luxembourg Gardens is where students, starving artists and tourists
"looking for the 'authentic' Paris" "sit elbow-to-elbow" at "long communal tables" to eat "decent, inexpensive" ("if uninspired") "comfort
meals" in an "unpretentious" room adorned by a cubbyholed napkin
holder where the likes of Baudelaire and Hemingway once kept their
linen; old-timers opine it "hasn't changed in 40 years" – "even the
waitresses seem the same" with their "genuine rude service."

Pomponette (A la) ●🛇 *Bistro*
| ▽ 17 | 15 | 14 | €46 |

18ᵉ | 42, rue Lepic (Abbesses/Blanche) | 01-46-06-08-36 |
www.alapomponette.fr
"A real institution, managed by the fourth generation" of the clan
that opened it in 1909, this bistro serves "good, if not light" comfort

food amid "very Montmartre decor" – "the walls are adorned by works of local painters who were short of cash (and sometimes of talent)"; the "honest neighborhood ambiance" is accented by monthly concerts ("you may wait awhile for your check since your waiter may be busy dancing").

Pomze ⑤ *New French*

18	17	19	€50

8ᵉ | 109, bd Haussmann (Miromesnil/St-Augustin) | 01-42-65-65-83 | www.pomze.com

"Admirers of William Tell" and apple addicts are thrilled to the core by this "wonderfully inventive" "concept" eatery in the 8th, where the New French menu "is built around *la pomme* in all its forms", adding "subtle flavors" to dishes from starters to dessert; augmenting them is an impressive selection of – what else? – "the best ciders" from around France; N.B. there's also a ground-floor gourmet shop.

Potager du Roy (Le) ⑤M *Classic French*

19	17	16	€53

Versailles | 1, rue du Maréchal-Joffre (Versailles-Rive Gauche RER) | 01-39-50-35-34

Visitors to Versailles hail this "lovely retreat" near the palace, where the chef makes "exceptional" Traditional French "cuisine with a touch of originality", giving "a place of honor to vegetables" (the name refers to the royal garden); the decor is equally "classic" – though perhaps the tables are "a little too close together" – and while it's "a little dear", you won't need a king's ransom to pay the bill.

Pouilly Reuilly ⑤ *Bistro*

–	–	–	M

Le Pré-St-Gervais | 68, rue André Joineau (Hoche) | 01-48-45-14-59

It's just east of the city in Le Pré-Saint-Gervais, but suburban surveyors say this "old favorite" can be "out of this world" for "heavy", "typical bistro food" (think organ meats, blood sausage and giant éclairs); as they walk through to the post-war dining room, customers get a close-up look at the kitchen – but be advised that it stops taking orders after 9:45 PM.

Poule au Pot (La) ◑M *Bistro*

23	19	23	€46

1ᵉʳ | 9, rue Vauvilliers (Châtelet-Les Halles/Louvre-Rivoli) | 01-42-36-32-96 | www.lapouleaupot.fr

There's "a chicken in every pot" – or nearly – at this "classic spot" in Les Halles, a "local place" where peckish diners can count on "large portions" of the "signature dish", as well as onion soup, bone marrow, profiteroles and other bistro faves; the service is "very amiable", right up until closing time at 5 AM.

Pramil M *Bistro/New French*

–	–	–	M

3ᵉ | 9, rue du Vertbois (Temple) | 01-42-72-03-60

Just steps from the busy Place de la République, this cozy bistro with white-painted beams and pots of white orchids all over the small chic dining room pulls a mixed crowd of discerning regulars for the suave contemporary bistro cooking of chef Alain Pramil; the menu follows the seasons, but dishes like a salad of *ficoide glaciale* (a fleshy, slightly acidic succulent) with roasted tomatoes and shrimp or onglet de veau with potato purée show off his style.

⚡ Pré Catelan (Le) ⑤Ⓜ *Haute Cuisine*   27 | 28 | 26 | €159

16ᵉ | Bois de Boulogne, Route de Suresnes (Pont-de-Neuilly/ Porte Maillot) | 01-44-14-41-14 | www.precatelanparis.com

"Haute Cuisine of the highest order", "impeccable" service and, of course, that "beautiful location" in the Bois de Boulogne – small wonder that a "phenomenal dining experience" awaits at this "elegant, enduring" classic; though redone in contemporary tones of beige, bronze and gray, the decor retains its "magical" imperial aura, and while the "prices are budget-busting", most declare "cost be damned" because "lunch in the garden on a summer afternoon is pure bliss."

Press Café ⑤ *Bistro*   - | - | - | I

2ᵉ | 89, rue Montmartre (Sentier) | 01-40-26-07-30 | www.presscafe.net

A stone's throw from the offices of Agence France-Presse (hence, its name), this "nice neighborhood bistro" in the 2nd arrondissement delights journalists and other hard-pressed locals with its "exceptional service and food"; the latter consists of simple cuisine – foie gras, hand-cut beef tartare, chocolate mousse – at prices so low they're newsworthy.

Pré Verre (Le) ⑤Ⓜ *New French*   22 | 13 | 16 | €38

5ᵉ | 8, rue Thénard (Maubert-Mutualité) | 01-43-54-59-47 | www.lepreverre.com

Diners "who like to be surprised" "wait in line" for a table at this "young, animated" Latin Quarter New French, which "has achieved cult culinary status by reinventing classics" with a "fusion of spices" that "get you traveling without moving" – and all for an "unbeatable price" too; but no matter how "crowded" and "noisy" the "narrow" main room gets, claustrophobic clients should "avoid at all costs" the "low-ceilinged basement."

Procope (Le) ◗ *Classic French*   16 | 22 | 16 | €55

6ᵉ | 13, rue de l'Ancienne Comédie (Odéon) | 01-40-46-79-00 | www.procope.com

"You have to eat in this 17th-century establishment once, just to check it off your list" – for this Classic French in Saint-Germain is practically "a museum" with its "portrait-laden walls, apartment-sized rooms" and antiques (you "like the idea of dining next to Voltaire's desk"?); once patronized by "luminaries of literature, the arts" and politics, it's "now frequented largely by tourists" – "the servers are clearly fed up with them" – and critics call the cuisine "great for history buffs, but not for gourmets."

P'tit Troquet (Le) ⑤ *Bistro*   22 | 17 | 23 | €40

7ᵉ | 28, rue de l'Exposition (Ecole Militaire) | 01-47-05-80-39

Now, "this is the bistro atmosphere you crave when you arrive in Paris" declare devotees of this "wife-, husband- and daughter-run little restaurant" "in an unassuming alleyway near the Eiffel Tower"; the service is "very nice" and the food "simply delightful"; true, the decor of flea-market finds is a tad "tired", but "with traditional food at reasonable prices becoming increasingly rare" these days, small wonder the place has been "discovered by tourists (so go late and eat with the French)."

	FOOD	DECOR	SERVICE	COST

Publicis Drugstore ● *Brasserie* | 11 | 11 | 10 | €35 |

8ᵉ | 133, av des Champs-Elysées (Charles de Gaulle-Etoile/George V) | 01-44-43-77-64 | www.publicisdrugstore.com

Boasting an "idyllic location on the Champs" within the glass-fronted Publicis entertainment/shopping complex, this "hip, modern" French take on an American coffee shop serves an eclectic brasserie menu throughout the day; "the decor is a little too bat cave-ish", and the food "banal, but the Parisians love it, so you have to try it."

Pure Café ❍ *Eclectic* | - | - | - | M |

11ᵉ | 14, rue Jean Macé (Faidherbe-Chaligny) | 01-43-71-47-22

There are no guarantees you'll spot actress Julie Delpy, but still this "classic cafe", featured in the film *Before Sunset*, makes a "lovely, casual date" (or reunion) place, thanks to its "fresh, delicious" Eclectic fare, "inexpensive drinks" from a horseshoe-shaped bar and "relaxed setting", courtesy of its "off-the-beaten-track location" in the 11th.

Pur'Grill *New French* | 19 | 18 | 18 | €83 |

2ᵉ | Park Hyatt Paris-Vendôme | 5, rue de la Paix (Opéra) | 01-58-71-12-34 | www.paris.vendome.hyatt.com

With "impressive circular design" (by American-in-Paris Ed Tuttle, who's done several Aman resorts), the Park Hyatt's "stylish" dinner-only eatery offers a "view of the artists of the kitchen" as they grill "tasty meats" and other New French fare; but some purists pout the decor's "impersonal" and the "prices are a bit steep for the offerings."

Quai (Le) *New French* | - | - | - | M |

7ᵉ | Quai Anatole France - Port de Solférino (Solférino) | 01-44-18-04-39 | www.restaurantlequai.com

"Nothing better than being on a barge on a beautiful day" say sea-faring surveyors of this houseboat moored at the foot of the Musée d'Orsay; "charming servers" offer "enjoyable" New French lunches, in a glass-enclosed room or outside on the Seine-side terrace where the splendid view lets "you wave to the *bateaux-mouches* passing by."

Quai Ouest ❍ *Eclectic* | 13 | 14 | 11 | €47 |

Saint-Cloud | 1200, quai Marcel Dassault (Pont-de-St-Cloud) | 01-46-02-35-54

If everyone likes the "nice view" of the Seine from this "huge hangar-like" ship in suburban Saint-Cloud, opinions are mixed when it comes to the Eclectic menu; if amiable mateys maintain it's "better than what you usually find at other barge restaurants", cynical sailors snap the kitchen "could do better", and so could the "slow" staff; but then, "you come here not for the food, but for the setting" and to "see and be seen" by the TV-industry and trendy types.

Quai-Quai 🗷 M *Classic French* | - | - | - | M |

1ᵉʳ | 74, quai des Orfèvres (Pont Neuf) | 01-46-33-69-75 | www.quaiquai-restaurant.com

A trio of new owners (who also run Cinq Mars) has given this long-running bistro with two entrances – one on the wharf, the other on the Place Dauphine – a new lease on life; they've installed a high-quality French comfort-food menu (poached egg and lentil salad, filet mignon with sage-seasoned mashed potatoes, pain perdu) and redone the decor with colorful pillows and sayings scrawled across the walls.

404 (Le) ◑ *Moroccan* | 22 | 25 | 20 | €43 |

3ᵉ | 69, rue des Gravilliers (Arts et Métiers) | 01-42-74-57-81

It's like a "berber's tent deep in the medina" at this "lively" Moroccan near Arts et Métiers, with "exotic", "sumptuous" decor like "the inside of a genie bottle", "frenzied music" and a "sexy, moody, party atmosphere"; just "prepare to be sardined" into the "cool crowd" that packs the place seven days a week for "tasty, reasonably priced" couscous and tagines, and avoid the first seating if you don't want to be "rushed out" before your mint tea arrives.

Quedubon *Bistro/Wine Bar* | - | - | - | M |

19ᵉ | 22, rue du Plateau (Buttes Chaumont) | 01-42-38-18-65

Run by Gilles Bénard (ex Chez Ramulaud), this young, gray-hued wine bar near the Parc de Buttes Chaumont has quickly become a neighborhood institution; what everyone loves is the excellent selection of *vins* by the glass – many of them organic – and simple eats, including Basque charcuterie, perfectly aged cheeses and a couple of hot bistro dishes that change daily, while always remaining affordable.

Quincy (Le) 🗷⇗ *Bistro* | - | - | - | M |

12ᵉ | 28, av Ledru-Rollin (Gare de Lyon/Quai de la Rapée) | 01-46-28-46-76 | www.lequincy.fr

"It doesn't get any more local than this" cry converts to this "cozy", "very Parisian" veteran bistro near the Gare de Lyon, which delights with traditional French dishes like "great snails and frogs' legs", and chef-owner Michel Bosshard, who "comes to the table and helps you decide what to order"; fans fear that after four decades, he "will need to retire soon, so rush to try it before it's too late."

Quinzième (Le) 🗷 *New French* | - | - | - | E |

15ᵉ | 14, rue Cauchy (Javel) | 01-45-54-43-43 | www.restaurantlequinzieme.com

"In a quiet corner of the 15th, near the Parc André Citroën" lies "the restaurant everyone's talking about" these days – "TV chef Cyril Lignac's" first physical kitchen; fans find the New French fare quite "pleasing to the palate", while opponents argue it's "overpriced, overrated and overexposed in the media" – but none of that stops media mavens from flocking to the "lovely" contemporary digs.

	FOOD	DECOR	SERVICE	COST

Racines (Les) 🚫 *Wine Bar/Bistro* | - | - | - | M |

2ᵉ | 8, Passage des Panoramas (Grands Boulevards) | 01-40-13-06-41 | www.morethanorganic.com

The romantic Passage des Panoramas, an ancient arcade in the 2nd arrondissement, is the picturesque location of one of the hottest *bistrots à vins* in Paris; a mélange of vinophiles, boutique-owners and fashion types mix it up over pours – many of them organic – and plates of cheese and charcuterie plus a few hot Classic French dishes and pastas, made with quality produce (the meat comes from star butcher Hugo Desnoyer and vegetables from chef Alain Passard's farm).

Ragueneau (Le) ◑🚫 *Classic French/Tearoom* | - | - | - | I |

1ᵉʳ | 202, rue St-Honoré (Palais Royal-Musée du Louvre) | 01-42-60-29-20 | www.ragueneau.fr

"A few meters from the Louvre and La Comédie Française", this theatrical-looking venue named for the poetry-loving pastry chef in *Cyrano de Bergerac* is ideal for a cuppa in the main floor tea salon, but it also serves "pretty good" Classic French food in the upstairs dining room; "it may not be gastronomy, but it's good value" for the money; N.B. there's live jazz on Friday nights, but it's closed Saturday and Sunday evenings.

Ravi ◑ *Indian* | ▽ 21 | 20 | 19 | €48 |

7ᵉ | 50, rue de Verneuil (Rue du Bac) | 01-42-61-17-28 | www.restaurant-ravi.com

"Definitely known only to the locals", "this tiny – we mean tiny – treasure in Saint-Germain" offers "dark ambiance" and "detailed decor" of carved wooden screens and artwork to back up its "delicious" Indian cuisine; while "adorable", the staff sometimes seems "on vacation"; nevertheless, subcontinental supporters swear "if you want a romantic dinner, there's nowhere better."

Rech (Le) 🚫Ⓜ *Seafood* | - | - | - | E |

17ᵉ | 62, av des Ternes (Charles de Gaulle-Etoile/Ternes) | 01-45-72-29-47 | www.rech.fr

Proprietor Alain Ducasse has recently installed Jacques Maximin as the head chef here, and fish fans are flipping over the "great rebirth of this great old place" just off the Place des Ternes; gently "upgraded", it "keeps the best of the old", from the "fabulous" seafood to the softly lit 1920s blond-wood interior on the second floor; the first is a more casual cafe, with "nice *coquillages.*"

Réconfort (Le) ◑ *New French* | - | - | - | M |

3ᵉ | 37, rue de Poitou (St-Sébastien Froissart) | 01-49-96-09-60 | www.lereconfort.com

"Few restaurants so surely justify their name" – 'comfort' – as this "apartmentlike" eatery in the northern Marais; "hidden inside of an old novel", the menu offers "simple modern French food without too many frills"; a "lively crowd" sometimes gets "noisy", but "subtle lighting" makes it "a place to stare into your date's eyes and chat late into the evening."

Réfectoire (Le) *Bistro* — | — | — | M

11ᵉ | 80, bd Richard Lenoir (Richard Lenoir/St-Ambroise) |
01-48-06-74-85 | www.lerefectoire.com

A "kitschy atmosphere" – the "chairs, tables and so on are quite close
to that of French public school" cafeterias (*réfectoires*) – makes this
11th-arrondissement bistro a "cool, undiscovered place"; the "creative kitchen's" offerings are "accompanied by a lively staff", and all
told, even grown-ups find it "thoroughly enjoyable", especially if
they "try the restrooms", a true sound-and-light show.

☑ Régalade (La) ☒ *Bistro* — 25 | 17 | 20 | €51

14ᵉ | 49, av Jean Moulin (Alésia) | 01-45-45-68-58

Nostalgists naturally say it "isn't what it used to be", but scores support the sentiment that this "consummate bistro" is now "even better
than under its legendary previous chef-owner", Yves Camdeborde;
chef Bruno Doucet's "country French" cuisine with a Basque influ-
ence is "hearty and generous" – "where else will a waiter put down
a two-ft.-long terrine and bucket of cornichons just for starters?" –
and the staff has actually gotten "friendly"; sure it's "noisy" and
prices have drifted up, but it's "still a winner" and "well worth the
trip to the southern confines of the 14th"; N.B. closed weekends.

🆕 Reginette ☒ *Pizza* — | — | — | M

8ᵉ | 66, av des Champs-Elysées (Franklin D. Roosevelt/
St-Philippe-du-Roule) | 01-83-56-65-55

Adjacent to the famous Regine's nightclub, off the Champs, this
vest-pocket pizzeria packs 'em in with pies that would make a Neapolitan proud, turned out by a sassy pizzaiolo who puts on a good
show for office workers at noon and couples coming by for a quick
pre-movie meal; Naples has never seen a dessert pizza like the one
here spread with Nutella, however – and would surely blink twice at
the prices too (though they're moderate for the area).

☑ Relais d'Auteuil
"Patrick Pignol" ☒Ⓜ *Haute Cuisine* — 27 | 20 | 26 | €137

16ᵉ | 31, bd Murat (Michel-Ange-Molitor/Porte d'Auteuil) |
01-46-51-09-54

"If you're adventuresome", join the "well-to-do neighborhood
clientele" that congregates at this Haute Cuisine table out toward
the Porte d'Auteuil, which, while "outrageously expensive", is
considered "one of the best in Paris" for the eponymous chef-
owner's traditional French food and "outstanding wine"; the "warm
welcome of Madame Pignol" now comes in newly renovated (post-
Survey) quarters done up in stainless steel – it's a "really lovely"
experience, all 'round.

☑ Relais de l'Entrecôte (Le) ❶ *Steak* — 22 | 14 | 18 | €39

6ᵉ | 20, rue St-Benoît (St-Germain-des-Prés) | 01-45-49-16-00
8ᵉ | 15, rue Marbeuf (Franklin D. Roosevelt) | 01-49-52-07-17
www.relais-entrecote.com

They're "one-trick ponies, but it's a great trick" maintain meat eaters of these two "cafeterialike" carnivores' caves in the 6th and 8th,

where the "only item on the menu is steak" "with plate-licking secret sauce", salad and "frites that just keep coming", plus a "side of grumpy waitresses"; skeptics sneer it's "France's answer to Outback Steakhouse", complete "with lines snaking outside the door daily", but it's ideal "for people who can't make up their minds what to order."

Relais de Venise (Le) ◑ *Steak* 24 16 19 €37

17ᵉ | 271, bd Péreire (Porte Maillot) | 01-45-74-27-97

"No surprises" await at this steakhouse at Porte Maillot, an "address handed down from generation to generation", where "the wait for a table is interminable" and then the "friendly but abrupt" waitresses are almost too "quick"; the fixed menu stars an "eternal entrecôte" with "mysterious sauce" that has "spies the world over trying to find out the recipe", along with "terrific frites" ("whatever you do, don't ask for ketchup!"); P.S. the "bargain price" includes "second helpings."

Relais du Parc (Le) ⊠ *Classic/New French* 19 18 16 €73

16ᵉ | Hôtel Le Parc | 55-57, av Raymond Poincaré (Trocadéro/Victor Hugo) | 01-44-05-66-10 | www.leparcparishotel.com

"Ducasse meets current chef" (Spoon alum Alexandre Nicolas) at this "expensive" hotel venue near Trocadéro, where the fare these days tends toward bourgeois comfort classics; with its white clapboard walls and seasonally changing colors, the decor channels a New England frame of mind, but the crowd is definitely *très Parisien*, particularly on the "beautiful outdoor patio."

Relais Louis XIII ⊠ Ⓜ *Haute Cuisine* 25 24 25 €104

6ᵉ | 8, rue des Grands-Augustins (Odéon/St-Michel) | 01-43-26-75-96 | www.relaislouis13.com

"Feel like Louis himself and dine like a king" at this "wonderful, atavistic" table in Saint-Germain, with a "romantic châteaulike setting", "outstanding Haute Cuisine" and "wine list that doesn't disappoint", proffered by an "impeccable" staff; sure, it seems "stuffy" and "unadventurous" to modernists (and "expensive" to everybody), but "staunch fans" feel it's just the "sort of place Americans dream about – and too rarely experience – in Paris."

Relais Plaza (Le) ◑ *Brasserie/Eclectic* 23 22 22 €76

8ᵉ | Plaza-Athénée | 25, av Montaigne (Alma Marceau/ Franklin D. Roosevelt) | 01-53-67-64-00 | www.plaza-athenee-paris.com

"Celebrities and a chic clientele" add a "touch of glamour" to this "sophisticated, intimate" art deco "brasserie deluxe"; "the more casual dining experience of the Plaza-Athénée", it's run by the same chefs behind the main restaurant, and their "seductive" Eclectic fare inspires clients to confide "you feel like you're cheating – Alain Ducasse–inspired dishes at a fraction of the price."

Réminet (Le) *New French* - - - E

5ᵉ | 3, rue des Grands-Degrés (Maubert-Mutualité/St-Michel) | 01-44-07-04-24 | www.lereminet.com

This longtime Latin Quarter charmer in the 5th, overlooking the Ile Saint-Louis, has returned under new management, which has created a vaulted basement dining room (though insiders prefer the main floor) and a different New French menu, which includes roast scallops with mushroom risotto and cannelés with poached pineapple; the wine list ranges across regions to include large and small producers.

Rendez-vous des Chauffeurs (Au) 🛱Ⓜ *Bistro*

FOOD	DECOR	SERVICE	COST
-	-	-	I

18ᵉ | 11, rue des Portes-Blanches (Marcadet-Poissonniers) | 01-42-64-04-17

Nothing apparently changes (not even the menu) at this century-old "bistro with a real sense of neighborhood" – specifically, an untouristy part of the 18th; a "convivial" "hole-in-the-wall", it has "no decor" to speak of – just copious portions of "simply wonderful food" (including hand-cut fries that some call "the best in the world") at "very gentle prices."

Repaire de Cartouche (Le) 🛱Ⓜ *Bistro*

FOOD	DECOR	SERVICE	COST
16	12	12	€41

11ᵉ | 8, bd Filles du Calvaire (St-Sébastien Froissart) | 01-47-00-25-86

There's a "nice local feel, with few tourists" that pervades this "relaxed" venue in the 11th, a site for family groups who are fans of the "rich", traditional bistro cooking; but the decor's "banal" and the service "glacial" ("maybe I came at a bad time?"), leaving some to suggest it's "not worth the 40-odd euros."

Restaurant (Le) 🛱Ⓜ *Classic French*

FOOD	DECOR	SERVICE	COST
▽ 26	27	26	€76

6ᵉ | L'Hôtel | 13, rue des Beaux-Arts (St-Germain-des-Prés) | 01-44-41-99-01 | www.l-hotel.com

Philippe Belissent, "a chef from Ledoyen", assumed command of the venue a while back, and "what a great surprise!" – it now offers "a dreamy dinner in the dreamy decor" of the "luxuriant" Left Bank hotel "where Oscar Wilde spent his last days"; "if only he could have lived to enjoy" the "creative", "light Classic French cuisine" ("foams and emulsions abound but not to excess"), served amid the "lushly" louche look of a low-lit space with leopard print accents, small tables and cushy chairs that "will make anyone look divine"; "servers are at the ready, but never pretentious", so if you don't mind hefty prices, hie thee to this "hedonistic experience."

Restaurant de la Tour 🛱 *Classic French*

FOOD	DECOR	SERVICE	COST
▽ 21	21	23	€54

15ᵉ | 6, rue Desaix (Dupleix/La Motte-Picquet-Grenelle) | 01-43-06-04-24

"A charming place, with owners who seem genuinely pleased to welcome customers", this newly revamped (post-Survey) site dishes up highly "delicious" Classic French fare, including "foie gras, langoustines, boned pigeon, wild boar stew and crêpes suzette"; dominated by a "business crowd at lunch", it's close to the Eiffel Tower, so "expect Americans and Brits" as well, all attracted by the "prettily priced" prix fixes.

Restaurant du Marché 🛱Ⓜ *Bistro*

FOOD	DECOR	SERVICE	COST
-	-	-	M

15ᵉ | 59, rue de Dantzig (Porte de Versailles) | 01-48-28-31-55

Celebrating its 42nd year, this long-standing, low-key bistro in the 15th draws locals with oft-changing, "good, unpretentious country cuisine" and vaguely rustic, classic decor of red banquettes, pewter bar and the archetypical blackboard; Saturday morning cooking classes are led by chef-owner Francis Lévêque.

Restaurant du Musée d'Orsay M *Classic French*

17 | 23 | 17 | €35

7ᵉ | Musée d'Orsay | 1, rue de la Légion d'Honneur (Solférino) | 01-45-49-47-03 | www.museedorsay.fr

When Manet and Monet start to merge in your mind, the Musée d'Orsay's eatery offers a "regal" "respite from museum overload" with a "stunning" river view and belle epoque decor of "painted ceilings, crystal chandeliers and mirrored walls" that is "just as interesting" as the institution itself; the Classic French fare is a bit "institutional" too, but even if "the food's better on an airplane, you couldn't ask for a prettier place to sit after a day of Impressionist art."

Restaurant du Palais Royal Ⓩ *Classic French*

19 | 20 | 19 | €63

1ᵉʳ | 110, Galerie de Valois (Bourse/Palais Royal-Musée du Louvre) | 01-40-20-00-27 | www.restaurantdupalaisroyal.com

"What better decor than the leaf-dappled shade of the Jardins du Palais-Royal?" sigh surveyors seduced by the "magnificent terrace" of this Classic French overlooking one of the city's prettiest gardens; some find it might be a little "too expensive" for food that's just "above average", but all reviewers agree that it is absolutely "idyllic on a beautiful summer evening."

Restaurant Manufacture Ⓩ *Bistro*

▽ 21 | 18 | 19 | €40

Issy-les-Moulineaux | 20, esplanade de la Manufacture (Corentin-Celton/Porte de Versailles) | 01-40-93-08-98 | www.restaurantmanufacture.com

A "canteen for the TV-industry types working nearby", this "cool" loft space in Issy-les-Moulineaux has a "superb" setting (and camera-worthy terrace) dating from its former life as a tobacco factory; the "original" bistro food is "a clever mix of traditional products and modern flavors" – all told, it manufactures "one of the best price/value ratios in the suburbs"; N.B. closed on weekends.

Restaurant Paul M *Bistro*

20 | 17 | 18 | €36

1ᵉʳ | 15, pl Dauphine (Pont-Neuf) | 01-43-54-21-48

"Pretend you are in 1940s Paris" at this "quiet oasis" "on a lovely square on the Ile de la Cité", a "landmark setting" where former neighbors Yves Montand and Simone Signoret used to dine on Classic French fare; it's still served today, from "sublime breakfasts" to dinners in the traditional, mirrored bistro setting or under the stars – "an outdoor table and almost anything grilled will never disappoint" you here.

Reuan Thai *Thai*

- | - | - | I

11ᵉ | 36, rue de l'Orillon (Belleville) | 01-43-55-15-82

It's a short trip from Belleville to Bangkok, thanks to this "tasty" Thai table, a "great find" for "flavorful" fare, including curries and coconut ice cream, served by a "busy" but "friendly" staff; low prices seal the deal.

	FOOD	DECOR	SERVICE	COST

Réveil du 10e (Le) *Bistro*
	-	-	-	M

10ᵉ | 35, rue du Château d'Eau (Château d'Eau/Jacques Bonsergent) | 01-42-41-77-59

Head for the increasingly trendy 10th to try this retro-looking site (a 1960s vintage cafe) enhanced with a newly added year-round terrace; it's a "wonderful neighborhood bistro" that charms with hearty eats and, despite its small size, a "terrific wine selection", including *beaucoup de* Beaujolais by the glass.

Ribouldingue 🚫Ⓜ *Classic French*
	18	15	14	€40

5ᵉ | 10, rue St-Julien-le-Pauvre (St-Michel) | 01-46-33-98-80

A few "just don't get it", but most find "fascinating" "the exquisite way the chef prepares organs" at this offal-oriented Classic French ("I'm pretty sure I ate cow's udders and liked them"); if the decor's "a bit rummage"-sale–like, it's because it's left over from the previous tenant; besides, what they saved on redesign is reflected in the bill: "it's rare to find these prices" in the touristy Latin Quarter.

Rice and Fish 🚫⇄ *Japanese*
	-	-	-	M

2ᵉ | 22, rue Greneta (Réaumur Sébastopol) | 01-73-70-46-09

With an interior that recalls the classic American diner, this snug duplex in the 2nd is the first Parisian showcase of Japanese-Californian cooking, with two Yankee hand-rollers behind the counter who learned their craft in San Francisco; it's ideal for lunch or an early supper of such sushi specialties as eel temeki and soft-shell crab roll – or maybe 'le krunchy' with tempura shrimp and secret sauce.

River Café *Classic/New French*
	14	15	11	€48

Issy-les-Moulineaux | 146, quai de Stalingrad (Issy-Val de Seine RER) | 01-40-93-50-20 | www.lerivercafe.net

"Rare-for-Paris waterfront dining" is the daily special on this "nice houseboat" "permanently moored" in Issy-les-Moulineaux with "mini-terraces on each side"; but seafarers snap the combo of Classic and New French cooking is "not inspirational" and "you have to have time to spare" because the deck hands are in no hurry to serve.

Robe et le Palais (La) 🚫 *Wine Bar/Bistro*
	19	14	17	€38

1ᵉʳ | 13, rue des Lavandières-Ste-Opportune (Châtelet-Les Halles) | 01-45-08-07-41

Boasting an appropriate "ambiance of cases of grand crus" (literally), this *bistrot à vins* is a "favorite" in the 1st, since its status as a "great place to discover new wines" is supplemented by the "simple but good" fare; the staff, however, leaves "a hot-and-cold impression": "service is slow, but the waiters are friendly."

Robert et Louise Ⓜ *Bistro*
	21	14	16	€39

3ᵉ | 64, rue Vieille-du-Temple (Rambuteau) | 01-42-78-55-89

"Guests from all over the world sit together at long tables" at "this palace of meat" in the Marais – a fiftysomething, "extremely popular" place for its "great steaks" cooked over an open fire "right in front of you", along with other traditional bistro dishes; the setting amounts to a "hole-in-the-wall, with a kitchen the size of a closet",

	FOOD	DECOR	SERVICE	COST

but the welcome is "warm"; just avoid the bathroom, which is, to put it politely, rather "rustic."

Roi du Pot-au-Feu (Le) 🅜 *Bistro*
- | - | - | M

9ᵉ | 34, rue Vignon (Havre-Caumartin/Madeleine) | 01-47-42-37-10

"Real pot-au-feu" fans make pilgrimage to this "cramped" bistro for princely portions of the "hearty" "traditional dish" and other "beefy" "French staples"; while its 1930s setting almost "seems too kitschy", it's a "must-do" "for a meal to put you to sleep or to last you all day" shopping nearby on the Grands Boulevards.

Rollin (Le) 🅜🅜 *Classic French*
- | - | - | M

11ᵉ | 92, av Ledru-Rollin (Ledru-Rollin) | 01-48-06-51-92

Overlooking the Place de la Bastille, this airy, loftlike New French caters to a sophisticated crowd that appreciates its minimalist decor, classic French cuisine and wines from small producers; eating at the bar is a good option for solo diners, while the highly reasonable prices are just plain good.

Romantica (La) 🅜 *Italian*
▽ 23 | 20 | 19 | €59

Clichy | 73, bd Jean Jaurès (Mairie-de-Clichy) | 01-47-37-29-71 | www.claudiopuglia.com

Latin food lovers say this idyllic Italian in the Clichy suburbs "lives up to its name", with a flower-filled courtyard, "very friendly" service and "excellent" pasta; "don't miss the house specialty", tagliolini flambéed tableside in a Parmesan wheel, but "be warned" that this filling dish might leave you "too sleepy to be romantic afterwards."

Rosa Bonheur 🅜 *Southwest*
- | - | - | M

19ᵉ | 2, allee de la Cascade, Parc des Buttes-Chaumont (Botzaris) | 01-42-00-00-45 | www.rosabonheur.fr

The newest tenant of this pretty belle epoque pavilion in the most arcadian of Paris' parks has hit a winning formula with its rotisserie that supplies the menu's main courses – Camargue-style roast chicken, leg of lamb, pork ribs – all served with organic vegetables; the hip young crowd is a sign of how this corner of the city is renewing itself, while the servers reflect the tongue-in-cheek pastoralism that makes this place a good time, especially in summer out on the terrace; N.B. Sunday brunch has already become a local institution.

Rose Bakery 🅜 *British/French*
17 | 12 | 13 | €27

3ᵉ | 30, rue Debelleyme (Filles du Calvaire) | 01-49-96-54-01

9ᵉ | 46, rue des Martyrs (Notre-Dame-de-Lorette) | 01-42-82-12-80

A "media favorite" that "emphasizes market freshness", this Anglo-French tearoom/bakery/takeaway on the hippest street in the 9th offers "original", often organic fare from morning until early evening (it's especially "great for brunch"); but the rose is not without its thorns: if "long on food, it's short on ambiance", and "much too small for its enthusiastic clientele (you can spend a lot of time waiting)" – though its 3rd-arrondissement offshoot might ease the squeeze.

| | FOOD | DECOR | SERVICE | COST |

Rose de France *Bistro*
- | **-** | **-** | **M**

1er | 24, pl Dauphine (Pont Neuf/Cité) | 01-43-54-10-12 |
www.larosedefrance.com

Located on a calm, tree-lined square on the Ile de la Cité, this
"small" but "warm and welcoming" bistro beckons with "a choice of
French classics with new wave flair"; the "co-owner will advise
on the wines" – some are even from his own vineyard – and the experience is especially "charming" if you snag a seat outside on the
year-round terrace.

Rosimar ⓈSpanish
- | **-** | **-** | **M**

16^e | 26, rue Poussin (Michel-Ange-Auteuil/Porte d'Auteuil) |
01-45-27-74-91

"Almost everyone's a regular, yet newcomers are well treated" at
this "neighborhood place" "in the heart of the 16th" arrondissement; "authentic Catalan cuisine", "world-class paella" (order it
when you book) and a "heartwarming welcome" make up for the
"mirrored" but "gloomy decor."

Rôtisserie d'en Face (La) ⓈBistro
21 | **18** | **20** | **€51**

6^e | 2, rue Christine (Odéon/St-Michel) | 01-43-26-40-98 |
www.jacques-cagna.com

Surveyors whose appetites are richer than their wallets make a
habit of Jacques Cagna's "casual", "always buzzing" bistro in
Saint-Germain supplying "simple, excellently prepared food for a
fraction of the price" of the chef-owner's Haute Cuisine table
nearby; but if the menu is full of "solid" Gallic "staples" (notably
"rotisserie chicken to beat the band"), Yankee critics cavil the
clientele is too close to home – seems like "every person in the
restaurant is American!"

Rôtisserie du Beaujolais (La) *Bistro*
23 | **18** | **21** | **€47**

5^e | 19, quai de la Tournelle (Jussieu/Pont-Marie) | 01-43-54-17-47 |
www.tourdargent.com

Overlooking the Seine, this "bustling" bistro might be "next to La
Tour d'Argent", but it's "completely different" from its grandiose
parent; it's "one heck of a lot more reasonable", with "down-home"
Beaujolais fare, including "perfectly cooked meat" from a rotisserie
overlooking the room, and a "cramped but charming" ambiance
made even more "homey" by the "owners' cat, named Beaujolais,
often sleeping next to the bar" ("admire the feline and you'll get
a better table").

Rotonde (La) ❂Brasserie
15 | **14** | **14** | **€49**

6^e | 105, bd du Montparnasse (Vavin) | 01-43-26-48-26 |
www.rotondemontparnasse.com

In Montparnasse, a "neighborhood populated by famous cafes
from a bygone era", this "elegant old-time brasserie" is a "favorite" for its "ruby-red decor" and "padded little nooks"; while critics carp the cuisine's "correct" but "not exceptional", at least
the "genuinely surly but efficient waiters" add to the authentic
atmosphere of yore.

	FOOD	DECOR	SERVICE	COST

Rouge St-Honoré ● *Eclectic*

▽ 13 | 14 | 14 | €34

1er | 34, pl du Marché St-Honoré (Pyramides/Tuileries) | 01-42-61-16-09 | www.rouge-saint-honore.com

Although they've diversified somewhat, the menu's still "based on the tomato and its derivatives" at this "cute" Eclectic with grocery-store–like decor; "perfectly adequate for somewhere cheap and cheerful, it's nothing to get excited about" – though the location overlooking the Place du Marché Saint-Honoré is "pleasant for sitting outside on a warm evening."

Royal Madeleine *Classic French*

19 | 16 | 17 | €55

8e | 11, rue du Chevalier St-Georges (Madeleine) | 01-42-60-14-36 | www.royalmadeleine.com

On a side street "near the Madeleine", this "charming bistro" boasts a recently renovated (post-Survey), "typically Parisian" dining room "with garnet velvet banquettes, period engravings" and a vintage zinc bar; an "amiable" staff serves "refreshingly down to earth" Classic French dishes, and if it's "a little expensive", that's not surprising given the "good-quality" fare, "warm" decor and "froufrou neighborhood."

Rubis (Le) 🗷 *Wine Bar/Bistro*

15 | 10 | 15 | €27

1er | 10, rue du Marché St-Honoré (Tuileries) | 01-42-61-03-34

Here's one ruby (*rubis*) that's a real "gem" declare devotees who haunt this "essential" wine bar steps from the Place du Marché Saint-Honoré; it "hasn't changed in 25 years", but still overflows with "atmosphere, true French personality", a "sublime value-for-money lunch" of classic Gallic fare (or just charcuterie and cheese plates at night) and an inexpensive selection of Beaujolais that's drunk liberally around "barrels on the sidewalk when it's nice out."

Rucola (La) 🗷 *Italian*

- | - | - | M

17e | 198, bd Malesherbes (Wagram) | 01-44-40-04-50 | www.larucola.fr

"In a neighborhood filled with mediocre Italian food", the "elegant" offerings of this table ("no pizzas!") attract lots of locals; but the candlelit dining room, decorated with wines in open bins, "welcomes even tourists as prodigal sons and daughters" to this section of the 17th.

Rughetta (La) ● *Italian*

- | - | - | M

18e | 41, rue Lepic (Abbesses/Blanche) | 01-42-23-41-70

"Always packed with the young crowd and celebrities" from the neighborhood, this "lively" Montmartre trattoria serves "very good" pizza and pasta that are redolent of Rome; so what if "the personnel is not always nice" and the decor is minimal – "the terrace is really cool in the summer."

Sale e Pepe ●🗷M *Italian*

- | - | - | M

18e | 30, rue Ramey (Château Rouge/Jules Joffrin) | 01-46-06-08-01

"You'll feel at home as heaping portions of pasta are served onto your plate from a steaming sauté pan" at this "affordable" "cozy"

Sicilian in the 18th, where "a bubbly Italian duo greets you" then treats you to "delicious thin-crust pizzas as well as pastas" made with "fresh ingredients"; "but don't expect a menu, as the chef typically brings out whatever he's compelled to prepare."

Salon d'Hélène 🖂Ⓜ *Southwest* `19` `18` `17` `€70`

6ᵉ | 4, rue d'Assas (Sèvres-Babylone) | 01-42-22-00-11 | www.helenedarroze.com

"More casual than her fine-dining restaurant" on the floor above, Hélène Darroze's tapas bar-like canteen in the 6th is "popular with the young slick crowd" that covets her "dreamy" "small-portioned" Southwest French–inspired plates, including "the best foie gras on earth"; "the food's quite good, but it's not worth the ticket with the non-decor and frosty service" snarl cynics (though others find the staff "affable" enough); P.S. sybarites suggest "if your wallet and schedule allow, indulge in the lunchtime tasting menu" – 10 courses for 88€.

Salon du Panthéon 🖂 *Bistro* `-` `-` `-` `M`

5ᵉ | Cinéma du Panthéon | 13, rue Victor Cousin (Cluny La Sorbonne/Luxembourg RER) | 01-56-24-88-80 | www.cinemadupantheon.fr

Located on the top floor of the Cinéma du Panthéon, this smart '60s-style cafe was decorated by screen goddess Catherine Deneuve (with an antiques dealer's help); ever since its autumn 2007 premiere, it's been pulling a hip crowd that loves to lounge on the generously spaced sofas, lingering over a drink or a light meal of bistro bites; N.B. closed on weekends.

Samiin *Korean* `-` `-` `-` `M`

7ᵉ | 74, av de Breteuil (Sèvres-Lecourbe) | 01-47-34-58-96 | www.samiin.com

"Delicious Korean cuisine in a lovely setting" is the lure at this original little place near the Ecole Militaire; "the female servers are charming and helpful", and prices are "so reasonable for the quality and creativity" of the homestyle fare.

Sardegna a Tavola 🖂 *Italian* `▽` `21` `12` `12` `€55`

12ᵉ | 1, rue de Cotte (Ledru-Rollin) | 01-44-75-03-28

It's not rare to be surrounded by Italian families enjoying this crowded, "superb" Sardinian out in the 12th; regulars ignore the "brusque" service and concentrate on the "finesse" of the "creative preparations" and regional wines, saying "enormous portions" ("sharing's encouraged") make the "inflated prices" a little easier to swallow.

Sarladais (Le) 🖂 *Southwest* `-` `-` `-` `E`

8ᵉ | 2, rue de Vienne (St-Augustin) | 01-45-22-23-62 | www.lesarladais.com

Patrons who venture into this venue "off the beaten path" near the Gare Saint-Lazare are "amazed" to dig into a "tremendous cassoulet" and other seafood-oriented, "consistent" classics from the Southwest; the staff "serves with easy assurance", and the "warmly decorated" digs make it "dependable" for a business lunch or "quiet meal with a friend."

| | FOOD | DECOR | SERVICE | COST |

Saudade ☒ *Portuguese* — | — | — | M

1ᵉʳ | 34, rue des Bourdonnais (Châtelet-Les Halles) | 01-42-36-03-65 | www.restaurantsaudade.com

Perfect for "anyone who loves cod in all its preparations", this long-running Lusitanian near Châtelet is considered by many to be the best outpost of Portugal in Paris; perhaps the azulejo-tiled dining room is "ready for an update", but you still get "guaranteed atmosphere", especially when the live music plays on fado night.

Saut du Loup (Le) ◑ *New French* 14 | 17 | 15 | €51

1ᵉʳ | Musée des Arts Décoratifs | 107, rue de Rivoli (Palais Royal-Musée du Louvre/Tuileries) | 01-42-25-49-55 | www.lesautduloup.com

Tucked away inside the Musée des Arts Décoratifs, this "fashionable" New French offers "gorgeous views" over the Louvre courtyard; while the menu is "good", it "doesn't have many surprises", so enjoy the "nifty" setting instead – a "chic" black-and-white dining room decked out with designer furniture – or, "if the weather's nice, opt for the terrace" with that "Parisian dreamscape" of the I.M. Pei pyramid, the Jardins du Carrousel and the Tuileries.

Sauvignon (Au) *Sandwiches/Wine Bar* 14 | 13 | 13 | €35

7ᵉ | 80, rue des Sts-Pères (Sèvres-Babylone) | 01-45-48-49-02

"A chic crowd" that spends more shopping than eating "grabs a quick lunch" or après-store munchie at this "delightful" *bar à vins* with "lovely *tartines*" (open-face sandwiches) "and a wonderful selection of wines by the glass"; "such a deal you will not find elsewhere", "especially considering the neighborhood" (the tony 7th).

Saveurs de Flora (Les) ☒ *New French* 21 | 21 | 20 | €66

8ᵉ | 36, av George V (George V) | 01-40-70-10-49 | www.lessaveursdeflora.com

Chef-owner Flora Mikula's hideaway just off the Champs-Elysées "feels almost like somebody's private dining room" with "a cozy atmosphere" created by wallpaper, mirrors and candlelight; her "personal", "inventive-but-not-over-the top" New French fare is served by a "warm", if often "overwhelmed" staff; though it's not cheap, most find it "reasonably priced", given the expensive neighborhood.

Saveurs du Marché (Aux) ☒ *Bistro* — | — | — | M

Neuilly-sur-Seine | 4, rue de l'Eglise (Pont-de-Neuilly) | 01-47-45-72-11

This "good little" place in posh suburban Neuilly boasts fresh, often organic products from the nearby local *marché* (market) and "pleasing" Classic French dishes by chef-owner David Cheleman, who cut his teeth working with Jean-Pierre Vigato (Apicius); be aware, this black-and-beige bistro is "unfortunately not open during the weekend."

Sawadee ☒ *Thai* — | — | — | M

15ᵉ | 53, av Emile Zola (Charles Michels) | 01-45-77-68-90

Its friendly "multilingual staff" makes this "excellent Thai" in a "somewhat concrete corner" of the 15th a "place one returns to with pleasure", even if "the menu hasn't changed in years"; the pretty dining room with golden Buddhas offers a bit of Bangkok to boot.

Scheffer (Le) ⊠ *Bistro* | 18 | 13 | 19 | €36 |

16ᵉ | 22, rue Scheffer (Trocadéro) | 01-47-27-81-11

"The old owner is gone, taking some of his posters with him, but they've done a great job of maintaining the old atmosphere, good food and low prices" at this "terrific bistro near Trocadéro"; a "simple place", it's often "noisy" and "jam-packed", but it proves that getting "value for money" "is not impossible" in the "snooty 16th."

Scoop Ⓜ *Eclectic* | ▽ 17 | 12 | 12 | €28 |

1ᵉʳ | 154, rue St-Honoré (Louvre-Rivoli/Palais Royal-Musée du Louvre) | 01-42-60-31-84 | www.scoopcafe.com

Here's a scoop: when shopping on the Rue Saint-Honoré, refresh yourself with the Eclectic offerings of this "charming ice cream place", which also serves "ample salads" and "absolutely fabulous burgers"; aiming for "an American-style ambiance", the "narrow" red-and-white space "doesn't have enough style" some scold, but "you get your money's worth."

Sébillon ◑ *Brasserie* | 15 | 14 | 14 | €52 |

Neuilly-sur-Seine | 20, av Charles de Gaulle (Les Sablons/Porte Maillot) | 01-46-24-71-31 | www.rest-gj.com

A "Parisian-style brasserie in Neuilly", this "noisy" veteran has been "serving traditional French meals" since World War I; however, old-timers advise "go for one reason only: the famous, eat-as-much-as-you-can lamb" carved tableside, as the "rest of the menu is mediocre", and both the decor and "the service were a lot better 30 years ago" (and in our previous Survey).

16 Haussmann (Le) ⊠ *New French* | 18 | 18 | 17 | €70 |

9ᵉ | Hôtel Ambassador | 16, bd Haussmann (Chaussée d'Antin/Richelieu-Drouot) | 01-44-83-40-58 | www.16haussmann.com

The nouveau-"baroque" decor, redone post-Survey in more muted tones, makes a fitting backdrop for the "innovative" New French cooking at this "luxury hotel restaurant" steps from the Opéra Garnier; clients get "cozy" in the "comfortable chairs" and "well-spaced tables", unperturbed at the slightly "absentminded service" and "high-end" prices (though some say it all "would be better if the exchange rate were better" too).

☒ Senderens *Brasserie/New French* | 26 | 22 | 23 | €115 |

8ᵉ | 9, pl de la Madeleine (Madeleine) | 01-42-65-22-90 | www.senderens.fr

"Isn't it refreshing when a 70-year-old chef breaks all conventions and reinvents what a restaurant should be?"; that's what happened when chef-owner Alain Senderens transformed "the venerable Lucas Carton" in the 8th into a "more casual *brasserie de luxe*, with "creative" New French cuisine and "modernized" design (think a tented ceiling, Corian-topped tables and metallic leather chairs); many "miss Carton's decor and superior service", especially since "the price tag is [still] not insignificant", but almost all agree the "food's fabulous", and find this fresh "formula a winner."

Sens ● *Mediterranean*

FOOD	DECOR	SERVICE	COST
-	-	-	E

8ᵉ | 23, rue de Ponthieu (Franklin D. Roosevelt) | 01-42-25-95-00 | www.sensparis.com

The Pourcel twins, chef-owners behind Montpellier's famed Jardin des Sens, take on the affluent Golden Triangle with this slick see-and-be-seen venue; the futuristic gray decor, topped by a glass-roofed bar, creates a chic background to the designer thread-garbed clientele consuming "good" seafood-oriented Med specialties, brought by befittingly blasé staffers.

Sensing ☒ *New French*

FOOD	DECOR	SERVICE	COST
24	21	21	€71

6ᵉ | 19, rue Brea (Notre-Dame-des-Champs/Vavin) | 01-43-27-08-80 | www.restaurant-sensing.com

"Be sure to ask for the rear dining room" (it's where the fashionable folks flock) at this "affordable high-end restaurant" owned by chef-restaurateur "Guy Martin from Grand Véfour"; most find the New French fare "a gastronomic delight, so gorgeous we actually took photos", and the "staff is astonishingly friendly"; we're sensing some dissent over the tobacco-brown and limestone decor – "so-phisticated" vs. "kinda cold" – but overall, this "trendy anti-bistro" is "a grand addition" to Montparnasse.

7ème Sud ● *Mediterranean/Moroccan*

FOOD	DECOR	SERVICE	COST
15	15	14	€33

7ᵉ | 159, rue de Grenelle (La Tour-Maubourg) | 01-44-18-30-30
16ᵉ | 56, rue de Boulainvilliers (La Muette) | 01-45-20-18-32 Ⓜ

"Very BCBG" (French for 'preppy'), this pair, each an "understated" "cross between a cafe and a restaurant" in the 7th and 16th ar-rondissements, is "always a good time" if you're "loud, hip and young"; big at brunch, the "sunny" Med-Moroccan menu is "on the high side of average" and the "service is nice – even toward Americans who don't speak French well"; no wonder many "wish they could be a regular" here.

Sept Quinze (Le) *New French*

FOOD	DECOR	SERVICE	COST
∇ -	14	18	M

15ᵉ | 29, av Lowendal (Cambronne/Ségur) | 01-43-06-23-06

"Reservations are a must since the locals dine frequently" at this "bustling, lively restaurant on the border between the 7th and the 15th" arrondissements (hence the name); a new owner jazzed up the decor last year (outdating the score) and installed a Malian chef who turns out New French fare, with a few Classic touches; since it "sometimes can get noisy", "choose the terrace" if weather permits.

Severo (Le) ☒ *Steak*

FOOD	DECOR	SERVICE	COST
20	12	16	€46

14ᵉ | 8, rue des Plantes (Mouton-Duvernet) | 01-45-40-40-91

"Meat eaters and wine drinkers unite" at this small site in the 14th, where the owner, "formerly a butcher", emphasizes beef (in fact that's all he serves) and ages it too, serving it with some of "the best varietals in France"; the atmosphere is "typical Parisian" bistro, from the blackboards on the walls to the "service that lacks friendliness."

	FOOD	DECOR	SERVICE	COST

🆕 Shan Gout Ⓜ *Chinese* | - | - | - | M |

12ᵉ | 22, rue Hector-Malot (Gare de Lyon) | 01-43-40-62-14

Though this small dining room near the Gare de Lyon has almost zero decor aside from a few red lanterns dangling from the ceiling, it's become a hit because of the short-but-excellent menu by a talented young Chinese chef who has cooked his way through many of Paris' better Sino spots; the kitchen uses no MSG and prides itself on its fresh, authentic Sichuan dishes, including vegetable-stuffed ravioli and shrimp cooked in egg whites, offered at moderate prices.

Shu Ⓢ *Japanese* | - | - | - | E |

6ᵉ | 8, rue Suger (Odéon/St-Michel) | 01-46-34-25-88

Japanese chef-owner Osamu Ukai's refined cooking has instantly won this tiny young Latin Quarter dining room a loyal following among 6th-arrondissement locals; within its snug, subterranean and simply decorated surrounds, it serves elaborate dishes at dinner, with the specialty being kushiage – skewers of deep-fried meats, fish and vegetables.

Sinago (Le) Ⓢ *Cambodian* | - | - | - | I |

9ᵉ | 17, rue de Maubeuge (Cadet/Notre-Dame-de-Lorette) | 01-48-78-11-14

Converts to Cambodian cuisine caution you "must reserve" ahead for this "friendly neighborhood favorite" in the 9th; it's a Phnom-enal address for "excellent", "fresh" Khmer dishes, even if the narrow room with slightly incongruous decor of wood paneling and rigging from an old Breton boat is "mediocre."

6 New York Ⓢ *New French* | 17 | 17 | 18 | €55 |

16ᵉ | 6, av de New York (Alma Marceau) | 01-40-70-03-30

As "modern" as Manhattan – but with "wonderful views of the Eiffel Tower" across the Seine to prove where you really are – this "aptly named", "chic" table in the 16th boasts "contemporary", "sober" surrounds and a "good-looking" staff to back up the "innovative" French cuisine; though a Food score drop confirms culinary "standards have slipped recently", it still draws an "upper-crust clientele" that doesn't mind the "stiff prices."

Sizin ◑Ⓢ *Turkish* | - | - | - | M |

9ᵉ | 47, rue St-Georges (St-Georges) | 01-44-63-02-28 | www.sizin-restaurant.com

"Not your corner kebab joint" bellow Byzantine experts of this "superb value-for-money" "family restaurant" in the 9th, decorated with old postcards of Istanbul; a "warm, welcoming staff serves fine Turkish cuisine" and wines as "authentic" as they are unusual.

Sobane Ⓢ *Korean* | - | - | - | M |

9ᵉ | 5, rue de la Tour d'Auvergne (Anvers/Cadet) | 01-48-78-02-91

Just on the edge of the 9th (aka Bobo-land), this cozy Korean has become a local hit with its homestyle dishes, some of which include specially imported vegetables; popular choices include galbi-gouhi (grilled beef) and green-tea tiramisu, and the prix fixe lunch and dinner menus offer good value; courteous service and a calm, if slightly cramped, setting make this an ideal address for a tête-à-tête.

NEW Société (La) ● *Classic French*
FOOD	DECOR	SERVICE	COST
-	-	-	E

6ᵉ | 4, pl St-Germain-des-Prés (St-Germain-des-Prés) | 01-53-63-60-60 | www.societe-restaurant.com

With one of the best locations in Paris, right in the heart of Saint-Germain-des-Prés, the Costes strike again with this stunning arrival boasting a Shanghai-in-the-'30s look by French designer Christian Liaigre; it's cast with the same pretty waitresses as the brothers' other restaurants, attracts a similarly see-and-be-seen crowd and offers the same seen-it-before expensive menu of French comfort food and a few vaguely Asian dishes.

Sormani ⊠ *Italian*
FOOD	DECOR	SERVICE	COST
23	16	20	€76

17ᵉ | 4, rue du Général Lanrezac (Charles de Gaulle-Etoile) | 01-43-80-13-91

"Everyone raves" that this "institution" near the Etoile is one of "the best Italians in Paris"; with "divine" dishes often "bathed in truffles", it's "as close to Italy as you are going to get without going there" (but don't expect an economic advantage, since the "prices are astounding"); the Venetian-style, "lively red decor partially offsets" the "oppressive" air generated by the number of "business and older patrons."

Sot l'y Laisse (Le) ⊠ Ⓜ *Bistro*
FOOD	DECOR	SERVICE	COST
-	-	-	M

11ᵉ | 70, rue Alexandre Dumas (Alexandre Dumas) | 01-40-09-79-20

Named for a particularly choice piece of poultry, this yellow-toned, "lovely discovery in a lost corner of Paris" south of Père Lachaise is a "charming bistro", with fare that combines "finesse and simplicity" and a "superb wine list"; all's served with "remarkable gentility" in "truly warm" digs.

⊠ Soufflé (Le) ⊠ *Classic French*
FOOD	DECOR	SERVICE	COST
22	17	22	€50

1ᵉʳ | 36, rue du Mont-Thabor (Concorde) | 01-42-60-27-19

"Beloved by natives and tourists alike", this 1st-arrondissement "institution" is known, like the name says, for "soufflés in more possibilities than you thought were possible" – "you can even get a three-course menu" of the puffers – "baked with loving hands" and "served with panache" amid an atmosphere of "old-school charm"; the savvy "steer clear of the rest of the Classic French menu", and eventually the egg-white "novelty wears off" – but when the need strikes, this is a "sure cure for your soufflé jones."

NEW Soya Cantine Bio *Vegetarian*
FOOD	DECOR	SERVICE	COST
-	-	-	I

11ᵉ | 20, rue de la Pierre Levée (Parmentier) | 01-48-06-33-02

For veggie fans, this trendy eatery near the Place de la République offers plates of all-organic produce – the tofu-carrot lasagnas are a must – served and cooked with a smile by Christelle Dhuit and her green team in a high-ceilinged industrial venue made of cement, glass and wood; there's also a wide selection of organic wines, vegetable juices and smoothies, all at very reasonable prices.

	FOOD	DECOR	SERVICE	COST

Spoon Paris ⌧ *Eclectic/New French* — 22 | 20 | 22 | €74

8e | Hôtel Marignan | 12, rue de Marignan (Franklin D. Roosevelt) | 01-40-76-34-44 | www.spoon.tm.fr

"An adventure in world-influenced cuisine" "à la Alain Ducasse" lures "young" international types to this hotel venue with a "clean, modern setting" just off the Champs; "you are in control" as you "mix and match" the Eclectic–New French "dishes paired in and across columns" on the menu, which was recently (post-Survey) redone to favor healthier, environmentally sustainable ingredients; yes, these "small tastes" come at "fairly large prices" – but most say "just splurge and do it."

Square (Le) ⌧ *Classic French* — - | - | - | M

7e | 31, rue St-Dominique (Invalides/Solférino) | 01-45-51-09-03 | www.restaurant-lesquare.com

This "chic" "hot spot" covers all the right angles with a "noisy", "friendly vibe" provided by a "young crowd" and "charming servers"; while the Classic French food is "perfectly fine", folks come "more for fun than cuisine"; still, the prix fixes offer a "bang for your buck" that's "nice in a neighborhood" (the 7th) where "reasonable" is rare.

Square de Marcardet ⌧Ⓜ *Classic/New French* — - | - | - | M

18e | 227 bis, rue Marcardet (Guy Moquet) | 01-53-11-08-41 | www.le-square.fr

A hipster crowd makes a straight line for this casual, "excellent" address in the faraway 18th, where huge blackboards present the day's offerings, an inventive mix of Classic and New French cuisine; "a fine time" can be had wherever one perches: the bar area with banquettes, the dining room with wooden bistro tables overlooking a patio garden or the garden itself, with vine-covered walls.

Square Trousseau (Le) ● *Bistro* — ∇ 19 | 19 | 17 | €43

12e | 1, rue Antoine Vollon (Bastille/Ledru-Rollin) | 01-43-43-06-00

"Off the beaten track", this "friendly bistro" "just across from the charming Square Trousseau" is a "nice neighborhood place", with "charming", "old-fashioned classic" decor (banquettes, zinc bar, etc.), a kitchen that "brings a new twist to the standards (our favorite: the veal shank with honey)" and "swift, sharp staffers"; a "lively crowd" heads for the "patio seating in the warmer weather"; N.B. a recent management change may outdate the above scores.

Stella (Le) ● *Brasserie* — 20 | 16 | 18 | €49

16e | 133, av Victor Hugo (Rue de la Pompe/Victor Hugo) | 01-56-90-56-00

"The chicest brasserie in Paris" – "it's located in the wealthy 16th" – swings with smart-looking "neighborhood foodies" dining on "an ever-fresh supply of seafood", "fabulous steak tartare" and other "clichés of French cooking", attended to by a staff that "comes and goes with incredible speed" and evinces a "fun, slap-on-the-bottom, malicious air"; "low-key and easy", it's especially "worth it on those evenings when everything else is closed."

	FOOD	DECOR	SERVICE	COST

⊠ Stella Maris ⊠ *Classic French* | 26 | 17 | 21 | €95 |

8ᵉ | 4, rue Arsène Houssaye (Charles de Gaulle-Etoile) | 01-42-89-16-22 | www.stellamaris.abemadi.com

A "hidden jewel off the Champs-Elysées" enthuse admirers of this "inventive" establishment owned by Tateru Yoshino, a "Japanese chef who breathes elegant Asian undertones into Classic French fare" – just try the cabbage pâté to experience his "exquisite" creativity; admittedly, "prices have gone up", many find the "minimalist decor more suited to business than romance" and the service, though "warm", often "drags as the evening wears on"; but these things only slightly mar a mostly "magical" time.

Stéphane Gaborieau-Le Pergolèse ⊠ *Haute Cuisine* | - | - | - | VE |

16ᵉ | 40, rue Pergolèse (Argentine) | 01-45-00-21-40 | www.lepergolese.com

After working in luxury hotels in Lyon and the south of France, chef-owner Stéphane Gaborieau now runs this plush old-timer in the 16th, and is "slowly introducing his own flavors" into the classic Haute Cuisine menu; the wood-paneled dining room with oil paintings on the walls and crisp linen tablecloths is "intimate and quiet", even "romantic"; expect suave service and steep prices.

Stéphane Martin ⊠ Ⓜ *Classic French* | - | - | - | M |

15ᵉ | 67, rue des Entrepreneurs (Charles Michels/Commerce) | 01-45-79-03-31 | www.stephanemartin.com

"With chef-owner Stéphane Martin doing fantastic things in the kitchen", this Classic French is "a great non-touristy place" in the "unassuming" 15th; both the decor and service have a "warm feel", and if the latter's a tad "rushed on weekends", this remains "a find!"

Stresa (Le) ⊠ *Italian* | 22 | 16 | 19 | €87 |

8ᵉ | 7, rue Chambiges (Alma Marceau) | 01-47-23-51-62

The "stars" come out to this "wonderful" Italian in the 8th, where it's "tough to get a table" unless "you know someone"; the refined cuisine is "recommended for cognoscenti", though prices are so high the figures "while in euros, seem to be in lira", and some say simply "do not go" unless you get off on "clients who spend their time looking at each other in an aquarium of mirrors"; N.B. closed weekends.

Studio (The) ● *Tex-Mex* | - | - | - | M |

4ᵉ | 41, rue du Temple (Hôtel-de-Ville/Rambuteau) | 01-42-74-10-38 | www.the-studio.fr

"If you're in the mood for Mexican in a funky setting" – a 17th-century courtyard, shared with a dance studio – then head to this Tex-Mex in the Marais; "coming from a Texan" surveyor, "this place may have the best in Paris" – or at least, "the closest to the real thing."

Suave ⊠ *Vietnamese* | - | - | - | I |

13ᵉ | 20, rue de la Providence (Corvisart/Tolbiac) | 01-45-89-99-27

Reservations are imperative at this "small" but "cute" site near Butte aux Cailles, often "crowded" with admirers of its "ample portions of

Vietnamese food – less spicy than [in the U.S.], but very good nevertheless"; "kind service" and a suave use of "fresh" ingredients make it stand out in a neighborhood filled with Asian eateries.

Sud (Le) *Mediterranean/Provence*   ▽ 16 | 18 | 16 | €52

17ᵉ | 91, bd Gouvion-St-Cyr (Porte Maillot) | 01-45-74-02-77 | www.lesud.fr

"Ah, the sound of crickets in the middle of a Paris winter" sigh surveyors who "feel like they're on vacation" at this Provençal oasis "next to the traffic jams of Porte Maillot"; "exotic Med cuisine and a mix of colors in the plate" reflect the "southern ambiance" of the "under-the-olive-trees" decor; acquired by the Frères Blanc group not too long ago, it seems "less good" to some, and the bill is "a little pricey"; nevertheless, the place can get as "crowded" as Aix in August.

Suffren (Le) ❶ *Brasserie*   14 | 12 | 13 | €43

15ᵉ | 84, av de Suffren (La Motte-Picquet-Grenelle) | 01-45-66-97-86

This family-owned, "bustling brasserie" in the 15th has long been a "popular" "neighborhood standard"; "regulars who stick to the classics and don't [challenge] the kitchen's creativity" report it "delivers what it promises: well-executed versions of basic French fare"; prices are higher and the staff's gotten "a little slower", but "great people-watching" from a large sun-filled terrace passes the time.

Table d'Anvers (La) 🗷 *Classic French*   17 | 16 | 15 | €55

9ᵉ | 2, pl d'Anvers (Anvers) | 01-48-78-35-21 | www.latabledanvers.com

"Discreet and low-key" ("the signature orchid on the table says it all"), this Classic French on the edge of Montmartre appeals to tourists and locals alike with its "copious meals"; however, cynics say it's "expensive for the type of food" – "basic, if well prepared."

∄ Table de Joël Robuchon (La) *Haute Cuisine*   26 | 21 | 25 | €119

16ᵉ | 16, av Bugeaud (Victor Hugo) | 01-56-28-16-16 | www.joel-robuchon.com

"Haute Cuisine presented by a master" sums up owner Joël Robuchon's "elegant" eatery in the 16th, which offers his "trademark" "food that tastes likes real food" (regulars recommend "ordering from the small-plates side of the menu" or "trying the tasting menu – a nonstop delight"); most like the "modern, without-excess" decor, even if the "ambiance is rather businesslike", and the "professional, yet unfussy service"; in short, "it's what a great restaurant should be: sophisticated, friendly and always on" – literally: it's "open every day and all year (even in August!)."

Table d'Eugène (La) 🗷🅼 *New French*   - | - | - | M

18ᵉ | 18, rue Eugène Sue (Jules Joffrin) | 01-42-55-61-64

Chef-owner Geoffroy Maillard has a hit with this eatery painted a soothing willow green and offering a chalkboard menu that shows off his cosmopolitan culinary imagination with such New French dishes as a grilled risotto cube garnished with wild mushrooms and boar braised in chocolate for seven hours; since 18tharrondissement locals know value when they see it, the place is already always packed.

	FOOD	DECOR	SERVICE	COST

Table d'Hédiard (La) 🅉 *New French* 22 | 17 | 21 | €50

8ᵉ | 21, pl de la Madeleine (Madeleine) | 01-43-12-88-99 |
www.hediard.fr

"Pick up groceries and get a quick bite to eat" at this New French "perched above a wonderful gourmet shop" in the 8th; all through the day, there's "light, fresh food and divine desserts" (though "it can be difficult to swallow the prices"); the "staff's attitude" ranges from "affected" to "attentive", but overall, it's a "wonderful place for resting those weary, overworked tourist feet."

Table du Baltimore (La) 🅉 *Haute Cuisine* − | − | − | VE

16ᵉ | M. Gallery Baltimore | 88 bis, av Kléber (Boissière) | 01-44-34-54-34 |
www.hotel-baltimore-paris.com

"Always reliable" for a "business lunch or dinner", this "luxurious hotel restaurant" near Trocadéro provides a "comfortable" setting (including "great air-conditioning, a rare thing in Paris"), "attentive service" and a "nice wine list"; but there are tempered tributes for the Haute Cuisine: "good, even very good, but not extraordinary."

Table du Lancaster (La) *Haute Cuisine* 23 | 23 | 23 | €109

8ᵉ | Hôtel Lancaster | 7, rue de Berri (Franklin D. Roosevelt/George V) |
01-40-76-40-18 | www.hotel-lancaster.fr

While fans of the Hôtel Lancaster's dining room judge the Asian-influenced Haute Cuisine "exciting" and "exotic", doubters dish their "disappointment" over the "too-predictable" offerings; but if the "food's slipped a little, the garden is still beautiful", as is the "civilized" interior and "quiet location away from the madness of the nearby Champs."

Table Lauriston (La) 🅉 *Classic French* 20 | 16 | 19 | €50

16ᵉ | 129, rue Lauriston (Trocadéro) | 01-47-27-00-07 |
www.restaurantlatablelauriston.com

Not far from Trocadéro, this Classic French finds fans aplenty for its "excellent, unpretentious" cooking by chef-owner Serge Barbey and its staffers, supervised by his wife, who "really listen to the customer" in a "convivial", silver-accented dining room; given this, and the swank 16th address, it's "a good buy."

🆉 Taillevent 🅉 *Haute Cuisine* 28 | 28 | 28 | €164

8ᵉ | 15, rue Lamennais (Charles de Gaulle-Etoile/George V) |
01-44-95-15-01 | www.taillevent.com

"You're at home the minute you enter" this "elegant", "spectacular modern art"-adorned townhouse in the 8th, which – though still mourning the loss of legendary owner Jean-Claude Vrinat – shines on as Paris' No. 1 for Food and Popularity; guests would "gladly borrow from the kids' college fund" to sample "service that's not just an art form, but a religion" as it delivers chef Alain Solivérès' "classic", sometimes "inventive", but always "decadent and luscious" Haute Cuisine, backed by "a prodigious wine list"; in short, "why wait for heaven, when you can go to Taillevent?"

	FOOD	DECOR	SERVICE	COST

Tan Dinh 🚫🚭 *Vietnamese* | 23 | 14 | 21 | €71 |

7ᵉ | 60, rue de Verneuil (Rue du Bac/Solférino) | 01-45-44-04-84
A "fashionable", "dedicated clientele" adds to the cachet of this "sedate Vietnamese charmer" in the 7th, where the cuisine is "delicate", the "service refined" and an "amazing wine list (particularly the Burgundies) keeps customers coming back"; malcontents mumble that the "portions are small" for the price – which, by the way, requires a pocketful of cash, because "they don't accept credit cards."

Tang 🚫 *Chinese* | 17 | 15 | 16 | €58 |

16ᵉ | 125, rue de la Tour (Rue de la Pompe) | 01-45-04-35-35
This chichi Chinese in the 16th enjoys a high-ranking reputation, and while many feel it's merited, thanks to the "solicitous" owner and "memorable" food from a "diversified menu", scores side with the sizable number of dissidents who declare it "too expensive" for dishes that are merely "good."

Tante Louise 🚫 *Burgundy/Classic French* | 22 | 18 | 20 | €70 |

8ᵉ | 41, rue Boissy-d'Anglas (Concorde/Madeleine) | 01-42-65-06-85 | www.bernard-loiseau.com
"Near the Madeleine", this "luxury bistro" specializing in "traditional Burgundian"-accented French cuisine "cooked to perfection" remains a "good bet for a business lunch or a date" and a "favorite standby" with "the American Embassy crowd nearby"; its "cozy" setting with wood paneling and big armchairs is ideal on "a coolish winter evening", even if the staff seems "attentive and perfunctory at the same time"; N.B. closed weekends.

Tante Marguerite 🚫 *Classic French* | ▽ 22 | 19 | 22 | €69 |

7ᵉ | 5, rue de Bourgogne (Assemblée Nationale/Invalides) | 01-45-51-79-42 | www.bernard-loiseau.com
"Located on a divine little square behind the Assemblée Nationale", this "beautiful neighborhood" bistro does a "good job" with "nice traditional French cuisine" brought to table by "well-trained" "servers who float through the dining room"; its "quiet, special" ambiance is popular with politicians at noon and locals at night; N.B. a recent chef change may outdate the above Food score.

Tastevin 🅼 *Classic French* | ▽ 24 | 20 | 24 | €69 |

Maisons-Laffitte | 9, av Eglé (Maisons-Laffitte RER) | 01-39-62-11-67
It may be "hard to get to without a car" but that doesn't stop clients who "come back religiously over the decades" to this family-run "historic restaurant" serving "well-prepared" Classic French cuisine in a century-old house and "beautiful" gardens in Maisons-Laffitte; admirers appreciate the "quiet" setting ("don't go if you're younger than 35") and "special personal service" in this "old-world" "treasure."

Taverne de Maître Kanter ● *Brasserie* | ▽ 16 | 18 | 15 | €35 |

1ᵉʳ | 16, rue Coquillière (Châtelet-Les Halles/Louvre-Rivoli) | 01-42-36-74-24 | www.tmk-leshalles.com
"Typical Alsatian fare in typical Alsatian surroundings" sums up this two-story Les Halles brasserie abounding in "fresh sauerkraut" and

"trays of shellfish"; it's pretty "basic, but a better standby than one might expect" – especially since "it's never closed."

Taverne du Sergent Recruteur (La) ☾ *Classic French*

FOOD	DECOR	SERVICE	COST
16	16	17	€37

4ᵉ | 41, rue St-Louis-en-l'Ile (Pont-Marie) | 01-43-54-75-42 | www.lesergentrecruteur.com

There are "more tourists jammed in [here] than in Notre Dame" at this Ile Saint-Louis veteran that "attempts to re-create Middle Ages communal dining" with "ye olde" decor of beamed stone walls, farm tools and long wood tables; "excellent baskets of charcuterie, [crudités] and cheese are provided when you sit down", but otherwise the Classic French fare's fairly "marginal" and some feel it's "from a former era and should be left there"; still, with "the right group and sufficient wine, it can be fun."

Taverne Henri IV (La) ⊠ *Wine Bar/Bistro*

FOOD	DECOR	SERVICE	COST
16	16	18	€40

1ᵉʳ | 13, pl du Pont-Neuf (Pont-Neuf) | 01-43-54-27-90

"Curators and carpenters sit side by side for a glass" at this "working man's wine bar" on the tip of Ile de la Cité, a "historical institution" and "an old favorite" of many (including writer Georges Simenon); to accompany the "nice selection of wines at good prices", present-day patrons tuck into "homey platters of country pâtés, cheeses" and charcuterie, noting the "owners have spruced up the tired old decor."

Temps au Temps (Le) ⊠Ⓜ *Bistro*

FOOD	DECOR	SERVICE	COST
25	16	25	€38

11ᵉ | 13, rue Paul Bert (Faidherbe-Chaligny) | 01-43-79-63-40 | www.tempsautemps.com

After six years, this "teeny" bistro in the 11th "remains a breath of fresh air", thanks to "fabulous food at a price you won't believe" – "a three-course meal for 30€"; reserve at least four days in advance, since the room with a big enameled clock face is usually "jam-packed with a total of 26 guests and one hard-working waitress" – in fact, some surveyors were "hesitant to share [their opinions], because I may not get in next time!"; N.B. the above ratings don't reflect the departure of chef-owner Sylvain Sentra.

Temps des Cerises (Le) ◖⊠ *Bistro*

FOOD	DECOR	SERVICE	COST
–	–	–	M

13ᵉ | 18, rue de la Butte aux Cailles (Corvisart/Place d'Italie) | 01-45-89-69-48

Egalitarians eat up this "lively legacy of the Paris Commune days", a Butte aux Cailles bistro "run as a cooperative" where "all the staffers, from chef to dishwasher, are owners" and patrons sit together at "large tables"; it's "genuine, gruff and earthy" – "please put in modern toilets!" – but the "generous portions" of "hearty traditional French fare" are cheap enough for the masses.

Terminus Nord ☾ *Brasserie*

FOOD	DECOR	SERVICE	COST
17	19	17	€45

10ᵉ | 23, rue de Dunkerque (Gare du Nord) | 01-42-85-05-15 | www.terminusnord.com

"Exuding the bustle and expectation of its namesake across the road", the Gare du Nord, this "classic" brasserie with its "fin de siècle decor" is "the perfect spot for Eurostar travelers" to "go back in time"; while the food quality can be "random", passengers profess that the "platters of briny seafood are always a safe bet" and the "rushed", white-aproned waiters are "fun to watch."

Terrasse Mirabeau (La) ⓩ *Bistro* — | — | — | M

16ᵉ | 5, pl de Barcelone (Javel/Mirabeau) | 01-42-24-41-51 | www.terrasse-mirabeau.com

What "a revelation" rave epicureans who "dream of going all the time" to this "upscale bistro – or is it a reasonably priced creative restaurant?" – in the 16th; the kitchen's "superb creativity", including "excellent terrines", matches the sleek, mirrored maroon-and-chocolate–colored decor with "real paintings on the tabletops" and big bay windows overlooking a "beautiful terrace."

Terres de Truffes ⓩ *Classic French* ▽ 19 | 14 | 17 | €81

8ᵉ | 21, rue Vignon (Madeleine) | 01-53-43-80-44 | www.terresdetruffes.com

According to funghi-philes "no place is better at delivering superb truffle dishes, from starter to dessert", than this "connoisseurs' mecca" near the Madeleine; however, dissidents declare it has to dig deeper: "since a management change, the former generosity is gone, the recipes have changed and the prices have gone up" – though a recent (post-Survey) chef change may quiet their complaints.

Terrines de Gérard Vié (Les) ⓩ Ⓜ *Bistro* — | — | — | M

6ᵉ | 97, rue du Cherche-Midi (Duroc) | 01-42-22-19-18

With downsizing the order of the day, it's no surprise that chef Gérard Vié has traded in the aristocratic confines of Versailles' Trianon Palace hotel for a traditional bistro in the 6th – so homey-looking it even has a country ham clamped into a slicing stand in the middle of the room; most customers start with one of the namesake terrines (rabbit, herring and foie gras among them), and then go on to a French classic like salt cod with whipped potatoes or lamb braised for seven hours; the wood bar houses a large selection of organic wines.

Terroir (Le) ⓩ *Bistro* — | — | — | E

13ᵉ | 11, bd Arago (Les Gobelins) | 01-47-07-36-99

"A perennial favorite" of "local people" and tourists on the trail of a "real French restaurant", this bistro in the 13th serves "no trendy nonsense, just top-rate traditional cooking" in "high-priced" but "incredible portions" ("try the terrine de maison and see if you can even eat anything else"); "hearty regional wines", plus a "warm welcome", round out the "marvelous" experience.

Tête Ailleurs (La) ⓩ *Mediterranean* — | — | — | M

4ᵉ | 20, rue Beautreillis (St-Paul/Sully Morland) | 01-42-72-47-80 | www.lateteailleurs.fr

Southern warmth is served at this "casual", "charming" Marais table with "delicious Mediterranean food" (including a "heavenly lamb") and an "eager-to-please staff" whose efforts make it "one of the friendliest places in town"; the "bright, arty decor" combines

| | FOOD | DECOR | SERVICE | COST |

rich orange shades with exposed-stone walls and natural light from a glass rooftop.

Thiou *Thai*
7^e | 49, quai d'Orsay (Invalides) | 01-40-62-96-50 🚫
8^e | 12, av George V (Alma Marceau) | 01-47-20-89-56

Petit Thiou 🚫 *Thai*
7^e | 3, rue Surcouf (Invalides) | 01-40-62-96-70

"When the mood moves you for a chic Asian dinner, come" to these venerable venues, which offer "the best Thai in Paris – and know it, judging by the prices" some quip; the "food is like the decor – smooth" and the scene "social-trendy"; some surveyors prefer Petit Thiou, as it's "less noisy" (and less expensive).

Thoumieux *New French*
7^e | Hôtel Thoumieux | 79, rue St-Dominique (Invalides/La Tour-Maubourg) | 01-47-05-49-75 | www.thoumieux.com

Owners Thierry Costes (also of the Hôtel Amour) and chef Jean-François Piège, ex Les Ambassadeurs, have given this 1920s-vintage brasserie in the 7th a top-to-bottom makeover, completely transforming the dark vieille-France interior with glamourous, multiply mirrored supper-club decor; the menu's changed entirely too – out goes the cassoulet and in come contemporary French dishes like squid à la carbonara or puffed-up pizzas with tuna and mozzarella – and this new incarnation is attracting a Costes-brothers crowd willing to pay their usual lofty prices.

NEW Tico *Bistro/New French*
8^e | 95, rue du Faubourg St-Honoré (St-Philippe-du-Roule) | 01-47-42-64-10 | www.tico-restaurant.fr

Not very far from the Elysée Palace on the chic Faubourg Saint-Honoré, this sleek-yet-friendly arrival provides an ideal setting for the talents of chef François Chambonnet (ex Michel Rostang), whose contemporary bistro cuisine puts an original slant on traditional French gastronomy; the low-key downstairs bar affords light snacking and expert cocktails to the tune of live music, and what's more, the ultramodern amenities include a special elevator that makes the entire space handicapped-accessible, a rarity in Paris.

Tierny & Co. 🚫Ⓜ *Bistro*
16^e | 137, av de Versailles (Exelmans/Mirabeau) | 01-46-47-72-00

It got a new name and an eponymous chef-owner a while back, but so far all else remains the same at this "lively" "neo-bistro" in the 16th on the way to Versailles; though "small", it's "well laid out", with low lighting, dark-wood tables and a long banquette to create a cozy atmosphere, plus a 34€ prix fixe to please the wallet.

Timbre (Le) 🚫Ⓜ *Bistro*
6^e | 3, rue Ste-Beuve (Notre-Dame-des-Champs/Vavin) | 01-45-49-10-40 | www.restaurantletimbre.com

Wanderers seeking "a wonderful little neighborhood spot" find this bistro near the Luxembourg Gardens offers "just the right combination of food and ambiance" – both provided by "original" English chef-owner Chris Wright, who's a joy to "watch juggling many dishes at once, and making each perfect" (and "surprisingly inexpensive"); yes, the "cramped" space is "absolutely a postage stamp [*timbre*] in size" – "but that's part of the charm."

Timgad (Le) *Moroccan*   20 | 19 | 18 | €49

17e | 21, rue Brunel (Argentine) | 01-45-74-23-70 | www.timgad-paris.com

Couscous critics call this "refined, exotic" table in the 17th "one of the best Moroccans in town", serving the "melt-in-the-mouth" Mahgreb mainstay and other dishes "of exemplary finesse"; "step in the restaurant and you're in the heart of Marrakech", thanks to "amazing" decor of hand-carved plaster and service of "authentic warmth"; but the "exceptional meal" does come with an "exceptional price."

Toi ● *New French*   - | - | - | M

8e | 27, rue du Colisée (Franklin D. Roosevelt/St-Philippe-du-Roule) | 01-42-56-56-58 | www.restaurant-toi.com

Newly redone in vivid pink, this club near the Champs offers "trendy" lounge dining in armchairs or on couches, "creative alcoholic concoctions" "and a young crowd"; even fans admit it's "more amusing than appetizing", given that the New French menu "isn't very long", but the arrival of a new chef may change all that.

Tokyo Eat ● M *New French*   14 | 17 | 13 | €41

16e | Palais de Tokyo | 13, av du President Wilson (Iéna) | 01-47-20-00-29 | www.palaisdetokyo.com

"Great in summer" – when you can sit out on the terrace and take in the superb views of the Seine and the Eiffel Tower – this "funky" New French in the Palais de Tokyo pulls patrons with its futuristic "high design", including "über-cool light fixtures"; but, as with many museum venues, the food and staff "leave less than an imperishable memory."

Tong Yen ● *Chinese*   15 | 11 | 13 | €56

8e | 1 bis, rue Jean Mermoz (Franklin D. Roosevelt) | 01-42-25-04-23

Managing to be "ultra-Parisian and cosmopolitan at the same time", this "well-known Asian" near the Champs offers "all the classics"; but despite its rep as "one of the best Chinese-Vietnamese-Thai in Paris", foes feel "the food and service have deteriorated" – though "delightful owner" Thérèse Luong "makes up for the staff's shortcomings" – and the '60s decor is "too old"; it's also "very dear for the quality of the cuisine, but when you receive presidents", a premium is perhaps understandable.

Tonnelle Saintongeaise   - | - | - | E
(La) Z *Classic French*

Neuilly-sur-Seine | 32, bd Vital-Bouhot (Pont-de-Levallois) | 01-46-24-43-15 | www.latonnellesaintongeaise.com

With its "charming location", complete with "a terrace right in the middle of Ile de la Jatte", this Classic French is a comfortable hangout (its covered courtyard is agreeable "even in stormy summer weather"); the menu offers "dishes that are simple but always adequate", including specialties from the chef's native Charente and hand-cut steak tartare that's a "must for raw-meat lovers."

Toque (La) ⊠ Classic French   — | — | — | E

17ᵉ | 16, rue de Tocqueville (Villiers) | 01-42-27-97-75
"Loyal followers" of chef-owner Jacky Joubert have been coming to his small establishment in the 17th for more than 30 years now to partake of "palate-pleasing, if traditional" French cuisine in an alcoved dining room underneath the clouds of a trompe l'oeil ceiling; a "thoughtful staff" completes the "warm", "conservative atmosphere" that's "perfect" "for a business meal" or just an "enjoyable evening."

☑ Tour d'Argent (La) ⊠ Ⓜ Haute Cuisine   25 | 28 | 26 | €145

5ᵉ | 15-17, quai de la Tournelle (Cardinal Lemoine/Pont-Marie) | 01-43-54-23-31 | www.latourdargent.com
Defiant (and dominant) devotees "don't care if it's considered uncool" – this Haute Cuisine table "is still one of the most magical of Parisian places", with its "spectacular views of Notre Dame"; "make sure you ask for a window table when you book, and for heaven's sake order the pressed duck" "with its numbered certificate" – though chef Stéphane Haissant has "finally updated" the menu with some "excellent" options, served by an initially "haughty", but truly "outstanding staff"; so let the grouches grimace she's "a grande dame in decline" – this tower remains "a reason to sell off your worldly goods for one meal here before you die."

Tournesol (Le) Bistro   ∇ 18 | 17 | 19 | €45

16ᵉ | 2, av de Lamballe (Passy) | 01-45-25-95-94
"One goes for the terrace and the trendy" scene say patrons of this "nice Passy bistro" – though the cooking is quite "competent" as well; the "quick" servers can "tease you in both French and English."

☑ Train Bleu (Le) Classic French   19 | 27 | 20 | €62

12ᵉ | Gare de Lyon (Gare de Lyon) | 01-43-43-09-06 | www.le-train-bleu.com
"Travel in style" at this "belle epoque masterpiece" in the Gare de Lyon, a "grande old dame" of a brasserie with "beautiful" painted scenes of the southern destinations served by the station; "though it's a little more expensive than you want", there's "surprisingly good" Classic French food and "tableside service" (e.g. "lamb from the trolley") – all of which puts you on "the right track to a great evening."

35° Ouest ⊠ Ⓜ Seafood   20 | 18 | 21 | €64

7ᵉ | 35, rue de Verneuil (Rue du Bac) | 01-42-86-98-88
This "little fish that could" makes a splash with an "intimate", modern "chic" setting near the Rue du Bac and a "small, carefully edited" seafood menu featuring "the freshest ingredients" in "original" preparations; it's "still undiscovered" by tourists, despite "smiling"

	FOOD	DECOR	SERVICE	COST

service and a "good-value" lunch menu – though dinner prices head rapidly upstream.

Tricotin ● *Asian*

–	–	–	I

13ᵉ | 15, av de Choisy (Porte de Choisy) | 01-45-84-74-44

Dumpling devotees line up for a table at this "superior" "canteen-style Asian" in Chinatown, where two dining rooms with different menus (but the same "minimal decor") are always "crowded" with admirers who dig their chopsticks into "amazingly good" (and "inexpensive") Chinese, Vietnamese or Thai dishes, plus "quality dim sum."

Troquet (Le) 🗷 Ⓜ *Basque/New French*

24	16	19	€45

15ᵉ | 21, rue François Bonvin (Sèvres-Lecourbe/Volontaire) | 01-45-66-89-00

It's worth traveling to an "unassuming" part of the 15th for this "incredible find" of a New French that "distills the best of Paris neighborhood eating", thanks to chef-owner Christian Etchebest's "excellent" Basque-inspired menu that "emphasizes market-fresh" ingredients; despite "nondescript" decor, "locals love it and with good reason" since it offers "incredible value for the money" and the "staff is casual and friendly."

🗷 Trou Gascon (Au) 🗷 *Southwest*

26	19	24	€75

12ᵉ | 40, rue Taine (Daumesnil) | 01-43-44-34-26 | www.autrougascon.fr

"Let's hear it for the Southwest!" shout supporters of Alain Dutournier's original "off-the-beaten-track" eatery in the 12th that's "worth every travel minute"; "a mixture of classics and innovations", its Gascon cuisine includes "the best confit de canard I've ever had", "transcendent cassoulet" and other "superb heart-attack food" served in "spare but elegant surroundings"; though the wine list's "a little short" of by-the-glass offerings, that's "made up for by a huge selection of Armagnacs", so for most "the real trick is to get up from the table after a meal" here.

Truc Café (Le) ● Ⓜ *Wine Bar/Bistro*

–	–	–	M

18ᵉ | 58, rue du Poteau (Jules Joffrin) | 01-42-52-64-09

Generously served Classic French dishes and an Italian-oriented wine list have made this *bistrot à vins* in a gentrifying Montmartre neighborhood a hit with a trendy young crowd; changing contemporary art exhibitions and a pretty, quiet little garden out back please as much as the smiling service and modest prices.

Truffe Noire (La) 🗷 *Classic French*

–	–	–	E

Neuilly-sur-Seine | 2, pl Parmentier (Les Sablons/Porte Maillot) | 01-46-24-94-14 | www.truffenoire.net

Neuilly's nobility and corporate types from La Défense get their dose of decadent eats at this "delightful" denizen that's maintained a "consistently high quality over the years"; within cool, contemporary decor of gray walls and Murano chandeliers, the "very Classic" French fare features the fabulous fungus in all its forms, so "it's expensive – but there's nothing better than a truffle", *n'est-ce pas?*

	FOOD	DECOR	SERVICE	COST

Truffière (La) 🚫Ⓜ Haute Cuisine
| 23 | 23 | 23 | €87 |

5ᵉ | 4, rue Blainville (Cardinal Lemoine/Place Monge) | 01-46-33-29-82 |
www.latruffiere.com

"Talk about old-fashioned dining": this "romantic" spot, "off the Rue
Mouffetard in an alley so narrow you can hardly get out of the taxi",
"sets the mood with old stone walls and beamed ceilings", "courteous servers" and a "sybaritic menu" of Haute Cuisine in which certain "expensive ingredients, as the name indicates, are used with
abandon" – "they even put truffles in the dessert soufflé"; yes, it's all
"a little dated" and pricey (the wine alone is "highway robbery"), but
the latter can be ameliorated at the lunch prix fixe, "a great deal."

Trumilou (Le) Bistro
| 19 | 12 | 18 | €31 |

4ᵉ | 84, quai de l'Hôtel de Ville (Hôtel-de-Ville/Pont-Marie) |
01-42-77-63-98 | www.letrumilou.com

"Other than its location across from the Seine, there's nothing
fancy" here – and that pleases budgeters who make a beeline for this
"boisterous", "friendly", "funky bargain of a place", serving "decent
old-style" bistro food in the 4th; sure, the "eclectic decor" is looking
"a little tattered", but it's "just the thing to soothe an artist's soul."

Tsé-Yang 🌑 Chinese
| 18 | 17 | 16 | €48 |

16ᵉ | 25, av Pierre 1er de Serbie (Alma Marceau/Iéna) | 01-47-20-70-22 |
www.tseyang.fr

Practically a time zone away from its Chinatown cousins, this "luxurious" 16th-arrondissement Asian draws an upscale clientele who
claim it's "the only restaurant where you eat *real* Chinese cuisine" –
that is, undiluted by Thai or Vietnamese offerings as is often the
case in Paris – served in a "transporting" black-and-gold room; still,
some snap it's "a bit too dear, given the quantities served."

Tsukizi 🚫Ⓜ Japanese
| - | - | - | M |

6ᵉ | 2 bis, rue des Ciseaux (Mabillon/St-Germain-des-Prés) |
01-43-54-65-19

"A lot of Japanese" clients and others "who miss real sushi" get a
"traditional" taste of Tokyo at this "tiny counter", a Saint-Germain
"hideaway" where expats slice and dice the "fresh products"; zealots
even praise the "Zen ambiance" (the critical just call it "cramped").

Uitr Seafood
| - | - | - | M |

15ᵉ | 1, pl Falguière (Pasteur/Pernety) | 01-47-34-12-24

This seafooder in the 15th is "the cheaper version of La Cagouille –
and you get what you pay for" say some, citing the "brief menu" and
nautical setting that's a bit "beat-up"; but merrier mateys maintain
the "cuisine's remarkable", with "very fresh" shellfish; occasional
jazz nights also encourage diners to drop anchor here.

Unico 🚫Ⓜ Argentinean
| - | - | - | E |

11ᵉ | 15, rue Paul Bert (Faidherbe-Chaligny) | 01-43-67-08-68 |
www.resto-unico.com

Calling all gauchos: this "trendy Argentine" in the hip Rue Paul Bert
tempts with "tender, perfectly prepared pampas-raised beef" and

"good Argentinean wines"; with its orange-hued, '70s-vintage decor – so retro it seems "postmodern" – and "bustling, warm" vibe, "this place is indeed *único.*"

Urbane ☒Ⓜ *Bistro* | - | - | - | M |

10ᵉ | 12, rue Arthur Groussier (Belleville/Goncourt) | 01-42-40-74-75

"Tucked away near Belleville", this "little gem", run by a Franco-Irish couple, takes a tasty, transformative approach to bistro classics ("made me realize that I do like boudin noir!"); "everyone loves" "the Sunday brunches, with their generous portions" and acoustic music, but the brown paper–covered tables, colored lights, framed photo-covered walls and "DJs also make it a hip hangout" anytime.

Vagenende ❶ *Brasserie* | 15 | 23 | 16 | €48 |

6ᵉ | 142, bd St-Germain (Mabillon/Odéon) | 01-43-26-68-18 | www.vagenende.fr

Aka "the poor man's Maxim's", this century-old brasserie in the 6th is "a feast for the eyes" with a "stunningly authentic", "almost edible" art nouveau interior; less mouthwatering is the "acceptable-but-ordinary" menu, despite an "outstanding" raw bar; still, the "bustling" ambiance, the "great-for-people-watching" location and the late-night service make it "fine for an off-hour meal, just to soak in the decor."

Vaudeville (Le) ❶ *Brasserie* | 18 | 21 | 17 | €54 |

2ᵉ | 29, rue Vivienne (Bourse) | 01-40-20-04-62 | www.vaudevilleparis.com

The "stylish clientele" enhances the "sparkling" "marble and mosaic" setting of this art deco spot "across from the Bourse", a "lively late-night brasserie" with a "special-occasion feel"; despite "desultory service", seafood lovers say this is "the best of the Groupe Flo" chain, with the "good", "basic" menu enhanced by "giant platters of *fruits de mer*" that have 'em rolling in the aisles.

Verre Bouteille (Le) ❶☒Ⓜ *Wine Bar/Bistro* | 13 | 12 | 14 | €37 |

17ᵉ | 85, av des Ternes (Porte Maillot) | 01-45-74-01-02 | www.leverrebouteille.com

"Simple and unpretentious", this wine bar in the 17th is "well-known to *noctambules*" for its long hours and well-liked by vinophiles for its "interesting wine list"; bad-mouthing bacchanalians call the "food basic", "the decor faded" and the "welcome not great"; but even if "being open late is its main advantage", it still pours a "good night out."

Verre Volé (Le) ❶ *Wine Bar/Bistro* | 16 | 15 | 18 | €30 |

10ᵉ | 67, rue de Lancry (République) | 01-48-03-17-34

Vino-inclined reviewers "run, don't walk" to this "jovial" wine bar on the Canal Saint-Martin and "while away the afternoon" or evening sampling the "intelligently and passionately chosen" young varietals alongside "simple" dishes such as oysters or charcuterie; the room is "*toute petite*" so it can be "hard to find a free table", but at least the cheek-to-jowl ambiance ensures it's always "high-spirited."

	FOOD	DECOR	SERVICE	COST

Versance (Le) 🗠Ⓜ *Classic/New French* — | - | - | E

2ᵉ | 16, rue Feydeau (Bourse) | 01-45-08-00-08 | www.leversance.fr
A "promising debut" declare disciples of young chef Samuel Cavagnis'
"elegant" yearling; his produce-driven French cuisine blends the traditional and the "inventive", as does the white-and-dove-gray decor,
which juxtaposes contemporary furniture with 19th-century moldings
and stained glass; maybe the staff needs "to be more professional",
but most agree that investing in this place near the old Bourse is "already a sure thing" (just make sure your portfolio's liquid).

Viaduc Café (Le) ◑ *Classic/New French* — | - | - | M

12ᵉ | 43, av Daumesnil (Bastille/Gare de Lyon) | 01-44-74-70-70
The trip is "hip" at this "lovely" eatery with stone walls and high ceilings built "under the arches of a former railroad viaduct" in the 12th;
it's "understandably popular" for its "original" decor and a "beautiful" large terrace open until the wee hours in summer, despite the
"just fair" Classic–New French cuisine; still, it's "not about the food"
here – "the whole point of the place is to get a tan and to be seen."

Vieux Chêne (Au) 🗠 *Bistro* — | - | - | M

11ᵉ | 7, rue du Dahomey (Faidherbe-Chaligny) | 01-43-71-67-69 |
www.vieuxchene.fr
Its "simple decor is little changed from its years as a working man's
bistro, but the food has a finesse that takes traditional dishes to the
next level" at this New French in the 11th; "the owners are always
nice", the prices consistently easygoing and be sure to cast your eye
over the vintage cognac collection; N.B. closed weekends.

Villa Corse (La) 🗠 *Corsica* 20 | 20 | 17 | €50

15ᵉ | 164, bd de Grenelle (Cambronne/La Motte-Picquet-Grenelle) |
01-53-86-70-81 ◑
16ᵉ | 141, av de Malakoff (Porte Maillot) | 01-40-67-18-44
The Ile de France meets the Ile de Beauté (as the French call
Corsica) at these stylish showcases in the 15th and 16th, both "hot
spots that are always busy with pretty young things" sampling the
"elaborate", "earthy" eats in "luxurious", "comfortable men's club-
like settings"; "service is attentive – but not always accurate", however, and some say the prices would make even a Napoleon retreat.

Villa des Ternes 🗠 *Bistro/Italian* — | - | - | M

17ᵉ | 35, rue Guersant (Porte Maillot/Porte de Champerret) |
01-45-74-23-86
On a quiet residential street near the Porte Maillot, this small enclave has a definitely Franco-Italian touch with its homemade pastas
and pizzas baked in a special oven joining some bistro favorites; the
red-and-white gingham-covered tablecloths and wood beams convey a cozy atmosphere, and service is always friendly and quick.

Village d'Ung et Li Lam ◑🗠 *Chinese/Thai* — | - | - | M

8ᵉ | 10, rue Jean Mermoz (Franklin D. Roosevelt) | 01-42-25-99-79
Village people call this original outpost in the 8th "a must in Paris",
as much for the "ultrakitsch decor" (kind of "Asia meets the

Champs-Elysées", with an aquarium on the ceiling) as for the "wholesome" – "if not well-spiced" – Chinese-Thai cuisine and the "smiling welcome"; N.B. closed weekends.

☑ Villaret (Le) ◐☒ *Bistro*   26 | 16 | 23 | €53
11ᵉ | 13, rue Ternaux (Oberkampf/Parmentier) | 01-43-57-89-76
It's worth traveling to an "out-of-the-way residential neighborhood" in the 11th to discover this "good example of the bistro-revival phenomenon", whose "inventive" "wonderfully prepared food" is absolutely "amazing"; views vary on the decor – "homey atmosphere, with exposed-stone walls" vs. "nonexistent" – but fans flip for the "friendly, fun service"; and if "prices are becoming a little high", perhaps that befits "one of the best bistros in Paris."

Villa Spicy ◐ *New French*   13 | 14 | 13 | €47
8ᵉ | 8, av Franklin D. Roosevelt (Franklin D. Roosevelt/ St-Philippe-du-Roule) | 01-56-59-62-59 | www.villaspicy.com
"Colorful decor" – refurbished a while back in cool tones and including a pseudo-veranda – beckons business types of the 8th to this reasonable eatery; the Med-inflected New French fare is "original" enough, but foes fume that "this boring and bland place" belies its name: "there's no spice in the food" or the "characterless service" – though the recent (post-Survey) arrival of a new chef may change their tune.

NEW Vin Chai Moi ☒ *Wine Bar/Bistro*   – | – | – | M
1ᵉʳ | 18, rue Duphot (Madeleine) | 01-40-15-06-69 | www.vin-chai-moi.fr
Steps from Place de la Madeleine, this contemporary French bistro by Luc Menier, former sommelier at Guy Savoy, features a vaulted tasting cellar, a street-level wine shop and a pretty, rustic first-floor dining room with varnished-wood tables, iron chairs and swag Bordeaux-hued curtains; the moderately priced menu features inventive modern French dishes such as escargot beignets in garlic butter, and there's an impressive selection of offbeat cocktails and wines by the glass too; its relaxing atmosphere is popular with the business set at lunch and stylish locals in the evening.

Vinci (Le) ☒ *Classic French/Italian*   – | – | – | E
16ᵉ | 23, rue Paul Valéry (Victor Hugo) | 01-45-01-68-18
Suits in the 16th know this "small" site "on a sleepy side street" as "one of the best deals in the neighborhood", "deserving its loyal clientele" with prix fixes that are "champion for value"; its Joël Robuchon–trained chef cooks up "excellent" dishes that combine "Italian inspiration" and Classic French savoir faire, served amid the "warm" ambiance created by well-spaced tables and reddish tones.

Vin dans les Voiles
(Le) ☒Ⓜ *Wine Bar/Bistro*   – | – | – | I
16ᵉ | 8, rue Chapu (Exelmans) | 01-46-47-83-98 | www.vindanslesvoiles.com
"If you want just a simple, casual [meal], with a nice selection of wines and an owner who's passionate about them, here's your per-

fect" place sing supporters of this *bistrot à vins* in the 16th; "charming and cozy", it offers an "often-changing menu and the prices are more than reasonable."

Vin et Marée *Seafood*   18 | 14 | 15 | €48

1ᵉʳ | 165, rue St-Honoré (Palais Royal-Musée du Louvre) | 01-42-86-06-96 ●
7ᵉ | 71, av de Suffren (La Motte-Picquet-Grenelle) | 01-47-83-27-12
11ᵉ | 276, bd Voltaire (Nation) | 01-43-72-31-23
14ᵉ | 108, av du Maine (Gaîté) | 01-43-20-29-50
16ᵉ | 183, bd Murat (Porte de St-Cloud) | 01-46-47-91-39

This "chain of simple" seafooders has cast a wide net throughout the city, and its clients trust the "consistent quality" of the "standard fare" from a "tuna steak big enough for Ahab" to a "gigantesque" baba "with a good bottle of rum generously left at the table"; some carp about the "inattentive" service that leaves them fishing around for a waiter, and the "spacious" settings that seem slightly "sterile" – though entirely smoke-free now.

20 de Bellechasse (Le) ●🇿 *Bistro*   19 | 17 | 18 | €58

7ᵉ | 20, rue de Bellechasse (Solférino) | 01-47-05-11-11

The owners (two "friendly guys") and a "young crowd" "full of locals" who all "know each other" get this "casual", "hip" bistro "buzzing"; the classic cooking – "enjoyable, fresh" and "well priced" considering the privileged 'hood near the Musée d'Orsay – adds to the appeal, so at times this "happening place" feels like a "crowded shoebox" (don't be surprised if people kick their Pradas off and "dancing ensues").

21 🇿🇲 *Seafood*   - | - | - | E

6ᵉ | 21, rue Mazarine (Odéon) | 01-46-33-76-90

Only premier *poissons* gain access to the kitchen of Paul Minchelli, who earned a following at his own eponymous restaurant prior to opening this table with a mysterious black exterior and just a '21' on the awning; it's strategically situated to snag the Saint-Germain elite who slide into black leather booths and order what many consider "the city's best fish, perfectly cooked" from a blackboard menu, at prices that leave some gasping for air; P.S. "reservations mandatory."

Vins des Pyrénées ● *Classic French*   16 | 15 | 16 | €34

4ᵉ | 25, rue Beautreillis (Bastille/St-Paul) | 01-42-72-64-94

"Near Bastille", this "unique wine bar" is a "nice neighborhood-type place" with an "at-home feeling" claim converts who concentrate on its "robust, hearty" Classic French fare and a "good vino list at reasonable prices" – dismissing as sour grapes those who find the "food, and especially the service, uneven."

🇿 Vin sur Vin *New French*   26 | 21 | 22 | €82

7ᵉ | 20, rue de Monttessuy (Alma Marceau/Ecole Militaire) | 01-47-05-14-20

Its "astonishing wine list" – 600 labels, baby – may be the main attraction at this "small storefront" decorated like "an elegant home"

	FOOD	DECOR	SERVICE	COST

in the 7th; but don't neglect the New French cuisine, which seems like "art" – "interesting", and full of "fine, fresh ingredients"; surveyors are mixed on the service: it possesses "a true passion for food and wine", but "where's the warmth?"; even so, this "out-of-the-way" place is "worth a trip."

☒ Violon d'Ingres (Le) ☒Ⓜ Bistro | 25 | 21 | 23 | €81 |

7ᵉ | 135, rue St-Dominique (Ecole Militaire) | 01-45-55-15-05 | www.leviolondingres.com

A while back, chef-owner Christian Constant did a "scaling-down" of his beloved Haute Cuisine table in the 7th, but "the conversion to a bistro hasn't changed the high quality of the food" ("Constant remains constant"); redone to be "sleek and modern, the narrow space obliges tables to be arranged like a railroad dining car, but the lack of intimacy is offset by a warm and informed staff"; though "better now", "prices remain high"; even so, most maintain "you can't visit Paris without dining here."

Voltaire (Le) ☒Ⓜ Bistro | 24 | 20 | 22 | €75 |

7ᵉ | 27, quai Voltaire (Rue du Bac) | 01-42-61-17-49

The atmosphere oozing "old-style French charm" and "old-world bistro fare done one better" make this "classic" "along the Seine" in the 7th a major "favorite"; many maintain it's "more of a [private] club than a restaurant", both because of its "elegant dark-wood decor" and its "popularity with celebrities" and a major Paris power crowd – so, you first-timers better "go with a regular or you'll feel like an intruder"; in addition, be sure to "dress chic" and be braced for "definitely pricey" tabs.

Wadja ☒ Bistro | 20 | 12 | 16 | €37 |

6ᵉ | 10, rue de la Grande-Chaumière (Vavin) | 01-46-33-02-02

This "unpretentious" neighborhood bistro in Montparnasse "is one of the places where you say, if I lived nearby, I'd eat here at least twice a week", since it has "consistently good" – even occasionally "innovative" – Classic French fare "and a surprising wine list" at prices offering "unbeatable value for the money"; hélas, the service can be "cliché French – meaning impatient and haughty."

Waknine ☒ New French | - | - | - | M |

16ᵉ | 9, av Pierre 1er de Serbie (Iéna) | 01-47-23-48-18 | www.waknine.fr

The welcoming armchairs "fill up at lunchtime" in this "chic", "charming" 16th-arrondissement address where "always smiling" servers deliver "slightly fusion" New French food; the room can get "noisy" at noon or during impromptu "TGIF wine gatherings", but there's a "softer ambiance at night" and at afternoon tea too.

Wally Le Saharien ☒Ⓜ North African | ▽ 15 | 14 | 14 | €38 |

9ᵉ | 36, rue Rodier (Anvers/Notre-Dame-de-Lorette) | 01-42-85-51-90

North African–born Wally is "a true prince of the desert", which partially explains why Parisians steer their caravans toward his longstanding place in the 9th, with its "museum"-like decor of ethnic rugs and objects (which recently underwent a complete overhaul, outdating the above Decor score) and "fancy" Algerian eats, including "unique dry couscous", that many call "the best I know"; still, malcontents mutter it's all a mirage, slamming "small portions that are nondescript in terms of flavor and presentation" and "prices that are too high for what you get."

Waly-Fay ◑ *African*

- - - I

11ᵉ | 6, rue Godefroy Cavaignac (Voltaire) | 01-40-24-17-79

Not far from the Bastille, this one-of-a-kind venue offers a wide array of affordable West African dishes like Creole blood sausage and curry colombo, produced by a melting-pot team that includes owner Joséphine from the Ivory Coast, a Senegalese cook and a Caribbean partner; open in the evenings only, it inhabits a cozy, jazzy, loftlike space in a former toy factory.

Water Bar Colette (Le) ⊠ *Italian/New French*

14 16 13 €36

1ᵉʳ | 213, rue St-Honoré (Tuileries) | 01-55-35-33-93 | www.colette.fr

"Rich women shopping in the neighborhood" maintain their figures with "light, fresh" Italian–New French nibbles accompanied by an assortment of "mineral waters with strange names" at this "spare" cafe in the "super-trendy" store Colette; detractors dismiss it as an "amusing but expensive" "fad" that won't die – "nice bottles, but a bit too much attitude"; perhaps the post-Survey installation of a more colorful design scheme has warmed things up.

Wepler ◑ *Brasserie*

14 11 12 €44

18ᵉ | 14, pl de Clichy (Place de Clichy) | 01-45-22-53-24 | www.wepler.com

Overlooking the busy Place de Clichy, this "typical, old-fashioned brasserie", one of the last independents in Paris, serves up "traditional French dishes", including "excellent shellfish platters", to an eclectic crowd of creative artists, shopkeepers, students and tourists; after 100-plus years, both the vintage decor and the kitchen unsurprisingly seem "faded" and the staff *stressé*, though "speedy" (not so bad, since many patrons are going to a show nearby); but amiable *amis* love it anyway: "it is what it is, even if it's not what it was."

☑ Willi's Wine Bar ⊠ *Wine Bar/Bistro*

20 17 19 €45

1ᵉʳ | 13, rue des Petits-Champs (Palais Royal-Musée du Louvre/Pyramides) | 01-42-61-05-09 | www.williswinebar.com

"If you're a wine lover, this is the place to go" opine oenophiles of this slightly "cramped" *bar à vins* in the 1st that stays "true to form after many years" under the eye of British owner Mark Williamson; "there are English-speakers in the house", including the staff, "but the food is French", and while it can be either "surprisingly good or so-so", no worries – "Willi's is a state of mind not to be missed."

Winch (Le) *Seafood*

- - - M

18ᵉ | 44, rue Damremont (Abbesses/Place de Clichy) | 01-42-23-04-63

It's smooth sailing at this seafooder with a laid-back loungelike decor of blue walls and black-and-white photos of Brittany, and "excellent" preparations that range from Breton fish stew to shrimp with mint and orange chutney; well "worth a visit" if you're touring Montmartre.

	FOOD	DECOR	SERVICE	COST

Wok Cooking *Asian*   — | — | — | M
11ᵉ | 25, rue des Taillandiers (Bastille) | 01-55-28-88-77

"You get to choose your own ingredients and sauces and watch them cook in front of you" at this "affordable" and "always crowded" Asian in the 11th; converts call it a "good concept", but cynics say just wok on by, wondering "why would you do this in Paris?"

W Restaurant (Le) 🖼 *New French*   — | — | — | E
8ᵉ | Hôtel Warwick | 5, rue de Berri (George V) | 01-45-61-82-08 | www.warwickhotels.com

A few steps off the Champs, this New French could well be "the best business"-lunch destination when quality cuisine can clinch the deal; the kitchen "deserves kudos" for the "fresh" fare prepared with a Mediterranean accent and proffered by "efficient service" – both of which "transcend" the "corporate-chic and cold decor" and the uninspiring "location at the back of an international hotel."

NEW Yam'Tcha 🅼 *Asian/New French*   — | — | — | E
1ᵉʳ | 4, rue Sauval (Louvre-Rivoli) | 01-40-26-08-07

Exposed-stone walls and an ancient beamed ceiling create a warm atmosphere at this Franco-Asian arrival on a side street off Les Halles; from her small, glassed-in corner kitchen, chef Adeline Grattard (ex Le Meurice, L'Astrance) cooks a single market menu daily that reflects both her French Haute Cuisine training and a recent stint in Hong Kong, while her husband, Chi Wah Chan, serves as tea steward (yam'tcha means 'to drink tea') for those opting to sample a different brew with each course; N.B. book well in advance.

Yen 🖼 *Japanese*   20 | 15 | 16 | €42
6ᵉ | 22, rue St-Benoît (St-Germain-des-Prés) | 01-45-44-11-18

Gourmands ready for "something other than sushi" nippon over to this Saint-Germain Japanese for "elaborate", "unconventional" offerings, including "the best soba in Paris", in a coolly "Zen atmosphere" where "the regulars go upstairs"; but cost-conscious customers complain that "small" portions and "expensive" tabs mean "you'll have a yen after eating here . . . for something to eat."

Yugaraj 🅼 *Indian*   23 | 17 | 18 | €53
6ᵉ | 14, rue Dauphine (Odéon/Pont-Neuf) | 01-43-26-44-91

"It's rare to find good Indian in Paris", but it "rivals anything in London or NYC" at this Saint-Germain subcontinental, whose "gourmet touch means we're not in the mere chicken vindaloo zone anymore" – in fact, pheasant biryani is more their speed, as are "great wines"; some feel the decor of Anglo-Indian antiquities "shows signs of fatigue, but this remains one of the best" of the breed in town.

Zébra Square ◐ *Classic French/Italian*   10 | — | 9 | €48
16ᵉ | 3, pl Clément-Ader (Avenue du Pdt Kennedy RER/Passy) | 01-44-14-91-91 | www.zebrasquare.com

"Très trendy", this "young"-feeling place "across from La Maison de la Radio" in the 16th has changed its stripes since its acquistion by chef-owner Thierry Burlot; he hopes to continue pulling in media mavens and the "BCBG crowd" (the French equivalent of preppy) with darker decor, lower noise level and a revamped Classic French–Italian menu (not reflected in the Food score).

☑ Ze Kitchen Galerie ⊠ *Eclectic*   25 | 20 | 20 | €65

6ᵉ | 4, rue des Grands-Augustins (Odéon/St-Michel) | 01-44-32-00-32 | www.zekitchengalerie.fr

"Co-chef/owner William Ledeuil has his finger and palate on the pulse of the modern diner" declare disciples of his still-"trendy" Eclectic eatery in Saint-Germain; a "pleasantly varied" "crowd that's the image of the area" (e.g. affluent, "hip" gallery-goers) devours "divine repasts" of "intelligent" "quasi Asian-French" fare, including "fish served *à la plancha* – on a grill at your table"; the art-adorned, loftlike space is "sleek, if a little cold", and so is the staff, some say, "unless they know you"; there's no denying, though, its "title as the best fusion food in Paris."

Zéphyr (Le) ❶ *Bistro*   − | − | − | M

20ᵉ | 1, rue du Jourdain (Jourdain) | 01-46-36-65-81 | www.lezephyrcafe.com

True, its name means 'gentle breeze', but reviewers blow hot and cold over this Belleville bistro; the "extremely inventive" fare is "scrumptious" to some palates, but overpriced to others; still, it's a popular place "to meet with close friends" and admire the superbly preserved "art deco setting – a treat for the eyes"; P.S. insiders say the *tour du chocolat* "dessert sampler is a must for any self-respecting chocolate lover."

Zeyer (Le) ❶ *Brasserie*   ▽ 16 | 16 | 19 | €59

14ᵉ | 62, rue d'Alésia (Alésia) | 01-45-40-43-88

"A monument of the 14th" for nearly a century, this "handsome brasserie" with retro-"art deco atmosphere" has "the same owner as Le Dôme", and serves much the "same fare – fresh fish, oysters and *fruits de mer*"; "a professionally run operation, it's out of the way, but don't be surprised if you want to come back."

Zinc-Zinc ❶⊠ *Bistro*   ▽ 16 | 15 | 13 | €34

Neuilly-sur-Seine | 209 ter, av de Gaulle (Pont-de-Neuilly) | 01-40-88-36-06 | www.zinczinc.com

Critics may cavil "the cuisine's too greasy and the room too noisy", but the majority of Neuilly natives find this "lively" bistro "always reliable"; it's especially "nice with the gang after work", when it serves "excellent tapas", and some welcome the weekday breakfast as well.

Zo ❶⊠ *Eclectic*   − | − | − | M

8ᵉ | 13, rue Montalivet (Champs-Elysées-Clémenceau) | 01-42-65-18-18 | www.restaurantzo.com

Fusionistas from the "posh neighborhood" around the Faubourg Saint-Honoré have made this "happening" table their "local hangout" with a "contemporary, light" Eclectic menu that meanders from the Mediterranean to Japan and a bar that specializes in fruity vodkas; for an eatery *à la mode,* it's "affordable", with surprisingly "nice service."

Zygomates (Les) 🗷Ⓜ *Bistro* ▽ | 20 | 16 | 21 | €44 |

12ᵉ | 7, rue de Capri (Daumesnil/Michel Bizot) | 01-40-19-93-04 | www.leszygomates.fr

The *zygomates* (the muscles used to smile) get a workout at this "cozy, welcoming" bistro in an "old butcher's shop" in the 12th; as "it only seats a few dozen people", it's always packed with a "local crowd" lapping up the "creative" takes on Classic French favorites at "great prices"; "crossing the city for it might be too much, but if you're looking for a restaurant in the area, it's very good."

INDEXES

French Cuisines

Includes names, locations and Food ratings.

BISTRO

Name	Rating
Absinthe | 1er	20
Accolade | 17^e	-
Affriolé | 7^e	22
Alfred | 1er	-
Ⓩ Allard | 6^e	21
Ⓩ Ami Louis | 3^e	25
Ampère | 17^e	-
Antoine | 16^e	-
AOC | 5^e	18
Ⓩ Ardoise | 1er	24
Assiette | 14^e	-
Astier | 11^e	21
Atelier Maître Albert | 5^e	21
BAM | 1er	-
Bar des Théâtres | 8^e	15
Bastide Odéon | 6^e	22
Ⓩ Benoît | 4^e	24
Beurre Noisette | 15^e	23
Biche au Bois | 12^e	20
Bis du Severo | 14^e	-
Bistral | 17^e	19
Bistro 121 | 15^e	-
Bistro de Breteuil | 7^e	16
Bistro/Deux Théâtres | 9^e	14
Bistro du 17ème | 17^e	18
Bistro Melrose | 17^e	-
Bistro Poulbot | 18^e	-
Bistro St. Ferdinand | 17^e	14
Bistrot d'à Côté | multi.	21
Bistrot d'André | 15^e	-
Ⓩ Bistrot de l'Oulette | 4^e	26
Bistrot de Paris | 7^e	16
Bistrot des Dames | 17^e	14
Bistrot des Vignes | 16^e	17
Bistrot d'Henri | 6^e	20
Bistrot du Cap | 15^e	-
Bistrot du Dôme | multi.	21
Bistrot du Passage | 17^e	-
Bistrot du Peintre | 11^e	18
Bistrot du Sommelier | 8^e	18
Bistrot Niel | 17^e	-
Bistrot Paul Bert | 11^e	23
Bistrot Vivienne | 2^e	18
Ⓩ Bon Accueil | 7^e	24
Boucherie Roulière | 6^e	-
Boulangerie | 20^e	23
Buisson Ardent | 5^e	19
Café Burq | 18^e	-
NEW Café Cartouche | 12^e	-
Café Constant | 7^e	24
Café d'Angel | 17^e	-
Café de l'Industrie | 11^e	12
Café de Mars | 7^e	17
Café des Musées | 3^e	-
Café du Commerce | 15^e	16
Café Moderne | 2^e	21
Café Ruc | 1er	15
Caméléon | 6^e	20
Camille | 3^e	16
Cantine/Troquet | 14^e	-
Carte Blanche | 9^e	-
Casier à Vin | 15^e	-
Cave Gourmande | 19^e	25
Cerisaie | 14^e	21
Chalet/l'Oasis | Boulogne	-
Chardenoux | 11^e	19
Charpentiers | 6^e	18
Chéri Bibi | 18^e	-
Chez André | 8^e	20
Chez Denise | 1er	24
Chez Fred | 17^e	-
Ⓩ Chez Georges | 2^e	24
Chez Gérard | Neuilly	19
NEW Chez Grenouille | 9^e	-
Chez Julien | 4^e	19
Chez L'Ami Jean | 7^e	24
Chez la Vieille | 1er	16
Chez Léna et Mimile | 5^e	15
Chez Léon | 17^e	13
Chez Maître Paul | 6^e	21
Chez Marcel | 6^e	-
NEW Chez Marie-Louise | 10^e	-
Chez Paul | 11^e	21
Chez Paul | 13^e	16
Chez Ramulaud | 11^e	16
Chez René | 5^e	21
Chez Savy | 8^e	18
Christine | 6^e	23
Christophe | 5^e	-
Cinq Mars | 7^e	19
NEW Claude Colliot | 4^e	-
Clou | 17^e	19
Ⓩ Comptoir/Relais | 6^e	26

Cotolettes | 4ᵉ	–
Cotte Roti | 12ᵉ	–
Coupe Gorge | 4ᵉ	–
Crus de Bourgogne | 2ᵉ	17
Cuizine | 11ᵉ	–
Cul de Poule | 9ᵉ	–
D'Chez Eux | 7ᵉ	25
Des Gars | 3ᵉ	–
2 Pieces Cuisine | 18ᵉ	–
Duc de Richelieu | 12ᵉ	–
Ebauchoir | 12ᵉ	–
Entétée | 14ᵉ	–
Entracte | 18ᵉ	–
Entredgeu | 17ᵉ	17
Epi d'Or | 1ᵉʳ	16
ℤ Epi Dupin | 6ᵉ	24
Epigramme | 6ᵉ	–
Escargot Montorgueil | 1ᵉʳ	21
Ferrandaise | 6ᵉ	21
Fines Gueules | 1ᵉʳ	–
Fins Gourmets | 7ᵉ	19
Firmin le Barbier | 7ᵉ	–
ℤ Fontaine de Mars | 7ᵉ	21
Fontaines | 5ᵉ	17
NEW Fourchette | 17ᵉ	–
Fous d'en Face | 4ᵉ	–
NEW Frenchie | 2ᵉ	–
Gauloise | 15ᵉ	15
Gavroche | 2ᵉ	17
Georgette | 9ᵉ	22
Glou | 3ᵉ	–
Gorille Blanc | 7ᵉ	21
Gourmets des Ternes | 8ᵉ	19
Grand Pan | 15ᵉ	–
Grille | 10ᵉ	17
Grille St-Germain | 6ᵉ	17
Hide | 17ᵉ	–
Itineraires | 5ᵉ	–
Jadis | 15ᵉ	–
Jardinier | 9ᵉ	–
Joséphine/Dumonet | 6ᵉ	23
NEW KGB | 6ᵉ	–
Laiterie/Clotilde | 7ᵉ	–
Lescure | 1ᵉʳ	17
ℤ Lyonnais | 2ᵉ	21
Maison du Jardin | 6ᵉ	24
Mathusalem | 16ᵉ	–
Memère Paulette | 2ᵉ	–
Mesturet | 2ᵉ	–
Miroir | 18ᵉ	–
Moissonnier | 5ᵉ	19
NEW Mon Oncle | 18ᵉ	–
ℤ Mon Vieil Ami | 4ᵉ	24
Moulin à Vent | 5ᵉ	19
Noces de Jeannette | 2ᵉ	–
Oeillade | 7ᵉ	14
Office | 9ᵉ	–
Olivades | 7ᵉ	17
Opportun | 14ᵉ	15
Oudino | 7ᵉ	–
Parc aux Cerfs | 6ᵉ	21
Pères et Filles | 6ᵉ	16
Perraudin | 5ᵉ	13
Petit Marguery | 13ᵉ	21
Petit Pascal | 13ᵉ	–
Petit Pergolèse | 16ᵉ	23
Petit Pontoise | 5ᵉ	22
Petit Prince Paris | 5ᵉ	–
Petit Rétro | 16ᵉ	16
Petit Riche | 9ᵉ	18
Polichinelle Cafe | 11ᵉ	–
Polidor | 6ᵉ	17
Pomponette | 18ᵉ	17
Pouilly Reuilly | St-Gervais	–
Poule au Pot | 1ᵉʳ	23
Pramil | 3ᵉ	–
Press Café | 2ᵉ	–
P'tit Troquet | 7ᵉ	22
Pure Café | 11ᵉ	–
Quai-Quai | 1ᵉʳ	–
Quincy | 12ᵉ	–
Réfectoire | 11ᵉ	–
ℤ Régalade | 14ᵉ	25
Rendez-vous/Chauff. | 18ᵉ	–
Repaire de Cartouche | 11ᵉ	16
Rest. du Marché | 15ᵉ	–
Rest. Manufacture | Issy-les-Moul.	21
Rest. Paul | 1ᵉʳ	20
Réveil du 10e | 10ᵉ	–
Robert et Louise | 3ᵉ	21
Roi du Pot-au-Feu | 9ᵉ	–
Rose de France | 1ᵉʳ	–
Rôtiss. d'en Face | 6ᵉ	21
Rôtiss. du Beaujolais | 5ᵉ	23
Salon du Panthéon | 5ᵉ	–
Saveurs du Marché | Neuilly	–
Scheffer | 16ᵉ	18
Sot l'y Laisse | 11ᵉ	–
Square Trousseau | 12ᵉ	19
Temps au Temps | 11ᵉ	25
Temps des Cerises | 13ᵉ	–
Terrasse Mirabeau | 16ᵉ	–

Terrines/Gérard Vié | 6ᵉ	–
Terroir | 13ᵉ	–
NEW Tico | 8ᵉ	–
Tierny & Co. | 16ᵉ	–
Timbre | 6ᵉ	24
Tournesol | 16ᵉ	18
Trumilou | 4ᵉ	19
Urbane | 10ᵉ	–
Vieux Chêne | 11ᵉ	–
Villa des Ternes | 17ᵉ	–
Z Villaret | 11ᵉ	26
NEW Vin Chai Moi | 1ᵉʳ	–
20 de Bellechasse | 7ᵉ	19
Z Violon d'Ingres | 7ᵉ	25
Voltaire | 7ᵉ	24
Wadja | 6ᵉ	20
Zéphyr | 20ᵉ	–
Zinc-Zinc | Neuilly	16
Zygomates | 12ᵉ	20

BRASSERIE

Aub. Dab | 16ᵉ	16
Ballon des Ternes | 17ᵉ	15
Boeuf sur le Toit | 8ᵉ	18
Z Bofinger | 4ᵉ	20
Bouillon Racine | 6ᵉ	16
Z Brass. Balzar | 5ᵉ	19
Brass. du Louvre | 1ᵉʳ	16
Brass. Flo | 10ᵉ	18
Brass. Julien | 10ᵉ	19
Brass. La Lorraine | 8ᵉ	17
Brass. L'Européen | 12ᵉ	–
Z Brass. Lipp | 6ᵉ	17
Brass. Lutétia | 6ᵉ	18
Brass. Mollard | 8ᵉ	19
Brass./l'Ile St. Louis | 4ᵉ	17
Charlot Roi des Coq. | 9ᵉ	15
Chez Francis | 8ᵉ	17
Chez Georges-Maillot | 17ᵉ	18
Chez Jenny | 3ᵉ	19
Chez Les Anges | 7ᵉ	23
Chien qui Fume | 1ᵉʳ	18
Closerie des Lilas | 6ᵉ	18
Z Comptoir/Relais | 6ᵉ	26
Congrès Maillot | 17ᵉ	18
Costes | 1ᵉʳ	18
Z Coupole | 14ᵉ	19
Durand Dupont | Neuilly	–
Editeurs | 6ᵉ	14
Flandrin | 16ᵉ	15
Gallopin | 2ᵉ	16

Garnier | 8ᵉ	22
Grand Café | 9ᵉ	13
Grand Colbert | 2ᵉ	19
Mama Shelter | 20ᵉ	–
Marty | 5ᵉ	16
Mascotte | 18ᵉ	–
Petit Bofinger | multi.	18
Petit Lutétia | 6ᵉ	19
Petit Zinc | 6ᵉ	18
Pétrus | 17ᵉ	21
Pied de Cochon | 1ᵉʳ	18
Publicis Drugstore | 8ᵉ	11
Relais Plaza | 8ᵉ	23
Rosa Bonheur | 19ᵉ	–
Rotonde | 6ᵉ	15
Sébillon | Neuilly	15
Z Senderens | 8ᵉ	26
Stella | 16ᵉ	20
Suffren | 15ᵉ	14
Tav. de Maître Kanter | 1ᵉʳ	16
Terminus Nord | 10ᵉ	17
Vagenende | 6ᵉ	15
Vaudeville | 2ᵉ	18
Wepler | 18ᵉ	14
Zeyer | 14ᵉ	16

CLASSIC

A et M | 16ᵉ	21
Agapes | 5ᵉ	–
Agassin | 7ᵉ	–
Aiguière | 11ᵉ	–
Aimant du Sud | 13ᵉ	–
Z Allard | 6ᵉ	21
Allobroges | 20ᵉ	22
Z Ami Louis | 3ᵉ	25
Arome | 8ᵉ	–
Aub. Bressane | 7ᵉ	20
Aub. du Champ/Mars | 7ᵉ	17
Aub. du Clou | 9ᵉ	16
Aub. Nicolas Flamel | 3ᵉ	23
Aub./Reine Blanche | 4ᵉ	19
Auguste | 7ᵉ	25
Autobus Imperial | 1ᵉʳ	–
Bacchantes | 9ᵉ	–
Bar Vendôme | 1ᵉʳ	23
Basilic | 7ᵉ	15
Beaujolais d'Auteuil | 16ᵉ	17
Berkeley | 8ᵉ	14
Biche au Bois | 12ᵉ	20
Bistro de Breteuil | 7ᵉ	16
Bistro d'Hubert | 15ᵉ	22

Menus, photos, voting and more – free at ZAGAT.com

Bistro Poulbot	18e	_
Bistro St. Ferdinand	17e	14
Bistrot d'à Côté	**multi.**	21
Bistrot d'André	15e	_
Bistrot d'Henri	6e	20
Bistrot Papillon	9e	14
Boeuf Couronné	19e	16
Z Bon Accueil	7e	24
Bon Saint Pourçain	6e	18
Boudoir	8e	_
Brass. Printemps	9e	11
Buisson Ardent	5e	19
Café Beaubourg	4e	16
NEW Café Cartouche	12e	_
Café Charbon	11e	15
Z Café de Flore	6e	15
Café de la Musique	19e	15
Café de la Paix	9e	19
Café de l'Esplanade	7e	16
Z Café/Deux Magots	6e	16
Café Faubourg	8e	22
Café Guitry	9e	_
Café Le Petit Pont	5e	14
Z Café Marly	1er	16
Café Rouge	3e	_
Café Terminus	8e	_
Cap Seguin	**Boulogne**	_
Caveau du Palais	1er	19
Cave de l'Os à Moëlle	15e	22
Caves Pétrissans	17e	19
Céladon	2e	21
Chai 33	12e	14
Chalet	**Neuilly**	_
Chalet/l'Oasis	**Boulogne**	_
Chalet des Iles	16e	14
Chartier	9e	13
NEW Chateau Poivre	14e	_
Chéri Bibi	18e	_
Chez Cécile	8e	_
Chez Clément	**multi.**	15
Chez Denise	1er	24
Chez Françoise	7e	17
Chez Gégène	**Joinville**	_
Chez Géraud	16e	20
Chez Grisette	18e	_
Chez Léna et Mimile	5e	15
Chez Nénesse	3e	_
Christine	6e	23
Cigale Récamier	7e	21
Citrus Etoile	8e	20
Closerie des Lilas	6e	18

Coco & Co.	6e	_
Comédiens	9e	_
Cordonnerie	1er	_
Cotolettes	4e	_
Coupe-Chou	5e	23
Dali	1er	_
Da Rosa	6e	19
Deux Canards	10e	18
2 Pieces Cuisine	18e	_
Drouant	2e	22
Ebouillanté	4e	_
Ecluse	**multi.**	16
NEW Enfants Terribles	8e	_
Z Espadon	1er	26
Ferme St-Simon	7e	23
Fermette Marbeuf	8e	18
Firmin le Barbier	7e	_
Flora Danica	8e	19
Flore en l'Ile	4e	18
Florimond	7e	24
Fontaine Gaillon	2e	22
Fouquet's	8e	18
Gare	16e	14
Z Gérard Besson	1er	25
Gitane	15e	_
Gourmand	1er	20
Grande Armée	16e	15
Grand Louvre	1er	18
Gourmand	**Neuilly**	_
Guirlande de Julie	3e	15
Hangar	3e	18
Hide	17e	_
Ile	**Issy-les-Moul.**	18
Ilot Vache	4e	18
Il Vino	7e	_
Jadis	15e	_
Jardin des Cygnes	8e	22
Jardins de Bagatelle	16e	17
Je Thé . . . Me	15e	_
Joséphine/Dumonet	6e	23
Z Jules Verne	7e	22
Z Ladurée	**multi.**	23
Lavinia	1er	17
Libre Sens	8e	_
Ma Bourgogne	4e	18
Macéo	1er	23
Maison/Amér. Latine	7e	18
Marlotte	6e	16
Martel	10e	_
Mathusalem	16e	_
Maupertu	7e	21

Maxim's | 8^e	18
Méditerranée | 6^e	21
Ζ Michel Rostang | 17^e	27
Monsieur Lapin | 14^e	18
Moulin/Galette | 18^e	15
Murat | 16^e	13
Natacha | 14^e	-
Nos Ancêtres Gaulois | 4^e	13
Obé | 8^e	23
Ζ Os à Moëlle | 15^e	25
Ourcine | 13^e	24
Papilles | 5^e	23
Passage/Carm. | 11^e	-
Ζ Passiflore | 16^e	26
Paul Chêne | 16^e	20
Pavillon Montsouris | 14^e	17
Pelouse | 19^e	-
Père Claude | 15^e	17
Pères et Filles | 6^e	16
Petit Châtelet | 5^e	-
Petit Colombier | 17^e	18
Petite Chaise | 7^e	19
Petite Tour | 16^e	-
Petit Pascal | 13^e	-
Petit Rétro | 16^e	16
Petit Riche | 9^e	18
Petit St. Benoît | 6^e	16
Petit Victor Hugo | 16^e	19
Pharamond | 1er	19
Pierre au Palais Royal | 1er	17
Potager du Roy | **Versailles**	19
Procope | 6^e	16
Quai-Quai | 1er	-
Ragueneau | 1er	-
Relais du Parc | 16^e	19
Restaurant | 6^e	26
Rest. de la Tour | 15^e	21
Rest. du Palais Royal | 1er	19
Rest. du Musée d'Orsay | 7^e	17
Rest. Paul | 1er	20
Ribouldingue | 5^e	18
River Café | **Issy-les-Moul.**	14
Robe et le Palais | 1er	19
Rollin | 11^e	-
Royal Madeleine | 8^e	19
Rubis | 1er	15
Saveurs du Marché | **Neuilly**	-
Sébillon | **Neuilly**	15
NEW Société | 6^e	-
Ζ Soufflé | 1er	22
Square | 7^e	-

Square/Marcardet | 18^e	-
Ζ Stella Maris | 8^e	26
Stéphane Martin | 15^e	-
Table d'Anvers | 9^e	17
Table Lauriston | 16^e	20
Tante Louise | 8^e	22
Tante Marguerite | 7^e	22
Tastevin | **Maisons-Laff.**	24
Tav./Sgt. Recruteur | 4^e	16
Temps des Cerises | 13^e	-
Terres de Truffes | 8^e	19
Terrines/Gérard Vié | 6^e	-
Thoumieux | 7^e	-
Tonn. Saintongeaise | **Neuilly**	-
Toque | 17^e	-
Ζ Train Bleu | 12^e	19
Truc Café | 18^e	-
Truffe Noire | **Neuilly**	-
Versance | 2^e	-
Viaduc Café | 12^e	-
Ζ Villaret | 11^e	26
Vinci | 16^e	-
Vins des Pyrénées | 4^e	16
Wadja | 6^e	20
Zébra Square | 16^e	10
Zygomates | 12^e	20

CONTEMPORARY

Accolade | 17^e	-
Afaria | 15^e	-
Agapé | 17^e	-
Agapes | 5^e	-
Agassin | 7^e	-
Alcazar | 6^e	19
Ζ Ambassadeurs | 8^e	28
Amuse Bouche | 14^e	17
Angle/Faubourg | 8^e	24
NEW Arc | 8^e	-
Arome | 8^e	-
Ζ Astrance | 16^e	28
Atelier Berger | 1er	21
Aub. du Clou | 9^e	16
Aub./Reine Blanche | 4^e	19
Avant Goût | 13^e	23
Avenue | 8^e	18
BAM | 1er	-
Bamboche | 7^e	19
Bath's | 17^e	20
Bigarrade | 17^e	-
BIOArt | 13^e	-
Bistro d'Hubert | 15^e	22

Boudoir | 8ᵉ	-
Bound | 8ᵉ	-
Ƶ Bouquinistes | 6ᵉ	23
Ƶ Braisière | 17ᵉ	27
Café de l'Esplanade | 7ᵉ	16
Café Lenôtre | 8ᵉ	18
Café M | 8ᵉ	19
Ƶ Café Marly | 1ᵉʳ	16
Café Pleyel | 8ᵉ	-
Caïus | 17ᵉ	19
Camélia | **Bougival**	20
Cap Seguin | **Boulogne**	-
Carte Blanche | 9ᵉ	-
Cartes Postales | 1ᵉʳ	24
Casa Olympe | 9ᵉ	24
Cazaudehore | **St-Germain-Laye**	22
Chamarré Mont. | 18ᵉ	-
Chateaubriand | 11ᵉ	22
NEW Chateau Poivre | 14ᵉ	-
Chez Catherine | 8ᵉ	23
Chez Michel | 10ᵉ	24
Chiberta | 8ᵉ	22
Citrus Etoile | 8ᵉ	20
NEW Claude Colliot | 4ᵉ	-
Clos des Gourmets | 7ᵉ	25
Clos Morillons | 15ᵉ	-
Clovis | 8ᵉ	-
Cocottes | 7ᵉ	21
Cottage Marcadet | 18ᵉ	-
Cou de la Girafe | 8ᵉ	15
Cristal de Sel | 15ᵉ	-
Ƶ Cristal Room | 16ᵉ	17
Cuisine | 7ᵉ	25
Dalva | 2ᵉ	-
NEW Derrière | 3ᵉ	-
Ƶ 1728 | 8ᵉ	19
Dôme du Marais | 4ᵉ	22
Eclaireur | 8ᵉ	-
Etc. | 16ᵉ	-
Famille | 18ᵉ	19
First | 1ᵉʳ	18
Gaigne | 4ᵉ	-
Gazzetta | 12ᵉ	-
Georgette | 9ᵉ	22
Glou | 3ᵉ	-
Gourmand | 1ᵉʳ	20
Ƶ Hélène Darroze | 6ᵉ	25
Hier & Aujourd'hui | 17ᵉ	-
Ƶ Hiramatsu | 16ᵉ	26
Hôtel Amour | 9ᵉ	8
Ile | **Issy-les-Moul.**	18
Itineraires | 5ᵉ	-
Jadis | 15ᵉ	-
NEW Jamin | 16ᵉ	-
Jean | 9ᵉ	19
Karl et Erich | 17ᵉ	-
Macéo | 1ᵉʳ	23
Magnolias | **Perreux**	25
Maison Blanche | 8ᵉ	20
Maison du Jardin | 6ᵉ	24
Maxan | 8ᵉ	-
NEW MBC | 17ᵉ	-
Montalembert | 7ᵉ	19
Montparnasse 25 | 14ᵉ	16
Murano | 3ᵉ	16
Musichall | 8ᵉ	15
Office | 9ᵉ	-
Ƶ Ombres | 7ᵉ	18
Ourcine | 13ᵉ	24
NEW Passage 53 | 2ᵉ	-
Pershing | 8ᵉ	17
Petite Cour | 6ᵉ	21
Petit Marché | 3ᵉ	22
Petit Pergolèse | 16ᵉ	23
Petit Poucet | **Levallois**	-
Pétrelle | 9ᵉ	-
Pinxo | 1ᵉʳ	21
Ploum | 10ᵉ	-
Pomze | 8ᵉ	18
Pramil | 3ᵉ	-
Pré Verre | 5ᵉ	22
Pur'Grill | 2ᵉ	19
Quai | 7ᵉ	-
Quinzième | 15ᵉ	-
Réconfort | 3ᵉ	-
Relais du Parc | 16ᵉ	19
Réminet | 5ᵉ	-
River Café | **Issy-les-Moul.**	14
Saut du Loup | 1ᵉʳ	14
Saveurs de Flora | 8ᵉ	21
16 Haussmann | 9ᵉ	18
Ƶ Senderens | 8ᵉ	26
Sensing | 6ᵉ	24
Sept Quinze | 15ᵉ	-
6 New York | 16ᵉ	17
Spoon Paris | 8ᵉ	22
Square/Marcardet | 18ᵉ	-
Table d'Eugène | 18ᵉ	-
Table d'Hédiard | 8ᵉ	22
NEW Tico | 8ᵉ	-
Toi | 8ᵉ	-
Tokyo Eat | 16ᵉ	14

Troquet	15ᵉ	24
Versance	2ᵉ	–
Viaduc Café	12ᵉ	–
Vieux Chêne	11ᵉ	–
Villa Spicy	8ᵉ	13
NEW Vin Chai Moi	1ᵉʳ	–
🄩 Vin sur Vin	7ᵉ	26
Waknine	16ᵉ	–
Water Bar Colette	1ᵉʳ	14
W Restaurant	8ᵉ	–
NEW Yam'Tcha	1ᵉʳ	–

HAUTE CUISINE

🄩 Alain Ducasse	8ᵉ	28
🄩 Ambassadeurs	8ᵉ	28
🄩 Ambroisie	4ᵉ	28
🄩 Apicius	8ᵉ	26
🄩 Arpège	7ᵉ	26
Astor	8ᵉ	16
🄩 Atelier Joël Robuchon	7ᵉ	28
🄩 Bristol	8ᵉ	27
🄩 Carré des Feuillants	1ᵉʳ	26
Cazaudehore	St-Germain-Laye	22
153 Grenelle	7ᵉ	–
🄩 Cinq	8ᵉ	28
🄩 Dominique Bouchet	8ᵉ	27
Elysées	8ᵉ	23
Gordon Ramsay	Versailles	–
🄩 Grande Cascade	16ᵉ	25
🄩 Grand Véfour	1ᵉʳ	28
🄩 Guy Savoy	17ᵉ	28
🄩 Hiramatsu	16ᵉ	26
🄩 Jacques Cagna	6ᵉ	26
Jadis	15ᵉ	–
🄩 Lapérouse	6ᵉ	21
🄩 Lasserre	8ᵉ	27
🄩 Laurent	8ᵉ	24
🄩 Meurice	1ᵉʳ	27
Paris	6ᵉ	20
🄩 Pavillon Ledoyen	8ᵉ	26
🄩 Pierre Gagnaire	8ᵉ	28
🄩 Pré Catelan	16ᵉ	27
🄩 Relais d'Auteuil	16ᵉ	27
Relais Louis XIII	6ᵉ	25
Stéphane Gaborieau	16ᵉ	–
Table du Baltimore	16ᵉ	–
Table du Lancaster	8ᵉ	23
🄩 Table/Joël Robuchon	16ᵉ	26
🄩 Taillevent	8ᵉ	28
🄩 Tour d'Argent	5ᵉ	25
Truffière	5ᵉ	23

REGIONAL

ALPINE

Chalet	Neuilly	–
Montagnards	1ᵉʳ	–

ALSACE/JURA

Alsace	8ᵉ	18
🄩 Bofinger	4ᵉ	20
Chez Jenny	3ᵉ	19
Chez Maître Paul	6ᵉ	21
Epicure 108	17ᵉ	–
Tav. de Maître Kanter	1ᵉʳ	16

AUVERGNE

Ambassade/Auv.	3ᵉ	20
Bath's	17ᵉ	20
Bistrot à Vins Mélac	11ᵉ	14
Chantairelle	5ᵉ	–
Chez Gérard	Neuilly	19
Lozère	6ᵉ	18
Mascotte	18ᵉ	–
Nemrod	6ᵉ	16
Parisiennes	11ᵉ	–

AVEYRON

Ambassade/Auv.	3ᵉ	20
Aub. Aveyronnaise	12ᵉ	–
Chez Savy	8ᵉ	18

BASQUE

Bascou	3ᵉ	20
Basilic	7ᵉ	15
Cantine/Troquet	14ᵉ	–
Chez L'Ami Jean	7ᵉ	24
Cul de Poule	9ᵉ	–
Pamphlet	3ᵉ	23
🄩 Régalade	14ᵉ	25
Troquet	15ᵉ	24

BRITTANY

Breizh Café	3ᵉ	–
Chez Michel	10ᵉ	24
Crêperie de Josselin	14ᵉ	22

BURGUNDY

Ma Bourgogne	4ᵉ	18
Tante Louise	8ᵉ	22

CORSICA

Alivi	4ᵉ	16
Cosi (Le)	5ᵉ	16
Main d'Or	11ᵉ	–
Villa Corse	multi.	20

GASCONY

- Ⓩ Braisière | 17e — 27
- Comte de Gascogne | Boulogne — -

LYON

- Aub. Pyrénées | 11e — 20
- Ⓩ Benoît | 4e — 24
- Chez Fred | 17e — -
- Chez Marcel | 6e — -
- Chez René | 5e — 21
- Duc de Richelieu | 12e — -
- Ⓩ Lyonnais | 2e — 21
- Moissonnier | 5e — 19
- Opportun | 14e — 15

NORTHERN FRANCE

- Graindorge | 17e — 22
- Petites Sorcières | 14e — -

PROVENCE

- Aimant du Sud | 13e — -
- Bastide Odéon | 6e — 22
- Bistro de l'Olivier | 8e — 18
- Casa Olympe | 9e — 24
- Chez Janou | 3e — 23
- Ⓩ Fish La Boiss. | 6e — 22
- Olivades | 7e — 17
- Petit Niçois | 7e — 16
- Sud | 17e — 16

SOUTHWEST

- Afaria | 15e — -
- Assiette | 14e — -
- Aub. Etchégorry | 13e — -
- Aub. Pyrénées | 11e — 20
- Ⓩ Bistrot de l'Oulette | 4e — 26
- Café Faubourg | 8e — 22
- Cerisaie | 14e — 21
- Chez L'Ami Jean | 7e — 24
- Chez Papa | multi. — 17
- D'Chez Eux | 7e — 25
- Diapason | 18e — -
- Domaine/Lintillac | multi. — 18
- Fins Gourmets | 7e — 19
- Ⓩ Fontaine de Mars | 7e — 21
- Ⓩ Hélène Darroze | 6e — 25
- Il Etait une Oie | 17e — -
- J'Go | multi. — 14
- Languedoc | 5e — -
- Maison Courtine | 14e — 24
- Mesturet | 2e — -
- Oulette | 12e — 19
- Pamphlet | 3e — 23

- Pasco | 7e — 22
- Rosa Bonheur | 19e — -
- Salon d'Hélène | 6e — 19
- Sarladais | 8e — -
- Ⓩ Trou Gascon | 12e — 26

SEAFOOD

- Antoine | 16e — -
- Autour du Mont | 15e — -
- Autour/Saumon | multi. — 17
- Ballon et Coquillages | 17e — -
- Bar à Huîtres | multi. — 17
- Bistrot de Marius | 8e — 21
- Bistrot du Cap | 15e — -
- Bistrot du Dôme | multi. — 21
- Brass. L'Européen | 12e — -
- Brass. Lutétia | 6e — 18
- Cagouille | 14e — 25
- Ⓩ 144 Petrossian | 7e — 25
- Ⓩ Coupole | 14e — 19
- Dessirier | 17e — 20
- Divellec | 7e — 24
- Dôme | 14e — 22
- Duc | 14e — 23
- Ecailler du Bistrot | 11e — 19
- Ecume Saint-Honoré | 1er — -
- Fables/Fontaine | 7e — 24
- Ⓩ Fish La Boiss. | 6e — 22
- Fontaine Gaillon | 2e — 22
- Frégate | 12e — 24
- Garnier | 8e — 22
- Gaya | 7e — 23
- Goumard | 1er — 24
- Huîtrier | 17e — 20
- Jarrasse | Neuilly — -
- Luna | 8e — 17
- Maison Prunier | 16e — 21
- Marée | 8e — 23
- Marée Denfert/Passy | multi. — -
- Marée de Versailles | Versailles — 19
- Marius | 16e — 18
- Marius et Janette | 8e — 25
- Méditerranée | 6e — 21
- Petit Zinc | 6e — 18
- Pétrus | 17e — 21
- Pichet de Paris | 8e — 16
- Rech | 17e — -
- Sarladais | 8e — -
- Stella | 16e — 20
- Terminus Nord | 10e — 17
- 35° Ouest | 7e — 20

Uitr | 15e	–
Vin et Marée | **multi.**	18
21 | 6e	–
Wepler | 18e	14
Winch | 18e	–

SHELLFISH

Ballon des Ternes | 17e	15
Ballon et Coquillages | 17e	–
Bar à Huîtres | **multi.**	17
Charlot Roi des Coq. | 9e	15
Dôme | 14e	22
Ecaille de Fontaine | 2e	–
Ecailler du Bistrot | 11e	19
Ecume Saint-Honoré | 1er	–
Garnier | 8e	22
Huîtrerie Régis | 6e	22
Huîtrier | 17e	20
Marée de Versailles | **Versailles**	19
Marius | 16e	18
Marius et Janette | 8e	25
Pichet de Paris | 8e	16
Rech | 17e	–
Stella | 16e	20
Uitr | 15e	–

STEAK

(See also Steakhouses in Other Cuisines)

Boeuf Couronné | 19e	16
Boucherie Roulière | 6e	–
Devèz | 8e	16
Gavroche | 2e	17
Gourmets des Ternes | 8e	19
Hippopotamus | **multi.**	11
Louchebem | 1er	15
Relais de Venise | 17e	24
Z Relais/l'Entrecôte | **multi.**	22
Ribouldingue | 5e	18
Severo | 14e	20

WINE BARS/BISTROS

Ami Pierre | 11e	17
Bacchantes | 9e	–
Baratin | 20e	16
Baron Rouge | 12e	–
Bistrot à Vins Mélac | 11e	14
Bistrot du Sommelier | 8e	18
NEW Bistro Volnay | 2e	–
Bons Crus | 1er	–
Bourguignon du Marais | 4e	23
Café Burq | 18e	–
Café du Passage | 11e	–
Cantine de Quentin | 10e	–
Cave de l'Os à Moëlle | 15e	22
Caves Pétrissans | 17e	19
Chai 33 | 12e	14
Chez Grisette | 18e	–
Cloche des Halles | 1er	–
Clown Bar | 11e	17
Coude Fou | 4e	19
Couleurs de Vigne | 15e	–
Crémerie | 6e	–
Crudus | 1er	–
NEW Cru Rollin | 11e	–
Dix Vins | 15e	–
Ecluse | **multi.**	16
Enoteca | 4e	20
Fines Gueules | 1er	–
Jeu de Quilles | 14e	–
Juvéniles | 1er	16
Lavinia | 1er	17
Legrand Filles | 2e	–
Louis Vin | 5e	19
Mauzac | 5e	–
Passage/Carm. | 11e	–
Poisson Rouge | 10e	–
Quedubon | 19e	–
Racines | 2e	–
Robe et le Palais | 1er	19
Rubis | 1er	15
Sauvignon | 7e	14
Tav. Henri IV | 1er	16
Truc Café | 18e	–
Verre Bouteille | 17e	13
Verre Volé | 10e	16
NEW Vin Chai Moi | 1er	–
Vin dans les Voiles | 16e	–
Z Willi's Wine | 1er	20

Other Cuisines

Includes names, locations and Food ratings.

AMERICAN

Breakfast/America	multi.	15
Buffalo Grill	multi.	10
Coffee Parisien	multi.	16
Floors	18ᵉ	-
Joe Allen	1ᵉʳ	13
Meating	17ᵉ	17

ARGENTINEAN

Anahï	3ᵉ	19
El Palenque	5ᵉ	19
Unico	11ᵉ	-

ARMENIAN

Diamantaires	9ᵉ	-

ASIAN

Asian	8ᵉ	16
Bon	16ᵉ	-
𝗭 Buddha Bar	8ᵉ	16
Epicure 108	17ᵉ	-
Passy Mandarin	multi.	20
Tricotin	13ᵉ	-
Wok Cooking	11ᵉ	-

ASIAN FUSION

Guilo-Guilo	18ᵉ	-
Mood	8ᵉ	-
Nabulione	7ᵉ	-
𝗭 Passiflore	16ᵉ	26

BAKERIES

BE Boulangépicier	multi.	19
Boulangerie Eric Kayser	multi.	16
Rose Bakery	multi.	17

BELGIAN

Graindorge	17ᵉ	22
Léon/Bruxelles	multi.	16

BRITISH

Rose Bakery	multi.	17

BURGERS

Coffee Parisien	multi.	16
Ferdi	1ᵉʳ	-
Floors	18ᵉ	-
Indiana Café	multi.	7
Joe Allen	1ᵉʳ	13

CAMBODIAN

Coin/Gourmets	multi.	22
Kambodgia	16ᵉ	-
Mousson	1ᵉʳ	-
Sinago	9ᵉ	-

CAVIAR

Caviar Kaspia	8ᵉ	25
𝗭 144 Petrossian	7ᵉ	25
Maison du Caviar	8ᵉ	22
Maison Prunier	16ᵉ	21

CHINESE

(* dim sum specialist)

Chen Soleil d'Est	15ᵉ	-
Chez Ly	17ᵉ	-
Chez Vong	1ᵉʳ	21
Davé	1ᵉʳ	18
Diep	8ᵉ	21
Elysées Hong Kong	16ᵉ	-
Lao Tseu	7ᵉ	-
Mirama	5ᵉ	20
New Nioullaville*	11ᵉ	16
Nouveau Village	13ᵉ	18
Pates Vivantes	multi.	-
NEW Shan Gout	12ᵉ	-
Tang	16ᵉ	17
Tong Yen	8ᵉ	15
Tsé-Yang	16ᵉ	18
Village d'Ung	8ᵉ	-
NEW Yam'Tcha	1ᵉʳ	-

COFFEE SHOPS/ DINERS

Breakfast/America	multi.	15
Coffee Parisien	multi.	16
Floors	18ᵉ	-
Publicis Drugstore	8ᵉ	11

DANISH

Copenhague	8ᵉ	18
Flora Danica	8ᵉ	19
Petite Sirène/Copen.	9ᵉ	-

DESSERT

𝗭 Angelina	1ᵉʳ	20
A Priori Thé	2ᵉ	16
BAM	1ᵉʳ	-

OTHER CUISINES

Enoteca | 4e	20
Enzo | 14e	-
Fellini | S | multi.	21
Findi | 8e	16
Finzi | 8e	13
Fontanarosa | 15e	-
Giulio Rebellato | N | 16e	20
Gli Angeli | 3e	18
Grand Venise | 15e	25
I Golosi | 9e	17
Il Barone | 14e	21
Il Viccolo | 6e	-
L'Assaggio | N | 1er	23
Lei | 7e	21
Mori Venice | N | 2e	17
Ostéria | 4e	22
Paolo Petrini | N | 17e	-
Paris Seize | 16e	18
Perron | 7e	18
Pizza Chic | 6e	-
Pizzeria d'Auteuil | 16e	-
Pizzetta | 9e	-
Romantica | Clichy	23
Rucola | 17e	-
Rughetta | 18e	-
Sale e Pepe | S | 18e	-
Sardegna a Tavola | S | 12e	21
Sormani | 17e	23
Stresa | 8e	22
Villa des Ternes | N | 17e	-
Vinci | 16e	-
Water Bar Colette | 1er	14
Zébra Square | 16e	10

JAPANESE

(* sushi specialist)

Aida | 7e	23
Azabu | 6e	24
Benkay* | 15e	24
Bizan* | 2e	-
Bound | 8e	-
Ferdi | 1er	-
Foujita* | 1er	-
Guilo-Guilo | 18e	-
Higuma | 1er	15
Hotaru* | 9e	-
Inagiku | 5e	18
Isami* | 4e	25
Issé* | 1er	23
Kai | 1er	-
Kaïten* | 8e	-
Kifune* | 17e.	-

NEW Kiku | 9e	-
Kinugawa/Hanawa* | multi.	23
Lô Sushi* | 8e	15
Matsuri | multi.	14
Orient-Extrême* | 6e	18
Oto-Oto* | 6e	-
Ozu* | 16e	23
Ploum | 10e	-
Rice and Fish* | 2e	-
Shu | 6e	-
Tsukizi* | 6e	-
Yen | 6e	20

JEWISH

Pitchi Poï | 4e	-

KOREAN

Samiin | 7e	-
Sobane | 9e	-

LEBANESE

Al Dar | multi.	21
Al Diwan | 8e	21
Escale du Liban | 4e	-
Fakhr el Dine | 16e	24
Liza | 2e	24
Mont Liban | 17e	-
Noura | multi.	19

MEDITERRANEAN

Ami Pierre | 11e	17
Casier à Vin | 15e	-
Gazzetta | 12e	-
Il Vino | 7e	-
Pasco | 7e	22
Sens | 8e	-
7ème Sud | multi.	15
Sud | 17e	16
Tête Ailleurs | 4e	-

MEXICAN

Anahuacalli | 5e	21

MIDDLE EASTERN

Chez Marianne | 4e	18

MOROCCAN

Al Mounia | 16e	17
Andy Wahloo | 3e	14
Atlas | 5e	20
Chez Omar | 3e	21
Comptoir | 1er	21

OTHER CUISINES

El Mansour | 8e	17
Etoile Marocaine | 8e	-
Mansouria | 11e	22
Martel | 10e	-
Oum el Banine | 16e	-
Parisiennes | 11e	-
404 | 3e	22
7ème Sud | multi.	15
Timgad | 17e	20

NOODLE SHOPS

Higuma | 1er	15
Pates Vivantes | 9e	-

NORTH AFRICAN

Boule Rouge | 9e	-
Wally Le Saharien | 9e	15

PAKISTANI

New Jawad | 7e	18

PAN-LATIN

Barrio Latino | 12e	12

PIZZA

Al Taglio | 11e	-
Amici Miei | 11e	19
Bartolo | 6e	17
Briciola | 3e	-
Da Mimmo | 10e	-
Enzo | 14e	-
Mama Shelter | 20e	-
Pizza Chic | 6e	-
Pizzeria d'Auteuil | 16e	-
Pizzetta | 9e	-
NEW Reginette | 8e	-
Rughetta | 18e	-
Sale e Pepe | 18e	-

POLISH

Pitchi Poï | 4e	-

PORTUGUESE

Saudade | 1er	-

RUSSIAN

Caviar Kaspia | 8e	25
Daru | 8e	-
Maison du Caviar | 8e	22

SANDWICHES

BE Boulangépicier | multi.	19
NEW Bob's Kitchen | 3e	-
Boulangerie Eric Kayser | multi.	16
Cosi | 6e	19

Dame Tartine | 4e	14
Ferme | 1er	-
Lina's | multi.	16
Sauvignon | 7e	14

SEAFOOD

Autour/Saumon | multi.	17
Bar à Huîtres | 17e	17
Copenhague | 8e	18
Des Gars | 3e	-
Ecume Saint-Honoré | 1er	-
Garnier | 8e	22
Sens | 8e	-
Vin et Marée | 1er	18

SEYCHELLES

Coco de Mer | 5e	-

SOUP

BE Boulangépicier | multi.	19
Couleurs de Vigne | 15e	-
Laiterie/Clotilde | 7e	-

SOUTHEAST ASIAN

Baan-Boran | 1er	20
Banyan | 15e	19
Blue Elephant | 11e	20
Chez Ly | 17e	-
Chieng Mai | 5e	16
Davé | 1er	18
Diep | 8e	21
Erawan | 15e	17
Khun Akorn | 11e	-
Kim Anh | 15e	-
Lac-Hong | 16e	20
Lao Lane Xang | 13e	-
Lao Siam | 19e	15
Nouveau Village | 13e	18
Palanquin | 6e	18
Paradis Thai | 13e	15
Reuan Thai | 11e	-
Sawadee | 15e	-
Suave | 13e	-
Tan Dinh | 7e	23
Thiou/Petit Thiou | multi.	21
Tong Yen | 8e	15
Village d'Ung | 8e	-

SPANISH

(* tapas specialist)

Bellota-Bellota | 7e	19
Casa Tina* | 16e	-

Menus, photos, voting and more – free at ZAGAT.com

Chez Ramona* | 20e _|
Fogón* | 6e 21|
Rosimar | 16e _|

STEAKHOUSES

(See also Steak
under French Cuisines)
Anahï | 3e 19|
Buffalo Grill | **multi.** 10|
El Palenque | 5e 19|
Meating | 17e 17|
Unico | 11e _|

TEX-MEX

Indiana Café | **multi.** 7|
Studio | 4e _|

THAI

Baan-Boran | 1er 20|
Banyan | 15e 19|
Blue Elephant | 11e 20|
Chez Ly | 17e _|
Chieng Mai | 5e 16|
Erawan | 15e 17|
Ferdi | 1er _|
Khun Akorn | 11e _|
Lao Siam | 19e 15|
Nouveau Village | 13e 18|

Oth Sombath | 8e _|
Paradis Thai | 13e 15|
Reuan Thai | 11e _|
Sawadee | 15e _|
Thiou/Petit Thiou | **multi.** 21|
Village d'Ung | 8e _|

TURKISH

Sizin | 9e _|

VEGETARIAN

NEW Bob's Kitchen | 3e _|
NEW Cru Rollin | 11e _|
NEW Soya Cantine Bio | 11e _|

VIETNAMESE

Coin/Gourmets | **multi.** 22|
Davé | 1er 18|
Kambodgia | 16e _|
Kim Anh | 15e _|
Lac-Hong | 16e 20|
Mai Do | 6e _|
Palanquin | 6e 18|
Suave | 13e _|
Tan Dinh | 7e 23|

WEST AFRICAN

Waly-Fay | 11e _|

OTHER CUISINES

Locations

Includes names, cuisines and Food ratings.

Paris

1ST ARRONDISSEMENT

Absinthe	*Bistro*	20
Alfred	*Bistro*	-
🅩 Angelina	*Tea*	20
Angelo Procopio	*Italian*	-
🅩 Ardoise	*Bistro*	24
Atelier Berger	*New Fr.*	21
Autobus Imperial	*Classic Fr.*	-
Baan-Boran	*Thai*	20
BAM	*Bistro*	-
Barlotti	*Italian*	15
Bar Vendôme	*Classic Fr.*	23
Bons Crus	*Wine*	-
Boulangerie Eric Kayser	*Bakery/Sandwiches*	16
Brass. du Louvre	*Brass.*	16
Ca d'Oro	*Italian*	18
🅩 Café Marly	*Classic/New Fr.*	16
Café Ruc	*Bistro*	15
🅩 Carré des Feuillants	*Haute*	26
Carr's	*Irish*	-
Cartes Postales	*New Fr.*	24
Caveau du Palais	*Classic Fr.*	19
Chez Denise	*Bistro*	24
Chez la Vieille	*Bistro*	16
Chez Vong	*Chinese*	21
Chien qui Fume	*Brass.*	18
Cibus	*Italian*	-
Cloche des Halles	*Wine*	-
Coin/Gourmets	*Cambodian/Viet.*	22
Comptoir	*Eclectic/Moroccan*	21
Cordonnerie	*Classic Fr.*	-
Costes	*Eclectic*	18
Crudus	*Italian/Wine*	-
Dali	*Classic Fr.*	-
Davé	*Chinese/Viet.*	18
Djakarta	*Indonesian*	20
Ecluse	*Wine*	16
Ecume Saint-Honoré	*Shellfish*	-
Epi d'Or	*Bistro*	16
Escargot Montorgueil	*Bistro*	21
🅩 Espadon	*Classic Fr.*	26
Fellini	*Italian*	21
Ferdi	*Eclectic*	-
Ferme	*Sandwiches*	-

Fines Gueules	*Wine*	-
First	*New Fr.*	18
Foujita	*Japanese*	-
Fumoir	*Eclectic*	17
🅩 Gérard Besson	*Classic Fr.*	25
Goumard	*Seafood*	24
Gourmand	*Classic/New Fr.*	20
Grand Louvre	*Classic Fr.*	18
🅩 Grand Véfour	*Haute*	28
Higuma	*Japanese*	15
Hippopotamus	*Steak*	11
Issé	*Japanese*	23
Jean-Paul Hévin	*Dessert/Tea*	24
Joe Allen	*Amer.*	13
Juvéniles	*Wine*	16
Kai	*Japanese*	-
Kinugawa/Hanawa	*Japanese*	23
Kong	*Eclectic*	14
L'Assaggio	*Italian*	23
Lavinia	*Classic Fr.*	17
Léon/Bruxelles	*Belgian*	16
Lescure	*Bistro*	17
Louchebem	*Steak*	15
Macéo	*Classic/New Fr.*	23
Matsuri	*Japanese*	14
🅩 Meurice	*Haute*	27
Montagnards	*Alpine*	-
Mousson	*Cambodian*	-
Muscade	*Eclectic/Tea*	-
Paradis du Fruit	*Eclectic*	14
Pharamond	*Classic Fr.*	19
Pied de Cochon	*Brass.*	18
Pierre au Palais Royal	*Classic Fr.*	17
Pinxo	*New Fr.*	21
Poule au Pot	*Bistro*	23
Quai-Quai	*Classic Fr.*	-
Ragueneau	*Classic Fr./Tea*	-
Rest. du Palais Royal	*Classic Fr.*	19
Rest. Paul	*Bistro*	20
Robe et le Palais	*Wine*	19
Rose de France	*Bistro*	-
Rouge St-Honoré	*Eclectic*	13
Rubis	*Wine*	15
Saudade	*Portuguese*	-
Saut du Loup	*New Fr.*	14
Scoop	*Eclectic*	17
🅩 Soufflé	*Classic Fr.*	22

Tav. de Maître Kanter | *Brass.*	16
Tav. Henri IV | *Wine*	16
NEW Vin Chai Moi | *Wine*	–
Vin et Marée | *Seafood*	18
Water Bar Colette | *Italian/Fr.*	14
Z Willi's Wine | *Wine*	20
NEW Yam'Tcha | *Asian/New Fr.*	–

2ND ARRONDISSEMENT

A Priori Thé | *Tea*	16
Bistrot Vivienne | *Bistro*	18
NEW Bistro Volnay | *Wine*	–
Bizan | *Japanese*	–
Café Etienne Marcel | *Eclectic*	18
Café Moderne | *Bistro*	21
Céladon | *Classic Fr.*	21
Chez Clément | *Classic Fr.*	15
Z Chez Georges | *Bistro*	24
Crus de Bourgogne | *Bistro*	17
Dalva | *New Fr.*	–
Domaine/Lintillac | *Southwest*	18
Drouant | *Classic Fr.*	22
Ecaille de Fontaine | *Shellfish*	–
Fontaine Gaillon | *Classic Fr.*	22
NEW Frenchie | *Bistro*	–
Gallopin | *Brass.*	16
Gavroche | *Bistro*	17
Grand Colbert | *Brass.*	19
Hippopotamus | *Steak*	11
Legrand Filles | *Wine*	–
Lina's | *Sandwiches*	16
Liza | *Lebanese*	24
Z Lyonnais | *Lyon*	21
Memère Paulette | *Bistro*	–
Mesturet | *Southwest*	–
Mori Venice | *Italian*	17
Noces de Jeannette | *Bistro*	–
Noura | *Lebanese*	19
NEW Passage 53 | *New Fr.*	–
Passy Mandarin | *Asian*	20
Press Café | *Bistro*	–
Pur'Grill | *New Fr.*	19
Racines | *Wine*	–
Rice and Fish | *Japanese*	–
Vaudeville | *Brass.*	18
Versance | *Classic/New Fr.*	–

3RD ARRONDISSEMENT

Ambassade/Auv. | *Auvergne*	20
Z Ami Louis | *Bistro*	25
Anahï | *Argent.*	19

Andy Wahloo | *Moroccan*	14
Aub. Nicolas Flamel | *Classic Fr.*	23
Bar à Huîtres | *Seafood*	17
Bascou | *Basque*	20
NEW Bob's Kitchen | *Veg.*	–
Breizh Café | *Brittany*	–
Briciola | *Pizza*	–
Buffalo Grill | *Steak*	10
Café des Musées | *Bistro*	–
Café Rouge | *Classic Fr./Eclectic*	–
Camille | *Bistro*	16
Chez Janou | *Provence*	23
Chez Jenny | *Alsace*	19
Chez Nénesse | *Classic Fr.*	–
Chez Omar | *Moroccan*	21
NEW Derrière | *New Fr.*	–
Des Gars | *Bistro*	–
Gli Angeli | *Italian*	18
Glou | *Bistro*	–
Guirlande de Julie | *Classic Fr.*	15
Hangar | *Classic Fr.*	18
Indiana Café | *Tex-Mex*	7
Murano | *New Fr.*	16
Pamphlet | *Basque/Southwest*	23
Petit Marché | *New Fr.*	22
Pramil | *Bistro/New Fr.*	–
404 | *Moroccan*	22
Réconfort | *New Fr.*	–
Robert et Louise | *Bistro*	21
Rose Bakery | *British/Fr.*	17

4TH ARRONDISSEMENT

Alivi | *Corsica*	16
Z Ambroisie | *Haute*	28
Z As du Fallafel | *Israeli*	24
Aub./Reine Blanche | *Classic/New Fr.*	19
Autour/Saumon | *Seafood*	17
Bel Canto | *Italian*	13
Z Benoît | *Lyon*	24
Z Bistrot de l'Oulette | *Southwest*	26
Bistrot du Dôme | *Seafood*	21
Z Bofinger | *Brass.*	20
Bourguignon du Marais | *Wine*	23
Brass./l'Ile St. Louis | *Brass.*	17
Breakfast/America | *Amer.*	15
Café Beaubourg | *Classic Fr.*	16
Chez Clément | *Classic Fr.*	15
Chez Julien | *Bistro*	19
Chez Marianne | *Mideast.*	18
NEW Claude Colliot | *Bistro/New Fr.*	–

Cotolettes	*Bistro*	–	Cosi (Le)	*Corsica*	16
Coude Fou	*Wine*	19	Coupe-Chou	*Classic Fr.*	23
Coupe Gorge	*Bistro*	–	Délices d'Aphrodite	*Greek*	18
Curieux Spaghetti	*Italian*	–	El Palenque	*Argent.*	19
Dalloyau	*Dessert/Tea*	23	Fontaines	*Bistro*	17
Dame Tartine	*Sandwiches*	14	Hippopotamus	*Steak*	11
Dôme du Marais	*New Fr.*	22	Inagiku	*Japanese*	18
Ebouillanté	*Classic Fr./Tea*	–	Itineraires	*Bistro*	–
Enoteca	*Italian*	20	Languedoc	*Southwest*	–
Escale du Liban	*Lebanese*	–	Louis Vin	*Wine*	19
Flore en l'Ile	*Classic Fr.*	18	Maharajah	*Indian*	17
Fous d'en Face	*Bistro*	–	Marty	*Brass.*	16
Gaigne	*New Fr.*	–	Mauzac	*Wine*	–
☑ Georges	*Eclectic*	18	Mavrommatis	*Greek*	19
Hippopotamus	*Steak*	11	Mirama	*Chinese*	20
Ilot Vache	*Classic Fr.*	18	Moissonnier	*Lyon*	19
Isami	*Japanese*	25	Moulin à Vent	*Bistro*	19
Léon/Bruxelles	*Belgian*	16	Papilles	*Classic Fr.*	23
Loir dans/Théière	*Dessert/Tea*	16	Paradis du Fruit	*Eclectic*	14
Ma Bourgogne	*Burgundy*	18	Pates Vivantes	*Chinese*	–
Mariage Frères	*Dessert/Tea*	21	Perraudin	*Bistro*	13
☑ Mon Vieil Ami	*Bistro*	24	Petit Châtelet	*Classic Fr.*	–
Nos Ancêtres Gaulois	*Classic*	13	Petit Pontoise	*Bistro*	22
Ostéria	*Italian*	22	Petit Prince Paris	*Bistro*	–
Petit Bofinger	*Brass.*	18	Pré Verre	*New Fr.*	22
Pitchi Poï	*Jewish/Polish*	–	Réminet	*New Fr.*	–
Studio	*Tex-Mex*	–	Ribouldingue	*Classic Fr.*	18
Tav./Sgt. Recruteur	*Classic Fr.*	16	Rôtiss. du Beaujolais	*Bistro*	23
Tête Ailleurs	*Med.*	–	Salon du Panthéon	*Bistro*	–
Trumilou	*Bistro*	19	☑ Tour d'Argent	*Haute*	25
Vins des Pyrénées	*Classic Fr.*	16	Truffière	*Haute*	23

5TH ARRONDISSEMENT	6TH ARRONDISSEMENT
Agapes	*Classic/New Fr.*	–	Alcazar	*New Fr.*	19
Al Dar	*Lebanese*	21	☑ Allard	*Bistro*	21
Anahuacalli	*Mex.*	21	Azabu	*Japanese*	24
AOC	*Bistro*	18	Bartolo	*Pizza*	17
Atelier Maître Albert	*Bistro*	21	Bastide Odéon	*Provence*	22
Atlas	*Moroccan*	20	Bistrot d'Henri	*Bistro*	20
Bar à Huîtres	*Seafood*	17	Bon Saint Pourçain	*Classic Fr.*	18
☑ Brass. Balzar	*Brass.*	19	Boucherie Roulière	*Bistro*	–
Breakfast/America	*Amer.*	15	Bouillon Racine	*Brass.*	16
Buisson Ardent	*Bistro*	19	☑ Bouquinistes	*New Fr.*	23
Café Le Petit Pont	*Classic Fr.*	14	☑ Brass. Lipp	*Brass.*	17
Chantairelle	*Auvergne*	–	Brass. Lutétia	*Brass.*	18
Chez Léna et Mimile	*Bistro*	15	☑ Café de Flore	*Classic Fr.*	15
Chez René	*Lyon*	21	☑ Café/Deux Magots	*Classic*	16
Chieng Mai	*Thai*	16	Caméléon	*Bistro*	20
Christophe	*Bistro*	–	Casa Bini	*Italian*	21
Coco de Mer	*Seychelles*	–	Charpentiers	*Bistro*	18
Coin/Gourmets	*Cambodian/Viet.*	22	Cherche Midi	*Italian*	19

Chez Clément	*Classic Fr.*	15	Petit Lutétia	*Brass.*	19
Chez Maître Paul	*Alsace*	21	Petit St. Benoît	*Classic Fr.*	16
Chez Marcel	*Lyon*	-	Petit Zinc	*Brass.*	18
Christine	*Bistro*	23	Pizza Chic	*Pizza*	-
Closerie des Lilas	*Classic Fr.*	18	Polidor	*Bistro*	17
Coco & Co.	*Classic Fr.*	-	Procope	*Classic Fr.*	16
Coffee Parisien	*Amer.*	16	☑ Relais/l'Entrecôte	*Steak*	22
☑ Comptoir/Relais	*Bistro/Brass.*	26	Relais Louis XIII	*Haute*	25
Cosi	*Sandwiches*	19	Restaurant	*Classic Fr.*	26
Crémerie	*Wine*	-	Rôtiss. d'en Face	*Bistro*	21
Dalloyau	*Dessert/Tea*	23	Rotonde	*Brass.*	15
Da Rosa	*Classic Fr.*	19	Salon d'Hélène	*Southwest*	19
Ecluse	*Wine*	16	Sensing	*New Fr.*	24
Editeurs	*Brass.*	14	Shu	*Japanese*	-
Emporio Armani	*Italian*	19	NEW Société	*Classic Fr.*	-
☑ Epi Dupin	*Bistro*	24	Terrines/Gérard Vié	*Bistro*	-
Epigramme	*Bistro*	-	Timbre	*Bistro*	24
Ferrandaise	*Bistro*	21	Tsukizi	*Japanese*	-
☑ Fish Lá Boiss.	*Provence*	22	Vagenende	*Brass.*	15
Fogón	*Spanish*	21	21	*Seafood*	-
Grille St-Germain	*Bistro*	17	Wadja	*Bistro*	20
☑ Hélène Darroze		25	Yen	*Japanese*	20
New Fr./Southwest			Yugaraj	*Indian*	23
Hippopotamus	*Steak*	11	☑ Ze Kitchen Galerie	*Eclectic*	25
Huîtrerie Régis	*Shellfish*	22		
Il Viccolo	*Italian*	-	**7TH ARRONDISSEMENT**	
Indiana Café	*Tex-Mex*	7	Affriolé	*Bistro*	22
☑ Jacques Cagna	*Haute*	26	Agassin	*Classic/New Fr.*	-
J'Go	*Southwest*	14	Aida	*Japanese*	23
Joséphine/Dumonet	*Bistro*	23	☑ Arpège	*Haute*	26
NEW KGB	*Bistro/Eclectic*	-	☑ Atelier Joël Robuchon	*Haute*	28
☑ Ladurée	*Classic Fr./Tea*	23	Aub. Bressane	*Classic Fr.*	20
☑ Lapérouse	*Haute*	21	Aub. du Champ/Mars	*Classic*	17
Léon/Bruxelles	*Belgian*	16	Auguste	*Classic Fr.*	25
Lozère	*Auvergne*	18	Bamboche	*New Fr.*	19
Lup	*Eclectic*	-	Basilic	*Basque*	15
Mai Do	*Viet.*	-	Bellota-Bellota	*Spanish*	19
Maison du Jardin	*Bistro*	24	Bistro de Breteuil	*Bistro*	16
Mariage Frères	*Dessert/Tea*	21	Bistrot de Paris	*Bistro*	16
Marlotte	*Classic Fr.*	16	☑ Bon Accueil	*Bistro*	24
Méditerranée	*Seafood*	21	Café Constant	*Bistro*	24
Nemrod	*Auvergne*	16	Café de l'Esplanade		16
Noura	*Lebanese*	19	*Classic/New Fr.*		
Orient-Extrême	*Japanese*	18	Café de Mars	*Bistro*	17
Oto-Oto	*Japanese*	-	Caffè Toscano	*Italian*	19
Palanquin	*Viet.*	18	153 Grenelle	*Haute*	-
Paradis du Fruit	*Eclectic*	14	☑ 144 Petrossian	*Seafood*	25
Parc aux Cerfs	*Bistro*	21	Chez Françoise	*Classic Fr.*	17
Paris	*Haute*	20	Chez L'Ami Jean	*Basque/Bistro*	24
Pères et Filles	*Bistro*	16	Chez Les Anges	*Brass.*	23
Petite Cour	*New Fr.*	21	Cigale Récamier	*Classic Fr.*	21
			Cinq Mars	*Bistro*	19

Clos des Gourmets	New Fr.	25
Cocottes	New Fr.	21
Cuisine	New Fr.	25
D'Chez Eux	Bistro/Southwest	25
Deux Abeilles	Dessert/Tea	21
Divellec	Seafood	24
Domaine/Lintillac	Southwest	18
Fables/Fontaine	Seafood	24
Ferme St-Simon	Classic Fr.	23
Fins Gourmets	Southwest	19
Firmin le Barbier	Bistro	-
Florimond	Classic Fr.	24
☑ Fontaine de Mars	Southwest	21
Gaya	Seafood	23
Gorille Blanc	Bistro	21
Il Vino	Classic Fr./Med.	-
☑ Jules Verne	Haute	22
Laiterie/Clotilde	Bistro	-
Lao Tseu	Chinese	-
Lei	Italian	21
Lina's	Sandwiches	16
Maison/Amér. Latine	Classic	18
Matsuri	Japanese	14
Maupertu	Classic Fr.	21
Montalembert	New Fr.	19
Nabulione	Asian/Eclectic	-
New Jawad	Indian/Pakistani	18
Oeillade	Bistro	14
Olivades	Provence	17
☑ Ombres	New Fr.	18
Oudino	Bistro	-
Pasco	Med./Southwest	22
Perron	Italian	18
Petite Chaise	Classic Fr.	19
Petit Niçois	Provence	16
P'tit Troquet	Bistro	22
Quai	New Fr.	-
Ravi	Indian	21
Rest. du Musée d'Orsay	Classic	17
Samiin	Korean	-
Sauvignon	Sandwiches/Wine	14
7ème Sud	Med./Moroccan	15
Square	Classic Fr.	-
Tan Dinh	Viet.	23
Tante Marguerite	Classic Fr.	22
Thiou/Petit Thiou	Thai	21
Thoumieux	Classic Fr.	-
35° Ouest	Seafood	20
Vin et Marée	Seafood	18
20 de Bellechasse	Bistro	19
☑ Vin sur Vin	New Fr.	26

| ☑ Violon d'Ingres | Bistro | 25 |
| Voltaire | Bistro | 24 |

8TH ARRONDISSEMENT

☑ Alain Ducasse	Haute	28
Al Diwan	Lebanese	21
Alsace	Alsace	18
☑ Ambassadeurs	Haute/New Fr.	28
Angle/Faubourg	Classic/New Fr.	24
Annapurna	Indian	18
☑ Apicius	Haute	26
NEW Arc	New Fr.	-
Arome	Classic/New Fr.	-
Asian	Asian	16
Astor	Haute	16
Avenue	New Fr.	18
Bar des Théâtres	Bistro	15
BE Boulangépicier	Sandwiches	19
Berkeley	Eclectic	14
Bistro de l'Olivier	Provence	18
Bistrot de Marius	Seafood	21
Bistrot du Sommelier	Wine	18
Black Calavados	Eclectic	-
Bocconi	Italian	20
Boeuf sur le Toit	Brass.	18
Boudoir	Classic/New Fr.	-
Boulangerie Eric Kayser	Bakery/Sandwiches	16
Bound	Japanese/New Fr.	-
Brass. La Lorraine	Brass.	17
Brass. Mollard	Brass.	19
☑ Bristol	Haute	27
☑ Buddha Bar	Asian	16
Café Faubourg	Classic Fr.	22
Café Lenôtre	New Fr.	18
Café M	New Fr.	19
Café Pleyel	New Fr.	-
Café Terminus	Classic Fr.	-
Caviar Kaspia	Russian	25
Chez André	Bistro	20
Chez Catherine	New Fr.	23
Chez Cécile	Classic Fr.	-
Chez Clément	Classic Fr.	15
Chez Francis	Brass.	17
Chez Papa	Southwest	17
Chez Savy	Aveyron	18
Chiberta	New Fr.	22
☑ Cinq	Haute	28
Citrus Etoile	Classic/New Fr.	20
Clovis	New Fr.	-
Copenhague	Danish	18
Cou de la Girafe	New Fr.	15

Menus, photos, voting and more – free at ZAGAT.com

Dalloyau	*Dessert/Tea*	23
Daru	*Russian*	-
Devèz	*Steak*	16
Diep	*Asian*	21
☑ 1728	*New Fr.*	19
☑ Dominique Bouchet	*Haute*	27
Eclaireur	*New Fr.*	-
Ecluse	*Wine*	16
El Mansour	*Moroccan*	17
Elysées	*Haute*	23
NEW Enfants Terribles	*Classic*	-
Etoile Marocaine	*Moroccan*	-
Eugène	*Eclectic*	-
Fermette Marbeuf	*Classic Fr.*	18
Findi	*Italian*	16
Finzi	*Italian*	13
Flora Danica	*Classic Fr./Danish*	19
Fouquet's	*Classic Fr.*	18
Garnier	*Brass./Seafood*	22
Gourmets des Ternes	*Bistro*	19
Hippopotamus	*Steak*	11
Indiana Café	*Tex-Mex*	7
Indra	*Indian*	-
Jardin des Cygnes	*Classic Fr.*	22
Kaïten	*Japanese*	-
Kinugawa/Hanawa	*Japanese*	23
☑ Ladurée	*Classic Fr./Tea*	23
Ladurée Le Bar	*Eclectic*	-
☑ Lasserre	*Haute*	27
☑ Laurent	*Haute*	24
Léon/Bruxelles	*Belgian*	16
Libre Sens	*Classic Fr.*	-
Lina's	*Sandwiches*	16
Lô Sushi	*Japanese*	15
Luna	*Seafood*	17
Maison Blanche	*New Fr.*	20
Maison du Caviar	*Russian*	22
Marée	*Seafood*	23
Mariage Frères	*Dessert/Tea*	21
Marius et Janette	*Seafood*	25
Market	*Eclectic*	22
Maxan	*New Fr.*	-
Maxim's	*Classic Fr.*	18
Mood	*Asian Fusion*	-
Musichall	*New Fr.*	15
Obé	*Classic Fr.*	23
Oth Sombath	*Thai*	-
Paradis du Fruit	*Eclectic*	14
☑ Pavillon Ledoyen	*Haute*	26
Pershing	*Eclectic/New Fr.*	17
Pichet de Paris	*Seafood*	16

☑ Pierre Gagnaire	*Haute*	28
Pomze	*New Fr.*	18
Publicis Drugstore	*Brass.*	11
NEW Reginette	*Pizza*	-
☑ Relais/l'Entrecôte	*Steak*	22
Relais Plaza	*Brass./Eclectic*	23
Royal Madeleine	*Classic Fr.*	19
Sarladais	*Southwest*	-
Saveurs de Flora	*New Fr.*	21
☑ Senderens	*Brass./New Fr.*	26
Sens	*Med.*	-
Spoon Paris	*Eclectic/New Fr.*	22
☑ Stella Maris	*Classic Fr.*	26
Stresa	*Italian*	22
Table d'Hédiard	*New Fr.*	22
Table du Lancaster	*Haute*	23
☑ Taillevent	*Haute*	28
Tante Louise	*Burgundy/Classic*	22
Terres de Truffes	*Classic Fr.*	19
Thiou/Petit Thiou	*Thai*	21
NEW Tico	*Bistro/New Fr.*	-
Toi	*New Fr.*	-
Tong Yen	*Chinese*	15
Village d'Ung	*Chinese/Thai*	-
Villa Spicy	*New Fr.*	13
W Restaurant	*New Fr.*	-
Zo	*Eclectic*	-

9TH ARRONDISSEMENT

Aub. du Clou	*Classic Fr.*	16
Autour/Saumon	*Seafood*	17
Bacchantes	*Wine*	-
BE Boulangépicier	*Sandwiches*	19
Bistro/Deux Théâtres	*Bistro*	14
Bistrot Papillon	*Bistro*	14
Boule Rouge	*African*	-
Brass. Printemps	*Classic Fr.*	11
Buffalo Grill	*Steak*	10
Café de la Paix	*Classic Fr.*	19
Café Guitry	*Classic Fr.*	-
Carte Blanche	*Bistro/New Fr.*	-
Casa Olympe	*New Fr.*	24
Charlot Roi des Coq.	*Brass.*	15
Chartier	*Classic Fr.*	13
NEW Chez Grenouille	*Bistro*	-
Comédiens	*Classic Fr.*	-
Cul de Poule	*Bistro*	-
Dell Orto	*Italian*	-
Diamantaires	*Armenian/Greek*	-
Domaine/Lintillac	*Southwest*	18
Georgette	*Bistro*	22
Grand Café	*Brass.*	13

Hotaru | *Japanese* —
Hôtel Amour | *New Fr.* 8
I Golosi | *Italian* 17
Indiana Café | *Tex-Mex* 7
Jardinier | *Bistro* —
Jean | *New Fr.* 19
J'Go | *Southwest* 14
NEW Kiku | *Japanese* —
Z Ladurée | *Classic Fr./Tea* 23
Léon/Bruxelles | *Belgian* 16
Lina's | *Sandwiches* 16
No Stress Café | *Eclectic* —
Office | *Bistro/New Fr.* —
Pates Vivantes | *Chinese* —
Petite Sirène/Copen. | *Danish* —
Petit Riche | *Bistro* 18
Pétrelle | *New Fr.* —
Pizzetta | *Italian* —
Roi du Pot-au-Feu | *Bistro* —
Rose Bakery | *British/Fr.* 17
16 Haussmann | *New Fr.* 18
Sinago | *Cambodian* —
Sizin | *Turkish* —
Sobane | *Korean* —
Table d'Anvers | *Classic Fr.* 17
Wally Le Saharien | *N African* 15

10TH ARRONDISSEMENT

Brass. Flo | *Brass.* 18
Brass. Julien | *Brass.* 19
Buffalo Grill | *Steak* 10
Cantine de Quentin | *Wine* —
NEW Chez Marie-Louise | *Bistro* —
Chez Michel | *Brittany/New Fr.* 24
Chez Papa | *Southwest* 17
Chez Prune | *Eclectic* 18
Da Mimmo | *Italian* —
Deux Canards | *Classic Fr.* 18
Grille | *Bistro* 17
Hippopotamus | *Steak* 11
Indiana Café | *Tex-Mex* 7
Martel | *Classic Fr./Moroccan* —
Ploum | *Japanese/New Fr.* —
Poisson Rouge | *Eclectic/Wine* —
Réveil du 10e | *Bistro* —
Terminus Nord | *Brass.* 17
Urbane | *Bistro* —
Verre Volé | *Wine* 16

11TH ARRONDISSEMENT

Aiguière | *Classic Fr.* —
Al Taglio | *Pizza* —

Amici Miei | *Pizza* 19
Ami Pierre | *Med.* 17
Astier | *Bistro* 21
Aub. Pyrénées | *Lyon/Southwest* 20
Bistrot à Vins Mélac | *Wine* 14
Bistrot du Peintre | *Bistro* 18
Bistrot Paul Bert | *Bistro* 23
Blue Elephant | *Thai* 20
Café Charbon | *Classic Fr.* 15
Café de l'Industrie | *Bistro* 12
Café du Passage | *Wine* —
NEW Caffé dei Cioppi | *Italian* —
Chardenoux | *Bistro* 19
Chateaubriand | *New Fr.* 22
Chez Paul | *Bistro* 21
Chez Ramulaud | *Bistro* 16
Clown Bar | *Wine* 17
NEW Cru Rollin | *Wine* —
Cuizine | *Bistro* —
Ecailler du Bistrot | *Seafood* 19
Indiana Café | *Tex-Mex* 7
Khun Akorn | *Thai* —
Léon/Bruxelles | *Belgian* 16
Main d'Or | *Corsica* —
Mansouria | *Moroccan* 22
New Nioullaville | *Chinese* 16
Paradis du Fruit | *Eclectic* 14
Parisiennes | *Med./Moroccan* —
Passage/Carm. | *Wine* —
Polichinelle Cafe | *Bistro* —
Pure Café | *Eclectic* —
Réfectoire | *Bistro* —
Repaire de Cartouche | *Bistro* 16
Reuan Thai | *Thai* —
Rollin | *Classic Fr.* —
Sot l'y Laisse | *Bistro* —
NEW Soya Cantine Bio | *Veg.* —
Temps au Temps | *Bistro* 25
Unico | *Argent.* —
Vieux Chêne | *Bistro* —
Z Villaret | *Bistro* 26
Vin et Marée | *Seafood* 18
Waly-Fay | *African* —
Wok Cooking | *Asian* —

12TH ARRONDISSEMENT

Aub. Aveyronnaise | *Aveyron* —
Baron Rouge | *Wine* —
Barrio Latino | *Pan-Latin* 12
Biche au Bois | *Bistro* 20
Brass. L'Européen | *Brass.* —

NEW Café Cartouche | *Bistro*	⌐
Chai 33 | *Wine*	14
Cotte Roti | *Bistro*	⌐
Duc de Richelieu | *Lyon*	⌐
Ebauchoir | *Bistro*	⌐
Frégate | *Seafood*	24
Gazzetta | *Med./New Fr.*	⌐
Hippopotamus | *Steak*	11
Lina's | *Sandwiches*	16
Oulette | *Southwest*	19
Quincy | *Bistro*	⌐
Sardegna a Tavola | *Italian*	21
NEW Shan Gout | *Chinese*	⌐
Square Trousseau | *Bistro*	19
Z Train Bleu | *Classic Fr.*	19
Z Trou Gascon | *Southwest*	26
Viaduc Café | *Classic/New Fr.*	⌐
Zygomates | *Bistro*	20

13TH ARRONDISSEMENT

Aimant du Sud | *Classic Fr.*	⌐
Aub. Etchégorry | *Southwest*	⌐
Avant Goût | *New Fr.*	23
BIOArt | *New Fr.*	⌐
Buffalo Grill | *Steak*	10
Cailloux | *Italian*	⌐
Chez Paul | *Bistro*	16
Entoto | *Ethiopian*	⌐
Lao Lane Xang | *Asian*	⌐
Nouveau Village | *Chinese/Thai*	18
Ourcine | *Classic/New Fr.*	24
Paradis Thai | *Thai*	15
Petit Marguery | *Bistro*	21
Petit Pascal | *Bistro*	⌐
Suave | *Viet.*	⌐
Temps des Cerises | *Bistro*	⌐
Terroir | *Bistro*	⌐
Tricotin | *Asian*	⌐

14TH ARRONDISSEMENT

Amuse Bouche | *New Fr.*	17
Apollo | *Eclectic*	⌐
Assiette | *Bistro*	⌐
Bar à Huîtres | *Seafood*	17
Bis du Severo | *Bistro*	⌐
Bistrot du Dôme | *Seafood*	21
Buffalo Grill | *Steak*	10
Cagouille | *Seafood*	25
Cantine/Troquet | *Basque/Bistro*	⌐
Cerisaie | *Southwest*	21
NEW Chateau Poivre | *Bistro*	⌐

Chez Clément | *Classic Fr.*	15
Chez Papa | *Southwest*	17
Z Coupole | *Brass.*	19
Crêperie de Josselin | *Brittany*	22
Dôme | *Seafood*	22
Duc | *Seafood*	23
Entétée | *Bistro*	⌐
Enzo | *Italian*	⌐
Hippopotamus | *Steak*	11
Il Barone | *Italian*	21
Indiana Café | *Tex-Mex*	7
Jeu de Quilles | *Wine*	⌐
Léon/Bruxelles | *Belgian*	16
Maison Courtine | *Southwest*	24
Marée Denfert/Passy | *Seafood*	⌐
Monsieur Lapin | *Classic Fr.*	18
Montparnasse 25 | *New Fr.*	16
Natacha | *Classic Fr.*	⌐
Opportun | *Lyon*	15
Paradis du Fruit | *Eclectic*	14
Pavillon Montsouris | *Classic Fr.*	17
Petites Sorcières | *Northern Fr.*	⌐
Z Régalade | *Bistro*	25
Severo | *Steak*	20
Vin et Marée | *Seafood*	18
Zeyer | *Brass.*	16

15TH ARRONDISSEMENT

Afaria | *New Fr./Southwest*	⌐
Autour du Mont | *Seafood*	⌐
Autour/Saumon | *Seafood*	17
Banyan | *Thai*	19
Benkay | *Japanese*	24
Beurre Noisette | *Bistro*	23
Bistro 121 | *Bistro*	⌐
Bistro d'Hubert | *Classic/New Fr.*	22
Bistrot d'André | *Bistro*	⌐
Bistrot du Cap | *Seafood*	⌐
Café du Commerce | *Bistro*	16
Casier à Vin | *Bistro/Med.*	⌐
Cave de l'Os à Moëlle | *Wine*	22
Chen Soleil d'Est | *Chinese*	⌐
Chez Clément | *Classic Fr.*	15
Chez Papa | *Southwest*	17
Clos Morillons | *New Fr.*	⌐
Couleurs de Vigne | *Wine*	⌐
Cristal de Sel | *New Fr.*	⌐
Dalloyau | *Dessert/Tea.*	23
Dix Vins | *Wine*	⌐
Erawan | *Thai*	17
Fellini | *Italian*	21

Fontanarosa	*Italian*	–
Gauloise	*Bistro*	15
Gitane	*Classic Fr.*	–
Grand Pan	*Bistro*	–
Grand Venise	*Italian*	25
Hippopotamus	*Steak*	11
Jadis	*Classic/New Fr.*	–
Je Thé . . . Me	*Classic Fr.*	–
Kim Anh	*Viet.*	–
❷ Os à Moëlle	*Classic Fr.*	25
Père Claude	*Classic Fr.*	17
Quinzième	*New Fr.*	–
Rest. de la Tour	*Classic Fr.*	21
Rest. du Marché	*Bistro*	–
Sawadee	*Thai*	–
Sept Quinze	*New Fr.*	–
Stéphane Martin	*Classic Fr.*	–
Suffren	*Brass.*	14
Troquet	*Basque/New Fr.*	24
Uitr	*Seafood*	–
Villa Corse	*Corsica*	20

16TH ARRONDISSEMENT

A et M	*Classic Fr.*	21
Al Dar	*Lebanese*	21
Al Mounia	*Moroccan*	17
Antoine	*Bistro/Seafood*	–
❷ Astrance	*New Fr.*	28
Aub. Dab	*Brass.*	16
Beaujolais d'Auteuil	*Classic Fr.*	17
Bellini	*Italian*	24
Bistrot des Vignes	*Bistro*	17
Bon	*Asian*	–
Casa Tina	*Spanish*	–
Chalet des Iles	*Classic Fr.*	14
Chez Géraud	*Classic Fr.*	20
Coffee Parisien	*Amer.*	16
❷ Cristal Room	*New Fr.*	17
Elysées Hong Kong	*Chinese*	–
Etc.	*New Fr.*	–
Fakhr el Dine	*Lebanese*	24
Flandrin	*Brass.*	15
Gare	*Classic Fr.*	14
Giulio Rebellato	*Italian*	20
Grande Armée	*Classic Fr.*	15
❷ Grande Cascade	*Haute*	25
❷ Hiramatsu	*Haute/New Fr.*	26
NEW Jamin	*New Fr.*	–
Jardins de Bagatelle	*Classic Fr.*	17
Kambodgia	*SE Asian*	–
Lac-Hong	*Viet.*	20

Lina's	*Sandwiches*	16
Maison Prunier	*Seafood*	21
Marée Denfert/Passy	*Seafood*	–
Marius	*Seafood*	18
Mathusalem	*Bistro*	–
Matsuri	*Japanese*	14
Murat	*Classic Fr.*	13
Noura	*Lebanese*	19
Oum el Banine	*Moroccan*	–
Ozu	*Japanese*	23
Paris Seize	*Italian*	18
❷ Passiflore	*Asian/Classic Fr.*	26
Passy Mandarin	*Asian*	20
Paul Chêne	*Classic Fr.*	20
Petite Tour	*Classic Fr.*	–
Petit Pergolèse	*Bistro*	23
Petit Rétro	*Bistro*	16
Petit Victor Hugo	*Classic Fr.*	19
Pizzeria d'Auteuil	*Italian*	–
❷ Pré Catelan	*Haute*	27
❷ Relais d'Auteuil	*Haute*	27
Relais du Parc	*Classic/New Fr.*	19
Rosimar	*Spanish*	–
Scheffer	*Bistro*	18
7ème Sud	*Med./Moroccan*	15
6 New York	*New Fr.*	17
Stella	*Brass.*	20
Stéphane Gaborieau	*Haute*	–
Table du Baltimore	*Haute*	–
❷ Table/Joël Robuchon	*Haute*	26
Table Lauriston	*Classic Fr.*	20
Tang	*Chinese*	17
Terrasse Mirabeau	*Bistro*	–
Tierny & Co.	*Bistro*	–
Tokyo Eat	*New Fr.*	14
Tournesol	*Bistro*	18
Tsé-Yang	*Chinese*	18
Villa Corse	*Corsica*	20
Vinci	*Classic Fr./Italian*	–
Vin dans les Voiles	*Wine*	–
Vin et Marée	*Seafood*	18
Waknine	*New Fr.*	–
Zébra Square	*Classic Fr./Italian*	10

17TH ARRONDISSEMENT

Accolade	*Bistro*	–
Agapé	*New Fr.*	–
Ampère	*Bistro/Eclectic*	–
Autour/Saumon	*Seafood*	17
Ballon des Ternes	*Brass.*	15
Ballon et Coquillages	*Seafood*	–

Bar à Huîtres	*Seafood*	17
Bath's	*Auvergne/New Fr.*	20
Bigarrade	*New Fr.*	-
Bistral	*Bistro*	19
Bistro du 17ème	*Bistro*	18
Bistro Melrose	*Bistro*	-
Bistro St. Ferdinand	*Bistro*	14
Bistrot d'à Côté	*Bistro*	21
Bistrot des Dames	*Bistro*	14
Bistrot du Passage	*Bistro*	-
Bistrot Niel	*Bistro*	-
🄩 Braisière	*Gascony*	27
Buffalo Grill	*Steak*	10
Café d'Angel	*Bistro*	-
Caïus	*New Fr.*	19
Caves Pétrissans	*Wine*	19
Chez Clément	*Classic Fr.*	15
Chez Fred	*Lyon*	-
Chez Georges-Maillot	*Brass.*	18
Chez Léon	*Bistro*	13
Chez Ly	*Chinese/Thai*	-
Clou	*Bistro*	19
Congrès Maillot	*Brass.*	18
Dessirier	*Seafood*	20
Ecluse	*Wine*	16
Entredgeu	*Bistro*	17
Epicure 108	*Alsace/Asian*	-
🆕 Fourchette	*Bistro*	-
Graindorge	*Northern Fr.*	22
🄩 Guy Savoy	*Haute*	28
Hide	*Bistro*	-
Hier & Aujourd'hui	*New Fr.*	-
Huîtrier	*Seafood*	20
Il Etait une Oie	*Southwest*	-
Karl et Erich	*New Fr.*	-
Kifune	*Japanese*	-
Léon/Bruxelles	*Belgian*	16
Lina's	*Sandwiches*	16
🆕 MBC	*New Fr.*	-
Meating	*Steak*	17
🄩 Michel Rostang	*Classic Fr.*	27
Mont Liban	*Lebanese*	-
Paolo Petrini	*Italian*	-
Paradis du Fruit	*Eclectic*	14
Petit Colombier	*Classic Fr.*	18
Pétrus	*Brass.*	21
Rech	*Seafood*	-
Relais de Venise	*Steak*	24
Rucola	*Italian*	-
Sormani	*Italian*	23
Sud	*Med./Provence*	16
Timgad	*Moroccan*	20
Toque	*Classic Fr.*	-
Verre Bouteille	*Wine*	13
Villa des Ternes	*Bistro/Italian*	-

18TH ARRONDISSEMENT

Bistro Poulbot	*Bistro*	-
Café Burq	*Wine*	-
Chamarré Mont.	*New Fr.*	-
Chéri Bibi	*Bistro*	-
Chez Grisette	*Wine*	-
Cottage Marcadet	*New Fr.*	-
2 Pieces Cuisine	*Bistro*	-
Diapason	*Southwest*	-
Entracte	*Bistro*	-
Famille	*New Fr.*	19
Floors	*Amer./Burgers*	-
Guilo-Guilo	*Japanese*	-
Mascotte	*Auvergne*	-
Miroir	*Bistro*	-
🆕 Mon Oncle	*Bistro*	-
Moulin/Galette	*Classic Fr.*	15
Pomponette	*Bistro*	17
Rendez-vous/Chauff.	*Bistro*	-
Rughetta	*Italian*	-
Sale e Pepe	*Italian*	-
Square/Marcardet	*Classic/New Fr.*	-
Table d'Eugène	*New Fr.*	-
Truc Café	*Wine*	-
Wepler	*Brass.*	14
Winch	*Seafood*	-

19TH ARRONDISSEMENT

Boeuf Couronné	*Classic Fr.*	16
Buffalo Grill	*Steak*	10
Café de la Musique	*Classic Fr.*	15
Cave Gourmande	*Bistro*	25
Chez Vincent	*Italian*	-
Lao Siam	*Thai*	15
Pelouse	*Classic Fr.*	-
Quedubon	*Bistro/Wine*	-
Rosa Bonheur	*Southwest*	-

20TH ARRONDISSEMENT

Allobroges	*Classic Fr.*	22
Baratin	*Wine*	16
Boulangerie	*Bistro*	23
Chez Ramona	*Spanish*	-
Mama Shelter	*Brass.*	-
Zéphyr	*Bistro*	-

LOCATIONS

Outlying Areas

BOUGIVAL

Camélia | *New Fr.* 20

BOULOGNE-BILLANCOURT

Cap Seguin | *Classic Fr.* -
Chalet/l'Oasis | *Bistro* -
Comte de Gascogne | *Gascony* -
Dalloyau | *Dessert/Tea* 23

CLICHY

Romantica | *Italian* 23

ISSY-LES-MOULINEAUX

Ile | *Classic/New Fr.* 18
Rest. Manufacture | *Bistro* 21
River Café | *Classic/New Fr.* 14

JOINVILLE-LE-PONT

Chez Gégène | *Classic Fr.* -

LA DÉFENSE

Matsuri | *Japanese* 14
Petit Bofinger | *Brass.* 18

LE PRÉ-ST-GERVAIS

Pouilly Reuilly | *Bistro* -

LEVALLOIS-PERRET

Mandalay | *Eclectic* -
Petit Poucet | *New Fr.* -

MAISONS-LAFFITTE

Tastevin | *Classic Fr.* 24

NEUILLY-SUR-SEINE

Bel Canto | *Italian* 13
Bistrot d'à Côté | *Bistro* 21
Café la Jatte | *Eclectic* 14
Chalet | *Alpine/Classic Fr.* -
Chez Gérard | *Auvergne* 19
Chez Livio | *Italian* 13
Coffee Parisien | *Amer.* 16
Durand Dupont | *Eclectic* -
Gourmand | *Classic Fr.* -
Jarrasse | *Seafood* -
Lina's | *Sandwiches* 16
Saveurs du Marché | *Bistro* -
Sébillon | *Brass.* 15
Tonn. Saintongeaise | *Classic Fr.* -
Truffe Noire | *Classic Fr.* -
Zinc-Zinc | *Bistro* 16

PERREUX-SUR-MARNE

Magnolias | *New Fr.* 25

SAINT-CLOUD

Quai Ouest | *Eclectic* 13

SAINT-GERMAIN-EN-LAYE

Cazaudehore | *Haute* 22

VERSAILLES

Gordon Ramsay | *Haute* -
Marée de Versailles | *Seafood* 19
Potager du Roy | *Classic Fr.* 19

VINCENNES

Petit Bofinger | *Brass.* 18

Special Features

Listings cover the best in each category and include names, locations and Food ratings. Multi-location restaurants' features may vary by branch.

ADDITIONS

(Properties added since the last edition of the book)

Arc | 8e | -
Bistrot du Passage | 17e | -
Bistro Volnay | 2e | -
Bizan | 2e | -
Bob's Kitchen | 3e | -
Café Cartouche | 12e | -
Café des Musées | 3e | -
Caffé dei Cioppi | 11e | -
Chateau Poivre | 14e | -
Chez Grenouille | 9e | -
Chez Marie-Louise | 10e | -
Claude Colliot | 4e | -
Cotolettes | 4e | -
Cru Rollin | 11e | -
Derrière | 3e | -
Ecume Saint-Honoré | 1er | -
Enfants Terribles | 8e | -
Fourchette | 17e | -
Frenchie | 2e | -
Jamin | 16e | -
KGB | 6e | -
Kiku | 9e | -
Lao Lane Xang | 13e | -
Mai Do | 6e | -
MBC | 17e | -
Mon Oncle | 18e | -
Office | 9e | -
Oto-Oto | 6e | -
Passage 53 | 2e | -
Pramil | 3e | -
Reginette | 8e | -
Rice and Fish | 2e | -
Rosa Bonheur | 19e | -
Shan Gout | 12e | -
Société | 6e | -
Soya Cantine Bio | 11e | -
Tico | 8e | -
Vin Chai Moi | 1er | -
Waly-Fay | 11e | -
Yam'Tcha | 1er | -

BREAKFAST

(See also Hotel Dining)

Alsace | 8e | 18
🛛 Angelina | 1er | 20
A Priori Thé | 2e | 16
Autour/Saumon | **multi.** | 17
Avenue | 8e | 18
Bar des Théâtres | 8e | 15
Berkeley | 8e | 14
🛛 Brass. Balzar | 5e | 19
Brass. La Lorraine | 8e | 17
Brass. Printemps | 9e | 11
Breakfast/America | **multi.** | 15
Café Beaubourg | 4e | 16
🛛 Café de Flore | 6e | 15
Café de la Musique | 19e | 15
Café de l'Esplanade | 7e | 16
🛛 Café/Deux Magots | 6e | 16
Café Lenôtre | 8e | 18
Café Le Petit Pont | 5e | 14
🛛 Café Marly | 1er | 16
Café Ruc | 1er | 15
Camille | 3e | 16
Cazaudehore | St-Germain-Laye | 22
Chez Clément | **multi.** | 15
Chez Prune | 10e | 18
Cloche des Halles | 1er | -
Congrès Maillot | 17e | 18
Couleurs de Vigne | 15e | -
🛛 Coupole | 14e | 19
Dalloyau | **multi.** | 23
Deux Abeilles | 7e | 21
Dôme | 14e | 22
Duc de Richelieu | 12e | -
Editeurs | 6e | 14
Ferme | 1er | -
Flandrin | 16e | 15
Flore en l'Ille | 4e | 18
Fontaines | 5e | 17
Fouquet's | 8e | 18
Gavroche | 2e | 17
Grand Café | 9e | 13
Grande Armée | 16e | 15
Grille St-Germain | 6e | 17
🛛 Ladurée | **multi.** | 23
Lina's | **multi.** | 16
Loir dans/Théière | 4e | 16
Ma Bourgogne | 4e | 18
Main d'Or | 11e | -
Mascotte | 18e | -

Murat | 16ᵉ	13
Nemrod | 6ᵉ	16
Noura | 16ᵉ	19
Pomze | 8ᵉ	18
Procope | 6ᵉ	16
Publicis Drugstore | 8ᵉ	11
Rest. Paul | 1ᵉʳ	20
Rotonde | 6ᵉ	15
Sauvignon | 7ᵉ	14
Suffren | 15ᵉ	14
Table d'Hédiard | 8ᵉ	22
Tav. de Maître Kanter | 1ᵉʳ	16
Terminus Nord | 10ᵉ	17
Tricotin | 13ᵉ	-
Vaudeville | 2ᵉ	18
Viaduc Café | 12ᵉ	-
Wepler | 18ᵉ	14
Zébra Square | 16ᵉ	10
Zeyer | 14ᵉ	16
Zinc-Zinc | Neuilly	16

BRUNCH

Alcazar | 6ᵉ	19
☑ Angelina | 1ᵉʳ	20
A Priori Thé | 2ᵉ	16
Asian | 8ᵉ	16
Barlotti | 1ᵉʳ	15
Barrio Latino | 12ᵉ	12
Berkeley | 8ᵉ	14
Blue Elephant | 11ᵉ	20
Bon | 16ᵉ	-
Breakfast/America | multi.	15
Café Beaubourg | 4ᵉ	16
Café Charbon | 11ᵉ	15
Café de la Musique | 19ᵉ	15
Café de l'Industrie | 11ᵉ	12
Café Etienne Marcel | 2ᵉ	18
Café la Jatte | Neuilly	14
Café Le Petit Pont | 5ᵉ	14
Carr's | 1ᵉʳ	-
Chai 33 | 12ᵉ	14
Chez Prune | 10ᵉ	18
Curieux Spaghetti | 4ᵉ	-
Durand Dupont | Neuilly	-
Editeurs | 6ᵉ	14
Ferme | 1ᵉʳ	-
Findi | 8ᵉ	16
Flora Danica | 8ᵉ	19
Flore en l'Ile | 4ᵉ	18
Fumoir | 1ᵉʳ	17
Gare | 16ᵉ	14
Jardin des Cygnes | 8ᵉ	22

Joe Allen | 1ᵉʳ	13
Lina's | multi.	16
Liza | 2ᵉ	24
Loir dans/Théière | 4ᵉ	16
Mariage Frères | 6ᵉ	21
Market | 8ᵉ	22
Murano | 3ᵉ	16
No Stress Café | 9ᵉ	-
Paradis du Fruit | multi.	14
Pershing | 8ᵉ	17
Pitchi Poï | 4ᵉ	-
Publicis Drugstore | 8ᵉ	11
Quai | 7ᵉ	-
404 | 3ᵉ	22
Réfectoire | 11ᵉ	-
Rouge St-Honoré | 1ᵉʳ	13
Scoop | 1ᵉʳ	17
Studio | 4ᵉ	-
Viaduc Café | 12ᵉ	-
Villa Spicy | 8ᵉ	13
Wepler | 18ᵉ	14
W Restaurant | 8ᵉ	-
Zébra Square | 16ᵉ	10

BUSINESS DINING

Agapé | 17ᵉ	-
Alfred | 1ᵉʳ	-
☑ Ami Louis | 3ᵉ	25
Angle/Faubourg | 8ᵉ	24
☑ Astrance | 16ᵉ	28
Auguste | 7ᵉ	25
Bistro St. Ferdinand | 17ᵉ	14
Bistrot Niel | 17ᵉ	-
NEW Bistro Volnay | 2ᵉ	-
Boeuf Couronné | 19ᵉ	16
Boeuf sur le Toit | 8ᵉ	18
Buisson Ardent | 5ᵉ	19
Café de l'Esplanade | 7ᵉ	16
Café Faubourg | 8ᵉ	22
Caves Pétrissans | 17ᵉ	19
Céladon | 2ᵉ	21
153 Grenelle | 7ᵉ	-
☑ 144 Petrossian | 7ᵉ	25
Chamarré Mont. | 18ᵉ	-
Chez André | 8ᵉ	20
Chez Les Anges | 7ᵉ	23
Chez Savy | 8ᵉ	18
Chiberta | 8ᵉ	22
Clos des Gourmets | 7ᵉ	25
Copenhague | 8ᵉ	18
Costes | 1ᵉʳ	18
Cuisine | 7ᵉ	25

Menus, photos, voting and more – free at ZAGAT.com

Dali | 1er	–
Dessirier | 17^e	20
Divellec | 7^e	24
Dôme | 14^e	22
Dôme du Marais | 4^e	22
Z Dominique Bouchet | 8^e	27
Drouant | 2^e	22
Duc | 14^e	23
Etc. | 16^e	–
Flora Danica | 8^e	19
Fouquet's | 8^e	18
Gaya | 7^e	23
Georgette | 9^e	22
Z Gérard Besson | 1er	25
Gordon Ramsay | **Versailles**	–
Goumard | 1er	24
Graindorge | 17^e	22
Z Guy Savoy | 17^e	28
Z Hélène Darroze | 6^e	25
Il Vino | 7^e	–
Issé | 1er	23
Itineraires | 5^e	–
NEW Jamin | 16^e	–
Z Jules Verne | 7^e	22
Z Lapérouse | 6^e	21
L'Assaggio | 1er	23
Macéo | 1er	23
Maison Blanche | 8^e	20
Mansouria | 11^e	22
Marée | 8^e	23
Marius | 16^e	18
Marty | 5^e	16
Maxan | 8^e	–
Meating | 17^e	17
Z Meurice | 1er	27
Montalembert | 7^e	19
Mori Venice | 2^e	17
Oth Sombath | 8^e	–
Paris | 6^e	20
Paris Seize | 16^e	18
Pasco | 7^e	22
Petit Bofinger | 4^e	18
Petit Marguery | 13^e	21
Petit Pergolèse | 16^e	23
Pétrus | 17^e	21
Pichet de Paris | 8^e	16
Pierre au Palais Royal | 1er	17
Z Pierre Gagnaire | 8^e	28
Pomze | 8^e	18
Pur'Grill | 2^e	19
Relais Louis XIII | 6^e	25

Salon d'Hélène | 6^e	19
Saveurs de Flora | 8^e	21
Sébillon | **Neuilly**	15
16 Haussmann | 9^e	18
Sormani | 17^e	23
Z Stella Maris | 8^e	26
Stresa | 8^e	22
Table du Lancaster | 8^e	23
Z Table/Joël Robuchon | 16^e	26
Table Lauriston | 16^e	20
Tan Dinh | 7^e	23
Tante Louise | 8^e	22
Terrasse Mirabeau | 16^e	–
Terrines/Gérard Vié | 6^e	–
Tierny & Co. | 16^e	–
Z Train Bleu | 12^e	19
35° Ouest | 7^e	20
Z Trou Gascon | 12^e	26
Vagenende | 6^e	15
Vaudeville | 2^e	18
Versance | 2^e	–
Villa Spicy | 8^e	13
Vin et Marée | **multi.**	18
Voltaire | 7^e	24
W Restaurant | 8^e	–

CELEBRITY CHEFS

Z Alain Ducasse | *Alain Ducasse* | 8^e	28
Z Ambroisie | *Bernard Pacaud* | 4^e	28
Z Apicius | *Jean-Pierre Vigato* | 8^e	26
Z Arpège | *Alain Passard* | 7^e	26
Z Astrance | *Pascal Barbot* | 16^e	28
Z Atelier Joël Robuchon | *Joël Robuchon* | 7^e	28
Z Benoît | *Alain Ducasse* | 4^e	24
Bistrot d'à Côté | *Michel Rostang* | **multi.**	21
Boulangerie Eric Kayser | *Eric Kayser* | 8^e	16
Z Bouquinistes | *Guy Savoy* | 6^e	23
Z Bristol | *Eric Frechon* | 8^e	27
Z Carré des Feuillants | *Alain Dutournier* | 1er	26
Chiberta | *Guy Savoy* | 8^e	22
Cocottes | *Christian Constant* | 7^e	21
Z Comptoir/Relais | *Yves Camdeborde* | 6^e	26
Dali | *Yannick Alléno* | 1er	–
Drouant | *Antoine Westermann* | 2^e	22
Elysées | *Eric Briffard* | 8^e	23
Z Espadon | *Michel Roth* | 1er	26
Gaya | *Pierre Gagnaire* | 7^e	23

Restaurant	Rating
Gordon Ramsay | *Gordon Ramsay* | **Versailles**	–
Z Grand Véfour | *Guy Martin* | 1er	28
Z Guy Savoy | *Guy Savoy* | 17e	28
Z Hélène Darroze | *Hélène Darroze* | 6e	25
Z Hiramatsu | *Hiroyuki Hiramatsu* | 16e	26
Z Jacques Cagna | *Jacques Cagna* | 6e	26
Z Jules Verne | *Alain Ducasse* | 7e	22
NEW KGB | *William Ledeuil* | 6e	–
Z Lasserre | *Jean-Louis Nomicos* | 8e	27
Z Lyonnais | *Alain Ducasse* | 2e	21
Mama Shelter | *Alain Senderens* | 20e	–
Market | *Jean-Georges Vongerichten* | 8e	22
Z Michel Rostang | *Michel Rostang* | 17e	27
Z Mon Vieil Ami | *Antoine Westermann* | 4e	24
Oth Sombath | *Oth Sombath* | 8e	–
Z Pavillon Ledoyen | *Christian Le Squer* | 8e	26
Petites Sorcières | *Ghislaine Arabian* | 14e	–
Z Pierre Gagnaire | *Pierre Gagnaire* | 8e	28
Pinxo | *Alain Dutournier* | 1er	21
Quinzième | *Cyril Lignac* | 15e	–
Rech | *Alain Ducasse* | 17e	–
Relais Plaza | *Alain Ducasse* | 8e	23
Salon d'Hélène | *Hélène Darroze* | 6e	19
Z Senderens | *Alain Senderens* | 8e	26
Sensing | *Guy Martin* | 6e	24
Spoon Paris | *Alain Ducasse* | 8e	22
Table du Lancaster | *Michel Troisgros* | 8e	23
Z Table/Joël Robuchon | *Joël Robuchon* | 16e	26
Z Taillevent | *Alain Solivérès* | 8e	28
Z Trou Gascon | *Alain Dutournier* | 12e	26
21 | *Paul Minchelli* | 6e	–
Z Violon d'Ingres | *Christian Constant* | 7e	25
Z Ze Kitchen Galerie | *William Ledeuil* | 6e	25

CHEESE TRAYS

Restaurant	Rating
Agapé | 17e	–
Agassin | 7e	–
Aiguière | 11e	–
Aimant du Sud | 13e	–
Z Alain Ducasse | 8e	28
Alivi | 4e	16
Z Ambroisie | 4e	28
Ampère | 17e	–
Angelo Procopio | 1er	–
Z Apicius | 8e	26
Arome | 8e	–
Z Arpège | 7e	26
Astier | 11e	21
Astor | 8e	16
Atelier Berger | 1er	21
Z Atelier Joël Robuchon | 7e	28
Aub. Dab | 16e	16
Bacchantes | 9e	–
Ballon des Ternes | 17e	15
Ballon et Coquillages | 17e	–
BAM | 1er	–
Bar à Huîtres | 17e	17
Bar Vendôme | 1er	23
Bath's | 17e	20
Beaujolais d'Auteuil | 16e	17
Bel Canto | 4e	13
Bigarrade | 17e	–
Bistral | 17e	19
Bistro 121 | 15e	–
Bistrot à Vins Mélac | 11e	14
Bistrot du Sommelier | 8e	18
NEW Bistro Volnay | 2e	–
NEW Bob's Kitchen | 3e	–
Boeuf Couronné | 19e	16
Z Bon Accueil | 7e	24
Bons Crus | 1er	–
Bouillon Racine | 6e	16
Bound | 8e	–
Bourguignon du Marais | 4e	23
Z Braisière | 17e	27
Brass. du Louvre | 1er	16
Brass. Flo | 10e	18
Brass. Lutétia | 6e	18
NEW Café Cartouche | 12e	–
Café de l'Industrie | 11e	12
Café du Passage | 11e	–
Café Faubourg | 8e	22
Café Terminus | 8e	–
NEW Caffé dèi Cioppi | 11e	–
Camélia | **Bougival**	20
Z Carré des Feuillants | 1er	26
Caveau du Palais | 1er	19
Cave de l'Os à Moëlle | 15e	22

Menus, photos, voting and more – free at ZAGAT.com

Caves Pétrissans	17e	19	Etc.	16e	-
Caviar Kaspia	8e	25	Ferme St-Simon	7e	23
Cazaudehore	St-Germain-Laye	22	Fermette Marbeuf	8e	18
Céladon	2e	21	Fins Gourmets	7e	19
Chantairelle	5e	-	Firmin le Barbier	7e	-
Chez André	8e	20	Fontaine Gaillon	2e	22
Chez Catherine	8e	23	Fontaines	5e	17
Chez Françoise	7e	17	Fouquet's	8e	18
Chez Fred	17e	-	Garnier	8e	22
Ⓩ Chez Georges	2e	24	Giulio Rebellato	16e	20
Chez Léon	17e	13	Glou	3e	-
Chez Les Anges	7e	23	Gordon Ramsay	Versailles	-
Chez Maître Paul	6e	21	Goumard	1er	24
Chez Nénesse	3e	-	Gourmand	1er	20
Chez Ramulaud	11e	16	Graindorge	17e	22
Chez René	5e	21	Grand Café	9e	13
Chiberta	8e	22	Ⓩ Grande Cascade	16e	25
Ⓩ Cinq	8e	28	Ⓩ Grand Véfour	1er	28
Citrus Etoile	8e	20	Grille	10e	17
Cloche des Halles	1er	-	Ⓩ Guy Savoy	17e	28
Closerie des Lilas	6e	18	Ⓩ Hélène Darroze	6e	25
Clou	17e	19	Hide	17e	-
Clovis	8e	-	Huîtrerie Régis	6e	22
Comédiens	9e	-	I Golosi	9e	17
Congrès Maillot	17e	18	Il Vino	7e	-
Copenhague	8e	18	Ⓩ Jacques Cagna	6e	26
Cordonnerie	1er	-	Jadis	15e	-
Cosi (Le)	5e	16	Jardin des Cygnes	8e	22
Cottage Marcadet	18e	-	Jarrasse	Neuilly	-
Cotte Roti	12e	-	Jean	9e	19
Crémerie	6e	-	Jeu de Quilles	14e	-
Crudus	1er	-	J'Go	6e	14
NEW Cru Rollin	11e	-	Joséphine/Dumonet	6e	23
Cuizine	11e	-	Karl et Erich	17e	-
Cul de Poule	9e	-	L'Assaggio	1er	23
Dali	1er	-	Ⓩ Lasserre	8e	27
Dalloyau	8e	23	Ⓩ Laurent	8e	24
NEW Derrière	3e	-	Lavinia	1er	17
Diapason	18e	-	Louchebem	1er	15
Divellec	7e	24	Macéo	1er	23
Dôme	14e	22	Magnolias	Perreux	25
Dôme du Marais	4e	22	Main d'Or	11e	-
Drouant	2e	22	Maison Blanche	8e	20
Duc de Richelieu	12e	-	Maison du Jardin	6e	24
Ecailler du Bistrot	11e	19	Mama Shelter	20e	-
Eclaireur	8e	-	Marée	8e	23
Elysées	8e	23	Marlotte	6e	16
Epicure 108	17e	-	Mascotte	18e	-
Epi d'Or	1er	16	Maupertu	7e	21
Epigramme	6e	-	Meating	17e	17
Ⓩ Espadon	1er	26	Memère Paulette	2e	-

Restaurant	Rating
Mesturet | 2ᵉ	–
🄕 Meurice | 1ᵉʳ	27
🄕 Michel Rostang | 17ᵉ	27
Moissonnier | 5ᵉ	19
NEW Mon Oncle | 18ᵉ	–
Montparnasse 25 | 14ᵉ	16
Murano | 3ᵉ	16
Nos Ancêtres Gaulois | 4ᵉ	13
No Stress Café | 9ᵉ	–
Office | 9ᵉ	–
Oudino | 7ᵉ	–
Paolo Petrini | 17ᵉ	–
Papilles | 5ᵉ	23
Paris | 6ᵉ	20
Passage/Carm. | 11ᵉ	–
🄕 Passiflore | 16ᵉ	26
Paul Chêne | 16ᵉ	20
🄕 Pavillon Ledoyen | 8ᵉ	26
Pavillon Montsouris | 14ᵉ	17
Pelouse | 19ᵉ	–
Petit Colombier | 17ᵉ	18
Petite Sirène/Copen. | 9ᵉ	–
Petites Sorcières | 14ᵉ	–
Petit Pascal | 13ᵉ	–
Pétrelle | 9ᵉ	–
Pichet de Paris | 8ᵉ	16
🄕 Pierre Gagnaire | 8ᵉ	28
Poisson Rouge | 10ᵉ	–
Polichinelle Cafe | 11ᵉ	–
Pomze | 8ᵉ	18
Poule au Pot | 1ᵉʳ	23
Press Café | 2ᵉ	–
Procope | 6ᵉ	16
Pure Café | 11ᵉ	–
Quai-Quai | 1ᵉʳ	–
Quedubon | 19ᵉ	–
Quinzième | 15ᵉ	–
Racines | 2ᵉ	–
Ragueneau | 1ᵉʳ	–
🄕 Relais d'Auteuil | 16ᵉ	27
Relais de Venise | 17ᵉ	24
Relais du Parc | 16ᵉ	19
Relais Louis XIII | 6ᵉ	25
Réminet | 5ᵉ	–
Rendez-vous/Chauff. | 18ᵉ	–
Rollin | 11ᵉ	–
Romantica | Clichy	23
Rosa Bonheur | 19ᵉ	–
Rose Bakery | multi.	17
Rôtiss. du Beaujolais | 5ᵉ	23
Royal Madeleine | 8ᵉ	19
Salon d'Hélène | 6ᵉ	19
Salon du Panthéon | 5ᵉ	–
Sardegna a Tavola | 12ᵉ	21
Sauvignon | 7ᵉ	14
Saveurs de Flora | 8ᵉ	21
Sébillon | Neuilly	15
16 Haussmann | 9ᵉ	18
NEW Société | 6ᵉ	–
Sot l'y Laisse | 11ᵉ	–
🄕 Soufflé | 1ᵉʳ	22
Stella | 16ᵉ	20
Stéphane Gaborieau | 16ᵉ	–
Table d'Eugène | 18ᵉ	–
Table du Baltimore | 16ᵉ	–
Table du Lancaster | 8ᵉ	23
🄕 Table/Joël Robuchon | 16ᵉ	26
Table Lauriston | 16ᵉ	20
Tante Louise | 8ᵉ	22
Tastevin | Maisons-Laff.	24
Tav. Henri IV | 1ᵉʳ	16
Terrines/Gérard Vié | 6ᵉ	–
Tête Ailleurs | 4ᵉ	–
Thoumieux | 7ᵉ	–
Tierny & Co. | 16ᵉ	–
Timbre | 6ᵉ	24
Tokyo Eat | 16ᵉ	14
🄕 Tour d'Argent | 5ᵉ	25
🄕 Train Bleu | 12ᵉ	19
🄕 Trou Gascon | 12ᵉ	26
Truffe Noire | Neuilly	–
Truffière | 5ᵉ	23
Vaudeville | 2ᵉ	18
Versance | 2ᵉ	–
Vieux Chêne | 11ᵉ	–
🄕 Villaret | 11ᵉ	26
Vin dans les Voiles | 16ᵉ	–
Vins des Pyrénées | 4ᵉ	16
🄕 Violon d'Ingres | 7ᵉ	25
Waknine | 16ᵉ	–
Wepler | 18ᵉ	14
🄕 Willi's Wine | 1ᵉʳ	20
Winch | 18ᵉ	–
W Restaurant | 8ᵉ	–
Zéphyr | 20ᵉ	–
Zo | 8ᵉ	–

CHILD-FRIENDLY

(Alternatives to the usual fast-food places; * children's menu available)

Restaurant	Rating
Aiguière* | 11ᵉ	–
Alcazar* | 6ᵉ	19
Ampère | 17ᵉ	–

Restaurant	Location	
Amuse Bouche*	14e	17
Anahuacalli*	5e	21
A Priori Thé*	2e	16
Asian*	8e	16
Z Atelier Joël Robuchon	7e	28
Atlas*	5e	20
Aub. Dab*	16e	16
Autour/Saumon*	multi.	17
Bar à Huîtres*	multi.	17
Bar Vendôme*	1er	23
BE Boulangépicier	8e	19
BIOArt*	13e	-
Bistro 121	15e	-
Bistro de Breteuil*	7e	16
Bistrot d'André*	15e	-
Bistrot du Dôme	14e	21
Boeuf sur le Toit*	8e	18
Z Bofinger*	4e	20
Brass. du Louvre*	1er	16
Brass. Julien*	10e	19
Brass. Lutétia*	6e	18
Brass. Mollard*	8e	19
Breakfast/America	multi.	15
Buffalo Grill*	multi.	10
Café de la Musique	19e	15
Café de la Paix*	9e	19
Chai 33*	12e	14
Chalet*	Neuilly	-
Chalet des Iles*	16e	14
Chez Clément*	multi.	15
Chez Jenny*	3e	19
Chez Livio*	Neuilly	13
Congrès Maillot*	17e	18
Z Coupole*	14e	19
Dame Tartine*	4e	14
Fouquet's*	8e	18
Gare*	16e	14
Gauloise*	15e	15
Gitane	15e	-
Hippopotamus*	multi.	11
Indiana Café*	multi.	7
J'Go*	9e	14
Z Ladurée	8e	23
Languedoc	5e	-
Léon/Bruxelles*	multi.	16
Monsieur Lapin	14e	18
Paradis Thai	13e	15
Pavillon Montsouris*	14e	17
Petit Bofinger*	multi.	18
Petite Cour	6e	21
Petite Sirène/Copen.	9e	-
Petite Tour*	16e	-
Petit Poucet*	Levallois	-
Pied de Cochon	1er	18
Procope	6e	16
Quai Ouest	St-Cloud	13
Z Relais/l'Entrecôte	multi.	22
Rest. du Palais Royal	1er	19
Rest. du Musée d'Orsay*	7e	17
River Café	Issy-les-Moul.	14
Rôtiss. d'en Face	6e	21
Rôtiss. du Beaujolais	5e	23
Rotonde*	6e	15
Sardegna a Tavola	12e	21
Sébillon*	Neuilly	15
Studio*	4e	-
Tang	16e	17
Tav. de Maître Kanter*	1er	16
Terminus Nord*	10e	17
Z Train Bleu*	12e	19
Trumilou	4e	19
Vagenende*	6e	15
Vaudeville*	2e	18
Viaduc Café*	12e	-
Village d'Ung*	8e	-
Villa Spicy*	8e	13
Wepler*	18e	14

CLOSED JULY/AUGUST

(Varies; call ahead to confirm dates)

Restaurant	Location	
Accolade	17e	-
A et M	16e	21
Affriolé	7e	22
Agapé	17e	-
Agapes	5e	-
Aida	7e	23
Alfred	1er	-
Allobroges	20e	22
Al Taglio	11e	-
Z Ambassadeurs	8e	28
Z Ami Louis	3e	25
Ami Pierre	11e	17
Anahï	3e	19
Angelo Procopio	1er	-
Angle/Faubourg	8e	24
Antoine	16e	-
AOC	5e	18
Z Apicius	8e	26
Z Astrance	16e	28
Aub. Aveyronnaise	12e	-
Aub. du Champ/Mars	7e	17
Aub. Pyrénées	11e	20

SPECIAL FEATURES

Restaurant	Score
Auguste | 7e	25
Autour du Mont | 15e	–
Autour/Saumon | multi.	17
Baratin | 20e	16
Bar des Théâtres | 8e	15
Bascou | 3e	20
Bel Canto | multi.	13
Ⓩ Benoît | 4e	24
Bigarrade | 17e	–
Bistral | 17e	19
Bistro de l'Olivier | 8e	18
Bistro Poulbot | 18e	–
Bistrot à Vins Mélac | 11e	14
Bistrot d'à Côté | 17e	21
Bistrot de Paris | 7e	16
Bistrot des Vignes | 16e	17
Bistrot du Dôme | 4e	21
Bistrot du Passage | 17e	–
Bistrot du Sommelier | 8e	18
Bistrot Papillon | 9e	14
Bistrot Paul Bert | 11e	23
NEW Bob's Kitchen | 3e	–
Boucherie Roulière | 6e	–
Boulangerie | 20e	23
Boule Rouge | 9e	–
Bourguignon du Marais | 4e	23
Café des Musées | 3e	–
Café Lenôtre | 8e	18
Café Moderne | 2e	21
NEW Caffé dei Cioppi | 11e	–
Caffé Toscano | 7e	19
Camélia | Bougival	20
Cantine de Quentin | 10e	–
Ⓩ Carré des Feuillants | 1er	26
Carte Blanche | 9e	–
Casa Olympe | 9e	24
Casier à Vin | 15e	–
Caves Pétrissans | 17e	19
Caviar Kaspia | 8e	25
153 Grenelle | 7e	–
Cerisaie | 14e	21
NEW Chateau Poivre | 14e	–
Chen Soleil d'Est | 15e	–
Chez Gérard | Neuilly	19
NEW Chez Grenouille | 9e	–
Chez Grisette | 18e	–
Chez L'Ami Jean | 7e	24
Chez la Vieille | 1er	16
Chez Marcel | 6e	–
NEW Chez Marie-Louise | 10e	–
Chez Nénesse | 3e	–
Chez René | 5e	21
Chez Savy | 8e	18
Chieng Mai | 5e	16
Cibus | 1er	–
Cinq Mars | 7e	19
Clos des Gourmets | 7e	25
Clou | 17e	19
Clovis | 8e	–
Coco & Co. | 6e	–
Copenhague | 8e	18
Cordonnerie | 1er	–
Cottage Marcadet | 18e	–
Cou de la Girafe | 8e	15
Couleurs de Vigne | 15e	–
Crémerie | 6e	–
Crêperie de Josselin | 14e	22
Crudus | 1er	–
NEW Cru Rollin | 11e	–
Cuisine | 7e	25
Cuizine | 11e	–
Daru | 8e	–
Dell Orto | 9e	–
2 Pieces Cuisine | 18e	–
Ⓩ 1728 | 8e	19
Ecaille de Fontaine | 2e	–
Ecailler du Bistrot | 11e	19
Ecume Saint-Honoré | 1er	–
Entétée | 14e	–
Enzo | 14e	–
Ⓩ Epi Dupin | 6e	24
Escargot Montorgueil | 1er	21
Ferdi | 1er	–
Ferme St-Simon | 7e	23
Florimond | 7e	24
Fontaine Gaillon | 2e	22
Frégate | 12e	24
Gaigne | 4e	–
Gaya | 7e	23
Gazzetta | 12e	–
Georgette | 9e	22
Ⓩ Gérard Besson | 1er	25
Giulio Rebellato | 16e	20
Glou | 3e	–
Gordon Ramsay | Versailles	–
Gourmand | 1er	20
Ⓩ Grand Véfour | 1er	28
Grand Venise | 15e	25
Grille | 10e	17
Hangar | 3e	18
Hide | 17e	–

Hier & Aujourd'hui | 17ᵉ	_
🅩 Hiramatsu | 16ᵉ	26
Huîtrerie Régis | 6ᵉ	22
Inagiku | 5ᵉ	18
Itineraires | 5ᵉ	_
Jadis | 15ᵉ	_
NEW Jamin | 16ᵉ	_
Jardinier | 9ᵉ	_
Jeu de Quilles | 14ᵉ	_
J'Go | 9ᵉ	14
Kai | 1ᵉʳ	_
Karl et Erich | 17ᵉ	_
NEW KGB | 6ᵉ	_
Laiterie/Clotilde | 7ᵉ	_
L'Assaggio | 1ᵉʳ	23
Mai Do | 6ᵉ	_
Maison du Jardin | 6ᵉ	24
NEW MBC | 17ᵉ	_
Miroir | 18ᵉ	_
Mori Venice | 2ᵉ	17
Mousson | 1ᵉʳ	_
Office | 9ᵉ	_
Oth Sombath | 8ᵉ	_
Oudino | 7ᵉ	_
Ourcine | 13ᵉ	24
Papilles | 5ᵉ	23
Paris | 6ᵉ	20
Passy Mandarin | 16ᵉ	20
Pates Vivantes | 9ᵉ	_
Paul Chêne | 16ᵉ	20
Petit Pascal | 13ᵉ	_
Pétrelle | 9ᵉ	_
Pétrus | 17ᵉ	21
Pizza Chic | 6ᵉ	_
Ploum | 10ᵉ	_
Pramil | 3ᵉ	_
P'tit Troquet | 7ᵉ	22
Relais de Venise | 17ᵉ	24
Ribouldingue | 5ᵉ	18
Rice and Fish | 2ᵉ	_
Rollin | 11ᵉ	_
Rose Bakery | 9ᵉ	17
Royal Madeleine | 8ᵉ	19
Sensing | 6ᵉ	24
7ème Sud | 16ᵉ	15
Severo | 14ᵉ	20
6 New York | 16ᵉ	17
Sot l'y Laisse | 11ᵉ	_
🅩 Soufflé | 1ᵉʳ	22
Stéphane Gaborieau | 16ᵉ	_
Suave | 13ᵉ	_

Table d'Eugène | 18ᵉ	_
Table du Lancaster | 8ᵉ	23
Table Lauriston | 16ᵉ	20
Tang | 16ᵉ	17
Tav. Henri IV | 1ᵉʳ	16
Temps au Temps | 11ᵉ	25
Tête Ailleurs | 4ᵉ	_
Tierny & Co. | 16ᵉ	_
35° Ouest | 7ᵉ	20
🅩 Trou Gascon | 12ᵉ	26
Versance | 2ᵉ	_
Vin dans les Voiles | 16ᵉ	_
21 | 6ᵉ	_
NEW Yam'Tcha | 1ᵉʳ	_
Yugaraj | 6ᵉ	23

DANCING

Barrio Latino | 12ᵉ	12
Bound | 8ᵉ	_
Café de Mars | 7ᵉ	17
Chez Clément | 17ᵉ	15
Chez Gégène | Joinville	_
🅩 Coupole | 14ᵉ	19
Musichall | 8ᵉ	15

DELIVERY

Affriolé | 7ᵉ	22
Aiguière | 11ᵉ	_
Al Taglio | 11ᵉ	_
Anahuacalli | 5ᵉ	21
Atlas | 5ᵉ	20
Autour/Saumon | multi.	17
Bistro 121 | 15ᵉ	_
NEW Bob's Kitchen | 3ᵉ	_
Caffé Toscano | 7ᵉ	19
Casier à Vin | 15ᵉ	_
Chez Vincent | 19ᵉ	_
Coco de Mer | 5ᵉ	_
Dalloyau | multi.	23
NEW Derrière | 3ᵉ	_
Escale du Liban | 4ᵉ	_
Findi | 8ᵉ	16
Fines Gueules | 1ᵉʳ	_
Issé | 1ᵉʳ	23
Jarrasse | Neuilly	_
Kifune | 17ᵉ	_
🅩 Ladurée | multi.	23
Lina's | multi.	16
Maharajah | 5ᵉ	17
Maison du Caviar | 8ᵉ	22
Matsuri | 16ᵉ	14

Mavrommatis | 5ᵉ	19
Mont Liban | 17ᵉ	-
Mousson | 1ᵉʳ	-
Pamphlet | 3ᵉ	23
Petite Tour | 16ᵉ	-
Polichinelle Cafe | 11ᵉ	-
Pomze | 8ᵉ	18
Relais Louis XIII | 6ᵉ	25
🆕 Soya Cantine Bio | 11ᵉ	-
Suffren | 15ᵉ	14
Urbane | 10ᵉ	-
Wally Le Saharien | 9ᵉ	15
Waly-Fay | 11ᵉ	-

DINING ALONE

(Other than hotels and places with counter service)

Agassin | 7ᵉ	-
Aimant du Sud | 13ᵉ	-
Alcazar | 6ᵉ	19
Alfred | 1ᵉʳ	-
Alsace | 8ᵉ	18
Ampère | 17ᵉ	-
Amuse Bouche | 14ᵉ	17
🆉 As du Fallafel | 4ᵉ	24
Assiette | 14ᵉ	-
Aub. Bressane | 7ᵉ	20
Azabu | 6ᵉ	24
Ballon des Ternes | 17ᵉ	15
BAM | 1ᵉʳ	-
Bar à Huîtres | multi.	17
Bar des Théâtres | 8ᵉ	15
Bistrot à Vins Mélac | 11ᵉ	14
Bistrot de Marius | 8ᵉ	21
Bistrot du Peintre | 11ᵉ	18
Boeuf sur le Toit | 8ᵉ	18
Bouillon Racine | 6ᵉ	16
Boulangerie Eric Kayser | 8ᵉ	16
Bourguignon du Marais | 4ᵉ	23
Brass./l'Ile St. Louis | 4ᵉ	17
Breakfast/America | multi.	15
Buisson Ardent | 5ᵉ	19
Ca d'Oro | 1ᵉʳ	18
Café Beaubourg | 4ᵉ	16
🆉 Café de Flore | 6ᵉ	15
Café de l'Industrie | 11ᵉ	12
🆉 Café/Deux Magots | 6ᵉ	16
Café du Commerce | 15ᵉ	16
Café du Passage | 11ᵉ	-
Café Lenôtre | 8ᵉ	18
🆉 Café Marly | 1ᵉʳ	16
Café Pleyel | 8ᵉ	-

Caméléon | 6ᵉ	20
Camille | 3ᵉ	16
Cantine/Troquet | 14ᵉ	-
Carr's | 1ᵉʳ	-
Charlot Roi des Coq. | 9ᵉ	15
Charpentiers | 6ᵉ	18
Chartier | 9ᵉ	13
Chez Catherine | 8ᵉ	23
🆉 Chez Georges | 2ᵉ	24
Chez Jenny | 3ᵉ	19
Chez la Vieille | 1ᵉʳ	16
Chez Maître Paul | 6ᵉ	21
Chez Marcel | 6ᵉ	-
Chez Marianne | 4ᵉ	18
Closerie des Lilas | 6ᵉ	18
Cocottes | 7ᵉ	21
Coffee Parisien | multi.	16
Congrès Maillot | 17ᵉ	18
Cosi | 6ᵉ	19
Cotte Roti | 12ᵉ	-
🆉 Coupole | 14ᵉ	19
Curieux Spaghetti | 4ᵉ	-
Deux Canards | 10ᵉ	18
Duc de Richelieu | 12ᵉ	-
Durand Dupont | Neuilly	-
Ecluse | multi.	16
Emporio Armani | 6ᵉ	19
Entracte | 18ᵉ	-
Epi d'Or | 1ᵉʳ	16
Escargot Montorgueil | 1ᵉʳ	21
Fakhr el Dine | 16ᵉ	24
Ferdi | 1ᵉʳ	-
Ferme | 1ᵉʳ	-
Fines Gueules | 1ᵉʳ	-
Fins Gourmets | 7ᵉ	19
🆉 Fish La Boiss. | 6ᵉ	22
Floors | 18ᵉ	-
Fous d'en Face | 4ᵉ	-
Fumoir | 1ᵉʳ	17
Gaigne | 4ᵉ	-
Gauloise | 15ᵉ	15
Georgette | 9ᵉ	22
Gourmand | 1ᵉʳ	20
Isami | 4ᵉ	25
Itineraires | 5ᵉ	-
Jarrasse | Neuilly	-
Jean | 9ᵉ	19
Je Thé . . . Me | 15ᵉ	-
Joe Allen | 1ᵉʳ	13
Joséphine/Dumonet | 6ᵉ	23
Karl et Erich | 17ᵉ	-

Kinûgawa/Hanawa | 8ᵉ	23
🗷 Ladurée | multi.	23
Laiterie/Clotilde | 7ᵉ	-
Languedoc | 5ᵉ	-
Lao Tseu | 7ᵉ	-
Legrand Filles | 2ᵉ	-
Lina's | multi.	16
Lô Sushi | 8ᵉ	15
Ma Bourgogne | 4ᵉ	18
Marée Denfert/Passy | 14ᵉ	-
Marty | 5ᵉ	16
Maupertu | 7ᵉ	21
Mauzac | 5ᵉ	-
Maxan | 8ᵉ	-
Moulin à Vent | 5ᵉ	19
Mousson | 1ᵉʳ	-
Nemrod | 6ᵉ	16
No Stress Café | 9ᵉ	-
Pamphlet | 3ᵉ	23
Papilles | 5ᵉ	23
Paradis Thai | 13ᵉ	15
Pasco | 7ᵉ	22
Pates Vivantes | 9ᵉ	-
Pères et Filles | 6ᵉ	16
Perraudin | 5ᵉ	13
Petit Bofinger | 4ᵉ	18
Petit Colombier | 17ᵉ	18
Petite Chaise | 7ᵉ	19
Petite Sirène/Copen. | 9ᵉ	-
Petites Sorcières | 14ᵉ	-
Petit Lutétia | 6ᵉ	19
Petit Marguery | 13ᵉ	21
Petit Pergolèse | 16ᵉ	23
Petit Rétro | 16ᵉ	16
Petit Riche | 9ᵉ	18
Polidor | 6ᵉ	17
Poule au Pot | 1ᵉʳ	23
P'tit Troquet | 7ᵉ	22
Racines | 2ᵉ	-
Repaire de Cartouche | 11ᵉ	16
Rest. du Marché | 15ᵉ	-
Roi du Pot-au-Feu | 9ᵉ	-
Rose Bakery | multi.	17
Rose de France | 1ᵉʳ	-
Rubis | 1ᵉʳ	15
Suffren | 15ᵉ	14
Table d'Eugène | 18ᵉ	-
Table d'Hédiard | 8ᵉ	22
Tan Dinh | 7ᵉ	23
Tav. Henri IV | 1ᵉʳ	16
Terminus Nord | 10ᵉ	17

Vagenende | 6ᵉ	15
Viaduc Café | 12ᵉ	-
Vieux Chêne | 11ᵉ	-
Vin et Marée | multi.	18
🗷 Vin sur Vin | 7ᵉ	26
Wepler | 18ᵉ	14
Wok Cooking | 11ᵉ	-
Zéphyr | 20ᵉ	-

ENTERTAINMENT

(Call for days and times of performances)

Annapurna | sitar | 8ᵉ	18
Asian | DJ | 8ᵉ	16
Avenue | DJ | 8ᵉ	18
Barlotti | DJ | 1ᵉʳ	15
Barrio Latino | salsa | 12ᵉ	12
Bar Vendôme | piano | 1ᵉʳ	23
Bel Canto | opera | multi.	13
Berkeley | DJ | 8ᵉ	14
Café Charbon | concerts | 11ᵉ	15
Café Faubourg | piano | 8ᵉ	22
Café Le Petit Pont | jazz | 5ᵉ	14
Carr's | Irish | 1ᵉʳ	-
Chez Cécile | jazz | 8ᵉ	-
Chez Françoise | live music | 7ᵉ	17
Chez Gégène | dancing | Joinville	-
Diamantaires | orchestra | 9ᵉ	-
Djakarta | Balinese | 1ᵉʳ	20
Jardin des Cygnes | piano | 8ᵉ	22
🗷 Lasserre | piano | 8ᵉ	27
Lup | live music | 6ᵉ	-
Maxim's | piano | 8ᵉ	18
Musichall | varies | 8ᵉ	15
Nos Ancêtres Gaulois | guitar | 4ᵉ	13
Passage/Carm. | debates | 11ᵉ	-
Polichinelle Cafe | concerts | 11ᵉ	-
Quai Ouest | clown | St-Cloud	13
Relais Plaza | jazz | 8ᵉ	23
Saudade | Fado | 1ᵉʳ	-
Zébra Square | DJ | 16ᵉ	10
Zo | DJ | 8ᵉ	-

FAMILY-STYLE

Aimant du Sud | 13ᵉ	-
🗷 Allard | 6ᵉ	21
Allobroges | 20ᵉ	22
Al Taglio | 11ᵉ	-
Ampère | 17ᵉ	-
🗷 Ardoise | 1ᵉʳ	24
Bartolo | 6ᵉ	17
NEW Bob's Kitchen | 3ᵉ	-

Cantine/Troquet | 14ᵉ	-
Chalet/l'Oasis | **Boulogne**	-
Chez Papa | **multi.**	17
Closerie des Lilas | 6ᵉ	18
Coco & Co. | 6ᵉ	-
Flore en l'Ile | 4ᵉ	18
Z Fontaine de Mars | 7ᵉ	21
Fous d'en Face | 4ᵉ	-
Joséphine/Dumonet | 6ᵉ	23
Mama Shelter | 20ᵉ	-
Marty | 5ᵉ	16
Z Mon Vieil Ami | 4ᵉ	24
Repaire de Cartouche | 11ᵉ	16
Villa des Ternes | 17ᵉ	-
Wok Cooking | 11ᵉ	-

FIREPLACES

Atelier Maître Albert | 5ᵉ	21
Aub. du Clou | 9ᵉ	16
Bon | 16ᵉ	-
Brass. L'Européen | 12ᵉ	-
Carr's | 1ᵉʳ	-
Cazaudehore | **St-Germain-Laye**	22
Chalet des Iles | 16ᵉ	14
Costes | 1ᵉʳ	18
Coupe-Chou | 5ᵉ	23
Z Cristal Room | 16ᵉ	17
Diamantaires | 9ᵉ	-
Z 1728 | 8ᵉ	19
Fontaine Gaillon | 2ᵉ	22
Gordon Ramsay | **Versailles**	-
Z Grande Cascade | 16ᵉ	25
Je Thé . . . Me | 15ᵉ	-
Montalembert | 7ᵉ	19
Murano | 3ᵉ	16
Nabulione | 7ᵉ	-
Nos Ancêtres Gaulois | 4ᵉ	13
Paradis Thai | 13ᵉ	15
Pavillon Montsouris | 14ᵉ	17
Petit Châtelet | 5ᵉ	-
Petit Colombier | 17ᵉ	18
Petit Poucet | **Levallois**	-
Petit Victor Hugo | 16ᵉ	19
Pétrelle | 9ᵉ	-
Z Pré Catelan | 16ᵉ	27
Quai Ouest | **St-Cloud**	13
Relais du Parc | 16ᵉ	19
River Café | **Issy-les-Moul.**	14
Robert et Louise | 3ᵉ	21
Romantica | **Clichy**	23
Sud | 17ᵉ	16
Tastevin | **Maisons-Laff.**	24

Truffière | 5ᵉ	23
Villa Corse | 16ᵉ	20
Yugaraj | 6ᵉ	23

HISTORIC PLACES

(Year opened; * building)

1407 | Aub. Nicolas Flamel* | 3ᵉ	23
1582 | Tour d'Argent | 5ᵉ	25
1608 | Ragueneau | 1ᵉʳ	-
1610 | Relais Louis XIII* | 6ᵉ	25
1640 | Cordonnerie* | 1ᵉʳ	-
1650 | Aiguière* | 11ᵉ	-
1680 | Petite Chaise | 7ᵉ	19
1686 | Procope | 6ᵉ	16
1728 | 1728* | 8ᵉ	19
1758 | Ambassadeurs* | 8ᵉ	28
1760 | Grand Véfour | 1ᵉʳ	28
1766 | Lapérouse | 6ᵉ	21
1800 | Andy Wahloo* | 3ᵉ	14
1800 | Black Calavados* | 8ᵉ	-
1823 | A Priori Thé* | 2ᵉ	16
1832 | Escargot Montorgueil | 1ᵉʳ	21
1842 | Laurent* | 8ᵉ	24
1845 | Polidor | 6ᵉ	17
1854 | Arc* | 8ᵉ	-
1854 | Petit Riche | 9ᵉ	18
1855 | Brass. du Louvre | 1ᵉʳ	16
1856 | Charpentiers | 6ᵉ	18
1862 | Café de la Paix | 9ᵉ	19
1862 | Ladurée | 8ᵉ	23
1864 | Bofinger | 4ᵉ	20
1867 | Brass. Mollard | 8ᵉ	19
1870 | Boeuf Couronné | 19ᵉ	16
1870 | Soya Cantine Bio* | 11ᵉ	-
1872 | Goumard | 1ᵉʳ	24
1876 | Gallopin | 2ᵉ	16
1880 | Aub. du Clou* | 9ᵉ	16
1880 | Brass. Lipp | 6ᵉ	17
1881 | Café Terminus | 8ᵉ	-
1885 | Café/Deux Magots | 6ᵉ	16
1886 | Brass. Balzar | 5ᵉ	19
1889 | Jules Verne* | 7ᵉ	22
1890 | Bouillon Racine | 6ᵉ	16
1890 | Brass. Julien | 10ᵉ	19
1890 | Passage/Carm. | 11ᵉ	-
1892 | Wepler | 18ᵉ	14
1893 | Maxim's | 8ᵉ	18
1895 | Caves Pétrissans | 17ᵉ	19
1896 | Chartier | 9ᵉ	13
1897 | Ladurée | 9ᵉ	23
1897 | Pouilly Reuilly | **St-Gervais**	-
1898 | Espadon | 1ᵉʳ	26

Menus, photos, voting and more – free at ZAGAT.com

1899 | Fouquet's | 8ᵉ	18
1900 | Brass./l'Ile St. Louis | 4ᵉ	17
1900 | Café Lenôtre* | 8ᵉ	18
1900 | Chez Gégène | **Joinville**	-
1900 | Gauloise | 15ᵉ	15
1900 | Grande Cascade | 16ᵉ	25
1900 | Noces de Jeannette | 2ᵉ	-
1900 | Pavillon Ledoyen | 8ᵉ	26
1900 | Pré Catelan | 16ᵉ	27
1900 | Rest. Paul | 1ᵉʳ	20
1900 | Table d'Eugène* | 18ᵉ	-
1900 | Vieux Chêne* | 11ᵉ	-
1901 | Petit St. Benoît | 6ᵉ	16
1901 | Train Bleu | 12ᵉ	19
1903 | Angelina | 1ᵉʳ	20
1903 | Bistrot de Paris | 7ᵉ	16
1903 | Perraudin | 5ᵉ	13
1903 | Rotonde | 6ᵉ	15
1904 | Vagenende | 6ᵉ	15
1905 | Bons Crus | 1ᵉʳ	-
1906 | Rendez-vous/Chauff. | 18ᵉ	-
1908 | Chardenoux | 11ᵉ	19
1909 | Bistrot d'André | 15ᵉ	-
1909 | Pomponette | 18ᵉ	17
1910 | Brass. Lutétia | 6ᵉ	18
1910 | Fontaine de Mars | 7ᵉ	21
1912 | Benoît | 4ᵉ	24
1913 | Marty | 5ᵉ	16
1913 | Zeyer | 14ᵉ	16
1914 | Sébillon | **Neuilly**	15
1918 | Daru | 8ᵉ	-
1919 | Chez Marcel | 6ᵉ	-
1919 | Lescure | 1ᵉʳ	17
1920 | Chez Julien | 4ᵉ	19
1920 | Closerie des Lilas | 6ᵉ	18
1920 | Hôtel Amour* | 9ᵉ	8
1920 | Maison Prunier | 16ᵉ	21
1920 | Petit Niçois | 7ᵉ	16
1920 | Tournesol | 16ᵉ	18
1922 | Boeuf sur le Toit | 8ᵉ	18
1922 | Café du Commerce | 15ᵉ	16
1923 | Chez Savy | 8ᵉ	18
1923 | Thoumieux | 7ᵉ	-
1924 | Ami Louis | 3ᵉ	25
1924 | Bristol | 8ᵉ	27
1925 | Biche au Bois | 12ᵉ	20
1925 | Grand Venise | 15ᵉ	25
1925 | Gourmand | **Neuilly**	-
1925 | Petit Lutétia | 6ᵉ	19
1925 | Rech | 17ᵉ	-
1925 | Terminus Nord | 10ᵉ	17
1926 | Chez Georges-Maillot | 17ᵉ	18
1927 | Caviar Kaspia | 8ᵉ	25
1927 | Coupole | 14ᵉ	19
1928 | Cazaudehore | St-Germain-Laye	22
1929 | Diamantaires | 9ᵉ	-
1929 | Jardin des Cygnes | 8ᵉ	22
1929 | Petit Colombier | 17ᵉ	18
1929 | Tante Louise | 8ᵉ	22
1929 | Zéphyr | 20ᵉ	-
1930 | Allard | 6ᵉ	21
1930 | Garnier | 8ᵉ	22
1930 | Tico* | 8ᵉ	-
1930 | Trumilou | 4ᵉ	19
1931 | Chez L'Ami Jean | 7ᵉ	24
1932 | Chiberta | 8ᵉ	22
1932 | Crus de Bourgogne | 2ᵉ	17
1935 | Epi d'Or | 1ᵉʳ	16
1935 | Poule au Pot | 1ᵉʳ	23
1935 | Truffe Noire | **Neuilly**	-
1936 | Relais Plaza | 8ᵉ	23
1937 | Chez André | 8ᵉ	20
1937 | Chez Léna et Mimile | 5ᵉ	15
1939 | Voltaire | 7ᵉ	24
1940 | Flandrin | 16ᵉ	15
1942 | Lasserre | 8ᵉ	27
1942 | Méditerranée | 6ᵉ	21
1943 | Royal Madeleine | 8ᵉ	19
1945 | Aub. Bressane | 7ᵉ	20
1945 | Bar des Théâtres | 8ᵉ	15
1945 | Chez Fred | 17ᵉ	-
1945 | Chez Paul | 11ᵉ	21
1945 | Pied de Cochon | 1ᵉʳ	18
1946 | Chez Maître Paul | 6ᵉ	21
1946 | Taillevent | 8ᵉ	28
1947 | Moulin à Vent | 5ᵉ	19
1948 | Rubis | 1ᵉʳ	15
1949 | Chez Françoise | 7ᵉ	17
1950 | Diapason | 18ᵉ	-
1950 | Terrasse Mirabeau* | 16ᵉ	-
1951 | Bartolo | 6ᵉ	17
1951 | Deux Canards | 10ᵉ	18
1951 | Petit Châtelet | 5ᵉ	-
1952 | Bistro 121 | 15ᵉ	-
1954 | Sauvignon | 7ᵉ	14
1955 | Copenhague | 8ᵉ	18
1956 | Maison du Caviar | 8ᵉ	22
1956 | Robert et Louise | 3ᵉ	21
1957 | Chez René | 5ᵉ	21
1958 | Publicis Drugstore | 8ᵉ	11
1959 | Fins Gourmets | 7ᵉ	19

1959 | Paul Chêne | 16e — 20
1959 | Relais de Venise | 17e — 24
1960 | Chez Léon | 17e — 13
1960 | Rest. de la Tour | 15e — 21
1960 | Truffière | 5e — 23

HOLIDAY MEALS

(Special prix fixe meals offered at major holidays)

Z Ambassadeurs | 8e — 28
Z Ambroisie | 4e — 28
Z Apicius | 8e — 26
Z Arpège | 7e — 26
Astor | 8e — 16
Z Atelier Joël Robuchon | 7e — 28
Z Benoît | 4e — 24
Z Bristol | 8e — 27
Z Café/Deux Magots | 6e — 16
Z 144 Petrossian | 7e — 25
Chen Soleil d'Est | 15e — -
Chiberta | 8e — 22
Z Cinq | 8e — 28
Z Coupole | 14e — 19
Daru | 8e — -
Diapason | 18e — -
Divellec | 7e — 24
Z Espadon | 1er — 26
Goumard | 1er — 24
Z Grande Cascade | 16e — 25
Z Guy Savoy | 17e — 28
Huîtrier | 17e — 20
Jardins de Bagatelle | 16e — 17
Z Jules Verne | 7e — 22
Z Lapérouse | 6e — 21
Z Lasserre | 8e — 27
Marée | 8e — 23
Maxim's | 8e — 18
Montparnasse 25 | 14e — 16
Paris | 6e — 20
Z Pavillon Ledoyen | 8e — 26
Z Pierre Gagnaire | 8e — 28
Potager du Roy | **Versailles** — 19
Z Pré Catelan | 16e — 27
Relais Louis XIII | 6e — 25
Romantica | **Clichy** — 23
Salon d'Hélène | 6e — 19
Z Senderens | 8e — 26
Sormani | 17e — 23
Table d'Anvers | 9e — 17
Z Taillevent | 8e — 28
Tan Dinh | 7e — 23

Z Tour d'Argent | 5e — 25
Z Trou Gascon | 12e — 26
Wally Le Saharien | 9e — 15

HOTEL DINING

Ambassador, Hôtel
  16 Haussmann | 9e — 18
Amour, Hôtel
  Hôtel Amour | 9e — 8
Astor, Hôtel
  Astor | 8e — 16
Balzac, Hôtel
  Z Pierre Gagnaire | 8e — 28
Bristol, Hôtel Le
  Z Bristol | 8e — 27
Castille Paris, Hôtel
  L'Assaggio | 1er — 23
Concorde St-Lazare, Hôtel
  Café Terminus | 8e — -
Costes, Hôtel
  Costes | 1er — 18
Crillon, Hôtel de
  Z Ambassadeurs | 8e — 28
  Obé | 8e — 23
El Dorado, Hôtel
  Bistrot des Dames | 17e — 14
Four Seasons George V
  Z Cinq | 8e — 28
Hôtel, L'
  Restaurant | 6e — 26
Hyatt, Hôtel
  Café M | 8e — 19
InterContinental Le Grand Hôtel
  Café de la Paix | 9e — 19
Lancaster, Hôtel
  Table du Lancaster | 8e — 23
Louvre, Hôtel du
  Brass. du Louvre | 1er — 16
Lutétia, Hôtel
  Brass. Lutétia | 6e — 18
  Paris | 6e — 20
Mama Shelter
  Mama Shelter | 20e — -
Marignan, Hôtel
  Spoon Paris | 8e — 22
Méridien Montparnasse, Le
  Montparnasse 25 | 14e — 16
Meurice, Hôtel
  Dali | 1er — -
  Z Meurice | 1er — 27

M. Gallery Baltimore
  Table du Baltimore | 16ᵉ | –⌐
Montalembert, Hôtel
  Montalembert | 7ᵉ | 19⌐
Murano Urban Resort
  Murano | 3ᵉ | 16⌐
Novotel Tour Eiffel, Hôtel
  Benkay | 15ᵉ | 24⌐
Parc, Hôtel Le
  Relais du Parc | 16ᵉ | 19⌐
Park Hyatt Paris-Vendôme
  Pur'Grill | 2ᵉ | 19⌐
Pershing Hall, Hôtel
  Pershing | 8ᵉ | 17⌐
Plaza Athénée
  🆉 Alain Ducasse | 8ᵉ | 28⌐
  Relais Plaza | 8ᵉ | 23⌐
Pont Royal
  🆉 Atelier Joël Robuchon | 7ᵉ | 28⌐
Prince de Galles, Hôtel
  Jardin des Cygnes | 8ᵉ | 22⌐
Relais Saint-Germain, Hôtel
  🆉 Comptoir/Relais | 6ᵉ | 26⌐
Renaissance Paris Vendôme
  Pinxo | 1ᵉʳ | 21⌐
Ritz, Hôtel
  Bar Vendôme | 1ᵉʳ | 23⌐
  🆉 Espadon | 1ᵉʳ | 26⌐
Sofitel Arc de Triomphe
  Clovis | 8ᵉ | –⌐
Sofitel Le Faubourg
  Café Faubourg | 8ᵉ | 22⌐
Terrass Hôtel
  Diapason | 18ᵉ | –⌐
Thoumieux, Hôtel
  Thoumieux | 7ᵉ | –⌐
Trianon Palace
  Gordon Ramsay | **Versailles** | –⌐
Vernet, Hôtel
  Elysées | 8ᵉ | 23⌐
Warwick, Hôtel
  W Restaurant | 8ᵉ | –⌐
Westin Hotel
  First | 1ᵉʳ | 18⌐
Westminster, Hôtel
  Céladon | 2ᵉ | 21⌐

JACKET REQUIRED

(* Tie also required)
🆉 Alain Ducasse* | 8ᵉ | 28⌐
🆉 Ambroisie* | 4ᵉ | 28⌐
🆉 Arpège* | 7ᵉ | 26⌐

🆉 Astrance | 16ᵉ | 28⌐
🆉 Carré des Feuillants* | 1ᵉʳ | 26⌐
🆉 Cinq | 8ᵉ | 28⌐
🆉 Espadon* | 1ᵉʳ | 26⌐
🆉 Grande Cascade | 16ᵉ | 25⌐
🆉 Grand Véfour | 1ᵉʳ | 28⌐
🆉 Lasserre | 8ᵉ | 27⌐
Maxim's* | 8ᵉ | 18⌐
🆉 Meurice | 1ᵉʳ | 27⌐
🆉 Michel Rostang* | 17ᵉ | 27⌐
🆉 Pavillon Ledoyen | 8ᵉ | 26⌐
🆉 Pré Catelan* | 16ᵉ | 27⌐
Relais Plaza | 8ᵉ | 23⌐
🆉 Taillevent* | 8ᵉ | 28⌐
🆉 Tour d'Argent* | 5ᵉ | 25⌐

LATE DINING

(Weekday closing hour)
Al Dar | 12 AM | **multi.** | 21⌐
Al Diwan | 12 AM | 8ᵉ | 21⌐
Alsace | 24 hrs. | 8ᵉ | 18⌐
Ami Pierre | 12 AM | 11ᵉ | 17⌐
Anahï | 12 AM | 3ᵉ | 19⌐
Andy Wahloo | 12 AM | 3ᵉ | 14⌐
Asian | 12 AM | 8ᵉ | 16⌐
🆉 Atelier Joël Robuchon | 12 AM | 7ᵉ | 28⌐
Aub. Dab | 2 AM | 16ᵉ | 16⌐
Avenue | 1 AM | 8ᵉ | 18⌐
Bacchantes | 12:30 AM | 9ᵉ | –⌐
Ballon des Ternes | 12 AM | 17ᵉ | 15⌐
Bar à Huîtres | varies | **multi.** | 17⌐
Bar des Théâtres | 1 AM | 8ᵉ | 15⌐
Barlotti | 12:30 AM | 1ᵉʳ | 15⌐
Barrio Latino | 12:45 AM | 12ᵉ | 12⌐
Berkeley | 1 AM | 8ᵉ | 14⌐
Bistro/Deux Théâtres | 12:30 AM | 9ᵉ | 14⌐
Bistro Melrose | 1 AM | 17ᵉ | –⌐
🆉 Bistrot de l'Oulette | 12 AM | 4ᵉ | 26⌐
Bistrot du Peintre | 12 AM | 11ᵉ | 18⌐
Black Calavados | 12 AM | 8ᵉ | –⌐
Blue Elephant | 12 AM | 11ᵉ | 20⌐
Boeuf Couronné | 12 AM | 19ᵉ | 16⌐
Boeuf sur le Toit | 1 AM | 8ᵉ | 18⌐
🆉 Bofinger | 12:30 AM | 4ᵉ | 20⌐
Boudoir | 12:30 AM | 8ᵉ | –⌐
Bound | 1 AM | 8ᵉ | –⌐
🆉 Brass. Balzar | 12 AM | 5ᵉ | 19⌐
Brass. Flo | 12:30 AM | 10ᵉ | 18⌐
Brass. Julien | 1 AM | 10ᵉ | 19⌐
Brass. La Lorraine | 1 AM | 8ᵉ | 17⌐

SPECIAL FEATURES

Name	Hours	Loc.	Rating
Brass. L'Européen	1 AM	12e	–
Z Brass. Lipp	1 AM	6e	17
Brass. Mollard	12:30 AM	8e	19
Z Buddha Bar	12:30 AM	8e	16
Café Beaubourg	12 AM	4e	16
Café Burq	12 AM	18e	–
Z Café de Flore	1:30 AM	6e	15
Café de la Musique	varies	19e	15
Café de l'Esplanade	12:45 AM	7e	16
Café de l'Industrie	12 AM	11e	12
Z Café/Deux Magots	1 AM	6e	16
Café du Commerce	12 AM	15e	16
Café du Passage	1 AM	11e	–
Café Etienne Marcel	12 AM	2e	18
Café Le Petit Pont	varies	5e	14
Z Café Marly	2 AM	1er	16
Café Ruc	1 AM	1er	15
Camille	12 AM	3e	16
Caviar Kaspia	1 AM	8e	25
Chai 33	12 AM	12e	14
Charlot Roi des Coq.	varies	9e	15
Chéri Bibi	12 AM	18e	–
Chez André	1 AM	8e	20
Chez Clément	1 AM	multi.	15
Chez Denise	5 AM	1er	24
Chez Francis	12:30 AM	8e	17
Chez Françoise	12 AM	7e	17
Chez Janou	12 AM	3e	23
Chez Jenny	12 AM	3e	19
Chez L'Ami Jean	12 AM	7e	24
Chez Michel	12 AM	10e	24
Chez Papa	1 AM	multi.	17
Chez Paul	12 AM	11e	21
Chez Paul	12 AM	13e	16
Chez Prune	1 AM	10e	18
Chez Vincent	12 AM	19e	–
Chien qui Fume	1 AM	1er	18
Christine	12 AM	6e	23
Coco de Mer	12 AM	5e	–
Coffee Parisien	varies	multi.	16
Congrès Maillot	2 AM	17e	18
Costes	24 hrs.	1er	18
Coude Fou	12 AM	4e	19
Coupe Gorge	12 AM	4e	–
Z Coupole	1:30 AM	14e	19
Curieux Spaghetti	12 AM	4e	–
Dell Orto	12 AM	9e	–
Devèz	12:30 AM	8e	16
Diep	12:30 AM	8e	21
Dôme	12:30 AM	14e	22
Duc de Richelieu	1 AM	12e	–
Durand Dupont	12 AM	Neuilly	–
Ecluse	1 AM	multi.	16
Editeurs	2 AM	6e	14
Escale du Liban	12 AM	4e	–
Fakhr el Dine	12 AM	16e	24
Fines Gueules	2 AM	1er	–
Flore en l'Ile	2 AM	4e	18
Fogón	12 AM	6e	21
Fouquet's	12 AM	8e	18
Fous d'en Face	12 AM	4e	–
Gallopin	12 AM	2e	16
Gavroche	1 AM	2e	17
Grand Café	24 hrs.	9e	13
Grand Colbert	1 AM	2e	19
Grande Armée	1 AM	16e	15
Grille St-Germain	12:30 AM	6e	17
Hippopotamus	varies	multi.	11
Hôtel Amour	11:30 PM	9e	8
Huîtrerie Régis	12 AM	6e	22
Il Vino	12 AM	7e	–
Indiana Café	1 AM	multi.	7
J'Go	varies	multi.	14
Joe Allen	12:30 AM	1er	13
Kaïten	12 AM	8e	–
Kong	12:30 AM	1er	14
Léon/Bruxelles	varies	multi.	16
Libre Sens	12 AM	8e	–
Lô Sushi	12 AM	8e	15
Ma Bourgogne	1 AM	4e	18
Main d'Or	12 AM	11e	–
Maison du Caviar	1 AM	8e	22
Mama Shelter	12 AM	20e	–
Martel	12 AM	10e	–
Mood	12 AM	8e	–
Murano	12 AM	3e	16
Murat	12 AM	16e	13
Musichall	5 AM	8e	15
Nabulione	12 AM	7e	–
New Jawad	12 AM	7e	18
New Nioullaville	12:30 AM	11e	16
Noura	12 AM	multi.	19
Opportun	12 AM	14e	15
Paradis du Fruit	1 AM	multi.	14
Paul Chêne	12 AM	16e	20
Pershing	12 AM	8e	17
Petit Bofinger	varies	4e	18
Petit Marché	12 AM	3e	22
Petit Prince Paris	12 AM	5e	–
Petit Riche	12:15 AM	9e	18
Petit Zinc	12 AM	6e	18

Pied de Cochon | 24 hrs. | 1er		18
Pierre au Palais Royal | 12 AM | 1er		17
Polidor | 12:30 AM | 6^e		17
Pomponette | 12 AM | 18^e		17
Poule au Pot | 5 AM | 1er		23
Procope | 1 AM | 6^e		16
Publicis Drugstore | 2 AM | 8^e		11
404 | 12 AM | 3^e		22
Rotonde | 1 AM | 6^e		15
Rouge St-Honoré | 12 AM | 1er		13
Sébillon | 12 AM | **Neuilly**		15
Sens | 11:30 PM | 8^e		-
NEW Société | 2 AM | 6^e		-
Stella | 1 AM | 16^e		20
Studio | 12:30 AM | 4^e		-
Suffren | 12 AM | 15^e		14
Tav. de Maître Kanter | 24 hrs. | 1er		16
Terminus Nord | 1 AM | 10^e		17
Tong Yen | 12:15 AM | 8^e		15
Tricotin | 12 AM | 13^e		-
Truc Café | 2 AM | 18^e		-
Vagenende | 1 AM | 6^e		15
Vaudeville | 1 AM | 2^e		18
Verre Bouteille | 4 AM | 17^e		13
Verre Volé | 12 AM | 10^e		16
Viaduc Café | 3 AM | 12^e		-
Village d'Ung | 12 AM | 8^e		-
Villa Spicy | 12 AM | 8^e		13
Vin et Marée | 12:30 AM | 1er		18
Waly-Fay | 2 AM | 11^e		-
Wepler | 1 AM | 18^e		14
Zéphyr | 12 AM | 20^e		-
Zeyer | 12:30 AM | 14^e		16
Zo | 12 AM | 8^e		-

MEET FOR A DRINK

Alcazar | 6^e		19
Z Angelina | 1er		20
Autobus Imperial | 1er		-
BAM | 1er		-
Bar des Théâtres | 8^e		15
Baron Rouge | 12^e		-
Bistrot à Vins Mélac | 11^e		14
Bistrot du Peintre | 11^e		18
Bistrot Paul Bert | 11^e		23
Black Calavados | 8^e		-
NEW Bob's Kitchen | 3^e		-
Bons Crus | 1er		-
Bourguignon du Marais | 4^e		23
Z Brass. Balzar | 5^e		19
Breakfast/America | 5^e		15

Z Buddha Bar | 8^e		16
Café Beaubourg | 4^e		16
Café Burq | 18^e		-
Café Charbon | 11^e		15
Z Café de Flore | 6^e		15
Café de la Musique | 19^e		15
Café de l'Esplanade | 7^e		16
Café de l'Industrie | 11^e		12
Z Café/Deux Magots | 6^e		16
Café du Passage | 11^e		-
Café la Jatte | **Neuilly**		14
Café Lenôtre | 8^e		18
Z Café Marly | 1er		16
Café Ruc | 1er		15
Carr's | 1er		-
Cave de l'Os à Moëlle | 15^e		22
Cloche des Halles | 1er		-
Closerie des Lilas | 6^e		18
Clown Bar | 11^e		17
Comptoir | 1er		21
Cosi | 6^e		19
Coude Fou | 4^e		19
Z Coupole | 14^e		19
Curieux Spaghetti | 4^e		-
Dalloyau | **multi.**		23
Dame Tartine | 4^e		14
Deux Abeilles | 7^e		21
Dix Vins | 15^e		-
Dôme | 14^e		22
Eclaireur | 8^e		-
Ecluse | **multi.**		16
Enoteca | 4^e		20
Ferdi | 1er		-
Ferme | 1er		-
Fines Gueules | 1er		-
First | 1er		18
Z Fish La Boiss. | 6^e		22
Fontaines | 5^e		17
Fouquet's | 8^e		18
Fous d'en Face | 4^e		-
Fumoir | 1er		17
Gavroche | 2^e		17
Grande Armée | 16^e		15
Indiana Café | **multi.**		7
Juvéniles | 1er		16
Z Ladurée | **multi.**		23
Legrand Filles | 2^e		-
Lina's | **multi.**		16
Loir dans/Théière | 4^e		16
Ma Bourgogne | 4^e		18
Mama Shelter | 20^e		-

SPECIAL FEATURES

Mauzac | 5ᵉ	—
Murano | 3ᵉ	16
Musichall | 8ᵉ	15
Nabulione | 7ᵉ	—
Nemrod | 6ᵉ	16
No Stress Café | 9ᵉ	—
Poisson Rouge | 10ᵉ	—
Publicis Drugstore | 8ᵉ	11
Racines | 2ᵉ	—
Rest. du Palais Royal | 1ᵉʳ	19
River Café | **Issy-les-Moul.**	14
Rubis | 1ᵉʳ	15
Salon du Panthéon | 5ᵉ	—
Sauvignon | 7ᵉ	14
Suffren | 15ᵉ	14
Viaduc Café | 12ᵉ	—
☑ Vin sur Vin | 7ᵉ	26
Wepler | 18ᵉ	14
☑ Willi's Wine | 1ᵉʳ	20
Zébra Square | 16ᵉ	10
Zo | 8ᵉ	—

NO AIR-CONDITIONING

Accolade | 17ᵉ	—
A et M | 16ᵉ	21
Afaria | 15ᵉ	—
Agapes | 5ᵉ	—
Aimant du Sud | 13ᵉ	—
Alfred | 1ᵉʳ	—
Alivi | 4ᵉ	16
Al Taglio | 11ᵉ	—
☑ Ami Louis | 3ᵉ	25
Ami Pierre | 11ᵉ	17
Amuse Bouche | 14ᵉ	17
Anahuacalli | 5ᵉ	21
☑ Angelina | 1ᵉʳ	20
Angelo Procopio | 1ᵉʳ	—
AOC | 5ᵉ	18
Apollo | 14ᵉ	—
A Priori Thé | 2ᵉ	16
Assiette | 14ᵉ	—
Atelier Berger | 1ᵉʳ	21
Aub. du Champ/Mars | 7ᵉ	17
Aub. Nicolas Flamel | 3ᵉ	23
Autour du Mont | 15ᵉ	—
Autour/Saumon | **multi.**	17
BAM | 1ᵉʳ	—
Bar à Huîtres | 17ᵉ	17
Baratin | 20ᵉ	16
Bascou | 3ᵉ	20
Biche au Bois | 12ᵉ	20

BIOArt | 13ᵉ	—
Bistro d'Hubert | 15ᵉ	22
Bistrot d'à Côté | **Neuilly**	21
Bistrot d'André | 15ᵉ	—
☑ Bistrot de l'Oulette | 4ᵉ	26
Bistrot de Marius | 8ᵉ	21
Bistrot de Paris | 7ᵉ	16
Bistrot des Dames | 17ᵉ	14
Bistrot d'Henri | 6ᵉ	20
Bistrot Vivienne | 2ᵉ	18
Bon Saint Pourçain | 6ᵉ	18
Brass./l'Ile St. Louis | 4ᵉ	17
Breakfast/America | 5ᵉ	15
Breizh Café | 3ᵉ	—
Ca d'Oro | 1ᵉʳ	18
Café Beaubourg | 4ᵉ	16
Café Burq | 18ᵉ	—
NEW Café Cartouche | 12ᵉ	—
Café Charbon | 11ᵉ	15
Café de Mars | 7ᵉ	17
Café Le Petit Pont | 5ᵉ	14
NEW Caffé dei Cioppi | 11ᵉ	—
Cagouille | 14ᵉ	25
Cailloux | 13ᵉ	—
Caméléon | 6ᵉ	20
Cantine/Troquet | 14ᵉ	—
Cap Seguin | **Boulogne**	—
Carr's | 1ᵉʳ	—
Caves Pétrissans | 17ᵉ	19
Cerisaie | 14ᵉ	21
Chalet | **Neuilly**	—
Chalet des Iles | 16ᵉ	14
Chantairelle | 5ᵉ	—
Chardenoux | 11ᵉ	19
NEW Chateau Poivre | 14ᵉ	—
Chéri Bibi | 18ᵉ	—
Chez Françoise | 7ᵉ	17
Chez Georges-Maillot | 17ᵉ	18
Chez Géraud | 16ᵉ	20
NEW Chez Grenouille | 9ᵉ	—
Chez Grisette | 18ᵉ	—
Chez Julien | 4ᵉ	19
Chez Léon | 17ᵉ	13
Chez Marcel | 6ᵉ	—
Chez Marianne | 4ᵉ	18
NEW Chez Marie-Louise | 10ᵉ	—
Chez Michel | 10ᵉ	24
Chez Nénesse | 3ᵉ	—
Chez Omar | 3ᵉ	21
Chez Paul | 11ᵉ	21
Chez Paul | 13ᵉ	16

Restaurant	Score
Chez Prune | 10e	18
Chez Ramona | 20e	-
Chez René | 5e	21
Christophe | 5e	-
Cibus | 1er	-
Cloche des Halles | 1er	-
Closerie des Lilas | 6e	18
Clou | 17e	19
Clown Bar | 11e	17
Coco de Mer | 5e	-
Coin/Gourmets | 5e	22
Cordonnerie | 1er	-
Cosi | 6e	19
Cotolettes | 4e	-
Cotte Roti | 12e	-
Coupe Gorge | 4e	-
Crémerie | 6e	-
Cristal de Sel | 15e	-
Crudus | 1er	-
NEW Cru Rollin | 11e	-
Crus de Bourgogne | 2e	17
Dalva | 2e	-
Dame Tartine | 4e	14
Dell Orto | 9e	-
Des Gars | 3e	-
Deux Abeilles | 7e	21
2 Pieces Cuisine | 18e	-
Devèz | 8e	16
Dix Vins | 15e	-
Djakarta | 1er	20
Dôme du Marais | 4e	22
Duc de Richelieu | 12e	-
Durand Dupont | Neuilly	-
Ebouillanté | 4e	-
Ecluse | 8e	16
Ecume Saint-Honoré | 1er	-
Entoto | 13e	-
Entracte | 18e	-
Epi d'Or | 1er	16
Z Epi Dupin | 6e	24
Epigramme | 6e	-
Ferdi | 1er	-
Fines Gueules | 1er	-
Fins Gourmets | 7e	19
Flandrin | 16e	15
Flore en l'Ile | 4e	18
Fouquet's | 8e	18
NEW Fourchette | 17e	-
Gauloise | 15e	15
Gavroche | 2e	17
Georgette | 9e	22
Gorille Blanc | 7e	21
Gourmets des Ternes | 8e	19
Graindorge | 17e	22
Z Grande Cascade | 16e	25
Grand Pan | 15e	-
Gourmand | Neuilly	-
Hier & Aujourd'hui | 17e	-
Hotaru | 9e	-
Huîtrerie Régis | 6e	22
Il Barone | 14e	21
Il Etait une Oie | 17e	-
Jadis | 15e	-
Jardins de Bagatelle | 16e	17
Jean | 9e	19
Khun Akorn | 11e	-
Louchebem | 1er	15
Z Lyonnais | 2e	21
Ma Bourgogne | 4e	18
Marée Denfert/Passy | multi.	-
Marius | 16e	18
Martel | 10e	-
Mascotte | 18e	-
Maupertu | 7e	21
Memère Paulette | 2e	-
Moissonnier | 5e	19
NEW Mon Oncle | 18e	-
Montagnards | 1er	-
Z Mon Vieil Ami | 4e	24
Moulin à Vent | 5e	19
Mousson | 1er	-
No Stress Café | 9e	-
Z Os à Moëlle | 15e	25
Ourcine | 13e	24
Pasco | 7e	22
Pavillon Montsouris | 14e	17
Pères et Filles | 6e	16
Perraudin | 5e	13
Petit Châtelet | 5e	-
Petite Sirène/Copen. | 9e	-
Petites Sorcières | 14e	-
Petit Lutétia | 6e	19
Petit Marché | 3e	22
Petit Marguery | 13e	21
Petit Niçois | 7e	16
Petit Pascal | 13e	-
Petit Poucet | Levallois	-
Pétrelle | 9e	-
Pharamond | 1er	19
Pitchi Poï | 4e	-
Pizza Chic | 6e	-
Poisson Rouge | 10e	-

SPECIAL FEATURES

Pomponette	18e	17
Pramil	3e	–
⛶ Pré Catelan	16e	27
Procope	6e	16
P'tit Troquet	7e	22
Pure Café	11e	–
Quedubon	19e	–
Quinzième	15e	–
Racines	2e	–
Réconfort	3e	–
Relais de Venise	17e	24
Rendez-vous/Chauff.	18e	–
Repaire de Cartouche	11e	16
Rest. du Marché	15e	–
Rest. du Palais Royal	1er	19
Rest. Paul	1er	20
Réveil du 10e	10e	-
Rice and Fish	2e	–
River Café	Issy-les-Moul.	14
Robert et Louise	3e	21
Roi du Pot-au-Feu	9e	–
Rollin	11e	–
Romantica	Clichy	23
Rose Bakery	3e	17
Rose de France	1er	–
Rughetta	18e	–
Sale e Pepe	18e	–
Sardegna a Tavola	12e	21
Sauvignon	7e	14
Scheffer	16e	18
Sept Quinze	15e	–
Sinago	9e	–
Sobane	9e	–
Sot l'y Laisse	11e	–
NEW Soya Cantine Bio	11e	–
Square/Marcardet	18e	–
Square Trousseau	12e	19
Tastevin	Maisons-Laff.	24
Tav. Henri IV	1er	16
Temps au Temps	11e	25
Temps des Cerises	13e	–
Terrasse Mirabeau	16e	–
Terrines/Gérard Vié	6e	–
Terroir	13e	–
Timbre	6e	24
Tokyo Eat	16e	14
Tonn. Saintongeaise	Neuilly	–
Tournesol	16e	18
⛶ Train Bleu	12e	19
Troquet	15e	24
Truc Café	18e	–

Truffe Noire	Neuilly	–
Tsukizi	6e	–
Uitr	15e	–
Vaudeville	2e	18
Verre Volé	10e	16
Vieux Chêne	11e	–
Vin et Marée	16e	18
Wadja	6e	20
Waknine	16e	–
⛶ Willi's Wine	1er	20
Winch	18e	–
NEW Yam'Tcha	1er	–
Zéphyr	20e	–
Zinc-Zinc	Neuilly	16
Zygomates	12e	20

OPEN SUNDAY

Agapes	5e	–
Alcazar	6e	19
Al Dar	16e	21
Al Diwan	8e	21
Alivi	4e	16
Allobroges	20e	22
Alsace	8e	18
Al Taglio	11e	–
Ambassade/Auv.	3e	20
⛶ Ambassadeurs	8e	28
⛶ Ami Louis	3e	25
Anahï	3e	19
Anahuacalli	5e	21
Antoine	16e	–
Apollo	14e	–
A Priori Thé	2e	16
⛶ Ardoise	1er	24
⛶ As du Fallafel	4e	24
Asian	8e	16
Assiette	14e	–
Astier	11e	21
⛶ Atelier Joël Robuchon	7e	28
Atelier Maître Albert	5e	21
Atlas	5e	20
Aub. Aveyronnaise	12e	–
Aub. Bressane	7e	20
Aub. du Clou	9e	16
Aub./Reine Blanche	4e	19
Autour/Saumon	9e	17
Avenue	8e	18
Azabu	6e	24
Ballon des Ternes	17e	15
Ballon et Coquillages	17e	–
Bamboche	7e	19

Banyan | **15ᵉ** — 19	Café de Mars | **7ᵉ** — 17
Bar à Huîtres | **multi.** — 17	Café des Musées | **3ᵉ** — -
Bar des Théâtres | **8ᵉ** — 15	🆉 Café/Deux Magots | **6ᵉ** — 16
Barlotti | **1ᵉʳ** — 15	Café du Commerce | **15ᵉ** — 16
Baron Rouge | **12ᵉ** — -	Café du Passage | **11ᵉ** — -
Barrio Latino | **12ᵉ** — 12	Café Etienne Marcel | **2ᵉ** — 18
Bar Vendôme | **1ᵉʳ** — 23	Café Faubourg | **8ᵉ** — 22
Basilic | **7ᵉ** — 15	Café la Jatte | **Neuilly** — 14
Beaujolais d'Auteuil | **16ᵉ** — 17	Café Lenôtre | **8ᵉ** — 18
Bel Canto | **4ᵉ** — 13	Café Le Petit Pont | **5ᵉ** — 14
Benkay | **15ᵉ** — 24	🆉 Café Marly | **1ᵉʳ** — 16
🆉 Benoît | **4ᵉ** — 24	Café Rouge | **3ᵉ** — -
Berkeley | **8ᵉ** — 14	Café Ruc | **1ᵉʳ** — 15
Bis du Severo | **14ᵉ** — -	Café Terminus | **8ᵉ** — -
Bistro 121 | **15ᵉ** — -	Cagouille | **14ᵉ** — 25
Bistro de Breteuil | **7ᵉ** — 16	Cailloux | **13ᵉ** — -
Bistro du 17ème | **17ᵉ** — 18	Camille | **3ᵉ** — 16
Bistro St. Ferdinand | **17ᵉ** — 14	Cantine de Quentin | **10ᵉ** — -
Bistrot de Marius | **8ᵉ** — 21	Carr's | **1ᵉʳ** — -
Bistrot des Vignes | **16ᵉ** — 17	Casa Bini | **6ᵉ** — 21
Bistrot d'Henri | **6ᵉ** — 20	Casa Tina | **16ᵉ** — -
Bistrot du Cap | **15ᵉ** — -	Caveau du Palais | **1ᵉʳ** — 19
Bistrot du Dôme | **multi.** — 21	Cave de l'Os à Moëlle | **15ᵉ** — 22
Bistrot du Peintre | **11ᵉ** — 18	Cazaudehore | **St-Germain-Laye** — 22
Bizan | **2ᵉ** — -	Céladon | **2ᵉ** — 21
Blue Elephant | **11ᵉ** — 20	Chai 33 | **12ᵉ** — 14
NEW Bob's Kitchen | **3ᵉ** — -	Chalet | **Neuilly** — -
Boeuf Couronné | **19ᵉ** — 16	Chalet/l'Oasis | **Boulogne** — -
🆉 Bofinger | **4ᵉ** — 20	Chalet des Iles | **16ᵉ** — 14
Bon | **16ᵉ** — -	Chamarré Mont. | **18ᵉ** — -
Boucherie Roulière | **6ᵉ** — -	Chardenoux | **11ᵉ** — 19
Bound | **8ᵉ** — -	Charlot Roi des Coq. | **9ᵉ** — 15
🆉 Brass. Balzar | **5ᵉ** — 19	Charpentiers | **6ᵉ** — 18
Brass. du Louvre | **1ᵉʳ** — 16	Chartier | **9ᵉ** — 13
Brass. Flo | **10ᵉ** — 18	**NEW** Chateau Poivre | **14ᵉ** — -
Brass. Julien | **10ᵉ** — 19	Cherche Midi | **6ᵉ** — 19
Brass. La Lorraine | **8ᵉ** — 17	Chéri Bibi | **18ᵉ** — -
Brass. L'Européen | **12ᵉ** — -	Chez André | **8ᵉ** — 20
Brass. Printemps | **9ᵉ** — 11	Chez Clément | **multi.** — 15
Brass./l'Ile St. Louis | **4ᵉ** — 17	Chez Francis | **8ᵉ** — 17
Breakfast/America | **multi.** — 15	Chez Françoise | **7ᵉ** — 17
Breizh Café | **3ᵉ** — -	Chez Gégène | **Joinville** — -
🆉 Bristol | **8ᵉ** — 27	Chez Georges-Maillot | **17ᵉ** — 18
🆉 Buddha Bar | **8ᵉ** — 16	Chez Janou | **3ᵉ** — 23
Buffalo Grill | **multi.** — 10	Chez Jenny | **3ᵉ** — 19
Ca d'Oro | **1ᵉʳ** — 18	Chez Julien | **4ᵉ** — 19
Café Beaubourg | **4ᵉ** — 16	Chez Léna et Mimile | **5ᵉ** — 15
Café Charbon | **11ᵉ** — 15	Chez Livio | **Neuilly** — 13
Café de la Musique | **19ᵉ** — 15	Chez Ly | **17ᵉ** — -
Café de la Paix | **9ᵉ** — 19	Chez Marianne | **4ᵉ** — 18
Café de l'Industrie | **11ᵉ** — 12	Chez Omar | **3ᵉ** — 21

Chez Papa | **multi.**	17
Chez Paul | 11e	21
Chez Paul | 13e	16
Chez Prune | 10e	18
Chez Ramona | 20e	-
Chien qui Fume | 1er	18
Christine | 6e	23
Christophe | 5e	-
Z Cinq | 8e	28
NEW Claude Colliot | 4e	-
Closerie des Lilas | 6e	18
Coco & Co. | 6e	-
Coin/Gourmets | 5e	22
Z Comptoir/Relais | 6e	26
Congrès Maillot | 17e	18
Cosi | 6e	19
Costes | 1er	18
Coude Fou | 4e	19
Coupe-Chou | 5e	23
Coupe Gorge | 4e	-
Z Coupole | 14e	19
Crêperie de Josselin | 14e	22
Cuisine | 7e	25
Curieux Spaghetti | 4e	-
Dali | 1er	-
Dalloyau | **multi.**	23
Dame Tartine | 4e	14
Da Rosa | 6e	19
Davé | 1er	18
Délices d'Aphrodite | 5e	18
NEW Derrière | 3e	-
Des Gars | 3e	-
Dessirier | 17e	20
Devèz | 8e	16
Diamantaires | 9e	-
Djakarta | 1er	20
Dôme | 14e	22
Drouant | 2e	22
Durand Dupont | **Neuilly**	-
Ebouillanté | 4e	-
Ecluse | **multi.**	16
Editeurs | 6e	14
Elysées | 8e	23
Elysées Hong Kong | 16e	-
Enoteca | 4e	20
Entoto | 13e	-
Entracte | 18e	-
Escale du Liban | 4e	-
Escargot Montorgueil | 1er	21
Z Espadon | 1er	26
Etoile Marocaine | 8e	-
Fables/Fontaine | 7e	24
Fakhr el Dine | 16e	24
Fellini | 1er	21
Ferdi | 1er	-
Ferme | 1er	-
Findi | 8e	16
Fines Gueules | 1er	-
Finzi | 8e	13
Firmin le Barbier | 7e	-
First | 1er	18
Z Fish La Boiss. | 6e	22
Flandrin | 16e	15
Floors | 18e	-
Flora Danica | 8e	19
Flore en l'Ile | 4e	18
Fogón | 6e	21
Z Fontaine de Mars | 7e	21
Fontaines | 5e	17
Fontanarosa | 15e	-
Foujita | 1er	-
Fouquet's | 8e	18
Fous d'en Face | 4e	-
NEW Frenchie | 2e	-
Fumoir | 1er	17
Gare | 16e	14
Garnier | 8e	22
Z Georges | 4e	18
Giulio Rebellato | 16e	20
Glou | 3e	-
Goumard | 1er	24
Grand Café | 9e	13
Grand Colbert | 2e	19
Grande Armée | 16e	15
Z Grande Cascade | 16e	25
Grand Louvre | 1er	18
Grille St-Germain | 6e	17
Guilo-Guilo | 18e	-
Gourmand | **Neuilly**	-
Guirlande de Julie | 3e	15
Higuma | 1er	15
Hippopotamus | **multi.**	11
Hôtel Amour | 9e	8
Huîtrerie Régis | 6e	22
Huîtrier | 17e	20
Ile | **Issy-les-Moul.**	18
Ilot Vache | 4e	18
Il Vino | 7e	-
Inagiku | 5e	18
Indiana Café | **multi.**	7
Jardin des Cygnes | 8e	22
Jardins de Bagatelle | 16e	17

Menus, photos, voting and more – free at ZAGAT.com

Jarrasse | **Neuilly**	–
J'Go | 6e	14
Joe Allen | 1er	13
Z Jules Verne | 7e	22
Khun Akorn | 11e	–
Kim Anh | 15e	–
Kong | 1er	14
Z Ladurée | **multi.**	23
Ladurée Le Bar | 8e	–
Languedoc | 5e	–
Lao Lane Xang | 13e	–
Lao Siam | 19e	15
Lao Tseu | 7e	–
Lei | 7e	21
Léon/Bruxelles | **multi.**	16
Libre Sens | 8e	–
Lina's | 16e	16
Liza | 2e	24
Loir dans/Théière | 4e	16
Lô Sushi | 8e	15
Louis Vin | 5e	19
Ma Bourgogne | 4e	18
Maharajah | 5e	17
Mai Do | 6e	–
Maison Blanche | 8e	20
Maison du Caviar | 8e	22
Mama Shelter | 20e	–
Marée | 8e	23
Marée Denfert/Passy | **multi.**	–
Mariage Frères | **multi.**	21
Marius et Janette | 8e	25
Market | 8e	22
Marlotte | 6e	16
Marty | 5e	16
Mascotte | 18e	–
Matsuri | **multi.**	14
Mauzac | 5e	–
Méditerranée | 6e	21
Mirama | 5e	20
Miroir | 18e	–
NEW Mon Oncle | 18e	–
Monsieur Lapin | 14e	18
Montalembert | 7e	19
Mont Liban | 17e	–
Z Mon Vieil Ami | 4e	24
Mood | 8e	–
Moulin/Galette | 18e	15
Murano | 3e	16
Murat | 16e	13
Muscade | 1er	–
Musichall | 8e	15
Nabulione | 7e	–
Nemrod | 6e	16
New Jawad | 7e	18
New Nioullaville | 11e	16
Noces de Jeannette | 2e	–
Nos Ancêtres Gaulois | 4e	13
No Stress Café | 9e	–
Noura | **multi.**	19
Nouveau Village | 13e	18
Obé | 8e	23
Z Ombres | 7e	18
Ozu | 16e	23
Paradis du Fruit | **multi.**	14
Paradis Thai | 13e	15
Parc aux Cerfs | 6e	21
Pasco | 7e	22
Passy Mandarin | **multi.**	20
Pavillon Montsouris | 14e	17
Pelouse | 19e	–
Père Claude | 15e	17
Pères et Filles | 6e	16
Perraudin | 5e	13
Pershing | 8e	17
Petit Bofinger | **Vincennes**	18
Petit Châtelet | 5e	–
Petite Chaise | 7e	19
Petite Cour | 6e	21
Petit Lutétia | 6e	19
Petit Marché | 3e	22
Petit Marguery | 13e	21
Petit Niçois | 7e	16
Petit Pontoise | 5e	22
Petit Poucet | **Levallois**	–
Petit Prince Paris | 5e	–
Petit Riche | 9e	18
Petit Zinc | 6e	18
Pétrus | 17e	21
Pharamond | 1er	19
Pied de Cochon | 1er	18
Pinxo | 1er	21
Pitchi Poï | 4e	–
Pizzeria d'Auteuil | 16e	–
Pizzetta | 9e	–
Poisson Rouge | 10e	–
Polichinelle Cafe | 11e	–
Polidor | 6e	17
Poule au Pot | 1er	23
Pramil | 3e	–
Procope | 6e	16
Publicis Drugstore | 8e	11
Pure Café | 11e	–

SPECIAL FEATURES

Pur'Grill | 2e	19	**NEW** Tico | 8e	-
Quai | 7e	-	Timgad | 17e	20
Quai Ouest | St-Cloud	13	Toi | 8e	-
404 | 3e	22	Tokyo Eat | 16e	14
Quedubon | 19e	-	Tong Yen | 8e	15
Ravi | 7e	21	Tournesol | 16e	18
Réconfort | 3e	-	☒ Train Bleu | 12e	19
Réfectoire | 11e	-	Tricotin | 13e	-
Relais de Venise | 17e	24	Truc Café | 18e	-
☒ Relais/l'Entrecôte | multi.	22	Trumilou | 4e	19
Relais Plaza | 8e	23	Tsé-Yang | 16e	18
Réminet | 5e	-	Uitr | 15e	-
Rest. du Musée d'Orsay | 7e	17	Vagenende | 6e	15
Rest. Paul | 1er	20	Vaudeville | 2e	18
Reuan Thai | 11e	-	Verre Volé | 10e	16
Réveil du 10e | 10e	-	Viaduc Café | 12e	-
River Café | Issy-les-Moul.	14	Villa Spicy | 8e	13
Robert et Louise | 3e	21	Vin et Marée | multi.	18
Rosa Bonheur | 19e	-	Vins des Pyrénées | 4e	16
Rose Bakery | multi.	17	☒ Vin sur Vin | 7e	26
Rose de France | 1er	-	Waly-Fay | 11e	-
Rôtiss. du Beaujolais | 5e	23	Wepler | 18e	14
Rotonde | 6e	15	Winch | 18e	-
Rouge St-Honoré | 1er	13	Wok Cooking | 11e	-
Royal Madeleine | 8e	19	**NEW** Yam'Tcha | 1er	-
Rughetta | 18e	-	Yugaraj | 6e	23
Samiin | 7e	-	Zébra Square | 16e	10
Saut du Loup | 1er	14	Zéphyr | 20e	-
Sauvignon | 7e	14	Zeyer | 14e	16
Scoop | 1er	17		
Sébillon | Neuilly	15		

OUTDOOR DINING

(G=garden; P=patio; S=sidewalk; T=terrace)

☒ Senderens | 8e	26
Sens | 8e	-
7ème Sud | multi.	15
Sept Quinze | 15e	-
NEW Shan Gout | 12e	-
NEW Société | 6e	-
NEW Soya Cantine Bio | 11e	-
Square Trousseau | 12e	19
Stella | 16e	20
Studio | 4e	-
Sud | 17e	16
Suffren | 15e	14
Table du Lancaster | 8e	23
☒ Table/Joël Robuchon | 16e	26
Tastevin | Maisons-Laff.	24
Tav. de Maître Kanter | 1er	16
Tav./Sgt. Recruteur | 4e	16
Terminus Nord | 10e	17
Thiou/Petit Thiou | 8e	21
Thoumieux | 7e	-

Absinthe | S, T | 1er	20
A et M | S | 16e	21
Aimant du Sud | S, T | 13e	-
☒ Alain Ducasse | P | 8e	28
Al Dar | S, T | multi.	21
Alivi | T | 4e	16
Alsace | S | 8e	18
Amici Miei | S | 11e	19
Ampère | S | 17e	-
Angelo Procopio | T | 1er	-
Antoine | T | 16e	-
AOC | T | 5e	18
A Priori Thé | P | 2e	16
Asian | S | 8e	16
Astier | S | 11e	21
Atlas | S | 5e	20
Aub. Aveyronnaise | P, S, T | 12e	-
Aub. Dab | S | 16e	16
Aub. du Clou | S, T | 9e	16

Aub. Étchégorry	S	13ᵉ	—

Aub. Étchégorry | S | 13ᵉ — —
Avenue | T | 8ᵉ — 18
Ballon des Ternes | S, T | 17ᵉ — 15
BAM | T | 1ᵉʳ — —
Barlotti | P, S | 1ᵉʳ — 15
Bartolo | S, T | 6ᵉ — 17
Bar Vendôme | P | 1ᵉʳ — 23
Basilic | G, T | 7ᵉ — 15
Beaujolais d'Auteuil | S | 16ᵉ — 17
BE Boulangépicier | S | 8ᵉ — 19
Berkeley | T | 8ᵉ — 14
BIOArt | T | 13ᵉ — —
Bistro de Breteuil | T | 7ᵉ — 16
Bistro d'Hubert | T | 15ᵉ — 22
Bistro du 17ème | S | 17ᵉ — 18
Bistro Melrose | S | 17ᵉ — —
Bistrot à Vins Mélac | S | 11ᵉ — 14
Bistrot d'à Côté | S | multi. — 21
Bistrot de Marius | S | 8ᵉ — 21
Bistrot des Dames | G | 17ᵉ — 14
Bistrot du Cap | T | 15ᵉ — —
Bistrot du Peintre | T | 11ᵉ — 18
Bistrot Niel | S, T | 17ᵉ — —
Bistrot Vivienne | T | 2ᵉ — 18
Bocconi | S | 8ᵉ — 20
Z Bon Accueil | S | 7ᵉ — 24
Bon Saint Pourçain | S | 6ᵉ — 18
Bourguignon du Marais | T | 4ᵉ — 23
Brass. du Louvre | T | 1ᵉʳ — 16
Brass./l'Ile St. Louis | T | 4ᵉ — 17
Z Bristol | G | 8ᵉ — 27
Buisson Ardent | S | 5ᵉ — 19
Café Beaubourg | T | 4ᵉ — 16
Café Charbon | S | 11ᵉ — 15
Z Café de Flore | S, T | 6ᵉ — 15
Café de la Musique | T | 19ᵉ — 15
Café de la Paix | S | 9ᵉ — 19
Café de l'Esplanade | S | 7ᵉ — 16
Café de l'Industrie | S | 11ᵉ — 12
Café de Mars | S | 7ᵉ — 17
Z Café/Deux Magots | G, T | 6ᵉ — 16
Café du Passage | S | 11ᵉ — —
Café Etienne Marcel | S | 2ᵉ — 18
Café Guitry | T | 9ᵉ — —
Café la Jatte | G, T | Neuilly — 14
Café Lenôtre | G, P | 8ᵉ — 18
Café Le Petit Pont | T | 5ᵉ — 14
Z Café Marly | T | 1ᵉʳ — 16
Café Ruc | S | 1ᵉʳ — 15
Cagouille | T | 14ᵉ — 25
Cailloux | S | 13ᵉ — —

Camille | S | 3ᵉ — 16
Cap Seguin | T | Boulogne — —
Casa Tina | S | 16ᵉ — —
Caves Pétrissans | T | 17ᵉ — 19
Cazaudehore | G, T | St-Germain-Laye — 22
Chai 33 | T | 12ᵉ — 14
Chalet/l'Oasis | G, T | Boulogne — —
Chalet des Iles | G, T | 16ᵉ — 14
Chantairelle | G | 5ᵉ — —
Charpentiers | S | 6ᵉ — 18
Cherche Midi | S | 6ᵉ — 19
Chez André | S | 8ᵉ — 20
Chez Francis | S | 8ᵉ — 17
Chez Gégène | S, T | Joinville — —
Chez Gérard | S | Neuilly — 19
Chez Janou | T | 3ᵉ — 23
Chez Léna et Mimile | T | 5ᵉ — 15
Chez Les Anges | S | 7ᵉ — 23
Chez Livio | T | Neuilly — 13
Chez Ly | S | 17ᵉ — —
Chez Marcel | S | 6ᵉ — —
Chez Marianne | S, T | 4ᵉ — 18
Chez Michel | S | 10ᵉ — 24
Chez Omar | T | 3ᵉ — 21
Chez Papa | S | multi. — 17
Chez Paul | S | 11ᵉ — 21
Chez Paul | S | 13ᵉ — 16
Chez Prune | S | 10ᵉ — 18
Chez Ramulaud | S | 11ᵉ — 16
Chez René | T | 5ᵉ — 21
Chez Savy | S | 8ᵉ — 18
Chez Vong | T | 1ᵉʳ — 21
Chien qui Fume | S, T | 1ᵉʳ — 18
Cigale Récamier | T | 7ᵉ — 21
Z Cinq | T | 8ᵉ — 28
Cloche des Halles | S, T | 1ᵉʳ — —
Clos des Gourmets | T | 7ᵉ — 25
Closerie des Lilas | T | 6ᵉ — 18
Clown Bar | S | 11ᵉ — 17
Comptoir | S | 1ᵉʳ — 21
Copenhague | T | 8ᵉ — 18
Cordonnerie | S | 1ᵉʳ — —
Costes | G, P | 1ᵉʳ — 18
Coupe-Chou | T | 5ᵉ — 23
Crus de Bourgogne | S | 2ᵉ — 17
Dalloyau | S, T | multi. — 23
Dame Tartine | T | 4ᵉ — 14
Da Mimmo | S | 10ᵉ — —
Da Rosa | T | 6ᵉ — 19
Daru | S | 8ᵉ — —

Délices d'Aphrodite | S | 5e | 18
Deux Abeilles | S | 7e | 21
Devèz | S | 8e | 16
Diapason | T | 18e | -
Duc de Richelieu | T | 12e | -
Durand Dupont | G | **Neuilly** | -
Ebauchoir | S | 12e | -
Editeurs | S | 6e | 14
El Mansour | S | 8e | 17
Entracte | T | 18e | -
Z Epi Dupin | S | 6e | 24
Z Espadon | G, T | 1er | 26
Eugène | S | 8e | -
Fables/Fontaine | T | 7e | 24
Findi | S | 8e | 16
Fins Gourmets | S | 7e | 19
Flandrin | S, T | 16e | 15
Flora Danica | G, T | 8e | 19
Flore en l'Ile | S, T | 4e | 18
Florimond | S | 7e | 24
Z Fontaine de Mars | S, T | 7e | 21
Fontaine Gaillon | T | 2e | 22
Fontaines | S, T | 5e | 17
Fontanarosa | T | 15e | -
Fouquet's | S, T | 8e | 18
Fous d'en Face | S | 4e | -
Fumoir | S | 1er | 17
Gallopin | S | 2e | 16
Gare | G, T | 16e | 14
Gauloise | S, T | 15e | 15
Z Georges | T | 4e | 18
Gitane | S | 15e | -
Gorille Blanc | S | 7e | 21
Gourmets des Ternes | S | 8e | 19
Grand Café | S | 9e | 13
Grande Armée | S | 16e | 15
Z Grande Cascade | T | 16e | 25
Grille St-Germain | S | 6e | 17
Gourmand | T | **Neuilly** | -
Guirlande de Julie | S, T | 3e | 15
Hangar | S | 3e | 18
Hippopotamus | T | 6e | 11
Ile | G, T | **Issy-les-Moul.** | 18
Issé | S | 1er | 23
Jardin des Cygnes | T | 8e | 22
Jardins de Bagatelle | G, T | 16e | 17
Jarrasse | S, T | **Neuilly** | -
Je Thé ... Me | S, T | 15e | -
Joe Allen | S, T | 1er | 13
Joséphine/Dumonet | S | 6e | 23
Kaïten | S, T | 8e | -

Khun Akorn | T | 11e | -
Kim Anh | T | 15e | -
L'Assaggio | P | 1er | 23
Z Laurent | G, T | 8e | 24
Legrand Filles | P | 2e | -
Lei | S | 7e | 21
Lescure | S, T | 1er | 17
Ma Bourgogne | S, T | 4e | 18
Main d'Or | S | 11e | -
Maison/Amér. Latine | G | 7e | 18
Maison Courtine | S | 14e | 24
Mama Shelter | T | 20e | -
Marée de Versailles | T | **Versailles** | 19
Marius | S, T | 16e | 18
Marius et Janette | S, T | 8e | 25
Market | S | 8e | 22
Marlotte | S, T | 6e | 16
Martel | S, T | 10e | -
Marty | S, T | 5e | 16
Mathusalem | S, T | 16e | -
Maupertu | S, T | 7e | 21
Mauzac | S | 5e | -
Mavrommatis | S, T | 5e | 19
Méditerranée | S, T | 6e | 21
Montalembert | S, T | 7e | 19
Moulin à Vent | S, T | 5e | 19
Moulin/Galette | P | 18e | 15
Murat | S | 16e | 13
Muscade | G | 1er | -
Nabulione | T | 7e | -
Natacha | S | 14e | -
Nemrod | S, T | 6e | 16
New Nioullaville | S | 11e | 16
No Stress Café | S, T | 9e | -
Noura | G | 6e | 19
Opportun | S | 14e | 15
Oulette | S, T | 12e | 19
Papilles | S, T | 5e | 23
Parc aux Cerfs | P | 6e | 21
Paris Seize | S | 16e | 18
Pasco | T | 7e | 22
Pavillon Montsouris | G, T | 14e | 17
Père Claude | S | 15e | 17
Pères et Filles | S, T | 6e | 16
Perraudin | P | 5e | 13
Pershing | P | 8e | 17
Petite Chaise | S | 7e | 19
Petite Cour | T | 6e | 21
Petit Marché | S | 3e | 22
Petit Marguery | T | 13e | 21
Petit Pontoise | S | 5e | 22

Name	Rating
Petit Poucet | G, P, T | **Levallois**	–
Petit Victor Hugo | S, T | **16ᵉ**	19
Pharamond | S, T | **1ᵉʳ**	19
Pichet de Paris | S | **8ᵉ**	16
Pitchi Poï | T | **4ᵉ**	–
Polichinelle Cafe | S | **11ᵉ**	–
Pomze | S, T | **8ᵉ**	18
⚂ Pré Catelan | G, T | **16ᵉ**	27
Publicis Drugstore | S, T | **8ᵉ**	11
Pure Café | S, T | **11ᵉ**	–
Pur'Grill | T | **2ᵉ**	19
Quai Ouest | T | **St-Cloud**	13
Rech | T | **17ᵉ**	–
Relais de Venise | S, T | **17ᵉ**	24
⚂ Relais/l'Entrecôte | S, T | **multi.**	22
Réminet | S | **5ᵉ**	–
Restaurant | P | **6ᵉ**	26
Rest. de la Tour | S | **15ᵉ**	21
Rest. du Marché | S, T | **15ᵉ**	–
Rest. du Palais Royal | G | **1ᵉʳ**	19
Rest. Manufacture | T | **Issy-les-Moul.**	21
Rest. Paul | S, T | **1ᵉʳ**	20
River Café | T | **Issy-les-Moul.**	14
Romantica | P, T | **Clichy**	23
Rotonde | S, T | **6ᵉ**	15
Rouge St-Honoré | T | **1ᵉʳ**	13
Rughetta | T | **18ᵉ**	–
Sauvignon | S | **7ᵉ**	14
Saveurs de Flora | S | **8ᵉ**	21
Sawadee | S, T | **15ᵉ**	–
Scoop | S | **1ᵉʳ**	17
16 Haussmann | T | **9ᵉ**	18
7ème Sud | S, T | **multi.**	15
Sept Quinze | S, T | **15ᵉ**	–
Square | S | **7ᵉ**	–
Square/Marcardet | G | **18ᵉ**	–
Square Trousseau | S | **12ᵉ**	19
Stella | S | **16ᵉ**	20
Stresa | S | **8ᵉ**	22
Studio | P | **4ᵉ**	–
Sud | P | **17ᵉ**	16
Suffren | S, T | **15ᵉ**	14
Table d'Anvers | S, T | **9ᵉ**	17
Tastevin | G | **Maisons-Laff.**	24
Temps au Temps | S, T | **11ᵉ**	25
Terrasse Mirabeau | T | **16ᵉ**	–
Terroir | S | **13ᵉ**	–
Thiou/Petit Thiou | S | **7ᵉ**	21
Tokyo Eat | T | **16ᵉ**	14
Tonn. Saintongeaise | G | **Neuilly**	–
Tournesol | S | **16ᵉ**	18
Troquet | S | **15ᵉ**	24
Trumilou | S | **4ᵉ**	19
Vagenende | S, T | **6ᵉ**	15
Vaudeville | S | **2ᵉ**	18
Viaduc Café | S, T | **12ᵉ**	–
Vieux Chêne | S | **11ᵉ**	–
Villa Spicy | S | **8ᵉ**	13
20 de Bellechasse | S | **7ᵉ**	19
Wepler | S | **18ᵉ**	14
Zébra Square | S, T | **16ᵉ**	10
Zéphyr | T | **20ᵉ**	–
Zo | S | **8ᵉ**	–

PARKING

(V=valet, *=validated)

Name	Rating
A et M | V | **16ᵉ**	21
Agapé | V | **17ᵉ**	–
⚂ Alain Ducasse | V | **8ᵉ**	28
Al Dar | V | **5ᵉ**	21
Al Diwan | V | **8ᵉ**	21
⚂ Ambassadeurs | V | **8ᵉ**	28
⚂ Ambroisie | V | **4ᵉ**	28
Antoine | V | **16ᵉ**	–
⚂ Apicius | V | **8ᵉ**	26
NEW Arc | V | **8ᵉ**	–
Arome | V | **8ᵉ**	–
Asian | V | **8ᵉ**	16
Astor | V | **8ᵉ**	16
Aub. Bressane | V | **7ᵉ**	20
Avenue | V | **8ᵉ**	18
Bar à Huîtres | V | **17ᵉ**	17
Barlotti | V | **1ᵉʳ**	15
Barrio Latino | V | **12ᵉ**	12
Bar Vendôme | V | **1ᵉʳ**	23
Bastide Odéon | V | **6ᵉ**	22
Bath's | V | **17ᵉ**	20
Benkay | V | **15ᵉ**	24
Berkeley | V | **8ᵉ**	14
BIOArt | V | **13ᵉ**	–
Bistro 121 | V | **15ᵉ**	–
Bistrot d'à Côté | V | **multi.**	21
Bistrot de Marius | V | **8ᵉ**	21
Bistrot de Paris | V | **7ᵉ**	16
Bistrot Niel | V | **17ᵉ**	–
Blue Elephant* | **11ᵉ**	20
Bocconi | V | **8ᵉ**	20
Boeuf Couronné | V | **19ᵉ**	16
Boeuf sur le Toit | V | **8ᵉ**	18
Bon | V | **16ᵉ**	–
⚂ Bouquinistes | V | **6ᵉ**	23
Brass. Flo | V | **10ᵉ**	18

Restaurant			Score
Brass. Julien	V	10e	19
Brass. La Lorraine	V	8e	17
Z Bristol	V	8e	27
Z Buddha Bar	V	8e	16
Café de l'Esplanade	V	7e	16
Café du Commerce	V	15e	16
Café Faubourg	V	8e	22
Café la Jatte	V	Neuilly	14
Café Lenôtre	V	8e	18
Café M	V	8e	19
Café Terminus	V	8e	–
Cap Seguin	V	Boulogne	–
Z Carré des Feuillants	V	1er	26
Caves Pétrissans	V	17e	19
Caviar Kaspia	V	8e	25
Céladon	V	2e	21
Chalet des Iles	V	16e	14
Chamarré Mont.	V	18e	–
Chen Soleil d'Est	V	15e	–
Chez Françoise	V	7e	17
Chez Fred	V	17e	–
Chez Georges-Maillot	V	17e	18
Chez Jenny	V	3e	19
Chez Les Anges	V	7e	23
Chez Livio	V	Neuilly	13
Chez Vong	V	1er	21
Chiberta	V	8e	22
Closerie des Lilas	V	6e	18
Clou	V	17e	19
Clovis	V	8e	–
Comte de Gascogne	V	Boulogne	–
Congrès Maillot	V	17e	18
Copenhague	V	8e	18
Costes	V	1er	18
Cou de la Girafe	V	8e	15
Z Cristal Room	V	16e	17
Dalloyau	V	8e	23
NEW Derrière	V	3e	–
Dessirier	V	17e	20
Diep	V	8e	21
Divellec	V	7e	24
Z 1728	V	8e	19
Drouant	V	2e	22
Duc	V	14e	23
El Mansour	V	8e	17
Elysées	V	8e	23
Escargot Montorgueil	V	1er	21
Z Espadon	V	1er	26
Etc.	V	16e	–
Findi	V	8e	16
First	V	1er	18
Flandrin	V	16e	15
Flora Danica	V	8e	19
Fontaine Gaillon	V	2e	22
Fouquet's	V	8e	18
Gare	V	16e	14
Garnier	V	8e	22
Z Georges	V	4e	18
Z Gérard Besson	V	1er	25
Gordon Ramsay	V	Versailles	–
Goumard	V	1er	24
Grand Colbert	V	2e	19
Grande Armée	V	16e	15
Z Grande Cascade	V	16e	25
Z Grand Véfour	V	1er	28
Grand Venise	V	15e	25
Z Guy Savoy	V	17e	28
Z Hélène Darroze	V	6e	25
Huîtrier	V	17e	20
Ile	V	Issy-les-Moul.	18
Z Jacques Cagna	V	6e	26
Jardin des Cygnes	V	8e	22
Jarrasse	V	Neuilly	–
Kinugawa/Hanawa	V	8e	23
Kong	V	1er	14
Lao Lane Xang	V	13e	–
Z Lapérouse	V	6e	21
L'Assaggio	V	1er	23
Z Lasserre	V	8e	27
Z Laurent	V	8e	24
Lei	V	7e	21
Liza	V	2e	24
Lup	V	6e	–
Z Lyonnais	V	2e	21
Maison Blanche	V	8e	20
Maison du Caviar	V	8e	22
Maison Prunier	V	16e	21
Mama Shelter	V	20e	–
Marée	V	8e	23
Marée Denfert/Passy	V	multi.	–
Marius	V	16e	18
Marius et Janette	V	8e	25
Market	V	8e	22
Marty	V	5e	16
Mathusalem	V	16e	–
Maxan	V	8e	–
Maxim's	V	8e	18
Meating	V	17e	17
Méditerranée	V	6e	21
Z Meurice	V	1er	27
Z Michel Rostang	V	17e	27

Montalembert | V | 7e	19	
Mori Venice | V | 2e	17	
Moulin à Vent | V | 5e	19	
Murano | V | 3e	16	
Murat | V | 16e	13	
Musichall | V | 8e	15	
Nabulione | V | 7e	-	
Obé | V | 8e	23	
Oth Sombath | V | 8e	-	
Ozu | V | 16e	23	
Paris | V | 6e	20	
Pasco* | 7e	22	
☑ Passiflore | V | 16e	26	
Paul Chêne | V | 16e	20	
☑ Pavillon Ledoyen | V | 8e	26	
Pavillon Montsouris | V | 14e	17	
Pershing | V | 8e	17	
Petit Pergolèse | V | 16e	23	
Petit Poucet | V | Levallois	-	
Pétrus | V | 17e	21	
☑ Pierre Gagnaire | V | 8e	28	
Pinxo | V | 1er	21	
☑ Pré Catelan | V | 16e	27	
Pur'Grill | V | 2e	19	
Quai Ouest | V | St-Cloud	13	
Quai-Quai | V | 1er	-	
Quinzième | V | 15e	-	
☑ Relais d'Auteuil | V | 16e	27	
Relais Plaza | V | 8e	23	
Réminet | V | 5e	-	
River Café | V | Issy-les-Moul.	14	
Romantica | V | Clichy	23	
Rôtiss. d'en Face | V | 6e	21	
Salon d'Hélène | V | 6e	19	
Saut du Loup | V | 1er	14	
Sébillon | V | Neuilly	15	
16 Haussmann | V | 9e	18	
☑ Senderens | V | 8e	26	
Sensing | V | 6e	24	
6 New York | V | 16e	17	
Sormani | V | 17e	23	
Spoon Paris | V | 8e	22	
Stella | V | 16e	20	
Sud | V | 17e	16	
Table d'Hédiard | V | 8e	22	
Table du Baltimore | V | 16e	-	
Table du Lancaster | V | 8e	23	
☑ Table/Joël Robuchon | V | 16e	26	
☑ Taillevent | V | 8e	28	
Tang | V | 16e	17	
Terrasse Mirabeau | V | 16e	-	

Thiou/Petit Thiou | V | 7e	21	
NEW Tico | V | 8e	-	
Timgad | V | 17e	20	
Toi | V | 8e	-	
Tong Yen | V | 8e	15	
☑ Tour d'Argent | V | 5e	25	
Truffe Noire | V | Neuilly	-	
Villa Corse | V | 15e	20	
Village d'Ung | V | 8e	-	
Villa Spicy | V | 8e	13	
Vin et Marée | V | multi.	18	
Winch | V | 18e	-	
W Restaurant | V | 8e	-	
Zébra Square | V | 16e	10	

PEOPLE-WATCHING

Absinthe | 1er	20	
☑ Alain Ducasse | 8e	28	
☑ Ami Louis | 3e	25	
Anahï | 3e	19	
Angelo Procopio | 1er	-	
Angle/Faubourg | 8e	24	
☑ Arpège | 7e	26	
Astor | 8e	16	
☑ Astrance | 16e	28	
☑ Atelier Joël Robuchon | 7e	28	
Avenue | 8e	18	
Barlotti | 1er	15	
☑ Benoît | 4e	24	
Berkeley | 8e	14	
NEW Bistro Volnay | 2e	-	
Black Calvados | 8e	-	
☑ Brass. Balzar | 5e	19	
☑ Brass. Lipp | 6e	17	
☑ Bristol | 8e	27	
Café Beaubourg | 4e	16	
☑ Café de Flore | 6e	15	
Café de l'Esplanade | 7e	16	
☑ Café/Deux Magots | 6e	16	
Café Etienne Marcel | 2e	18	
Café Guitry | 9e	-	
☑ 144 Petrossian | 7e	25	
Chateaubriand | 11e	22	
Chez Les Anges | 7e	23	
Chez Omar | 3e	21	
☑ Cinq | 8e	28	
Cinq Mars | 7e	19	
Copenhague | 8e	18	
Costes | 1er	18	
Cul de Poule | 9e	-	
Dali | 1er	-	

NEW Derrière | 3ᵉ	-
Divellec | 7ᵉ	24
Dôme | 14ᵉ	22
Drouant | 2ᵉ	22
Duc | 14ᵉ	23
Eclaireur | 8ᵉ	-
Elysées | 8ᵉ	23
Ƶ Epi Dupin | 6ᵉ	24
Ƶ Espadon | 1ᵉʳ	26
Etc. | 16ᵉ	-
Ferme St-Simon | 7ᵉ	23
Flandrin | 16ᵉ	15
Fouquet's | 8ᵉ	18
Gare | 16ᵉ	14
Gauloise | 15ᵉ	15
Ƶ Georges | 4ᵉ	18
Grande Armée | 16ᵉ	15
Ƶ Grand Véfour | 1ᵉʳ	28
Ƶ Guy Savoy | 17ᵉ	28
Ƶ Hélène Darroze | 6ᵉ	25
Itinéraires | 5ᵉ	-
Jarrasse | Neuilly	-
Joséphine/Dumonet | 6ᵉ	23
Kong | 1ᵉʳ	14
L'Assaggio | 1ᵉʳ	23
Ƶ Lasserre | 8ᵉ	27
Lup | 6ᵉ	-
Maison/Amér. Latine | 7ᵉ	18
Maison Blanche | 8ᵉ	20
Maison Prunier | 16ᵉ	21
Mama Shelter | 20ᵉ	-
Market | 8ᵉ	22
Méditerranée | 6ᵉ	21
Murano | 3ᵉ	16
Musichall | 8ᵉ	15
Nabulione | 7ᵉ	-
Ƶ Ombres | 7ᵉ	18
Oth Sombath | 8ᵉ	-
Ƶ Pavillon Ledoyen | 8ᵉ	26
Pétrelle | 9ᵉ	-
Ƶ Pierre Gagnaire | 8ᵉ	28
Poisson Rouge | 10ᵉ	-
Ƶ Pré Catelan | 16ᵉ	27
Publicis Drugstore | 8ᵉ	11
Quinzième | 15ᵉ	-
NEW Reginette | 8ᵉ	-
Relais Plaza | 8ᵉ	23
Restaurant | 6ᵉ	26
Salon d'Hélène | 6ᵉ	19
Salon du Panthéon | 5ᵉ	-
Saut du Loup | 1ᵉʳ	14

Ƶ Senderens | 8ᵉ	26
Sensing | 6ᵉ	24
6 New York | 16ᵉ	17
NEW Société | 6ᵉ	-
Sormani | 17ᵉ	23
Spoon Paris | 8ᵉ	22
Square Trousseau | 12ᵉ	19
Stresa | 8ᵉ	22
Table du Lancaster | 8ᵉ	23
Ƶ Table/Joël Robuchon | 16ᵉ	26
Ƶ Taillevent | 8ᵉ	28
Tan Dinh | 7ᵉ	23
Terrasse Mirabeau | 16ᵉ	-
Thiou/Petit Thiou | 7ᵉ	21
Tong Yen | 8ᵉ	15
Ƶ Tour d'Argent | 5ᵉ	25
Voltaire | 7ᵉ	24

POWER SCENES

Agapé | 17ᵉ	-
Ƶ Alain Ducasse | 8ᵉ	28
Ƶ Ambassadeurs | 8ᵉ	28
Ƶ Ambroisie | 4ᵉ	28
Ƶ Apicius | 8ᵉ	26
Ƶ Arpège | 7ᵉ	26
Assiette | 14ᵉ	-
Ƶ Atelier Joël Robuchon | 7ᵉ	28
Aub. Bressane | 7ᵉ	20
Bar des Théâtres | 8ᵉ	15
Bastide Odéon | 6ᵉ	22
Ƶ Benoît | 4ᵉ	24
Bistrot de Marius | 8ᵉ	21
Bistrot de Paris | 7ᵉ	16
Bistrot d'Henri | 6ᵉ	20
Bistrot Niel | 17ᵉ	-
Bon Saint Pourçain | 6ᵉ	18
Ƶ Brass. Balzar | 5ᵉ	19
Ƶ Brass. Lipp | 6ᵉ	17
Ƶ Bristol | 8ᵉ	27
Ƶ Café de Flore | 6ᵉ	15
Café Faubourg | 8ᵉ	22
Cagouille | 14ᵉ	25
Ƶ Carré des Feuillants | 1ᵉʳ	26
Caves Pétrissans | 17ᵉ	19
Caviar Kaspia | 8ᵉ	25
Cazaudehore | St-Germain-Laye	22
Céladon | 2ᵉ	21
Chen Soleil d'Est | 15ᵉ	-
Cherche Midi | 6ᵉ	19
Chez Les Anges | 7ᵉ	23
Chiberta | 8ᵉ	22

QUICK BITES

SPECIAL FEATURES

Bistrot à Vins Mélac | 11e	14
NEW Bob's Kitchen | 3e	-
Bons Crus | 1er	-
Boulangerie Eric Kayser | 8e	16
Brass. Printemps | 9e	11
Breakfast/America | **multi.**	15
Breizh Café | 3e	-
Z Buddha Bar | 8e	16
Buffalo Grill | **multi.**	10
Café Beaubourg | 4e	16
Z Café de Flore | 6e	15
Z Café/Deux Magots | 6e	16
Café du Commerce | 15e	16
Z Café Marly | 1er	16
Cave de l'Os à Moëlle | 15e	22
Chez Marianne | 4e	18
Chez Papa | **multi.**	17
Cloche des Halles | 1er	-
Clown Bar | 11e	17
Cocottes | 7e	21
Coffee Parisien | **multi.**	16
Congrès Maillot | 17e	18
Cosi | 6e	19
Crémerie | 6e	-
Crêperie de Josselin | 14e	22
Cul de Poule | 9e	-
Dalloyau | **multi.**	23
Dame Tartine | 4e	14
Da Rosa | 6e	19
Duc de Richelieu | 12e	-
Ebouillanté | 4e	-
Ecluse | **multi.**	16
Emporio Armani | 6e	19
Escale du Liban | 4e	-
Ferdi | 1er	-
Ferme | 1er	-
Fines Gueules | 1er	-
Fous d'en Face | 4e	-
Fumoir | 1er	17
Garnier | 8e	22
Indiana Café | **multi.**	7
Je Thé . . . Me | 15e	-
Joe Allen | 1er	13
Juvéniles | 1er	16
Laiterie/Clotilde | 7e	-
Léon/Bruxelles | **multi.**	16
Lina's | **multi.**	16
Loir dans/Théière | 4e	16
Lô Sushi | 8e	15
Ma Bourgogne | 4e	18
Maison du Caviar | 8e	22
Mama Shelter | 20e	-
Mariage Frères | **multi.**	21
Mauzac | 5e	-
Mesturet | 2e	-
Mirama | 5e	20
Murat | 16e	13
Nemrod | 6e	16
Noura | **multi.**	19
Papilles | 5e	23
Paradis du Fruit | 5e	14
Pates Vivantes | 9e	-
Petite Sirène/Copen. | 9e	-
Pinxo | 1er	21
Pizza Chic | 6e	-
Press Café | 2e	-
Publicis Drugstore | 8e	11
Quedubon | 19e	-
Ragueneau | 1er	-
Rest. du Musée d'Orsay | 7e	17
Rice and Fish | 2e	-
Rose Bakery | 9e	17
Rubis | 1er	15
Salon du Panthéon | 5e	-
Sauvignon | 7e	14
Scoop | 1er	17
Shu | 6e	-
Table d'Hédiard | 8e	22
Tav. Henri IV | 1er	16
Tsukizi | 6e	-
Viaduc Café | 12e	-
Z Vin sur Vin | 7e	26
Wok Cooking | 11e	-

QUIET CONVERSATION

Agassin | 7e	-
Aiguière | 11e	-
Aimant du Sud | 13e	-
Alfred | 1er	-
Alivi | 4e	16
Allobroges | 20e	22
Ambassade/Auv. | 3e	20
Ampère | 17e	-
Amuse Bouche | 14e	17
A Priori Thé | 2e	16
Assiette | 14e	-
Z Astrance | 16e	28
Atelier Berger | 1er	21
Z Atelier Joël Robuchon | 7e	28
Aub. du Clou | 9e	16
Aub. Pyrénées | 11e	20

Bamboche	7ᵉ	19	Dali	1ᵉʳ	-
Basilic	7ᵉ	15	Dalva	2ᵉ	-
Bellini	16ᵉ	24	Da Rosa	6ᵉ	19
🇿 Benoît	4ᵉ	24	Daru	8ᵉ	-
Bigarrade	17ᵉ	-	Délices d'Aphrodite	5ᵉ	18
Bistro d'Hubert	15ᵉ	22	Dessirier	17ᵉ	20
Bistro Poulbot	18ᵉ	-	Diapason	18ᵉ	-
Bistrot d'à Côté	multi.	21	Dix Vins	15ᵉ	-
Bistrot d'Henri	6ᵉ	20	Djakarta	1ᵉʳ	20
Bistrot du Peintre	11ᵉ	18	Ebouillanté	4ᵉ	-
NEW Bistro Volnay	2ᵉ	-	Ecaille de Fontaine	2ᵉ	-
Bizan	2ᵉ	-	El Mansour	8ᵉ	17
Boeuf sur le Toit	8ᵉ	18	Entoto	13ᵉ	-
Bon Saint Pourçain	6ᵉ	18	Entracte	18ᵉ	-
Bouillon Racine	6ᵉ	16	Epi d'Or	1ᵉʳ	16
Brass. Flo	10ᵉ	18	Epigramme	6ᵉ	-
Brass. Julien	10ᵉ	19	Erawan	15ᵉ	17
🇿 Brass. Lipp	6ᵉ	17	Escargot Montorgueil	1ᵉʳ	21
Brass. Mollard	8ᵉ	19	Fines Gueules	1ᵉʳ	-
Buisson Ardent	5ᵉ	19	Fins Gourmets	7ᵉ	19
Ca d'Oro	1ᵉʳ	18	Firmin le Barbier	7ᵉ	-
Café de l'Industrie	11ᵉ	12	Flora Danica	8ᵉ	19
🇿 Café/Deux Magots	6ᵉ	16	Flore en l'Ile	4ᵉ	18
Café du Passage	11ᵉ	-	🇿 Fontaine de Mars	7ᵉ	21
Café Faubourg	8ᵉ	22	Fontanarosa	15ᵉ	-
Café Lenôtre	8ᵉ	18	NEW Fourchette	17ᵉ	-
Café M	8ᵉ	19	Gallopin	2ᵉ	16
🇿 Café Marly	1ᵉʳ	16	Garnier	8ᵉ	22
Caméléon	6ᵉ	20	Gaya	7ᵉ	23
Camélia	Bougival	20	Georgette	9ᵉ	22
Cartes Postales	1ᵉʳ	24	🇿 Gérard Besson	1ᵉʳ	25
Cave Gourmande	19ᵉ	25	Gli Angeli	3ᵉ	18
Caviar Kaspia	8ᵉ	25	Goumard	1ᵉʳ	24
🇿 144 Petrossian	7ᵉ	25	Gourmand	1ᵉʳ	20
Chardenoux	11ᵉ	19	Graindorge	17ᵉ	22
Charpentiers	6ᵉ	18	Guirlande de Julie	3ᵉ	15
Chez Géraud	16ᵉ	20	Huîtrier	17ᵉ	20
Chez Les Anges	7ᵉ	23	Isami	4ᵉ	25
Chez Maître Paul	6ᵉ	21	Itineraires	5ᵉ	-
Chez René	5ᵉ	21	Jean	9ᵉ	19
Chiberta	8ᵉ	22	Joséphine/Dumonet	6ᵉ	23
Cigale Récamier	7ᵉ	21	🇿 Jules Verne	7ᵉ	22
Clos des Gourmets	7ᵉ	25	Karl et Erich	17ᵉ	-
Closerie des Lilas	6ᵉ	18	🇿 Ladurée	multi.	23
Copenhague	8ᵉ	18	Laiterie/Clotilde	7ᵉ	-
Costes	1ᵉʳ	18	🇿 Lapérouse	6ᵉ	21
Coupe-Chou	5ᵉ	23	L'Assaggio	1ᵉʳ	23
🇿 Coupole	14ᵉ	19	Legrand Filles	2ᵉ	-
Crus de Bourgogne	2ᵉ	17	Macéo	1ᵉʳ	23
Cuisine	7ᵉ	25	Magnolias	Perreux	25
Cuizine	11ᵉ	-	Maison Blanche	8ᵉ	20

Mansouria | 11e	
Marée | 8e	
Mariage Frères | **multi.**	
Marlotte | 6e	
Marty | 5e	
Maupertu | 7e	
Maxan | 8e	
Meating | 17e	
Méditerranée | 6e	
Montalembert | 7e	
Moulin/Galette | 18e	
Murano | 3e	
Muscade | 1er	
Nabulione | 7e	
No Stress Café | 9e	
Obé | 8e	
Oto-Oto | 6e	
Oulette | 12e	
Pamphlet | 3e	
Pasco | 7e	
Pelouse | 19e	
Pères et Filles | 6e	
Petit Colombier | 17e	
Petite Chaise | 7e	
Petite Sirène/Copen. | 9e	
Petit Lutétia | 6e	
Petit Marguery | 13e	
Petit Prince Paris | 5e	
Petit Rétro | 16e	
Pierre au Palais Royal | 1er	
Ƶ Pierre Gagnaire | 8e	
Polidor | 6e	
Potager du Roy | **Versailles**	
P'tit Troquet | 7e	
Quai-Quai | 1er	
Repaire de Cartouche | 11e	
Restaurant | 6e	
Rest. du Marché | 15e	
Rest. du Palais Royal | 1er	
Roi du Pot-au-Feu | 9e	
Rose de France | 1er	
Salon du Panthéon | 5e	
Sarladais | 8e	
Saudade | 1er	
Saut du Loup | 1er	
Sébillon | **Neuilly**	
16 Haussmann | 9e	
Sot l'y Laisse | 11e	
Ƶ Soufflé | 1er	
Ƶ Stella Maris | 8e	
Stresa | 8e	

Column values (left):
22, 23, 21, 16, 16, 21, –, 17, 21, 19, 15, 16, –, –, –, 23, –, 19, 23, 22, –, 16, 18, 19, –, 19, 21, –, 16, 17, 28, 17, 19, 22, –, 16, 26, –, 19, –, –, –, –, –, 14, 15, 18, –, 22, 26, 22

Table du Lancaster | 8e	23
Tan Dinh | 7e	23
Tante Louise | 8e	22
Tête Ailleurs | 4e	–
Thiou/Petit Thiou | 7e	21
Ƶ Trou Gascon | 12e	26
Tsé-Yang | 16e	18
Viaduc Café | 12e	–
NEW Vin Chai Moi | 1er	–
Vin dans les Voiles | 16e	–
Ƶ Vin sur Vin | 7e	26
Winch | 18e	–

ROMANTIC PLACES

Ƶ Alain Ducasse | 8e	28
Ƶ Allard | 6e	21
Ƶ Ambassadeurs | 8e	28
Ƶ Ambroisie | 4e	28
Ƶ Arpège | 7e	26
Astor | 8e	16
Ƶ Astrance | 16e	28
Bamboche | 7e	19
Bistro Poulbot | 18e	–
Blue Elephant | 11e	20
Boudoir | 8e	–
Bouillon Racine | 6e	16
Ƶ Bouquinistes | 6e	23
Brass. Flo | 10e	18
Brass. Julien | 10e	19
Ƶ Bristol | 8e	27
Buisson Ardent | 5e	19
Ƶ Café de Flore | 6e	15
Ƶ Café/Deux Magots | 6e	16
Café Lenôtre | 8e	18
Ƶ Café Marly | 1er	16
Casa Olympe | 9e	24
Caviar Kaspia | 8e	25
Ƶ 144 Petrossian | 7e	25
Chalet des Iles | 16e	14
Chamarré Mont. | 18e	–
Chardenoux | 11e	19
Chez Julien | 4e	19
Closerie des Lilas | 6e	18
Copenhague | 8e	18
Costes | 1er	18
Coupe-Chou | 5e	23
Ƶ Coupole | 14e	19
Ƶ Cristal Room | 16e	17
Crus de Bourgogne | 2e	17
Délices d'Aphrodite | 5e	18
Dôme | 14e	22

Menus, photos, voting and more – free at ZAGAT.com

El Mansour | 8ᵉ	17
Elysées | 8ᵉ	23
Epi d'Or | 1ᵉʳ	16
🆉 Espadon | 1ᵉʳ	26
Fakhr el Dine | 16ᵉ	24
First | 1ᵉʳ	18
Flora Danica | 8ᵉ	19
🆉 Fontaine de Mars | 7ᵉ	21
Gavroche | 2ᵉ	17
🆉 Georges | 4ᵉ	18
Gordon Ramsay | **Versailles**	-
🆉 Grande Cascade | 16ᵉ	25
🆉 Grand Véfour | 1ᵉʳ	28
Guilo-Guilo | 18ᵉ	-
Guirlande de Julie | 3ᵉ	15
🆉 Guy Savoy | 17ᵉ	28
🆉 Jacques Cagna | 6ᵉ	26
Jardins de Bagatelle | 16ᵉ	17
Joséphine/Dumonet | 6ᵉ	23
🆉 Jules Verne | 7ᵉ	22
🆉 Ladurée | **multi.**	23
🆉 Lapérouse | 6ᵉ	21
L'Assaggio | 1ᵉʳ	23
🆉 Lasserre | 8ᵉ	27
🆉 Laurent | 8ᵉ	24
Ma Bourgogne | 4ᵉ	18
Macéo | 1ᵉʳ	23
Maison/Amér. Latine | 7ᵉ	18
Maison Blanche | 8ᵉ	20
Mansouria | 11ᵉ	22
Marty | 5ᵉ	16
Maxim's | 8ᵉ	18
Méditerranée | 6ᵉ	21
🆉 Meurice | 1ᵉʳ	27
Moulin/Galette | 18ᵉ	15
Muscade | 1ᵉʳ	-
Nabulione | 7ᵉ	-
🆉 Pavillon Ledoyen | 8ᵉ	26
Pavillon Montsouris | 14ᵉ	17
Petit Prince Paris | 5ᵉ	-
Potager du Roy | **Versailles**	19
🆉 Pré Catelan | 16ᵉ	27
Relais Louis XIII | 6ᵉ	25
Restaurant | 6ᵉ	26
Rest. Paul | 1ᵉʳ	20
Romantica | **Clichy**	23
Rughetta | 18ᵉ	-
Sormani | 17ᵉ	23
Square Trousseau | 12ᵉ	19
🆉 Stella Maris | 8ᵉ	26
Tan Dinh | 7ᵉ	23

Tête Ailleurs | 4ᵉ	-
Timgad | 17ᵉ	20
🆉 Tour d'Argent | 5ᵉ	25
🆉 Train Bleu | 12ᵉ	19
🆉 Trou Gascon | 12ᵉ	26
Versance | 2ᵉ	-

SINGLES SCENES

Absinthe | 1ᵉʳ	20
A et M | 16ᵉ	21
Alsace | 8ᵉ	18
Amici Miei | 11ᵉ	19
Angle/Faubourg | 8ᵉ	24
Apollo | 14ᵉ	-
Astor | 8ᵉ	16
Aub. du Clou | 9ᵉ	16
Autobus Imperial | 1ᵉʳ	-
BAM | 1ᵉʳ	-
Bar des Théâtres | 8ᵉ	15
Barlotti | 1ᵉʳ	15
Baron Rouge | 12ᵉ	-
Barrio Latino | 12ᵉ	12
Berkeley | 8ᵉ	14
Bistro/Deux Théâtres | 9ᵉ	14
Bistrot à Vins Mélac | 11ᵉ	14
Bistrot d'à Côté | 17ᵉ	21
Black Calavados | 8ᵉ	-
Bon | 16ᵉ	-
🆉 Brass. Balzar | 5ᵉ	19
🆉 Buddha Bar | 8ᵉ	16
Café Beaubourg | 4ᵉ	16
Café Burq | 18ᵉ	-
🆉 Café de Flore | 6ᵉ	15
Café de la Paix | 9ᵉ	19
Café de l'Esplanade | 7ᵉ	16
🆉 Café/Deux Magots | 6ᵉ	16
Café du Passage | 11ᵉ	-
Café Etienne Marcel | 2ᵉ	18
Café la Jatte | **Neuilly**	14
Café Lenôtre | 8ᵉ	18
Café M | 8ᵉ	19
🆉 Café Marly | 1ᵉʳ	16
Café Ruc | 1ᵉʳ	15
Carr's | 1ᵉʳ	-
Cave de l'Os à Moëlle | 15ᵉ	22
Chateaubriand | 11ᵉ	22
Cherche Midi | 6ᵉ	19
Chez Gégène | **Joinville**	-
Cinq Mars | 7ᵉ	19
Closerie des Lilas | 6ᵉ	18
Clown Bar | 11ᵉ	17

Comédiens	9e	-
Costes	1er	18
Curieux Spaghetti	4e	-
Eclaireur	8e	-
Emporio Armani	6e	19
Enoteca	4e	20
Ferdi	1er	-
Floors	18e	-
Fumoir	1er	17
Grille St-Germain	6e	17
Joe Allen	1er	13
Kong	1er	14
Laiterie/Clotilde	7e	-
Loir dans/Théière	4e	16
Lô Sushi	8e	15
Lup	6e	-
Mama Shelter	20e	-
Murano	3e	16
Murat	16e	13
Musichall	8e	15
Pinxo	1er	21
Press Café	2e	-
Restaurant	6e	26
Rose Bakery	3e	17
Rubis	1er	15
Sauvignon	7e	14
Zo	8e	-

SLEEPERS

(Good food, but little known)

Affriolé	7e	22
Aida	7e	23
Allobroges	20e	22
Aub. Nicolas Flamel	3e	23
Auguste	7e	25
Avant Goût	13e	23
Azabu	6e	24
Bellini	16e	24
Benkay	15e	24
Beurre Noisette	15e	23
Bistro d'Hubert	15e	22
Z Bistrot de l'Oulette	4e	26
Boulangerie	20e	23
Bourguignon du Marais	4e	23
Z Braisière	17e	27
Café Faubourg	8e	22
Cagouille	14e	25
Cartes Postales	1er	24
Casa Olympe	9e	24
Cave de l'Os à Moëlle	15e	22
Cave Gourmande	19e	25

Cazaudehore	St-Germain-Laye	22
Chez Catherine	8e	23
Chez Les Anges	7e	23
Coin/Gourmets	multi.	22
Crêperie de Josselin	14e	22
Cuisine	7e	25
Divellec	7e	24
Dôme du Marais	4e	22
Duc	14e	23
Elysées	8e	23
Fakhr el Dine	16e	24
Fontaine Gaillon	2e	22
Frégate	12e	24
Garnier	8e	22
Georgette	9e	22
Z Gérard Besson	1er	25
Graindorge	17e	22
Z Grande Cascade	16e	25
Grand Venise	15e	25
Huîtrerie Régis	6e	22
Isami	4e	25
Issé	1er	23
Jardin des Cygnes	8e	22
Jean-Paul Hévin	1er	24
Kinugawa/Hanawa	multi.	23
L'Assaggio	1er	23
Liza	2e	24
Macéo	1er	23
Magnolias	Perreux	25
Maison Courtine	14e	24
Maison du Caviar	8e	22
Mansouria	11e	22
Marée	8e	23
Obé	8e	23
Z Os à Moëlle	15e	25
Ostéria	4e	22
Ourcine	13e	24
Ozu	16e	23
Pamphlet	3e	23
Papilles	5e	23
Pasco	7e	22
Z Passiflore	16e	26
Z Pavillon Ledoyen	8e	26
Petit Marché	3e	22
Petit Pergolèse	16e	23
Poule au Pot	1er	23
Z Relais d'Auteuil	16e	27
Relais Plaza	8e	23
Restaurant	6e	26
Romantica	Clichy	23

Sensing | 6ᵉ	24
Sormani | 17ᵉ	23
☑ Stella Maris | 8ᵉ	26
Stresa | 8ᵉ	22
Table d'Hédiard | 8ᵉ	22
Table du Lancaster | 8ᵉ	23
Tante Louise | 8ᵉ	22
Tante Marguerite | 7ᵉ	22
Tastevin | **Maisons-Laff.**	24
Temps au Temps | 11ᵉ	25
Timbre | 6ᵉ	24
Troquet | 15ᵉ	24
☑ Trou Gascon | 12ᵉ	26
Truffière | 5ᵉ	23
☑ Villaret | 11ᵉ	26
☑ Vin sur Vin | 7ᵉ	26
Yugaraj | 6ᵉ	23

TASTING MENUS

Agapé | 17ᵉ	-
Agapes | 5ᵉ	-
Aida | 7ᵉ	23
Aiguière | 11ᵉ	-
☑ Alain Ducasse | 8ᵉ	28
Allobroges | 20ᵉ	22
Al Mounia | 16ᵉ	17
Angle/Faubourg | 8ᵉ	24
☑ Apicius | 8ᵉ	26
Arome | 8ᵉ	-
☑ Arpège | 7ᵉ	26
Asian | 8ᵉ	16
Astor | 8ᵉ	16
☑ Astrance | 16ᵉ	28
Atelier Berger | 1ᵉʳ	21
Aub. Nicolas Flamel | 3ᵉ	23
Avant Goût | 13ᵉ	23
Baan-Boran | 1ᵉʳ	20
Bamboche | 7ᵉ	19
Bar à Huîtres | 3ᵉ	17
Bigarrade | 17ᵉ	-
Bistrot d'à Côté | 17ᵉ	21
Bistrot du Sommelier | 8ᵉ	18
Bizan | 2ᵉ	-
Blue Elephant | 11ᵉ	20
☑ Bristol | 8ᵉ	27
☑ Buddha Bar | 8ᵉ	16
Café de la Paix | 9ᵉ	19
Camélia | **Bougival**	20
☑ Carré des Feuillants | 1ᵉʳ	26
Cartes Postales | 1ᵉʳ	24
Casa Tina | 16ᵉ	-

Céladon | 2ᵉ	21
☑ 144 Petrossian | 7ᵉ	25
Chamarré Mont. | 18ᵉ	-
NEW Chateau Poivre | 14ᵉ	-
Chen Soleil d'Est | 15ᵉ	-
Chez Catherine | 8ᵉ	23
Chez Cécile | 8ᵉ	-
Chez L'Ami Jean | 7ᵉ	24
Chez Les Anges | 7ᵉ	23
Chez Marianne | 4ᵉ	18
Chez Michel | 10ᵉ	24
Chez Vincent | 19ᵉ	-
Chiberta | 8ᵉ	22
Chieng Mai | 5ᵉ	16
☑ Cinq | 8ᵉ	28
Clovis | 8ᵉ	-
Coco de Mer | 5ᵉ	-
Comte de Gascogne | **Boulogne**	-
Copenhague | 8ᵉ	18
☑ Cristal Room | 16ᵉ	17
Cuisine | 7ᵉ	25
D'Chez Eux | 7ᵉ	25
Des Gars | 3ᵉ	-
Diapason | 18ᵉ	-
☑ Dominique Bouchet | 8ᵉ	27
Elysées | 8ᵉ	23
☑ Espadon | 1ᵉʳ	26
Ferrandaise | 6ᵉ	21
Fogón | 6ᵉ	21
Fouquet's | 8ᵉ	18
Gaigne | 4ᵉ	-
Gazzetta | 12ᵉ	-
☑ Gérard Besson | 1ᵉʳ	25
Gordon Ramsay | **Versailles**	-
Graindorge | 17ᵉ	22
Grand Colbert | 2ᵉ	19
☑ Grande Cascade | 16ᵉ	25
☑ Grand Véfour | 1ᵉʳ	28
☑ Guy Savoy | 17ᵉ	28
☑ Hélène Darroze | 6ᵉ	25
☑ Hiramatsu | 16ᵉ	26
Il Vino | 7ᵉ	-
Inagiku | 5ᵉ	18
Issé | 1ᵉʳ	23
☑ Jacques Cagna | 6ᵉ	26
Jadis | 15ᵉ	-
Jean | 9ᵉ	19
Kinugawa/Hanawa | **multi.**	23
☑ Lapérouse | 6ᵉ	21
☑ Lasserre | 8ᵉ	27
☑ Laurent | 8ᵉ	24

Magnolias | **Perreux**	25
Maharajah | 5^e	17
Mansouria | 11^e	22
Marée | 8^e	23
Mavrommatis | 5^e	19
Maxan | 8^e	-
NEW MBC | 17^e	-
Z Meurice | 1er	27
Z Michel Rostang | 17^e	27
Mont Liban | 17^e	-
Montparnasse 25 | 14^e	16
Moulin/Galette | 18^e	15
Noura | 16^e	19
Olivades | 7^e	17
Orient-Extrême | 6^e	18
Z Os à Moëlle | 15^e	25
Oth Sombath | 8^e	-
Ozu | 16^e	23
Paris | 6^e	20
NEW Passage 53 | 2^e	-
Passy Mandarin | 16^e	20
Paul Chêne | 16^e	20
Z Pavillon Ledoyen | 8^e	26
Petit Colombier | 17^e	18
Petit Marguery | 13^e	21
Z Pierre Gagnaire | 8^e	28
Potager du Roy | **Versailles**	19
Z Pré Catelan | 16^e	27
Pur'Grill | 2^e	19
Quinzième | 15^e	-
Z Relais d'Auteuil | 16^e	27
Relais Louis XIII | 6^e	25
Réminet | 5^e	-
Restaurant | 6^e	26
Romantica | **Clichy**	23
Salon d'Hélène | 6^e	19
Saveurs de Flora | 8^e	21
Sawadee | 15^e	-
16 Haussmann | 9^e	18
Sensing | 6^e	24
Sobane | 9^e	-
Z Stella Maris | 8^e	26
Stéphane Gaborieau | 16^e	-
Table d'Anvers | 9^e	17
Table d'Eugène | 18^e	-
Table du Baltimore | 16^e	-
Table du Lancaster | 8^e	23
Z Table/Joël Robuchon | 16^e	26
Z Taillevent | 8^e	28
Tang | 16^e	17
Terrasse Mirabeau | 16^e	-

Z Train Bleu | 12^e	19
Troquet | 15^e	24
Truffe Noire | **Neuilly**	-
Truffière | 5^e	23
Z Villaret | 11^e	26
NEW Vin Chai Moi | 1er	-
Z Violon d'Ingres | 7^e	25
Wally Le Saharien | 9^e	15
W Restaurant | 8^e	-
NEW Yam'Tcha | 1er	-

TEEN APPEAL

Absinthe | 1er	20
Alcazar | 6^e	19
Al Dar | **multi.**	21
Anahï | 3^e	19
Anahuacalli | 5^e	21
Z Angelina | 1er	20
Annapurna | 8^e	18
Apollo | 14^e	-
Z As du Fallafel | 4^e	24
Asian | 8^e	16
Aub. du Clou | 9^e	16
Autobus Imperial | 1er	-
Avant Goût | 13^e	23
Avenue | 8^e	18
BAM | 1er	-
Bar des Théâtres | 8^e	15
Baron Rouge | 12^e	-
Barrio Latino | 12^e	12
Bartolo | 6^e	17
Bascou | 3^e	20
Berkeley | 8^e	14
BIOArt | 13^e	-
Bistrot à Vins Mélac | 11^e	14
Bistrot d'André | 15^e	-
Z Bistrot de l'Oulette | 4^e	26
Bistrot des Dames | 17^e	14
Bistrot du Peintre | 11^e	18
Blue Elephant | 11^e	20
Bon | 16^e	-
Boulangerie | 20^e	23
Breakfast/America | **multi.**	15
Breizh Café | 3^e	-
Z Buddha Bar | 8^e	16
Buffalo Grill | **multi.**	10
Café Beaubourg | 4^e	16
Café Burq | 18^e	-
Café Charbon | 11^e	15
Café de la Musique | 19^e	15
Café de l'Esplanade | 7^e	16

Menus, photos, voting and more – free at ZAGAT.com

Café de l'Industrie | 11e	12
Café de Mars | 7e	17
Café du Commerce | 15e	16
Café du Passage | 11e	-
Café la Jatte | **Neuilly**	14
Café Lenôtre | 8e	18
Z Café Marly | 1er	16
Café Rouge | 3e	-
Café Ruc | 1er	15
Cailloux | 13e	-
Cantine/Troquet | 14e	-
Carr's | 1er	-
Chalet des Iles | 16e	14
Chartier | 9e	13
Chez Clément | **multi.**	15
Chez L'Ami Jean | 7e	24
Chez Marianne | 4e	18
Chez Omar | 3e	21
Chez Papa | **multi.**	17
Chez Paul | 11e	21
Chez Prune | 10e	18
Chez Vong | 1er	21
Clown Bar | 11e	17
Coco & Co. | 6e	-
Coco de Mer | 5e	-
Cocottes | 7e	21
Coffee Parisien | **multi.**	16
Coin/Gourmets | 5e	22
Comptoir | 1er	21
Cosi | 6e	19
Costes | 1er	18
Coude Fou | 4e	19
Z Coupole | 14e	19
Crêperie de Josselin | 14e	22
Curieux Spaghetti | 4e	-
Dame Tartine | 4e	14
Délices d'Aphrodite | 5e	18
Dix Vins | 15e	-
Durand Dupont | **Neuilly**	-
Ebouillanté | 4e	-
Emporio Armani | 6e	19
Enoteca | 4e	20
Entoto | 13e	-
Entracte | 18e	-
Erawan | 15e	17
Ferme | 1er	-
Z Fish La Boiss. | 6e	22
Floors | 18e	-
Fogón | 6e	21
Z Fontaine de Mars | 7e	21
Fontaines | 5e	17
Fous d'en Face | 4e	-
Fumoir | 1er	17
Z Georges | 4e	18
Gli Angeli | 3e	18
Grande Armée | 16e	15
Grille St-Germain | 6e	17
Hangar | 3e	18
Hippopotamus | **multi.**	11
Ile | **Issy-les-Moul.**	18
Indiana Café | **multi.**	7
Isami | 4e	25
Joe Allen | 1er	13
Kong | 1er	14
Lao Siam | 19e	15
Léon/Bruxelles | **multi.**	16
Lina's | **multi.**	16
Loir dans/Théière | 4e	16
Lô Sushi | 8e	15
Lup | 6e	-
Ma Bourgogne | 4e	18
Mama Shelter | 20e	-
Mauzac | 5e	-
Mavrommatis | 5e	19
Mirama | 5e	20
Montagnards | 1er	-
Murat | 16e	13
No Stress Café | 9e	-
Ostéria | 4e	22
Paradis du Fruit | 5e	14
Paradis Thai | 13e	15
Pates Vivantes | 9e	-
Petite Sirène/Copen. | 9e	-
Pied de Cochon | 1er	18
Pizza Chic | 6e	-
Polidor | 6e	17
Press Café | 2e	-
Quai Ouest | **St-Cloud**	13
404 | 3e	22
Réfectoire | 11e	-
Rendez-vous/Chauff. | 18e	-
River Café | **Issy-les-Moul.**	14
Rose Bakery | **multi.**	17
Rubis | 1er	15
Sardegna a Tavola | 12e	21
Sauvignon | 7e	14
16 Haussmann | 9e	18
Sept Quinze | 15e	-
Spoon Paris | 8e	22
Square Trousseau | 12e	19
Tav. de Maître Kanter | 1er	16
Thiou/Petit Thiou | 7e	21

Tricotin | 13e	–
Trumilou | 4e	19
Vagenende | 6e	15
Vaudeville | 2e	18
Viaduc Café | 12e	–
Villa Spicy | 8e	13
Water Bar Colette | 1er	14
Wok Cooking | 11e	–
Yen | 6e	20
Zébra Square | 16e	10
Zéphyr | 20e	–
Zo | 8e	–

THEME RESTAURANTS

Aub. Nicolas Flamel | 3e	23
Bar à Huîtres | multi.	17
Barrio Latino | 12e	12
Bel Canto | multi.	13
Bellota-Bellota | 7e	19
Bistrot d'André | 15e	–
Breakfast/America | multi.	15
Breizh Café | 3e	–
Z Buddha Bar | 8e	16
Café de la Musique | 19e	15
Chez Clément | multi.	15
Coco & Co. | 6e	–
Coco de Mer | 5e	–
Cocottes | 7e	21
Il Vino | 7e	–
Léon/Bruxelles | multi.	16
Lina's | multi.	16
Monsieur Lapin | 14e	18
Montagnards | 1er	–
Nos Ancêtres Gaulois | 4e	13
Paradis du Fruit | 5e	14
Pomze | 8e	18
Rouge St-Honoré | 1er	13
Wok Cooking | 11e	–

TRANSPORTING EXPERIENCES

Anahï | 3e	19
Annapurna | 8e	18
Asian | 8e	16
Atlas | 5e	20
Benkay | 15e	24
Bigarrade | 17e	–
Blue Elephant | 11e	20
Breizh Café | 3e	–
Z Buddha Bar | 8e	16
Café la Jatte | Neuilly	14

Cerisaie | 14e	21
Chalet des Iles | 16e	14
Chen Soleil d'Est | 15e	–
Chez Gégène | Joinville	–
Chez Vong | 1er	21
Coco de Mer | 5e	–
Délices d'Aphrodite | 5e	18
Djakarta | 1er	20
Enoteca | 4e	20
Entoto | 13e	–
Erawan | 15e	17
Etoile Marocaine | 8e	–
Fakhr el Dine | 16e	24
Fogón | 6e	21
Guilo-Guilo | 18e	–
Il Vino | 7e	–
Isami | 4e	25
Jardins de Bagatelle | 16e	17
Mansouria | 11e	22
Mavrommatis | 5e	19
Monsieur Lapin | 14e	18
Saudade | 1er	–
Z Soufflé | 1er	22
Z Stella Maris | 8e	26
Tan Dinh | 7e	23
Timgad | 17e	20
Tricotin | 13e	–
Tsé-Yang | 16e	18
Wally Le Saharien | 9e	15
Yen | 6e	20

TRENDY

Afaria | 15e	–
Agapé | 17e	–
Aida | 7e	23
Alcazar | 6e	19
Z Ami Louis | 3e	25
Anahï | 3e	19
Andy Wahloo | 3e	14
Angle/Faubourg | 8e	24
Z Astrance | 16e	28
Z Atelier Joël Robuchon | 7e	28
Aub. du Clou | 9e	16
Avenue | 8e	18
Barlotti | 1er	15
Black Calavados | 8e	–
Bon | 16e	–
Bound | 8e	–
Briciola | 3e	–
Café Beaubourg | 4e	16
Café Burq | 18e	–

Café Charbon | 11e — 15
☑ Café de Flore | 6e — 15
Café de l'Esplanade | 7e — 16
Café des Musées | 3e — -
Café du Passage | 11e — -
Café Etienne Marcel | 2e — 18
Café Guitry | 9e — -
Café Rouge | 3e — -
Cailloux | 13e — -
Caméléon | 6e — 20
Cantine de Quentin | 10e — -
☑ 144 Petrossian | 7e — 25
Chateaubriand | 11e — 22
Cherche Midi | 6e — 19
Chéri Bibi | 18e — -
Chez Julien | 4e — 19
Chez Les Anges | 7e — 23
Chez Omar | 3e — 21
Chez Paul | 11e — 21
Chez Prune | 10e — 18
Chez Ramona | 20e — -
Chez Ramulaud | 11e — 16
Chez Vong | 1er — 21
Chieng Mai | 5e — 16
Cocottes | 7e — 21
☑ Comptoir/Relais | 6e — 26
Costes | 1er — 18
☑ Cristal Room | 16e — 17
Crudus | 1er — -
Cul de Poule | 9e — -
Curieux Spaghetti | 4e — -
Dalva | 2e — -
NEW Derrière | 3e — -
Dix Vins | 15e — -
Durand Dupont | Neuilly — -
Eclaireur | 8e — -
Famille | 18e — 19
Ferdi | 1er — -
☑ Fish La Boiss. | 6e — 22
☑ Fontaine de Mars | 7e — 21
Fouquet's | 8e — 18
NEW Frenchie | 2e — -
Fumoir | 1er — 17
Gare | 16e — 14
Gazzetta | 12e — -
☑ Georges | 4e — 18
Gli Angeli | 3e — 18
Grande Armée | 16e — 15
Grand Pan | 15e — -
Guilo-Guilo | 18e — -
Hangar | 3e — 18

Ile | Issy-les-Moul. — 18
Il Viccolo | 6e — -
NEW KGB | 6e — -
Kong | 1er — 14
Laiterie/Clotilde | 7e — -
Legrand Filles | 2e — -
Maison Blanche | 8e — 20
Mama Shelter | 20e — -
Market | 8e — 22
Martel | 10e — -
Miroir | 18e — -
NEW Mon Oncle | 18e — -
Mori Venice | 2e — 17
Murano | 3e — 16
Musichall | 8e — 15
Nabulione | 7e — -
Ozu | 16e — 23
Pizza Chic | 6e — -
Poisson Rouge | 10e — -
Quai-Quai | 1er — -
404 | 3e — 22
Quinzième | 15e — -
Racines | 2e — -
Réfectoire | 11e — -
NEW Reginette | 8e — -
Relais Plaza | 8e — 23
Restaurant | 6e — 26
Rest. Manufacture | Issy-les-Moul. — 21
Ribouldingue | 5e — 18
River Café | Issy-les-Moul. — 14
Rose Bakery | multi. — 17
Rughetta | 18e — -
Salon du Panthéon | 5e — -
Saut du Loup | 1er — 14
Sensing | 6e — 24
Sormani | 17e — 23
Spoon Paris | 8e — 22
Stresa | 8e — 22
Table du Lancaster | 8e — 23
Tong Yen | 8e — 15
Truc Café | 18e — -
Unico | 11e — -
Voltaire | 7e — 24
Water Bar Colette | 1er — 14
☑ Ze Kitchen Galerie | 6e — 25

VIEWS

Absinthe | 1er — 20
Agapes | 5e — -
Alfred | 1er — -
Alivi | 4e — 16

SPECIAL FEATURES

Restaurant	Rating
Alsace | 8ᵉ	18
Ⓩ Angelina | 1ᵉʳ	20
Antoine | 16ᵉ	-
NEW Arc | 8ᵉ	-
Aub. Etchégorry | 13ᵉ	-
Aub./Reine Blanche | 4ᵉ	19
Autobus Imperial | 1ᵉʳ	-
Autour/Saumon | 9ᵉ	17
Avenue | 8ᵉ	18
Bar Vendôme | 1ᵉʳ	23
Basilic | 7ᵉ	15
Bel Canto | 4ᵉ	13
Benkay | 15ᵉ	24
BIOArt | 13ᵉ	-
Bistro de Breteuil | 7ᵉ	16
Bistrot du Cap | 15ᵉ	-
Bistrot du Passage | 17ᵉ	-
Bistrot Vivienne | 2ᵉ	18
Ⓩ Bon Accueil | 7ᵉ	24
Ⓩ Bouquinistes | 6ᵉ	23
Bourguignon du Marais | 4ᵉ	23
Brass. du Louvre | 1ᵉʳ	16
Brass. L'Européen | 12ᵉ	-
Brass./l'Ile St. Louis | 4ᵉ	17
Café Beaubourg | 4ᵉ	16
Ⓩ Café de Flore | 6ᵉ	15
Café de la Musique | 19ᵉ	15
Café de l'Esplanade | 7ᵉ	16
Café Faubourg | 8ᵉ	22
Café la Jatte | Neuilly	14
Café Lenôtre | 8ᵉ	18
Café Le Petit Pont | 5ᵉ	14
Ⓩ Café Marly | 1ᵉʳ	16
Café Rouge | 3ᵉ	-
Cagouille | 14ᵉ	25
Cantine de Quentin | 10ᵉ	-
Cap Seguin | Boulogne	-
Caveau du Palais | 1ᵉʳ	19
Caviar Kaspia | 8ᵉ	25
Cazaudehore | St-Germain-Laye	22
Chalet/l'Oasis | Boulogne	-
Chalet des Iles | 16ᵉ	14
Chamarré Mont. | 18ᵉ	-
Chantairelle | 5ᵉ	-
Charlot Roi des Coq. | 9ᵉ	15
Chez Clément | 8ᵉ	15
Chez Francis | 8ᵉ	17
Chez Fred | 17ᵉ	-
Chez Gégène | Joinville	-
Chez Julien | 4ᵉ	19
Chez Léna et Mimile | 5ᵉ	15
NEW Chez Marie-Louise | 10ᵉ	-
Chez Paul | 13ᵉ	16
Chez Prune | 10ᵉ	18
Chien qui Fume | 1ᵉʳ	18
Ⓩ Cinq | 8ᵉ	28
Cloche des Halles | 1ᵉʳ	-
Clos des Gourmets | 7ᵉ	25
Comptoir | 1ᵉʳ	21
Copenhague | 8ᵉ	18
Dalloyau | 6ᵉ	23
Dame Tartine | 4ᵉ	14
D'Chez Eux | 7ᵉ	25
Diapason | 18ᵉ	-
Divellec | 7ᵉ	24
Duc de Richelieu | 12ᵉ	-
Durand Dupont | Neuilly	-
Ⓩ Espadon | 1ᵉʳ	26
Fables/Fontaine | 7ᵉ	24
First | 1ᵉʳ	18
Floors | 18ᵉ	-
Flora Danica | 8ᵉ	19
Flore en l'Ile | 4ᵉ	18
Ⓩ Fontaine de Mars | 7ᵉ	21
Fontaine Gaillon | 2ᵉ	22
Fontaines | 5ᵉ	17
Fouquet's | 8ᵉ	18
Fous d'en Face | 4ᵉ	-
Fumoir | 1ᵉʳ	17
Ⓩ Georges | 4ᵉ	18
Gli Angeli | 3ᵉ	18
Gordon Ramsay | Versailles	-
Grand Café | 9ᵉ	13
Grande Armée | 16ᵉ	15
Ⓩ Grande Cascade | 16ᵉ	25
Ⓩ Grand Véfour | 1ᵉʳ	28
Guirlande de Julie | 3ᵉ	15
Ile | Issy-les-Moul.	18
Il Vino | 7ᵉ	-
Isami | 4ᵉ	25
Jardins de Bagatelle | 16ᵉ	17
Ⓩ Jules Verne | 7ᵉ	22
Khun Akorn | 11ᵉ	-
Kinugawa/Hanawa | 8ᵉ	23
Kong | 1ᵉʳ	14
Ⓩ Ladurée | 8ᵉ	23
Ⓩ Lapérouse | 6ᵉ	21
L'Assaggio | 1ᵉʳ	23
Ⓩ Lasserre | 8ᵉ	27
Lavinia | 1ᵉʳ	17
Legrand Filles | 2ᵉ	-
Léon/Bruxelles | multi.	16

Mai Do | 6ᵉ	-
Maison/Amér. Latine | 7ᵉ	18
Maison Blanche | 8ᵉ	20
Marius | 16ᵉ	18
Market | 8ᵉ	22
Marty | 5ᵉ	16
Maupertu | 7ᵉ	21
Mavrommatis | 5ᵉ	19
Méditerranée | 6ᵉ	21
Moissonnier | 5ᵉ	19
Montalembert | 7ᵉ	19
Moulin/Galette | 18ᵉ	15
Muscade | 1ᵉʳ	-
Nabulione | 7ᵉ	-
Z Ombres | 7ᵉ	18
Ozu | 16ᵉ	23
Papilles | 5ᵉ	23
Parc aux Cerfs | 6ᵉ	21
Pasco | 7ᵉ	22
Z Pavillon Ledoyen | 8ᵉ	26
Pershing | 8ᵉ	17
Petit Châtelet | 5ᵉ	-
Petite Cour | 6ᵉ	21
Petit Marché | 3ᵉ	22
Petit Pergolèse | 16ᵉ	23
Petit Poucet | **Levallois**	-
Petit Zinc | 6ᵉ	18
Pied de Cochon | 1ᵉʳ	18
Pitchi Poï | 4ᵉ	-
Poisson Rouge | 10ᵉ	-
Pouilly Reuilly | **St-Gervais**	-
Poule au Pot | 1ᵉʳ	23
Procope | 6ᵉ	16
Pure Café | 11ᵉ	-
Quai | 7ᵉ	-
Quai Ouest | **St-Cloud**	13
Quai-Quai | 1ᵉʳ	-
Relais de Venise | 17ᵉ	24
Z Relais/l'Entrecôte | 6ᵉ	22
Réminet | 5ᵉ	-
Rest. de la Tour | 15ᵉ	21
Rest. du Palais Royal | 1ᵉʳ	19
Rest. du Musée d'Orsay | 7ᵉ	17
Rest. Paul | 1ᵉʳ	20
River Café | **Issy-les-Moul.**	14
Romantica | **Clichy**	23
Rosa Bonheur | 19ᵉ	-
Rose de France | 1ᵉʳ	-
Rotonde | 6ᵉ	15
Rouge St-Honoré | 1ᵉʳ	13
Saut du Loup | 1ᵉʳ	14

Sawadee | 15ᵉ	-
Sébillon | **Neuilly**	15
NEW Soya Cantine Bio | 11ᵉ	-
Square | 7ᵉ	-
Square/Marcardet | 18ᵉ	-
Square Trousseau | 12ᵉ	19
Suffren | 15ᵉ	14
Table d'Anvers | 9ᵉ	17
Table d'Hédiard | 8ᵉ	22
Table du Lancaster | 8ᵉ	23
Tastevin | **Maisons-Laff.**	24
Tav. Henri IV | 1ᵉʳ	16
Terrasse Mirabeau | 16ᵉ	-
Terres de Truffes | 8ᵉ	19
Thiou/Petit Thiou | 7ᵉ	21
Tonn. Saintongeaise | **Neuilly**	-
Z Tour d'Argent | 5ᵉ	25
Tournesol | 16ᵉ	18
Z Train Bleu | 12ᵉ	19
Truc Café | 18ᵉ	-
Trumilou | 4ᵉ	19
Vaudeville | 2ᵉ	18
Vin et Marée | 1ᵉʳ	18
Voltaire | 7ᵉ	24
Waknine | 16ᵉ	-
Wepler | 18ᵉ	14
Z Willi's Wine | 1ᵉʳ	20

VISITORS ON EXPENSE ACCOUNT

Agapé | 17ᵉ	-
Z Ambroisie | 4ᵉ	28
Z Ami Louis | 3ᵉ	25
Z Arpège | 7ᵉ	26
Assiette | 14ᵉ	-
Z Atelier Joël Robuchon | 7ᵉ	28
Auguste | 7ᵉ	25
Z Benoît | 4ᵉ	24
Café Faubourg | 8ᵉ	22
Z Carré des Feuillants | 1ᵉʳ	26
Caviar Kaspia | 8ᵉ	25
Chamarré Mont. | 18ᵉ	-
Chen Soleil d'Est | 15ᵉ	-
Chez Les Anges | 7ᵉ	23
Chiberta | 8ᵉ	22
Clovis | 8ᵉ	-
Copenhague | 8ᵉ	18
Cuisine | 7ᵉ	25
Dessirier | 17ᵉ	20
Divellec | 7ᵉ	24
Dôme | 14ᵉ	22

☑ Dominique Bouchet | 8ᵉ	27
Drouant | 2ᵉ	22
Duc | 14ᵉ	23
Eclaireur | 8ᵉ	-
Etc. | 16ᵉ	-
Ferme St-Simon | 7ᵉ	23
Flora Danica | 8ᵉ	19
Fouquet's | 8ᵉ	18
Frégate | 12ᵉ	24
Garnier | 8ᵉ	22
Gaya | 7ᵉ	23
☑ Gérard Besson | 1ᵉʳ	25
Gordon Ramsay | **Versailles**	-
Goumard | 1ᵉʳ	24
☑ Grand Véfour | 1ᵉʳ	28
☑ Guy Savoy | 17ᵉ	28
☑ Hélène Darroze | 6ᵉ	25
Il Vino | 7ᵉ	-
☑ Jacques Cagna | 6ᵉ	26
Jarrasse | **Neuilly**	-
Joséphine/Dumonet | 6ᵉ	23
☑ Jules Verne | 7ᵉ	22
Kifune | 17ᵉ	-
L'Assaggio | 1ᵉʳ	23
☑ Lasserre | 8ᵉ	27
☑ Laurent | 8ᵉ	24
Maison Blanche | 8ᵉ	20
Mansouria | 11ᵉ	22
Marée | 8ᵉ	23
Marius | 16ᵉ	18
Maxim's | 8ᵉ	18
Meating | 17ᵉ	17
☑ Michel Rostang | 17ᵉ	27
Obé | 8ᵉ	23
Oth Sombath | 8ᵉ	-
Oulette | 12ᵉ	19
☑ Pavillon Ledoyen | 8ᵉ	26
Petit Colombier | 17ᵉ	18
Pétrus | 17ᵉ	21
Pierre au Palais Royal | 1ᵉʳ	17
☑ Pierre Gagnaire | 8ᵉ	28
Pomze | 8ᵉ	18
☑ Pré Catelan | 16ᵉ	27
Relais Louis XIII | 6ᵉ	25
Relais Plaza | 8ᵉ	23
☑ Senderens | 8ᵉ	26
☑ Stella Maris | 8ᵉ	26
Table d'Anvers | 9ᵉ	17
Table du Lancaster | 8ᵉ	23
☑ Table/Joël Robuchon | 16ᵉ	26
☑ Taillevent | 8ᵉ	28

Tante Marguerite | 7ᵉ	22
Terrasse Mirabeau | 16ᵉ	-
☑ Tour d'Argent | 5ᵉ	25
☑ Trou Gascon | 12ᵉ	26
W Restaurant | 8ᵉ	-

WATERSIDE

BIOArt | 13ᵉ	-
Brass./l'Ile St. Louis | 4ᵉ	17
Buffalo Grill | 13ᵉ	10
Cap Seguin | **Boulogne**	-
Chalet des Iles | 16ᵉ	14
Chez Gégène | **Joinville**	-
NEW Chez Marie-Louise | 10ᵉ	-
Chez Prune | 10ᵉ	18
Gourmand | **Neuilly**	-
Petit Poucet | **Levallois**	-
Poisson Rouge | 10ᵉ	-
Quai | 7ᵉ	-
Quai Ouest | **St-Cloud**	13
Quai-Quai | 1ᵉʳ	-
River Café | **Issy-les-Moul.**	14

WINNING WINE LISTS

Agapé | 17ᵉ	-
☑ Alain Ducasse | 8ᵉ	28
☑ Ambassadeurs | 8ᵉ	28
☑ Ambroisie | 4ᵉ	28
☑ Atelier Joël Robuchon | 7ᵉ	28
Bistrot du Sommelier | 8ᵉ	18
Bistrot Paul Bert | 11ᵉ	23
NEW Bistro Volnay | 2ᵉ	-
Bourguignon du Marais | 4ᵉ	23
☑ Bristol | 8ᵉ	27
Café Burq | 18ᵉ	-
Café Lenôtre | 8ᵉ	18
Cagouille | 14ᵉ	25
☑ Carré des Feuillants | 1ᵉʳ	26
Cave de l'Os à Moëlle | 15ᵉ	22
Caves Pétrissans | 17ᵉ	19
☑ 144 Petrossian | 7ᵉ	25
Chai 33 | 12ᵉ	14
Chez Géraud | 16ᵉ	20
☑ Cinq | 8ᵉ	28
Coupe Gorge | 4ᵉ	-
Crémerie | 6ᵉ	-
Dessirier | 17ᵉ	20
Divellec | 7ᵉ	24
Drouant | 2ᵉ	22
Ecluse | **multi.**	16
Elysées | 8ᵉ	23

Enoteca | 4ᵉ	20	Oth Sombath | 8ᵉ	-
Ferme St-Simon | 7ᵉ	23	Oulette | 12ᵉ	19
Fines Gueules | 1ᵉʳ	-	Paris | 6ᵉ	20
Z Fish La Boiss. | 6ᵉ	22	**Z** Pavillon Ledoyen | 8ᵉ	26
Fogón | 6ᵉ	21	Petit Marguery | 13ᵉ	21
Z Gérard Besson | 1ᵉʳ	25	Pierre au Palais Royal | 1ᵉʳ	17
Z Grande Cascade | 16ᵉ	25	**Z** Pierre Gagnaire | 8ᵉ	28
Z Grand Véfour | 1ᵉʳ	28	Poisson Rouge | 10ᵉ	-
Z Guy Savoy | 17ᵉ	28	Quedubon | 19ᵉ	-
Z Hélène Darroze | 6ᵉ	25	Racines | 2ᵉ	-
Il Vino | 7ᵉ	-	Relais Louis XIII | 6ᵉ	25
Z Jacques Cagna | 6ᵉ	26	Saudade | 1ᵉʳ	-
Joséphine/Dumonet | 6ᵉ	23	**Z** Senderens | 8ᵉ	26
Z Jules Verne | 7ᵉ	22	Spoon Paris | 8ᵉ	22
L'Assaggio | 1ᵉʳ	23	**Z** Stella Maris | 8ᵉ	26
Z Lasserre | 8ᵉ	27	Table d'Anvers | 9ᵉ	17
Z Laurent | 8ᵉ	24	**Z** Taillevent | 8ᵉ	28
Lavinia | 1ᵉʳ	17	Tante Marguerite | 7ᵉ	22
Legrand Filles | 2ᵉ	-	Tav. Henri IV | 1ᵉʳ	16
Macéo | 1ᵉʳ	23	**Z** Tour d'Argent | 5ᵉ	25
Marée | 8ᵉ	23	**Z** Trou Gascon | 12ᵉ	26
Maxim's | 8ᵉ	18	Vieux Chêne | 11ᵉ	-
Z Meurice | 1ᵉʳ	27	Vin dans les Voiles | 16ᵉ	-
Z Michel Rostang | 17ᵉ	27	**Z** Vin sur Vin | 7ᵉ	26
Montparnasse 25 | 14ᵉ	16	Yugaraj | 6ᵉ	23

Wine Vintage Chart

This chart is based on our 0 to 30 scale. The ratings (by U. of South Carolina law professor **Howard Stravitz**) reflect vintage quality and the wine's readiness to drink. A dash means the wine is past its peak or too young to rate. Loire ratings are for dry whites.

Whites	95	96	97	98	99	00	01	02	03	04	05	06	07	08
France:														
Alsace	24	23	23	25	23	25	26	23	21	24	25	24	26	-
Burgundy	27	26	23	21	24	24	24	27	23	26	27	25	25	24
Loire Valley	-	-	-	-	-	23	24	26	22	24	27	23	23	24
Champagne	26	27	24	23	25	24	21	26	21	-	-	-	-	-
Sauternes	21	23	25	23	24	24	29	25	24	21	26	23	27	25
California:														
Chardonnay	-	-	-	-	23	22	25	26	22	26	29	24	27	-
Sauvignon Blanc	-	-	-	-	-	-	-	25	26	25	27	25	-	
Austria:														
Grüner V./Riesl.	24	21	26	23	25	22	23	25	26	25	24	26	24	22
Germany:	21	26	21	22	24	20	29	25	26	27	28	25	27	25

Reds	95	96	97	98	99	00	01	02	03	04	05	06	07	08
France:														
Bordeaux	26	25	23	25	24	29	26	24	26	24	28	24	23	25
Burgundy	26	27	25	24	27	22	24	27	25	23	28	25	24	-
Rhône	26	22	24	27	26	27	26	-	26	24	27	25	26	-
Beaujolais	-	-	-	-	-	-	-	-	24	-	27	24	25	23
California:														
Cab./Merlot	27	25	28	23	25	-	27	26	25	24	26	23	26	24
Pinot Noir	-	-	-	-	24	23	25	26	25	26	24	23	27	25
Zinfandel	-	-	-	-	-	-	25	23	27	22	22	21	21	25
Oregon:														
Pinot Noir	-	-	-	-	-	-	-	26	24	25	26	26	25	27
Italy:														
Tuscany	24	-	29	24	27	24	27	-	25	27	26	25	24	-
Piedmont	21	27	26	25	26	28	27	-	25	27	26	25	26	-
Spain:														
Rioja	26	24	25	-	25	24	28	-	23	27	26	24	25	-
Ribera del Duero/ Priorat	26	27	25	24	25	24	27	20	24	27	26	24	26	-
Australia:														
Shiraz/Cab.	24	26	25	28	24	24	27	27	25	26	26	24	22	-
Chile:	-	-	24	-	25	23	26	24	25	24	27	25	24	-
Argentina:														
Malbec	-	-	-	-	-	-	-	-	-	25	26	27	24	-

Menus, photos, voting and more – free at ZAGAT.com

Take us with you.
ZAGAT Mobile

You choose the phone and we'll help you choose the place. Access Zagat dining & travel content on your **iPhone, BlackBerry, Android, Windows Mobile** and **Palm smartphones.**

Text **EAT to 78247** for more information or visit us online at **www.zagat.com/mobile**